State and Revolution in Finland

Historical Materialism Book Series

The Historical Materialism Book Series is a major publishing initiative of the radical left. The capitalist crisis of the twenty-first century has been met by a resurgence of interest in critical Marxist theory. At the same time, the publishing institutions committed to Marxism have contracted markedly since the high point of the 1970s. The Historical Materialism Book Series is dedicated to addressing this situation by making available important works of Marxist theory. The aim of the series is to publish important theoretical contributions as the basis for vigorous intellectual debate and exchange on the left.

The peer-reviewed series publishes original monographs, translated texts, and reprints of classics across the bounds of academic disciplinary agendas and across the divisions of the left. The series is particularly concerned to encourage the internationalization of Marxist debate and aims to translate significant studies from beyond the English-speaking world.

For a full list of titles in the Historical Materialism Book Series available in paperback from Haymarket Books, visit:
https://www.haymarketbooks.org/series_collections/1-historical-materialism

State and Revolution in Finland

Risto Alapuro

Haymarket Books
Chicago, IL

First published in 2018 by Brill Academic Publishers, The Netherlands
© 2018 Koninklijke Brill NV, Leiden, The Netherlands

Published in paperback in 2019 by
Haymarket Books
P.O. Box 180165
Chicago, IL 60618
773-583-7884
www.haymarketbooks.org

ISBN: 978-1-64259-052-4

Distributed to the trade in the US through Consortium Book Sales and Distribution (www.cbsd.com) and internationally through Ingram Publisher Services International (www.ingramcontent.com).

This book was published with the generous support of Lannan Foundation and Wallace Action Fund.

Special discounts are available for bulk purchases by organizations and institutions. Please call 773-583-7884 or email info@haymarketbooks.org for more information.

Cover design by Jamie Kerry and Ragina Johnson.

Printed in the United States.

10 9 8 7 6 5 4 3 2 1

Library of Congress Cataloging-in-Publication data is available.

To Aappo and Mikko

Contents

Acknowledgements XI
Maps, Tables and Figures XIII

1 **The Formation of a Small Polity** 1
   1 The Problem 1
   2 A Comparative Perspective 2
   3 What Is to Be Explained 11
   4 Plan of the Book 13

PART 1
State-Making and the Class Structure

2 **Dominant Groups and State-Making** 19
   1 The Early Nineteenth Century 19
   2 Economic Integration 28
   3 The Late Nineteenth Century 34

3 **The Agrarian Class Structure and Industrial Workers** 38
   1 The Industrial and Agricultural Revolutions in Finland 38
   2 Freeholding Peasants and Agrarian Workers 40
   3 The Link between Industrial and Agrarian Workers 45
   4 Crofters 46

4 **Territorial Integration** 49
   1 Finnish Regions up to 1809 49
   2 Reorientation from Stockholm to St. Petersburg 56
   3 Territorial Integration in the Late Nineteenth Century 58
   4 Core-Periphery Interaction – the County of Viipuri and Eastern Finland 63
   5 South-Western Finland as a Core Region 66
   6 Declining Ostrobothnia 70
   7 Division of Labour and State Penetration in Northern Finland 73
   8 Summary 74

PART 2
National Integration and Class Integration

5   Finnish Nationalism   79
   1   The Dual Nature of Nationalism in Nineteenth-Century Europe   79
   2   Finland in a European Perspective   83
   3   The Consolidation of a National Culture   85
   4   Conclusion   91

6   Before the Revolution: Organisation, Mobilisation, and the Role of Russia   94
   1   Early Mass Organisation   94
   2   The Finno-Russian Conflict   103
   3   The General Strike of 1905, Parliamentary Reform, and the Rise of Agrarian Socialism   106

7   Regional Consolidation of Party Support   118
   1   Regions as Loci of Party Systems   118
   2   The South-Western Core Region   120
   3   The County of Viipuri   122
   4   Ostrobothnia   122
   5   Eastern Finland   124
   6   Northern Finland   125
   7   Conclusions   126

PART 3
The Abortive Revolution

8   On Preconditions for Revolutionary Situations   131

9   The Abortive Revolution of 1917–1918   137
   1   Socialists within the Polity   137
   2   The Rise of Multiple Sovereignty   146
   3   The Revolutionary Situation   152
   4   The Aftermath   160
   5   The Social and Regional Basis for the Revolution   162
   6   On the Character of the Finnish Revolution   168
   7   Breakdown of Society or Contest for State Power?   172

CONTENTS IX

10 State and Nation after the Failed Revolution 179
    1 The Failed Revolution and the Nation 179
    2 The Persistence of the Volcanic Model of the Finnish Revolution 183
    3 On the State, the Nation, and Class Balance 185
    4 The Lapua Movement, 1930–2 189
    5 The Mass Movement and the Dominant Classes in Finnish Fascism 194

PART 4
The Finnish State and Revolution in a European Perspective

11 Eastern European Revolutionary Movements 201
    1 National Movements in the Baltic Provinces 202
    2 Revolution in the Baltic Provinces, 1905 and 1917–18 210
    3 Challenges in East-Central Europe 221
    4 Fascism in Eastern Europe 231

12 The Formation of Finland in Europe 236
    1 Economic Consolidation 236
    2 The Formation of State and Nation 239
    3 Political Organisation and Mobilisation before 1917 241
    4 Revolutionary Situations in Small European Polities 244
    5 State and Revolution in Finland 246

Postscript to the Second Printing 250
    1 A Personal Note 250
    2 A Recapitulation 252
    3 The Reception of the Comparative Perspective 254
    4 Structures and Actors 260
    5 The Associational Tradition in the Political Process 264
    6 Causes and Scripts 266

Bibliography 269
Index 298

Acknowledgements

The most fundamental debts for the completion of this book are owed to two persons. Erik Allardt's emphasis on structural conflicts in social analysis and the comparative scope of his teaching have provided a basis from which this project has grown. No less important have been Erik's comments and personal support during many years, as well as the stimulating setting for research and the exchange of ideas provided by the Research Group for Comparative Sociology at the University of Helsinki.

More specifically, the roots of this book go back to the academic year 1973–4, which I spent in the Center for Research on Social Organization of the University of Michigan, Ann Arbor. Peasants and political conflicts were, in exciting ways, central issues in Charles Tilly's work. In the intellectual milieu surrounding him it was natural to come to grips with big structures and large processes without feeling them to be too huge. Since the inception of this book, years later, Chuck's continuing encouragement and advice have greatly facilitated the progress of the work up to publication.

Many other friends and colleagues have helped me with valuable criticism. Matti Alestalo, Edmund Dahlström, Max Engman, Michael Hechter, Antti Karisto, Pauli Kettunen, Matti Klinge, Klaus Mäkelä, Andreas Moritsch, Veijo Notkola, Gert von Pistohlkors, Seppo Pöntinen, Per Schybergson, Hannu Soikkanen, Henrik Stenius, Irma Sulkunen, Jukka-Pekka Takala, Hannu Uusitalo, and Matti Viikari have read the manuscript or essential parts of it. Their comments and suggestions not only corrected many of my errors but also led to a restructuring of the whole work and to repeated efforts at clarifying my argument. Gavin Bingham and, as copyeditor, Anne Canright, with their care and effort, greatly contributed to improving the language and the entire presentation. I also wish to thank Jutta Scherrer for giving me the opportunity to present the preliminary, and in many ways obscure, idea of the character of the revolutionary process in Finland in her seminar at the École des Hautes Études en Sciences Sociales in Paris in 1981.

I completed the major part of this study while a research fellow of the Academy of Finland. I am grateful also to the Emil Aaltonen Foundation, the Finnish Cultural Foundation, and the Kone Foundation for their financial support.

Parts of some chapters have previously appeared in *Mobilization, Center-Periphery Structures and Nation-Building*, edited by Per Torsvik and published by Universitetsforlaget in 1981 (Chapter 3); *The Politics of Territorial Identity: Studies in European Regionalism*, edited by Stein Rokkan and Derek W. Urwin and published by Sage in 1982 (Chapters 4, 5, and 7); *Who Were the Fascists: Social Roots of European Fascism*, edited by Stein Ugelvik Larsen, Bernt Hagtvet and Jan Petter Myklebust and published by Universitetsforlaget in 1980 (Chapter 10); and *The Breakdown of Democratic Regimes: Europe*, edited by Juan J. Linz and Alfred Stepan and published by Johns Hopkins University Press in 1978 (Chapter 10). The latter article was written with Erik Allardt; I have drawn here from the section I originally prepared myself. All the materials utilised here are reproduced with the permission of the publishers. Maps 4, 6, 7, 8, and 9 are reprinted, with permission, from Engman 1978, Jutikkala 1959, Lento 1951, and Kero 1974.

Maps, Tables and Figures

Maps

1. Finland, the Baltic Provinces of Russia, and Scandinavia in the nineteenth century (including the border between Sweden and Russia in 1721 and 1743)   21
2. Main Finnish regions and the line between the Reds and the Whites in the revolution of 1918   52
3. The counties of Finland at the beginning of the twentieth century   53
4. Regional distribution of passport-holding Finns living in Russia in 1881, by domicile in Finland   57
5. The Finnish railway network by 1918, with the Saimaa Canal   60
6. Urban industrial workers, 1884–1885 and 1938   61
7. Rural industrial workers, 1884–1885 and 1938   62
8. Net internal migration to 1920, by county of birth   69
9. Overseas emigration from Finland, 1870–1914, by commune   71
10. The Baltic Provinces (Estland, Livland, Kurland) and the border between Estonia and Latvia after 1917   204

Tables

1. Percentage distribution of Finnish population by industry, 1820–1920   26
2. Percentage distribution of Finnish population by estate, 1890   36
3. Indicators of market penetration in the countryside, 1870–1910   42
4. Agrarian households in Finland by class, 1815–1901   43
5. Production of sawn goods by county, 1860 and 1900   64
6. Population and migration in Finland by county, late nineteenth and early twentieth centuries   65
7. Finnish regions in terms of core-periphery position and class relations   75
8. Distribution of seats in Parliament won in Finnish general elections, 1907, 1916, and 1917   108
9. Rural and urban party support in Finnish general elections, 1907, 1916, and 1917   109
10. Regional variations in political mobilization in the Finnish countryside, 1907–1932   120
11. Distribution of seats in Parliament won in selected Finnish general elections, 1919–1933   187

Figure

1   Finnish cities, 1815 and 1920, ranked by population   67

CHAPTER 1

The Formation of a Small Polity

1   The Problem

More than two decades ago Barrington Moore, in his *Social Origins of Dictatorship and Democracy*, examined the paths different states have followed when moving into the modern age and assessed the ensuing variation in political systems. Concentrating on a few big countries where a certain social process had 'worked itself out',[1] he deliberately neglected the small countries:

> The fact that the smaller countries depend economically and politically on big and powerful ones means that the decisive causes of their politics lie outside their own boundaries. It also means that their political problems are not really comparable to those of larger countries. Therefore a general statement about the historical preconditions of democracy or authoritarianism covering small countries as well as large would very likely be so broad as to be abstractly platitudinous.[2]

When inverted, Moore's observation encapsulates the basic problem examined in this book. What *are* the decisive factors conditioning twentieth-century politics in smaller countries that are economically and politically dependent on big ones? Even though the question was dismissed by Moore, it is worth asking simply because most countries *are* small, and most people live in polities that are dependent on distant centres of power. In what ways, then, has dependence on powerful states influenced preconditions, forms, and outcomes of collective action in small polities? How has it affected the occurrence of revolutions, other large-scale conflicts, and the institutionalisation of political systems when these polities enter into an era of mass politics?

In this study answers to these questions will be sought based on the experience of Finland, one of the smaller European polities economically and politically dependent on big centres. It is also one of the countries called 'successor states' between the world wars. The state structures and internal conflicts of these polities, which formed a geographically connected area between Russia

---

1   Moore 1966, p. xii.
2   Moore 1966, p. xiii.

and other major European powers, were dramatically affected by World War I, and the countries reached a critical point in their political development at one and the same moment.

These characteristics set this group of polities apart from other small countries for which this perspective is also relevant, namely the Third World countries that have won independence from colonial rule in the twentieth century. Although it is true that dependence through capitalist commercialisation and interstate competition has powerfully shaped state-making and political conflicts in both classes of polities, only the European cases were dependent on backward empires, only they were geographically contiguous with the metropoles themselves, and only they experienced a simultaneous, sudden, and complete collapse of the metropolitan country. John Dunn's distinction between world war and decolonisation as the two major nondomestic processes related to the important revolutionary challenges in the twentieth century captures the main difference between the European and the other cases.[3]

The focus here is on Finland, which means that the problems will be dealt with in the context of a single country. The main thrust of the book will concern the nature of political and economic dependence and the particular political consequences it had in the Finnish case. At the end of the book a few comparisons with other Eastern European polities will be made to show the distinctiveness of certain Finnish features. Because Finland is an example of a whole class of countries, analysis of the Finnish experience, together with the comparisons with other countries, should help to put political development in this class of countries into perspective. The analysis may throw some light more generally on the development of politics in the dependent Eastern European countries and, ultimately, on how the political and economic impact of the big powers is reflected in the internal processes of the smaller countries.

2   A Comparative Perspective

From what perspective should early twentieth-century politics in Finland and other small Eastern European polities be viewed? If the small countries really are a case apart, various well-known models of political development cannot be used, because they are based, explicitly or implicitly, on the experience of

---

3 Dunn 1977, p. 98. Actually, Dunn speaks of revolutionary success and of big and small countries alike. The outcome in the small polities was presumably much more dependent on outside forces than in the large ones.

the large European national states.⁴ Moreover, it is by no means obvious that even the forms of collective action found in small countries are the same as those in big, established European states. Thus, if the causes of political transformation in the small European states are substantially different from those in the larger ones, then both the 'phases' or 'sequences' of political development and the nature of collective action in the two cases may likewise differ markedly.

During the years since Moore's work appeared, the problem of comparability has been approached in at least two new systematic ways. First, it has been pointed out that even in large states political transformation is dependent on the capitalist world-economy and on processes involving other states or the international state system. In this view Moore's distinction is not as unambiguous as he assumed it to be. The analysis of the relationship between states and the international system should not be confined to small polities but should be extended to large ones – as Theda Skocpol has forcefully maintained in her comparison of the French, Russian, and Chinese revolutions.⁵ Immanuel Wallerstein's and Perry Anderson's delineations of the rise of the European world-economy and the European state system can also be seen in this light.⁶ In both these analyses the emergence of the various individual states depends on their relations to the entire emerging structure: the trajectories of particular states are conditioned by their different relations to the system as a whole.

This perspective obviously suggests one way in which Finland can be compared with other states, even large ones. For example, it would appear useful to view the Finnish revolution of 1917–18 as the outcome of the interplay of domestic and international processes and in this sense similar to the 'great' revolutions examined in Skocpol's study. This approach, unlike theories of political development, does not imply that similarities between large and small countries must be found. Rather, it facilitates comparisons that should enable us to determine what was specific to the Finnish experience itself. For Finland, the significance of the international context is obvious; therefore, looking at other European states and their emergence in an international perspective may help to identify the key features of Finland's development. This does not necessarily mean that 'general statements' will be applicable to Finland, but it may help us see how the internal and external factors important throughout Europe were linked together in this particular case.

---

4   See Tilly 1975c.
5   Skocpol 1979. Also Skocpol 1982, pp. 367–73; Østerud 1978b, pp. 176–8.
6   Wallerstein 1974–80; P. Anderson 1974.

This approach alone, however, is not sufficient. It hardly suggests more than a general course for considering a northeastern latecomer state such as Finland. In order to determine what was specifically Finnish as opposed to what was common with other countries, notably the other small Eastern European polities, the emergence of Finland should be viewed more concretely and in a large perspective.

Perhaps the most ambitious effort in this, second, direction is Stein Rokkan's 'conceptual map of Europe'.[7] In commenting on Barrington Moore's decision to concentrate on leading countries, Rokkan argued that the analysis should not be restricted to large and powerful leading polities when examining specific regions such as Europe. 'On the contrary, the purpose is to account for variations among *all* the distinctive polities in the region, and this requires direct attention to the possible consequences of such factors as size, economic resource potential and location in the international power system'.[8] Thus Rokkan developed schemes that account for variations in the Western European party systems and in the scope for state-making in Europe.

In his conceptual map of Europe, state-making patterns vary along two major axes of development. On the West-East axis indicating the economic resource bases of the state-making centres, Finland is a region where surplus was extracted from agricultural labour and not, as in the West, from a highly monetised economy. Together with the Baltic territories, Bohemia, Poland, and Hungary, Finland was a 'landward buffer' in which both territorial centres and city networks were weakly developed. On the North-South axis measuring conditions for rapid cultural integration – that is, nation-building – Finland falls in the same class as Sweden, Denmark, Norway, and Iceland. In these northern countries, national Protestant churches marked off religious and linguistic areas into which cultural penetration could occur fairly easily. In the South, in contrast, religious 'supraterritoriality' created obstacles for cultural integration.[9] It is in this perspective – of an alliance between statemakers and landowners for extracting food and manpower and of separate cultural identities developing into political entities – that the major characteristics of Finnish state formation should be viewed.

Clearly, this model relates Finland to other political entities in Europe and provides a starting point for comparing state-making in Finland with state-making elsewhere in Europe. It helps us to see that the Finnish state-making

---

7 Allardt 1981b, p. 264.
8 Rokkan 1969, p. 60.
9 Rokkan 1973, pp. 80–4; Rokkan 1980, pp. 178–183; Tilly 1981, pp. 10–13.

experience resembles that not only in the fringe between Russia and the other major European powers but also in Scandinavia. Nonetheless, this approach has a major problem: by placing Finland or any other polity in a European context, it fails to take into account the way the entities interact. The international system is seen as the sum total of its component parts rather than as an environment affecting, perhaps in contradictory ways, the destinies of single entities. The model is essentially taxonomic; it does not really address Moore's problem, that is, the special features of *internal* developments in small polities that result from their *dependence* on big ones. Basically, as Charles Tilly puts it, it treats national experiences as 'cases' that result from different combinations of certain central variables.[10]

> Sweden, to take an obvious instance, is not simply a 'case' located somewhere in the northern reaches of a giant cross-tabulation. The Sweden which appears on Rokkan's conceptual map is a shrunken remainder of the expansive power which at one time or another dominated Norway, Finland, Estonia, Livonia, and other important parts of the North. Can we reconstruct the political development of Sweden – or, for that matter, of Norway, Finland, Estonia and Livonia – without taking that interaction directly into account?[11]

Tilly himself has explicitly suggested that small polities should be viewed as dependent on big ones. He also proposes a dichotomy exemplified by the above distinction between Sweden, on the one hand, and Norway, Finland, Estonia (Estland), and Livonia (Livland), on the other. The distinction represents the first two steps in the general movement toward a worldwide state system that originated in Europe.

The first phase was the formation of the first great national states. This involved commercial and military competition followed by economic penetration into the remainder of Europe and parts of the world outside Europe. The expansive processes were facilitated by the absence of important concentrations of power immediately outside the areas in which the substantial states were forming, as well as by the availability of new territories for expansion, conquest, and extraction of resources. What took place in this period, from approximately 1500 to 1700, was the consolidation of a system of states acknowledging, and to some extent guaranteeing, one another's existence. The Treaty

---

10   Tilly 1981, 16. Also Allardt 1981b, pp. 269–70.
11   Tilly 1981, 16.

of Westphalia (1648) played an important part in laying the foundation for the European state system.[12] By the end of the period, the substantial powers in Europe included such national states as England, France, Brandenburg-Prussia, and Sweden, as well as three empires: the Russian, the Austro-Hungarian, and the Ottoman.

Whereas the first phase in the development toward a worldwide state system involved the formation of a few early national states and empires with ethnically distinct centres, the second phase consisted of the division of most of Europe into distinct national states through wars, alliances, and a great variety of other manoeuvres. The earlier phase in state-making seriously constrained the second. New states increasingly came into being as a result of wars between established members of the state system. The Treaty of Westphalia, the Congress of Vienna (1815), and the Treaty of Versailles (1919) constitute dramatic demonstrations of this point.[13] And Finland is a good example of such a new state: the two major landmarks in its movement toward statehood were the Napoleonic Wars and World War I.

This pattern of the emergence of a system of a few early states followed by the regrouping of the remainder of Europe into a system of states subject to the constraints of the initial system (which by no means remained immutable) helps to place the Finnish and other Eastern European experience in perspective. It is the final phase of the process that concerns us here, however. In this phase, it is most important that the three great multinational empires, Russia, Austria-Hungary, and the Ottoman Empire, were dismembered. Each of them created somewhat different preconditions for the consolidation of national minorities.[14] The so-called successor states of the empires in the late 1800s and early 1900s include Finland, Estonia, Latvia, Lithuania, Poland, Czechoslovakia, Hungary, Romania, Bulgaria, Yugoslavia, and Albania. Many of these countries were 'unhistoric nations', in the sense that they were not linked to existing or even historically remembered polities. This was the last wave of creation of distinct national states in Europe, and it came about as a consequence of international crisis and/or conflict between the established members.

The distinction implies that state-making processes in the latecomer states were different from those in the early substantive states. In the early cases, the only political units that could survive were ones privileged with a relatively protected position in time and space, the availability of extractable resources, a

---

12 Tilly 1975b, pp. 30, 44–5; Tilly 1975c, pp. 636–7. See also Kiernan 1965, pp. 32–6.
13 Tilly 1975b, pp. 46, 74–5; Tilly 1975c, pp. 636–7.
14 The Poles, of course, were divided among various empires, as were the Romanians to a certain extent.

continuous supply of political entrepreneurs, success in war, homogeneity (initial or created) of the subject population, and strong coalitions between the central power and major segments of the landed elite.[15] The transformation of these states was largely a by-product of attempts by the central power to consolidate its position and to respond to challenges both external and internal. The state-making process, then, was intimately bound up with the conduct of war, the building of armies, the levying and regularisation of taxes, and the growth of the administrative apparatus. Tilly conceives of early state-making as a process in which the state-makers who were trying to survive and expand were forced to create standing armies for use against rivals elsewhere as well as rebels at home: 'States have grown up as warmaking organizations'.[16] The maintenance of armies made it necessary to squeeze more revenue from the populace, and the very existence of the army in turn facilitated this process, thereby contributing to the consolidation of central power. At the same time, various coalitions were formed between the central power and the major dominant classes.

In short, the main processes that brought the national state to a dominant position were not only coercive and extractive; they were also *internal*. It is true that the creation of standing armies resulted from struggles between states, and therefore external threats ultimately played an important role. But the relation of the rulers to the ruled *within* the state was decisive. Territorial consolidation, centralisation, differentiation of the instruments of government, and monopolisation of the means of coercion (that is, the fundamental state-making processes) were all imposed on the subject population by the emerging central power and its main allies.[17] This view is in line with other conceptions of European state formation. It is congruent with Max Weber's formulations on big (European) states. He views them in terms of his conception of the state as an apparatus of domination, which provides a model for analysing, above all, the internal processes of a political unit.[18] According to Perry Anderson, to take another example, the absolutist states in the West emerged in response to the internal decomposition of feudalism. As a new apparatus of feudal domination against the peasant masses, absolutism succeeded in obtaining the widespread commutation of dues. The same priority of the intra-state power relations was true in the East, despite the fact that there absolutism was largely a result of external pressures. The more advanced societies of the West were able to

---

15 Tilly 1975b, p. 40.
16 Tilly, Tilly and Tilly 1975, pp. 259–63 (quotation from p. 259).
17 Tilly 1975b, pp. 42, 71; Tilly 1975c, pp. 632–3.
18 Weber 1948, pp. 77–8, 82–3; Collins 1968, p. 48.

plunder the more retarded areas of Eastern Europe. To protect themselves, the countries of the East had to raise armies, and strong armies required strong states.[19]

This centuries-long process did not repeat itself in the second phase of state-making. The later the state-making process, the less adequate the above processes are for explaining the formation, survival, or growth of the state. New states were more or less *created* by existing ones,[20] as a result of crises and rivalries in the international state system, which led to wars and the break-up of empires subject to protracted pressures.

This difference meant that relations between the major local classes and the central power evolved differently. In other words, the connection between (1) *state structures* and (2) *class relations* was not the same as in the early substantive states. In the small dependent polities, class relations were not as institutionalised in political structures, which were in any case recent or otherwise weak. This difference then shaped the nature of local political organisation and collective action, which were reflected both in (3) *national integration* – that is, cultural homogenisation and nation-building – and in (4) *class integration* – that is, class-based collective action.

First, the position of the state apparatus vis-à-vis the subject population was dissimilar in the established states as contrasted with the latecomers. In the former the state apparatus had been consolidated over the course of centuries and had come to correspond to class relations in the core areas. In the latter this apparatus was often of recent origin or had been imposed by the metropolitan country. Prior to independence, the position of the dominant groups was usually guaranteed by the metropolitan power, and inherited administrative institutions and state structures did not necessarily correspond to purely local power relations. The post-World War I Baltic countries constitute an excellent example of this situation. The relationship between the dominant groups and the subject population was much less institutionalised, and the state less autonomous, than in the early national states.

It is in this context of political structures that the second factor, class relations, should be viewed. In the last century the expansion of the Western capitalist market dissolved feudal ties and reshaped agrarian class structures in Eastern Europe. Large numbers of emancipated peasants were allotted minuscule holdings or no land at all, except in the Balkans, where backward small farming became predominant. The consolidation of large capitalist estates was

---

19   P. Anderson 1974, pp. 18, 196–202; Gourevitch 1978, pp. 427–8.
20   Tilly 1975c, p. 636.

not immediately accompanied by the growth of an industrial proletariat in the cities. It was common to see class boundaries imposed along ethnic lines: in a number of minority areas, local peasantries were confronted with non-native landlords. The level of literacy was much lower than in the West and Scandinavia, and popular organisation was weak.[21] All in all, large strata of the peasantry in minority regions were hurt by economic dependence on the developed West. Examples of the effect of this class structure on collective action are the extensive peasant unrest in the Baltic Provinces of Russia in 1905 and the great Romanian peasant revolt in 1907.

Third, ethnic considerations played a much more prominent role in the later cases. The formation of the state was given momentum by the aspirations of ethnically distinct groups, or, more precisely, by the actions of their elites. In the earlier phase of state-making, national consciousness, participation, and commitment generally developed only after strong states had been formed, as a consequence of deliberate actions on the part of the central power.[22] In the Eastern European latecomer states, the process was reversed: ethnic similarities led to the emergence of a national consciousness before the formation of the state.[23] This difference should be borne in mind when assessing the role of nationalism in the two cases.

Fourth, in the nineteenth century and the beginning of the twentieth, class-based collective action took place in different conditions in the two classes of countries. During this period there were increasing demands for the extension of political rights in Europe, the working-class movement being the main challenger in the old and new states alike. If, following Charles Tilly,[24] collective action is conceived of as resulting from changing combinations of interests, organisation, mobilisation, and opportunity, it is particularly the opportunity that distinguishes the latecomer states from the earlier (Western) European national states. The difference merits attention because the bulk of the relevant literature has, more or less implicitly, taken the experience of the early Western European states as their starting point.

The Western experience suggests that collective action was the result of a gradual but painful process running from common interests through organisation and mobilisation to collective action. This conception pervades the writings of several analysts of political transformations and revolutions: it is

---

21 Berend and Ránki 1974, pp. 25–58; Orridge and Williams 1982, pp. 24, 29, 32.
22 Tilly 1975b, p. 70.
23 Chlebowczyk 1980, pp. 21–2, 214; Eley 1981, pp. 96–105; Orridge 1982, pp. 44–5.
24 Tilly 1978, pp. 7–8.

present in Barrington Moore's great book; it figures in the Tilly's analysis of the rebellious century extending from 1830 to 1930 in France, Italy, and Germany; and it is a central theme in E.P. Thompson's book on the making of the English working class.[25] Political rights were gradually won through hard and often protracted struggles in which the workers slowly learned to organise, mobilise, and act collectively against state machineries, first in strikes and then, after gaining some rights, in elections fought with their own parties.[26] Each step of the expansion of rights 'usually occurred in response to the demand of some well-defined contender or coalition of contenders'.[27] 'Organization gave working people the strength to demand their rights. The acquisition of those rights brought expanded use of them in formulating new demands or pursuing old ones. The sequence ... is a general rule for collective action'.[28]

In the emerging latecomer polities, the character of collective action was different. The state apparatus was usually not 'internal' to the same extent, and therefore major crises did not result from demands made by ethnically distinct subject populations but rather arose from international conflicts and their impact on the fragile mother empires. Fluctuation between extreme repression and temporary liberalisation was much more likely than in the major Western states. Opportunities sometimes changed rapidly and quite independently of the strength of collective action. It may be argued, for example, that the Russo-Japanese War had a much greater impact on the introduction of universal suffrage in Finland in 1906 than did the demands of domestic contenders in preceding years. The collapse of the Russian and Austro-Hungarian empires in World War I and the effect of this on the constituent nationalities were the final results of this process.

It seems reasonable to hypothesise that different opportunity structures produced differences in organisation and mobilisation. In Finland the peculiar character of the early working-class movement, which played a decisive part in the abortive revolution of 1917–18, can be traced to the opportunities at the beginning of the century.

In sum, the state-making histories of the old and the new polities varied systematically, and Finland was undoubtedly one of the latter. Its state apparatus was dependent on the mother empire; it was economically dependent on the Western market; ethnic considerations played a prominent part in the state-

---

[25] Moore 1966; Tilly, Tilly and Tilly 1975; Thompson 1963.
[26] Abendroth 1965, esp. pp. 51–86; Tilly 1978, p. 113.
[27] Tilly 1978, pp. 170–1.
[28] Tilly, Tilly and Tilly 1975, p. 280.

making process; and finally, opportunities sometimes changed independent of the strength of domestic collective action. But, quite importantly, Finland resembled the other new polities in political dependence much more than in the character of the class structure or the nature of economic dependence. Among the smaller European regions experiencing a serious revolutionary challenge at the end of World War I, Finland was practically the only one to have a decidedly non-feudal class structure.[29] Finland's distinctiveness stems from the fact that, in the longer run, it was not just a minority region in a multinational empire; rather, it was a territory between *two* established members of the international state system. Before the nineteenth century, the Finnish-language areas that were to form the bulk of present-day Finland belonged to Sweden. Finland's class structure, which was similar to Sweden's and Norway's, had its origins in this earlier period. This fact has direct implications for the character of subsequent collective action, but it also implies that economic dependence on the Western market did not have the same consequences as in the East.

The specifically Finnish combination – a decisive similarity with Eastern successor states in political dependence on the one hand, and with Scandinavia in class structure and economic dependence on the other – makes the analysis of a political, economic, and cultural interface necessary. The Scandinavian countries cannot be omitted, even if the most important comparison is with Eastern Europe.

3 What Is to Be Explained

In the nineteenth century, Finland was characterised by nearly complete social tranquillity and a very conservative political system. But the first elections based on universal suffrage were held as early as 1907, and they gave the Social Democrats the largest share of seats in any European country, even though Finland was one of the most agrarian countries in Europe. Almost nine-tenths of the votes cast for the Social Democrats came from the countryside. Rural voters were in the majority in both absolute and relative terms, and the party was not only strongly supported but also well organised in the countryside. Dur-

---

29   Bohemia resembled Finland the most in this respect. Whereas peasant landownership was extensive in the Balkans, farms there were fragmented and scarcely viable compared to those of the Finnish landowning class. See Berend and Ránki 1974, pp. 49–52; and below, Chapter 3.

ing the following decade this party was gradually integrated into the prevailing political system. Nonetheless, in 1918, immediately after Finland became independent, it spearheaded an abortive revolution. Finally, a little over a decade later, a powerful fascist-type movement emerged and attempted to overthrow the Finnish parliamentary political system.

These are the main processes to be explained in this study: the entrance of the masses onto the political scene in 1907, the rise and failure of the revolution of 1918, and the fascist-type reaction of the early 1930s. These phenomena took place in a region that was or had just ceased to be a politically autonomous part of the Russian Empire and had close economic links with the West. To make sense of these processes, a number of questions must be answered. What were the roles of the external and internal forces in the formation of the Finnish state and in the creation of preconditions for collective action in it? How did the outside factors and their intertwining with domestic structures affect, first, early political mobilisation and, second, the outbreak of revolution in 1918? Finally, what was the impact of the failure of the revolution on state structures and conflicts in the 1920s and 1930s?

These questions may be viewed as problems involving relations between the state and class structures in Finland and the organisation at their intersection – an organisation reflected in the nature of national and class integration. All four processes should be viewed as dependent on external forces. In this perspective, the first phenomenon that needs to be examined is the consolidation of the Finnish state, and particularly its relation both to the system of established states in Europe and to the capitalist world economy. Second, the class structure and the impact of the world market on it are to be considered. Here the third and fourth processes, linked to the role of the various classes in the emerging Finnish state, become relevant. In what ways were political developments in the mother country mediated into the Finnish state and class structures, thus reshaping their mutual relations? What were the roles of domestic and non-domestic forces in Finnish nationalism and early twentieth-century politics? Moreover, how did the endogenous and exogenous factors influence the process of political mobilisation in 1917 and 1918, after the collapse of Imperial Russia? Finally, the consequences of the abortive revolution for the state and the classes in the newly independent republic will be assessed.

The class relations that were institutionalised in the Finnish state through specific forms of national and class integration during the nineteenth century will be delineated first. Then the picture will be fleshed out by an examination of the sudden disruptions in state control that came about because of interstate rivalries damaging to Russia. The question is, how did earlier Finnish structures and forms of integration become effective in the crisis, and what then happened to them? Reduced to its barest essentials, then, the theme of this book is the interplay between institutionalised domestic class relations and fluctuations in the controlling capacity of the state resulting from oscillations in the mother empire.

After considering these questions it will be possible to judge the relevance of other Eastern European cases for Finland, as well as the relevance of the Finnish case for them, in terms of classes, state formation, and problems of organisation.

4   Plan of the Book

The book is divided into four parts, dealing first with fundamental state-making processes and class relations (Part I), national integration and class integration (Part II), and the rupture of integration in the abortive revolution (Part III). Then an attempt is made to place Finnish developments in a European perspective (Part IV).

In Part I the formation of the Finnish state and its linkages with the development of the class structure are delineated. The process of state-making and the shifting relations among the upper classes bear the marks of Finland's position in the interface between Sweden and Russia. When the Finnish regions were transferred from Sweden to Russia and made into a separate political unit, the relations between the dominant groups were redefined. Then, a half-century later, they were completed and modified by capitalist development. In the consolidation of the economy, Finland benefited greatly from its Scandinavian social structure and its status as an 'overdeveloped' minority region in a multinational empire. From this double point of departure, a Western type of social structure and an Eastern type of dependence, Finland was able to start a process of economically autonomous development in the latter part of the nineteenth century (Chapter 2).

In this process close ties developed between the agrarian and the industrial proletariat. Finland's main industrial sector, forestry, was strongly and very directly linked to the countryside because the peasants owned the bulk of the forests. Consequently, the capitalist transformation was felt immediately and profoundly in both town and country (Chapter 3).

Another aspect of the process of state-making and, notably, of the formation of a national economy was territorial integration. During the Swedish period the Finnish regions interacted mainly with an external core, Stockholm. In the nineteenth century, however, after tentative and partial reorientation toward

St. Petersburg, a domestic core emerged. A geographical division of labour was established, which tied the various regions together in a more fundamental sense than ever before and accentuated a number of regional inequalities (Chapter 4).

Part II lays out the interrelationship between the state and the class structures in the process of organisation. The starting point is Finland's resemblance to Scandinavia, on the one hand, in its basic patterns of organisation and mobilisation, and to other minor nationalities in the large empires, on the other, in its opportunities for collective action.

The national movement was a struggle for self-assertion and liberation, but at the same time it served for the dominant classes as a 'civic religion' for the emerging state, thanks to the early foundation of the Finnish polity by the Russian imperial authorities. The latter aspect of the national movement was intensified by the strength of the Finnish-speaking peasantry; because the authority of the Swedish-speaking upper classes rested structurally on a fragile foundation, their national responsiveness was enhanced. It is mainly because of this combination – so it is argued – that national consolidation occurred in Finland, and nationalism advanced exceptionally calmly and steadily (Chapter 5).

Although the emerging party system closely resembled the Scandinavian one, the political opportunity granted by the first Russian revolution in 1905–6 made the main challenger, the worker movement, focus overwhelmingly on purely political and, more particularly, parliamentary action, at the expense of strikes and other forms of collective action based directly on productive relations. Strong agrarian support for the Social Democratic party worked in the same direction. The movement rapidly attained membership in the polity and became a powerful instrument in both class and national integration (Chapter 6).

The emergence of regionally varying party support is another indicator of national integration. The persistence of regional conflicts is manifest in the combinations of party support, which differed from region to region. But because all important parties played a national role, it is reasonable to view the regional combinations as the way in which local conflicts were fused on the emerging national level (Chapter 7).

In Part III the disruption of metropolitan control and its domestic consequences during and after World War I are brought into play. Arguably, it was the strong position of the rather reformist worker movement in the polity, combined with the opportunity for collective action provided by the breakdown of the Russian Empire, that led Finland into a revolutionary situation. The Finnish case illustrates the primacy of changes in conditions for contests concerning state power and suggests that whether or not the challengers consider themselves revolutionaries at the outset is of secondary importance (Chapters 8 and 9).

The failed revolution marked the creation of an independent country out of a grand duchy, and especially out of the national and class integration consolidated in the previous phase of state-making. The earlier national culture provided the instruments for defining and analysing the seemingly surprising and incomprehensible developments of 1917–18. From this perspective, the Finnish fascist movement of the early 1930s appears to be basically a general bourgeois reaction, an attempt to reassert the White victory of 1918 (Chapter 10).

Finally, Part IV (Chapters 11 and 12) focuses both on features that Finland had in common with other Eastern European minority regions and latecomer polities and on features that differentiated Finland from them. The country's interface position seems crucial: Finland emerges as a kind of mixed case in which, curiously enough, a class structure and political system of a Western type and a sudden collapse of an Eastern type coincided to ignite a revolution. The former had granted the Social Democrats a central place in the representative political institutions of the country; the latter granted them an extremely advantageous opportunity to use this power. The revolutionary situation emerged when the labour movement attempted to maintain power and the particular advantages it had gained in the face of a resolute bourgeois effort to recapture a monopoly on power. This was very unlike the Baltic Provinces, where the revolutionaries really seized power, or Hungary, where they simply accepted it – in both cases after war had destroyed the state apparatus.

PART 1

State-Making and the Class Structure

CHAPTER 2

Dominant Groups and State-Making

1   The Early Nineteenth Century

Purely external factors determined the creation of Finland as a distinct political entity. As Edward C. Thaden dryly puts it, 'Finnish autonomy, and even the existence of a Finnish nation, can be considered an incidental byproduct of wars between Sweden and Russia during the eighteenth and at the beginning of the nineteenth centuries'.[1]

Prior to 1809 the mainly Finnish-speaking territories east of the Gulf of Bothnia and north of the Gulf of Finland were an integral part of Sweden. As on the other side of the Gulf of Bothnia, the language of the elites was Swedish. The sea did not separate but rather united the eastern provinces with the hub of the state, and these were more oriented to Stockholm than to each other (see Chapter 4). The south-western region of what later became the Finnish state belonged more or less to the core of the Swedish kingdom, whereas the other regions remained at the periphery. The concept of Finland existed, but it was more a geographical term than a political one. Initially it referred to the south-western region, which had been strongly linked to the core of the state from the thirteenth century onward. Only later was it extended to cover the Finnish-speaking peripheries, which in the course of the subsequent centuries came under the firm control of the Swedish monarchs.[2] At the end of the eighteenth century about 15 percent of the total population consisted of Swedish-speakers, most of whom were engaged in farming and fishing on the coastal regions.

The most striking characteristic of Swedish society, in the Finnish regions as well as in the territory making up the present-day Swedish state, was a free peasantry, which constituted the backbone of the social structure. Thanks to class balance in the rural economy, the relations of production were never really feudalised. Moreover, during the eighteenth century the position of the landholding peasants was reinforced markedly. In the double process of increases in peasant property and of enclosures, a foundation was laid for the emergence of a strong market-oriented cultivator class as well as for the internal differentiation of the agricultural population.

---

1   Thaden 1984, p. 82.
2   Klinge 1982, pp. 23–49; Carlsson 1980.

The freeholders' proprietorship was strengthened, and tenants on crown land were allowed to buy their holdings. Peasants also acquired the right to purchase noble lands. At the same time, common lands were redistributed to the landholders, and the repartition of mixed strips and fields into larger shares was started.[3]

The extensiveness of peasant property in the Swedish kingdom strongly suggests that the dominance of the nobility was based less on landownership than on its central position in the bureaucracy – particularly when Sweden is compared to Eastern and Central Europe. By contemporary standards, Sweden was administered effectively, and the surplus from peasant producers was extracted indirectly, rather than directly by a land-controlling nobility.[4] Even in southwestern Finland, that is, in the Finnish-speaking region where manorial relationships were by far the most widespread, nobles and other gentlemen owned only one-fifth of the complete farms (in Swedish, *mantal*) at the beginning of the nineteenth century.[5]

The comparatively strong position of the peasantry was reflected in the political system. The four-chamber Swedish Diet was unique in Europe in that it included a separate Peasant Estate alongside the hereditary nobility, the occupational clergy, and the burghers – although the Peasant Estate did remain inferior to the other three chambers.

In 1809 eight eastern counties were separated from Sweden and incorporated into the Russian Empire. Although this area was populated mainly by Finnish-speakers, the new border was drawn not on linguistic lines but on strategic ones. In 1807 at Tilsit, the Russian tsar Alexander I had agreed on zones of influence with Napoleon. As a consequence Russia conquered Finland, a territory important for the defence of St. Petersburg, in 1808–9.[6] One century earlier Peter the Great had won Estland, Livland, and the regions surrounding

---

3 Østerud 1978a, pp. 130–6. One indication of the deep roots of peasant freeholding in Sweden is that the enclosures furthered independent family farming, rather than leading to a reduction in peasant land, as was the case in England. The Swedish enclosures were initiated by the state and were not linked to the agricultural revolution but preceded it (ibid., pp. 144–9).
4 Mäkelä and Viikari 1977, pp. 166–7.
5 Landownership by the nobles and other gentlemen is measured by combining two percentages for the years 1805–7: the proportion of *mantal* cultivated by tenant farmers in Finland Proper, Satakunta, Häme, and Uusimaa (Jutikkala 1939, 39), and the proportion held by manorial demesnes in the same regions (Jutikkala 1932, pp. 74–82). The percentages – which are not fully comparable – are 16.4 and 3.4, respectively.
6 Tommila 1984, pp. 7–12, 54; Klinge 1980a, pp. 38–9.

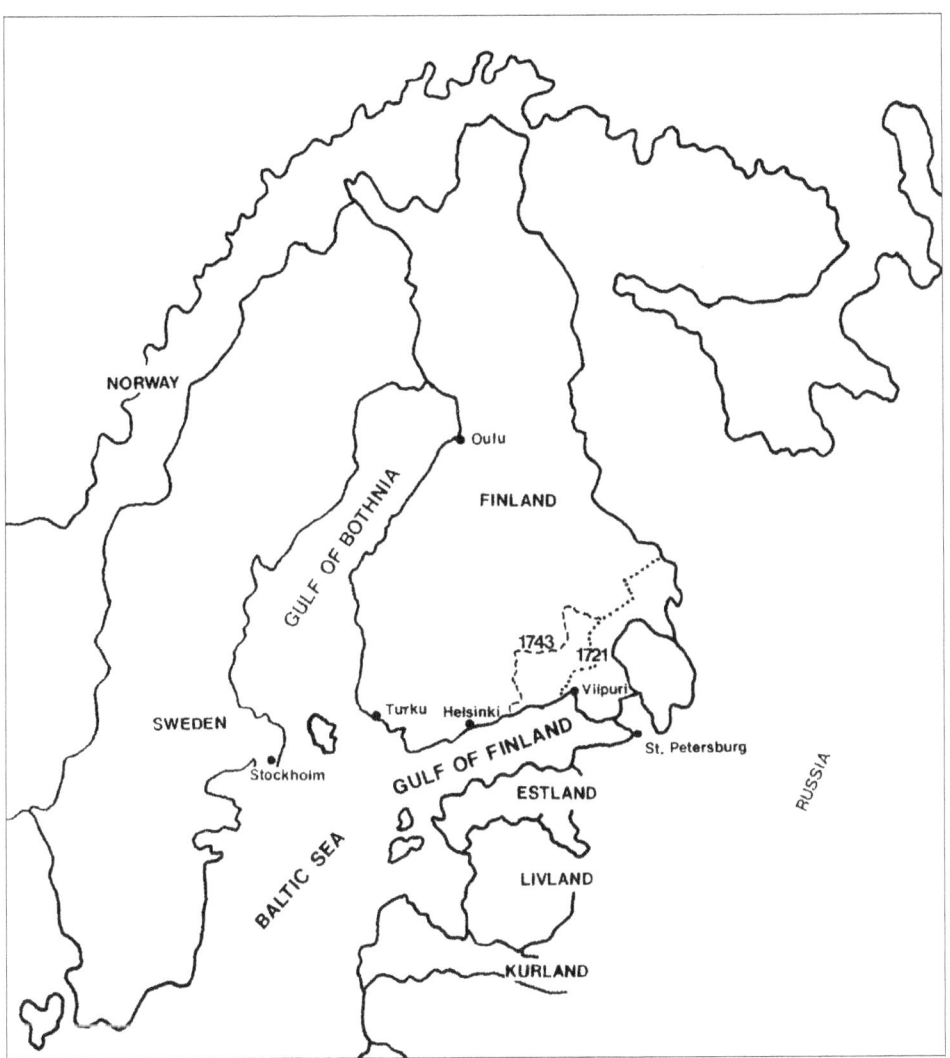

MAP 1   Finland, the Baltic Provinces of Russia, and Scandinavia in the nineteenth century (including the border between Sweden and Russia in 1721 and 1743)

the bottom of the Gulf of Finland from Sweden and established his new capital, St. Petersburg, in the newly acquired territories (see Map 1). From that time on, the protection of the new capital was of primary importance for Russia. During the eighteenth century, moreover, Sweden gradually lost her position as a great power. The conquest of Finland by Russia was the final phase in the shift in the balance of power between these two established members of the European state system.

Swedish sovereignty in the eastern counties ended in September 1809 with the Treaty of Hamina (in Swedish, Fredrikshamn), and the conquest was confirmed at the Congress of Vienna in 1815. The laws and privileges enjoyed hitherto by the people of the conquered territory were to remain unchanged under Russian rule. This was not exceptional: earlier Peter the Great had co-opted the established institutional structure in annexed regions. The pacification measures implemented in Finland in 1809 were similar to those adopted in the Baltic Provinces in 1710. The highest local authority was a Russian governor general. The local administration continued to operate as before, but under the surveillance of the governor general's office.[7] In the Finnish case, although there was no prior administrative authority covering the entire region, common administrative practices had evolved during the centuries of Swedish rule. These were strictly observed in the new political environment. As early as March 1809 the tsar met with the assembled Finnish estates in the cathedral city of Porvoo (Borgå) and declared his intention to make Finland an imperial grand duchy, a separate entity in governmental, financial, and religious affairs.

Alexander's interest in experiments with political and social reform had an influence on the rights granted to the Finns. He believed that Russia had much to learn from the institutional systems then prevailing in Russia's western borderlands. But foreign-policy considerations were still more important. Because of wars with Sweden, Turkey, and France and, in a broader perspective, because of Sweden's continuing military power, which allowed it to challenge his control of Finland, it seemed imperative to tie the new region to the central government by transferring the loyalties of the local elite to the new sovereign. This had occurred in the Baltic Provinces, and it was the goal in Finland.[8] 'The imperial policy of autonomy rested on the assumption that political loyalty and orthodoxy in the northwestern border zone could be best guaranteed through the employment of local elites and local traditions'.[9]

The goal was pursued by maintaining and even extending privileges, by building a central administration, and by creating a Finnish counterpart of the Swedish four-curia Diet. Among the institutions that were to remain unchanged were the fundamental laws, the Lutheran religion, and corporate privileges. Furthermore, the Finns were not subject to conscription, but they did become eligible for civil and military office in the empire (whereas Russians were not eligible for Finnish posts). The grand duchy had a separate budget and retained its own revenues. The local university in Turku (Åbo), which was

---

7   Jussila 1981, p. 32; Schweitzer 1984, pp. 202, 203.
8   Thaden 1981b, pp. 15–17; Thaden 1984, pp. 3, 60–1, 231–2.
9   Selleck 1961, p. 52.

later moved to Helsinki (Helsingfors), was given considerable privileges. Finland formed a separate customs area in the Russian foreign trade system. In economic affairs, only tariffs, trade relations with foreign countries, and some features of monetary policy were initially placed under Russian jurisdiction. The traditional administrative units – the counties and the communes – were retained, but they were integrated into a uniform domestic administration. As a further sign of favour, the south-western areas of Karelia around the city of Viipuri (Viborg), annexed by Russia in 1721 and 1743 (see Map 1), were united with the grand duchy in 1812.

From 1816 the highest domestic authority was the Senate. Its Economic Department served as the supreme administrative council, and its Judicial Department as the supreme court. The members were recruited primarily from the professional civil and judicial service. The Senate was chaired by the governor general, who was the highest official in Finland and commander-in-chief of the Russian troops stationed in the country. In St. Petersburg, Finnish matters were prepared and presented by the Committee for Finnish Affairs (between 1826 and 1857, the State Secretariat for Finnish Affairs), headed at first by a state secretary, and from 1834 on by a minister state secretary who figured among the ministers of the empire. Significantly, Finnish affairs were presented directly to the emperor, and the country was not subordinated to the central, ministerial government of Russia.[10]

The meaning of Finland's new position was far from self-evident at the outset. Its true importance and also a number of its institutional forms were established, especially in the first decades of the grand duchy, only through continued and determined efforts by Finnish leaders, for whom the consolidation of Finland's separate status remained a constant preoccupation.[11] The basis that made this work possible was laid in 1809 and the next few years, during which time Finland acquired for the first time a politically distinct status. Militarily its position was more secure than under Swedish rule, and personally members of the upper echelons of the administration had access to new offices under improved conditions.[12] Among all Russia's nineteenth-century borderlands, only Congress Poland enjoyed greater autonomy, and that was only until the insurrection of 1830–1.

The various initial measures rapidly produced the desired results. Nearly all important institutional and Swedish-speaking elites made public declarations of loyalty and gratitude, and organisation and recruitment for the new central

---

10   Jussila 1985, pp. 63, 66.
11   Schweitzer 1984, pp. 201–9; Jussila 1984, pp. 97–8.
12   Selleck 1961, pp. 35–7; Tommila 1984, pp. 51, 58–65, 75–6, 105, 113–31.

administration proceeded apace. For leaders of the Finnish nobility, trained in the Swedish royal service, it was relatively easy to transfer to the tsar personal loyalty developed in an earlier era.[13] Such shifts of allegiance were quite common during this period, particularly among the nobility. As E.J. Hobsbawm puts it, 'Before the "national" era … various "national" solidarities had only a casual connection, and were not supposed to have any special connection, with obligations to the state centre'.[14] In 1850, over one-fifth of the adult Finnish male nobility was in the Russian military service. During the entire period of Russian rule, the Imperial Army attracted about 3,300 Finns, mostly from the aristocracy.[15]

From the Russian point of view, the process was facilitated by the constitutional system introduced by the Swedish king, Gustav III, in 1772 and 1789. The Gustavian constitution presumed the existence of a strong royal executive governing by decree through an administrative hierarchy over which the Diet had very little control. This feature made it easier for the emperor to preserve the fundamental legislation. Moreover, Finland's autonomy was based ultimately on his generosity, not on formal recognition of fundamental laws. Finland never obtained from Alexander I or from his successors formal regulation of its relationship with Russia. The Finnish bureaucratic leaders were well aware that in the autocratic Russian Empire the constitution ultimately rested on a tenuous political balance and that the limitations of monarchy were self-imposed, or rather imposed by considerations of broader policy, over which Finns had no effective control.[16]

In a sense the Gustavian system facilitated cultural separation from Sweden. As a consequence of the war, Sweden's political system and cultural atmosphere changed greatly, and the former mother country became increasingly alien to the Finnish elites.[17]

The fact that the convening of the Diet depended on the monarch was extremely important for the domestic exercise of power. After 1809, the Diet was not summoned until 1863. Subsequently, however, it met at regular intervals. Without a parliament to serve as a public forum for political competition, the bureaucratically organised administration, with the Senate at its top, was needed to carry out important political tasks. And because the tsar remained

---

13   Korhonen 1963, pp. 190–214; Tommila 1984, pp. 83, 102; Selleck 1961, pp. 40, 42.
14   Hobsbawm 1972, p. 389.
15   Screen 1976, pp. 287–9; Kirby 1979, pp. 6–7.
16   Thaden 1984, 85, 230. Two basic studies are Korhonen 1963 and Jussila 1969; see also Selleck 1961, 41, 46–47, 53.
17   Klinge 1980b, pp. 13–14.

passive in local affairs, the actual exercise of political leadership devolved in large measure on the bureaucracy, with no clear division of political and administrative functions in the central government. Early nineteenth-century Finland was, in its upper echelons, a thoroughly bureaucratic society.[18]

In sum, then, when Russia created the Finnish polity, the position of the domestic bureaucracy was greatly strengthened. A central administration was built up, but its role was not limited to administrative affairs. By suspending the Diet for nearly half a century, the Russians indirectly endowed the top of the administration with vital political functions.

These arrangements were to change status and power relations among the dominant groups and to create new tensions. Paradoxically, the strengthening of the bureaucracy, which was the stronghold of the nobility, undermined the nobility's traditional position as the first and most powerful estate. Nobility was becoming more a reward than a prerequisite for bureaucratic success.[19] The erosion was symptomatic of a more general change affecting the dominant groups. In the bureaucratic society of the early nineteenth century, the four estates ceased to reflect adequately social differentiation. The basic social dividing line came to separate the 'gentry' from the masses. The bureaucracy constituted the core of the gentry (in Swedish, *ståndspersoner*; in Finnish, *säätyläiset*). In Swedish usage, the concept of the gentry initially referred to the nobility, the clergy, and their social equals. Later the term *other gentry* was used to refer to commoners who had entered the military and bureaucratic ranks and to any teachers or professionals who did not fall into the traditional 'learned estate' of the clergy. The gentry revolved around the civil service, which had an internal hierarchy and an official system of ranks. Ultimately the concept came to refer to a social identity recognised more by custom than by law. The gentry pattern included exposure to higher education, employment in the higher levels of the administration, personal association with other members of the gentry, an appropriate standard of living, and use of the Swedish language, which dominated all public services, higher education, and public life. In other words, the gentry was a status group in the Weberian sense.[20]

The existence of this status group is an indication of the stability that prevailed in the bureaucratic society of the time. Business and industrial activity were also under firm administrative control. The domestic government was the main source of commercial funds for business, and only the state could

---

18   Selleck 1961, pp. 25–6, 53–4; Wirilander 1974, pp. 105–6, 116, 120.
19   Jutikkala 1956, p. 124; Selleck 1961, pp. 25–26.
20   Selleck 1961, pp. 21–5; Wirilander 1974, pp. 33–6, 105–41, 153–9, 179–82, 409; Weber 1968, pp. 305–7, 935–8.

TABLE 1 Percentage distribution of Finnish population by industry, 1820–1920

Sector	1820	1870	1920
Agriculture and forestry	88%	83%	71%
Industry	4	6	15
Trade and communications	4	5	11
Unknown	4	6	3
Total	100%	100%	100%
N (thousands)	1,178	1,766	3,105

SOURCE: P. MANNINEN 1976, 81

create an adequate infrastructure. The character of the social structure helped to preserve social tranquillity. Nearly nine-tenths of the population worked in agriculture (see Table 1), and the agrarian population was made up mainly of landowning peasants and crofters (see Table 4, p. 43). Only the former had a recognised position in the political system, but in many cases the economic positions of the two groups were very much alike. The agrarian proletariat, in contrast, found itself under strict control owing to the hiring-out obligation and other regulations.[21]

Consequently, during this period the only visible social tension resulted not from challenges by subordinated groups but from the increased power and authority of the bureaucracy. This is a central point in Roberta Selleck's study of the Finnish political discussion during the half-century preceding the reconvening of the Diet in 1863.[22] Besides the civil hierarchy, the other main elite section in the gentry consisted of the clerical and academic groups. With the strengthening of the bureaucracy, their institutional position was slowly eroded, leading ultimately to dissatisfaction with and opposition to the civil hierarchy.

The Lutheran church and the national university were vested with powers of internal self-government and performed important political functions. The church, through its parish congregations, was responsible for local government in rural areas, as well as for public education – not only the basic instruction in literacy required of all Lutheran communicants, but also the secondary system

---

[21] Myllyntaus 1981, p. 178.
[22] Selleck 1961.

leading up to the university. There was a close link between the two institutions: both scholars and practising clerics made up the church elite.[23]

Recruitment patterns for the clergy and academic groups were similar and differed from those for the civil hierarchy. Just as there were family dynasties within the bureaucracy, so too was there much clerical-academic self- and inter-recruitment. Another peculiarity was the continuing entry into these groups by people from outside the gentry as a whole. The small flow of the sons of the independent peasantry and the petty bourgeoisie into (lower) church and university posts represented the only regular form of social mobility into the gentry during this period.[24]

The creation of a local bureaucratic hierarchy following the events of 1808–9 reduced the relative social status of the clerical and scholarly elites. The traditional academic emphasis on a broad classical education conflicted with the bureaucratic view that the university should provide vocational training for public service.[25] More important, because the church and university shaped public attitudes, not least of all through the educational system, bureaucratic leaders had to make use of the Second Estate in their efforts to maintain the precarious balance of imperial policy. These bureaucratic leaders thus eagerly claimed the right to exercise authoritative control based on their capacity to defend autonomy through a combination of rigid legalism, diplomacy, and strategic compromise. 'While it was generally sufficient to secure passive obedience from other social groups, the clerical and teaching personnel were required to play an active part in the execution of government policy by assisting in the control of public opinion'.[26] This was particularly important, at this time when public discussion was limited by official controls and the Diet did not convene, because the university provided virtually the only forum of debate outside the upper levels of the bureaucracy itself.

---

23   The institutional connections were gradually severed after 1809, but church and university men, sharing a similar educational background and a similar professional interest in the educational process, maintained close contacts even after formal separation (Selleck 1961, pp. 27–9; cf. Wirilander 1974, pp. 256–8, 329–35).

24   Waris 1940, pp. 216, 221–7; Selleck 1961, pp. 25, 29–31. Cf. Wirilander 1974, pp. 201–34, 351–5.

25   As training for the civil service became more important, the university curriculum could not be left in the hands of clergymen and scholars to the extent it had been before. Civil service training had been assigned to the university in the previous century, but a decisive move toward the dominance of bureaucratic considerations occurred after 1810 (Selleck 1961, pp. 74–7; cf. Tommila 1984, p. 132; and Wirilander 1974, pp. 234, 313, 336, 338, 344–5, 350, 360–3, 366).

26   Selleck 1961, p. 67.

For the members of the Second Estate, and especially for their leaders in the academic community, these processes implied a loss of freedom of action. Against various threats to their existence as an autonomous social corporation, politically conscious members of the academic community slowly began to assert alternative claims to status and authority:

> As institutional criticism of a liberal nature was prevented by censorship, these claims were expressed primarily in terms of cultural values. General education was opposed to routine administrative skill, and the capacity to contact the depths of the nation was described as more important than the ability to negotiate a defense of legal autonomy.[27]

To conclude, the creation of a separate Finnish polity did not evoke open social conflicts in the early nineteenth century. It did not change the relations between the rulers and the population, as had happened in the early European states; the earlier system of domination was preserved. But the change was significant for the Finnish elites. For the first time they were tied to each other through a domestic administration. The process of state-making, which was shaped above all by the country's dependent position, changed the relations between the elites and generated tension among them. As Selleck points out,[28] the very structure of Finland's autonomy tended to deflect frustrations arising out of Finno-Russian relations toward domestic targets, hastening the development of opposition within the ranks of the gentry – opposition not to the empire as such but rather to the local, governing elite of the grand duchy. This institutional tension played a part in the rise of the national movement from the 1840s on (see Chapter 5), and it was amplified and altered in the late nineteenth century as a consequence of the capitalist transformation.

2   Economic Integration

The early European national states grew up along with capitalism. In these countries, state-making and the development of capitalism were so closely intertwined that it is hard to distinguish their effects. In the Finnish case the relationship is much less problematic. Because the Finnish polity was created by external decision, economic consolidation could occur only after Finland had evolved politically. In the earliest phase of economic integration, then,

---

27   Ibid., p. 87.
28   Ibid., p. 34.

the state played the principal role, and it remained central when the capitalist transformation gave further momentum to the process.

Before the 1840s, the efforts of the state were directed more to maintaining the status quo than to creating an integrated economic unit. Industrial development was restrained by mercantilist restrictions, and the surplus extracted from the peasants provided the fiscal basis for nearly all the operations of the state. The largest public expenditure item was administration.[29] Under this passive policy a national market emerged rather slowly. There were agricultural regions of both over- and underproduction, but only weak commercial links existed between them. Similarly, the national market for industrial products was very modest. 'At present Finnish merchants have more extensive and more active relations with foreign countries than with each other', a geography manual stated in 1827.[30] Characteristically, the separation of the Finnish counties from Sweden did not lead to a sudden change in commercial relations with the former mother country. Sales to Stockholm of Finnish peasant produce remained important after 1809 in the western regions, and Finland's most important industrial activity, iron fabrication, was almost entirely dependent on Swedish ore until the 1860s. Until the 1840s commerce with Sweden resembled domestic trade more than foreign trade. Swedish currency was accepted along with the Russian silver and paper ruble and was even more widely used than the latter currency.[31] In the east, commercial ties with St. Petersburg were revitalised (see Chapter 4).

Only in the 1840s and 1850s did the state begin to actively support economic consolidation and growth. State revenues were increased in order to promote industry and the construction of the infrastructure, which in turn was supposed to stimulate trade in agricultural products. A monetary reform was carried out, the position of the Bank of Finland (founded in 1811) was reinforced, the tariff and land tax systems were reorganised, financing of industry was facilitated, vocational schools were founded, and the construction of roads and canals gained momentum. In the early 1840s the country was economically separated from Sweden as earlier tariff privileges were abolished and the Swedish currency was replaced by a domestic one.[32]

29   'Administration' included, above all, the maintenance of (former) officers in the army, abolished when the grand duchy was founded, as well as the maintenance of a small permanent detachment (Myllyntaus 1980, pp. 362–3).
30   Quoted in Mauranen 1980, p. 448.
31   Myllyntaus 1980, pp. 340, 347–8; Schybergson 1980a, pp. 412, 420–1; Schybergson 1980b, p. 451.
32   Myllyntaus 1980, pp. 338, 342, 353, 355, 358, 365; Schybergson 1980a, p. 432; Schybergson 1980b, p. 457; Mauranen 1980, p. 449.

The final steps in the repeal of mercantilist restrictions and in the construction of a national economy were taken between the late 1850s and the late 1870s. The process was accelerated by the crisis of the autocracy following the Crimean War and by the added strength of the domestic bourgeoisie and other interest groups. By revealing both the economic and military backwardness of the Russian autocracy, the war made internal reforms urgent and directed governmental attention to the loyalty of national minorities. To this end Alexander II, in 1856, initiated a liberal policy of reform in socially tranquil Finland. Gradually, however, this policy led to a crisis, because the established practices of consultation and administrative decree could no longer be employed without consultation with the four Finnish estates. Increasing Finnish demands finally brought the tsar to agree to the resumption and regularisation of Parliament from 1863 on – in the middle of the Polish crisis – and the basic economic legislation was revised.[33] By the end of the 1870s a separate Finnish currency had been introduced, all industries and trades freed from restrictions, the craft system and limitations on the free movement of labour abolished, active railway construction initiated, and the local administration modernised.

Of decisive importance, however, were the closing decades of the last century. Gross domestic product increased fivefold between 1860 and 1913, with the 1890s the period of most rapid growth. The growth rate was one of the fastest in Europe. At the same time, the share of industry and construction in the gross domestic product (GDP) increased from 13 to 25 percent, and the share of the primary sector fell from 65 to 47 percent. Self-financing played an important role in the growth of GDP.[34] Agriculture was linked to the rapidly expanding market, the main indication being the changeover from traditional arable cultivation to the much more commercial occupation of stock-raising. The land tax was replaced by various indirect taxes, mainly tariffs, as the main source of state revenue. In state expenditure, the construction of the infrastructure and the provision of social services, notably investments in railways and in education, came to predominate along with the administrative expenditures.[35]

In this way the main obstacles to capitalist transformation were removed – that is, the state itself began to acquire capitalist features. It no longer merely collected and distributed the surplus produce of the peasantry, as in the early nineteenth century. It now began to develop functions involved in the repro-

---

33 Suni 1979, pp. 59–63, 100–4; Seileck 1961, pp. 178–9.
34 Hjerppe and Pihkala 1977, p. 60; Hjerppe, Peltonen, and Pihkala 1984, p. 44; A. Kuusterä 1985, pp. 144–5.
35 Pihkala 1977.

duction of the capitalist mode of production.[36] The state had proceeded from controlling economic activity to promoting the process of accumulation both by establishing the legal and institutional framework conducive to growth and by carrying out economic activity. Thus a political unit that had been created by an external decision gradually became economically integrated.

This transformation was greatly accelerated by Finland's links to the international economic system.[37] Actually, as Iván T. Berend and György Ránki have pointed out – and as the importance of tariffs in state revenue makes clear in the Finnish case – it is just at the intersection of domestic and international forces that the state played its part in the capitalist transformation of the European peripheries and prepared the periphery in question to face the challenge of the industrialised West.[38] By the middle of the century, the industrial revolution in Western Europe had created a capitalist market of a type that had never existed before, with a pulling power that attracted whatever food and raw material the world could produce and that could transform backward agrarian regions within a few decades.[39] Finland was one of these regions, and wood was the resource exploited. Finland's resource endowment determined its role in the international division of labour, and wood processing became the country's leading industry. Between 1900 and 1909, wood industry products (essentially lumber) accounted for 44 percent of the total value of exports, or as much as 69 percent including forestry and the more advanced paper industry. At the same time, Finnish exports had one of the fastest growth rates among the peripheral countries of Europe, and the value of exports increased fifteenfold from 1860 to 1913. Finland was an 'open economy', the share of exports being twenty to twenty-five percent of the GDP from the 1890s on.[40]

Finland thus began to industrialise at about the same time as other countries in Eastern Europe, and its industrialisation was based on a low value-added export product. Linkages of the sawmill industry with other industrial sectors were modest. Production was based on the abundance of timber and on a cheap labour force. Most of Finland's sawn goods were exported to developed Western countries, notably Great Britain, and the exports were highly vulner-

---

36 Mäkelä and Viikari 1977, p. 168.
37 The preceding decades had prepared the way, of course. Between 1810 and 1870 the annual increase in the volume of foreign trade averaged two percent (Schybergson 1980b, p. 458).
38 Berend and Ránki 1982, pp. 59–73, 106, 141.
39 See P. Anderson 1974, p. 392; and Berend and Ránki 1982, p. 27.
40 Heikkinen and Hoffman 1982, pp. 60–70; Pihkala 1969, pp. 63, 74–5; Hirvonen and Hjerppe 1983, p. 32; Berend and Ránki 1982, pp. 114–15. The wood and paper industries accounted at that time for 83 percent of the value of industrial exports, which dominated the export trade.

able to international price fluctuations. In short, sawn goods were in many respects a staple product similar to those exported by weakly developed and dependent economies.[41]

Finland, however, escaped the so-called staple trap, that is, dependence arising from the dominance of a narrow range of exports based on raw materials. It followed the Scandinavian pattern more closely than that of the East-Central European agrarian peripheries.[42] Economic transformation contributed greatly to the process of state-making, and Finland emerged as an economic unit with a territorial division of labour and an autonomous economic core.[43]

What factors provided the initial impetus for Finland's 'self-sustained economic growth', especially from the 1880s and 1890s on?[44] A comprehensive answer is beyond the scope of this study, but clearly Finland's interface position determined its room for manoeuvre relative to both the Western capitalist market and Russia. First, as far as its Western-oriented export industry was concerned, the linkages of the sawmill industry with other sectors of the economy were the most significant. Activity in many other sectors was financed by the income of the sawmill industry, which was largely domestically owned.[45] The role of the independent peasantry was decisive in this respect. Finland's earlier history as a part of Sweden had led to the consolidation of a large freeholding peasantry. In the nineteenth century the nonfeudal class structure differentiated Finland from the other Eastern European agrarian peripheries. Unlike elsewhere, in Finland the peasants owned the bulk of the country's main industrial resource, the forests, especially in the most prosperous areas of Finland. Consequently, the rise of the forest industry benefited directly the upper stratum of the peasantry. Their position was quite different from that of other European peasants who owned less forest land and who did not experience the enormous rise in the price of land that occurred in Finland. Even compared to Sweden there was a clear difference.[46] A symbiotic relationship arose between farming, forestry, and the forest industry that enabled the spread of forest incomes to a large number of landowners, contributed to the changeover to stock-raising, increased purchasing power in the countryside, and stimulated

---

41 Hoffman 1980, pp. 110–12, 163–5, 173–4; Ahvenainen 1984, pp. 286–96. See also Berend and Ránki 1982, pp. 116–35.
42 Alestalo and Kuhnle 1987, pp. 12–18; Berend and Ránki 1982.
43 See Heikkinen and Hoffman 1982, pp. 82–7; and below, Chapter 4.
44 Heikkinen and Hjerppe 1981, p. 20; Hjerppe, Peltonen and Pihkala 1984, p. 44.
45 Hoffman 1980, p. 175.
46 Ibid.; Ahvenainen 1984, pp. 244–5; Jutikkala 1963, p. 344.

domestic industry.[47] Agrarian advance was connected with industrial development, and in this industrialisation direct foreign-investment capital played no important role.[48]

Second, compared to Russia, Finland was a developed region. In fact, Finland was one of the few relatively 'overdeveloped' minority regions within the multinational empires of the time.[49] Although most of the Finnish counties had been peripheral in the Swedish kingdom, their economic and educational levels were above those of Russia. Finland, long aided by considerable tariff privileges, became from the 1870s on not only an exporter of raw materials to the West but also an exporter of processed products to Russia. Between 1900 and 1909, Russia accounted for 28 percent of the total value of Finnish exports, but its share in the value of industrial exports, excluding sawmill industry products, was 73 percent. The main imports from Russia were grain products.[50] Exports to Russia, although they lagged behind those to Western Europe in volume, were of primary importance in stimulating manufacturing, for example the metal and the textile industries, which were the largest sectors after the wood industry. Metallurgy and textiles, along with papermaking, had much closer linkages with other industrial sectors than did the sawmill industry. This connection also facilitated economic consolidation in Finland.[51]

---

47 Hoffman 1980, pp. 170–2, 174–5; Soininen 1982, pp. 28, 47–50. Cf. Heikkinen and Hjerppe 1981, p. 22.
48 Hjerppe, Peltonen and Pihkala 1984, p. 45. Foreign loans were of significance, however, for example in the forest industry and in railway construction.
49 Only Bohemia, Croatia, and the Russian partition of Poland seem similar in this respect (Nairn 1977, pp. 185–7; Kiernan 1976, p. 120; Berend and Ránki 1982, pp. 107–8).
50 Pihkala 1969, pp. 74–5; Heikkinen and Hoffman 1982, pp. 67–70; Rasila 1982a, pp. 96–9.
51 Preferential tariff treatment in Russia had already helped the Finnish textile and metal industries in the early nineteenth century (Schybergson 1973, p. 59), but new tariffs, adopted simultaneously with the other post-Crimean War reforms in 1859, paved the way for the rapid and favourable development of trade. Several Finnish industries gained a highly advantageous position as compared with industries in Western European competitor countries. The cotton industry became the first modern manufacturing industry in Finland, and before 1850 about 75 percent of its production went to Russia (Schybergson 1980a, pp. 416–17). Similarly, the iron industry exported the bulk of its output to Russia and continuously increased the production of refined iron products as a share of total output. Russia also became the main market for the paper industry. In 1885, however, the Russian tariffs were readjusted, and Finland lost much of its relative advantage vis-à-vis Western countries. The textile industry had to reorient its production to the domestic market, and the export of certain processed products became unprofitable. In other respects, though, the new tariffs had no major negative impact (Hjerppe 1979, p. 131). Particularly in the 1880s, economic integration proceeded as a consequence of the consolidation of the domestic market. In this decade industrial and other domestic production was clearly

Finland's role in the emerging international division of labour cannot be explained solely by its interface position or natural resource endowment: of key importance was the continuously increasing demand for wood on the world market. The interface perspective does, however, throw light on those structures through which international market pressures were transmitted to Finland, and it is therefore essential for understanding the process of economic integration. Thanks to its 'Swedish' social structure, Finland was able to reduce the dangers arising from dependence on the export of a single product to the Western market. Moreover, the fact that Finland was 'overdeveloped' in relation to the mother country was decisive for exploiting the Russian connection. Given this constellation of domestic and international forces, the state could successfully operate to strengthen Finland's position both internally and externally.

3 The Late Nineteenth Century

During the latter half of the century, the capitalist transformation altered substantially the tensions that had emerged between the civil bureaucracy and the academic and clerical groups. Most important, the central role of the state in the process of industrialisation produced close connections between the bureaucratic elite and the bourgeoisie proper, which was made up of a growing number of owners and controllers of means of production. In economic policy the interests of industry were generally given priority over those of agriculture.[52] One major early indication of this partiality was corporate consultation in economic planning, as governmental, industrial, and commercial interests were reconciled in large economic commissions that laid the foundation for the great reforms of the 1850s and 1860s. There was also considerable interrecruitment between the bureaucratic and the commercial-industrial elites.[53]

---

   less dependent on foreign trade than previously (Hjerppe 1979, p. 27). Increasingly, the textile, machine, and other industries began to find outlets for their products in the domestic market (Hjerppe 1979, pp. 35, 131; Hjerppe 1981, p. 223; Hoffman 1980, pp. 34, 92, 116, 174–5; Heikkinen 1981, pp. 417–18). In a period in which domestic grain production was going through a profound crisis and agriculture was changing over to stock-raising, grain imports from Russia facilitated structural transformation. These imports were also advantageous to industry because they made it possible to keep wages low (Myllyntaus 1980, p. 349; Pipping 1969, p. 23).

52 Harmaja 1933, pp. 213, 219, 221. Cf. Pipping 1969, p. 23.
53 The economic elite came primarily from the gentry. The upper stratum of the burghers, i.e., the owners and managers of the large commercial houses, played a central role, espe-

Besides the bourgeoisie, another emerging group was the landowning and Finnish-speaking peasantry, whose wealthiest stratum was on a par with the landed gentry. Rapid economic rise was accompanied by political and cultural consolidation when the Diet was reconvened in 1863 and local government reformed in 1865 (see Chapter 3). In the late nineteenth century this group often allied itself with the clergy, then on the decline. At that time the educational system was divorced from the church, and local government from local parish administration. The decline of the clergy and its coalition with the peasantry are reflected in recruitment patterns. The sons of the gentry increasingly rejected clerical careers, and interrecruitment between academic and clerical groups decreased. Yet at the same time, socially mobile peasant sons joined the ranks of the clergy, which became the first gentry group with a Finnish-speaking majority.[54] As a church historian states, 'When the clergy realized that its hold on a large portion of the educated class was lost, it tried to find a closer connection with the peasant folk'.[55]

With the formation of two clusters among the dominant groups, earlier tensions were altered. The division emerged in the last decades of the century, after regular parliamentary meetings had begun to breathe new life into dormant political life. On one side were the bureaucracy and the bourgeoisie with their Swedish culture, on the other the church and the Finnish-speaking peasantry. In the Parliament the main cleavage was between most of the nobles and the burghers on the one hand, and the clergy and the independent peasantry on the other.

The economic tensions between the new bourgeoisie and the landowners were similar to those found in Scandinavia,[56] but in Finland they were reinforced by a cultural cleavage. Not surprisingly, these tensions are important for understanding the social basis of the national movement (Chapter 5); still, the cleavages should not be exaggerated. Economic development was undermining the gentry as a status group, but there was nonetheless a culture common to all dominant groups except the wealthy peasantry. In absolute numbers the gentry was small: in 1870, for example, it consisted of only 27,000 persons, fam-

---

cially in the sawmill industry, but the nobility and the bureaucracy produced members of the upper industrial and commercial stratum as well. There was also a movement from business to bureaucracy. Systematic information, however, covers only the period 1810–52 (Hoffman 1980, pp. 77–84; A. Kuusterä 1981; Mauranen 1981, pp. 200, 210; Schybergson 1977; Jutikkala 1974, pp. 24–48, 113; Noponen 1964, pp. 34–8; Waris 1940, pp. 258, 260).

54   Juva 1956, p. 123; Björklund 1939, pp. 33–7; Laaksonen 1962, pp. 36–7; Alapuro 1973a, p. 31; Elovainio 1972, p. 251.
55   Juva 1960, p. 359.
56   Rokkan 1970, pp. 108–9.

TABLE 2   Percentage distribution of Finnish population by estate, 1890

Estate	
Nobility	0.1%
Clergy	0.3
Burghers	3.1
Independent peasantry	26.1
Others	70.4
Total	100.0%
N (thousands)	2,380

SOURCE: *ÉLÉMENTS DÉMOGRAPHIQUES PRINCIPAUX DE LA FINLANDE POUR LES ANNÉES 1750–1890* 1899, 261, 262

ily members included, or 1.5 percent of the total population.[57] Twenty years later the share was somewhat higher, as may be seen from the first three figures in Table 2. All elites shared a similar background; they were educated at the same university and often knew one another.[58] And all were unanimous about the need to maintain and reinforce political autonomy. Conflicts between the landowners and the rising bourgeoisie seem to have been comparatively restricted. The landowning peasantry benefited from the leading industrial sector, sawmilling, and over a time a certain community of interests emerged.

These features should also be viewed in the context of the social tranquillity then prevailing. No challenge from below forced the dominant groups to close ranks. Apart from the last decade, the nineteenth century was a period in which internal social conflicts were practically unknown (see Chapter 6)[59] and external peace continued uninterrupted. The dominance of the landowning peasantry tended to mask the growth of the rural proletariat, and the urban proletariat increased significantly only in the 1890s. The ultimate guarantee of stability was provided by the empire, even if imperial troops were never needed

---

57 Wirilander 1974, p. 142.
58 Klinge 1980a, pp. 53, 64, 66. The number of students was small, around 600–50 in the 1870s, and only grew to about 1,250 at the turn of the century (Klinge 1967–8, 2: 3, 3: 2, 168).
59 The only region of peasant unrest in nineteenth-century Finland was the county of Viipuri. In this region, the so-called Old Finland, which was united with the 'new' Finland in 1812, Russian nobles had been granted land in the eighteenth century.

to put down local insurrections, as happened in Poland. Characteristically, only minor readjustments were made in corporate privileges. At the beginning of the twentieth century, Finland had essentially the same political system as it had in 1789.

A final indication of the growing strength of the local dominant groups and of Finland as a separate political unit was the creation of a national armed force. Up to the 1870s there was a peacetime Finnish detachment of between 1,600 and 4,500 men. In 1878, after general conscription had been introduced in Russia, the Parliament succeeded in obtaining approval for a separate Finnish army, a concession necessitated by the conflict in the Balkans and the concomitant Russian fear of Swedish intervention.[60] This army was also raised through general conscription and at full strength never exceeded 5,600 men.[61] Thus, whereas Alexander I's two other conquests, Bessarabia and Congress Poland, lost their original status in the course of the nineteenth century, Finland succeeded in preserving and even strengthening its original position.[62]

In the last decades of the century, territorial consolidation, centralisation, and differentiation of the instruments of government and economic integration occurred, as did monopolisation of the means of coercion. As to centralisation and the character of governmental institutions, Finland had not only a legal order but also a centralised administrative apparatus subject to this legal order – that is, the bureaucracy. In a word, Finnish leaders were increasingly in charge of, to use Weber's term, a modern state.[63]

---

60 Suni 1979, p. 98.
61 The rest of the conscripts remained in reserve. Young men were chosen by lot only to the extent necessary to keep the total active force at 5,600 (Lundin 1981, p. 420).
62 Jussila 1984, pp. 99–102; Polvinen 1984, p. 60.
63 According to Max Weber, the essential characteristics of the modern state are legal order, bureaucracy, binding authority over a territory, and monopolisation of the legitimate use of coercion (Weber 1968, p. 56; Bendix 1960, pp. 417–18).

CHAPTER 3

The Agrarian Class Structure and Industrial Workers

In the closing decades of the nineteenth century, capitalist development greatly speeded up the dissolution of traditional social structures. New divisions opened the way for conflicts within the agrarian population, and an industrial proletariat emerged. The two processes were linked in that Finland's industrialisation was based mainly on the exploitation of its forests.

1 The Industrial and Agricultural Revolutions in Finland

Stein Rokkan has argued that the considerable agrarian support the Social Democrats received in Finland resulted largely from the late start of emigration or, more specifically, from the rapid growth of the landless proletariat, which was a consequence of this late start.[1] This point becomes clear in the light of more fundamental processes, namely the industrial and demographic revolutions, which in Finland, as elsewhere in Eastern Europe, were chronologically distinct. There, because the onset of the population growth preceded industrialisation and economic growth, a large 'surplus' agrarian population was created before industrialisation could effectively absorb it.[2]

This situation was peculiar to the peripheral areas in the capitalist transformation of Europe. In the West – that is, in the core areas of capitalist development – the demographic revolution was a concomitant and constituent part of the industrial revolution itself. And not only that: population growth was inseparably linked to the simultaneous modernisation of the whole economy, which included both an industrial and a related agricultural revolutions.[3] Unlike Finland and the other Eastern regions, the countries of Western Europe industrialised at a fairly steady pace during the latter half of the nineteenth century and the beginning of the twentieth, deriving most of the required workforce from the growing landless population. In Sweden, for instance, industrial development (as well as emigration) absorbed the new agrar-

---

1 Rokkan 1981, pp. 69–70.
2 Berend and Ránki 1982, pp. 44–8.
3 Ibid., pp. 44–5.

ian proletariat, which was then becoming established as the population in the commercialising agricultural sector increased. The agricultural and industrial revolutions thus managed to keep pace with each other, as they did in Western Europe as a whole: the emerging rural proletariat was gradually dissipated. Sweden even experienced shortages of agricultural workers in the early years of the twentieth century.[4] In the West, in short, the problems of population increase were never as acute as they were in the East.

Eastern Europe, with its growing population, remained predominantly agricultural for a longer time. Instead of a 'balanced' process of industrialisation aided by an agricultural revolution, agricultural transformation preceded industrialisation. This development resulted from the almost unlimited market in the West for Eastern European cereals, meat, fruit, and other foodstuffs. The demand caused Eastern European agriculture to grow dependent on developed Western European capitalism and brought about several agrarian reforms that were aimed at transforming manorial estates into large capitalist farms. When the peasants were freed from feudal ties to their landlords, a new class of agricultural wage workers emerged, particularly in Hungary and Romania. These reforms took place near the middle of the century and immediately thereafter – well before the industrial take-off, and therefore well before the increase in population could be absorbed by industry. As a result, the industrial revolution was not directly associated with the capitalist transformation in agriculture but was delayed until the end of the nineteenth and the beginning of the twentieth centuries. With one-sided agrarian advance constituting the dynamic and decisive process, and with no strong links to an overall process of economic development 'carrying everything with it', development in Eastern Europe was thus mainly dependent on external factors.[5]

In Finland, however, the interaction of the industrial and agricultural revolutions was different than in the rest of Eastern Europe. Because Finland's capitalist transformation was based primarily on the rise of the forest industry, changes occurred immediately in the countryside. There new industrial centres grew up and there, unlike elsewhere, peasants owned the bulk of the best forest lands. The effects of industrialisation were therefore exceptionally direct and extensive in the rural areas.

This forestry-based industrialisation contributed to the virtual simultaneity of the capitalist transformation both in industry and in agriculture. The agricultural transformation occurred relatively late, even among the prosperous

---

4 Carlsson 1968, pp. 252–67; Jörberg 1975, pp. 104–6; Åkerman 1975, p. 173; Blum 1978, pp. 438–9.
5 See Berend and Ránki 1974, pp. 30–9, 53, 67 (quotation), 122–9, 135–47; and Blum 1978, p. 437.

peasants, only from the 1870s on – later than the great agrarian reforms in Eastern Europe or, for example, the agricultural revolution in Scandinavia.[6] Even as late as the 1860s, Finland experienced a disastrous famine that resulted in a population decline of eight percent and demonstrated that traditional arable farming practices were very much a dead end.[7] Thus late industrialisation and rapid population growth, as well as the linkage between the industrial and agricultural transformations, led in Finland to the *simultaneous* and *related* growth of the industrial and rural proletariat.

In other words, the situation in Finland was different not only from that in Sweden, where the rural proletariat had been absorbed as a result of industrial development, but also from that in Eastern Europe, where the industrial proletariat emerged only after land reforms had already given rise to a large landless proletariat.

Finnish conditions were aggravated, moreover, by the small scale of emigration. The rate of emigration, one indication of the breakup of traditional social arrangements, was lower than in Sweden. Those who left Finland for America between 1850 and 1910, for example, amounted to 7.7 percent of the 1910 population, whereas the corresponding figure for Sweden was 17.5 percent.[8] Furthermore, although emigration to America from East-Central Europe, as from Finland, began late, its relative importance was much greater.

2   Freeholding Peasants and Agrarian Workers

Large-scale peasant ownership of forest land, together with the employment that forestry and the sawmills provided for the landless, accentuated the spread of capitalism to the Finnish countryside. The integration into the developed capitalist market system in the late nineteenth century was felt immediately by the rural population.

Many landowning peasants prospered, and the changeover from arable farming to stock-raising and dairy farming – the central feature of the Finnish agricultural revolution – became easier than would otherwise have been the case. As a well-known commentator described the development, 'Capitalism and the spirit of capitalism [began], consciously or unconsciously, to penetrate into peasant agriculture ... The landowning peasant had to produce more

---

6   Jörberg 1973, pp. 393–406; Winberg 1975, pp. 33–5; Soininen 1974, p. 412; Østerud 1978a, pp. 189–94.
7   Strömmer 1969, p. 22; Soininen 1974, pp. 402–15.
8   Rasila 1970, p. 19.

for the market and to manage his farm like an enterprise; he had to begin to make calculations and to view economic activity from the point of profitability ... [In the process,] crofters, casual workers, and hired hands were increasingly exploited on the main farm'.[9] At the same time, in 1865, 1879, and 1883, restrictions on labour migration were removed, and hiring-out obligations were abolished. The everyday contacts between the freeholding peasant and his workers also appear to have changed. Contrary to earlier customs, the landowner and his family began to sleep and eat apart from the workers.[10] Moreover, from the end of the century on, the children of freeholders who could not become farmers themselves increasingly left agriculture, mainly for various middle-class occupations.[11]

These observations suggest, first, a transition from peasant to farmer, or a change in which the landowning peasant entered the market more fully than before and explored alternative uses for the factors of production. Second, they suggest that this transformation also altered the relationship between the landowner and other agrarian groups, workers and crofters, as the landowner had increasingly to maximise his returns in the context of the market, regardless of the immediate consequences of his action.[12]

Both suggestions are supported by several facts. First, owners of large farms received enough forest income to make the changeover to dairy farming markedly easier. As Lennart Jörberg says in a comparative account, 'The introduction of more modern production methods, new equipment and better buildings all demanded a great deal of capital. If they had relied wholly on agricultural yield, Finnish farmers could hardly have come by this capital. Instead they acquired it to a great extent from the sale of forests and timber'.[13] Most important in this respect, apparently, was the role forest incomes played in relieving the indebtedness caused by the preceding crisis of arable cultivation. In 1900, for example, private citizens, essentially peasants, received 90 percent of the proceeds from the sale of standing timber. From 1860 to 1900 timber prices rose three or four times as fast as consumer prices. No wonder, then, that incomes in the countryside were more unevenly distributed during the closing decades of the last century than in the previous period.[14]

---

9 Forsman 1912, pp. 19, 26.
10 Myllyntaus 1981, p. 181; Soikkanen 1961, p. 80.
11 According to Haapala's (1982, pp. 200–1) study of rural communities in the county of Häme.
12 See Wolf 1969, pp. xiv–xv, 286.
13 Jörberg 1973, pp. 400–1.
14 H. Kunnas 1973, pp. 87, 98; Hjerppe and Lefgren 1974, pp. 103–4. Cf. Hjerppe, Peltonen and Pihkala 1984, p. 43; M. Peltonen 1986, pp. 107–12.

TABLE 3   Indicators of market penetration in the countryside, 1870–1910

	1870	1880	1890	1900	1910
Total agrarian population, in thousands[a]	1,470	1,659	1,867	1,992	2,143
Area under cultivation, in thousands of hectares	–	830	980	1,568[b]	1,878[b]
Marketed roundwood, in thousands of solid cubic meters	2,090	3,370	5,500	11,400	15,970
Milk produced, in millions of kilograms	520	701	963	1,326	1,541
Rural savings banks	17	84	108	160	329

a Includes the population engaged in agriculture and forestry.
b In 1901. Then and in 1910 the definition of land under cultivation was broader than in the earlier period.
SOURCES: P. MANNINEN 1976, 81; SOININEN 1974, 130; *RECENSEMENT AGRICOLE DE 1910* 1916, 1; H. KUNNAS 1973, 110–111; VIITA 1965, 58–59; URBANS 1963, 449

Land prices also increased. One case study suggests that they increased in south-western Finland by over three and a half times in the period from 1850 until 1906–10;[15] a similar rise also occurred in central Finland:[16] further indications of the widening gap between landowners and others. It seems reasonable to agree with the conclusion of Hannu Soikkanen that, owing to the central role of wood processing, the impact of industrialisation on life in the countryside was greater in Finland than in other countries at a comparable level of development.[17]

A number of other economic indicators attest to this change (see Table 3). Gentry estates were increasingly transferred to the peasants throughout the nineteenth century, most markedly in its latter half. Differences between manors and wealthy peasant farms nearly disappeared. The area under cultivation was greatly increased. Milk production quadrupled between 1870 and 1910 and soon became the largest source of income for farmers, particularly through butter exports. Cooperative dairies controlled by wealthy peasants spread rapidly at the turn of the century, as did the number of professional farmers' societies and savings banks that mainly served peasant landowners.[18] At the same time, the farmers' tax burden fell significantly, for although their income increased, taxation remained at the previous level.

15   Kivialho 1927, pp. 118–21.
16   Markkanen 1977, pp. 60–2.
17   Soikkanen 1981, pp. 441–2.
18   See, e.g., Soininen 1982, pp. 40–6; and Alapuro 1980, p. 50.

TABLE 4   Agrarian households in Finland by class, 1815–1901

Class	1815	1870	1901	1815 (thousands)	1870 (thousands)	1901 (thousands)
Landowners	57%	39%	35%	75	83	103
Crofters[a]	28	32	17	38	68	49
Agricultural workers	15	29	48[b]	19	60	139[b]
Total	100%	100%	100%	132	211	291

a   Includes other tenant farmers as well.
b   In 1901 a number of scrapholders, who lived mainly by selling their labour power and who had previously been classified as crofters, were reclassified as agricultural workers. The relative increase in the number of households of agricultural workers and the relative decline in crofters' households is therefore somewhat exaggerated.
SOURCES: KILPI 1913, TABLES 33–36, 38, 54; GEBHARD 1913, 89, 92, 109

The political position of the freeholding peasants improved as well. Local government reforms instituted in 1865 guaranteed them power in local affairs. And at the national level they gained a great degree of influence once the Diet began to convene regularly after 1863 and the Peasant Estate for the first time gained equal status with the other estates.

These changes in themselves served to alter the relationship between the landowners and other agrarian groups. Moreover, not only was the wealth accruing from capitalist development distributed differentially among landowners and agricultural workers, but their relationship also changed directly.

The most important factor in this change was that the landowning population grew much more slowly than did the number of agricultural workers. During the last 30 years of the century, worker households grew in number from less than one-third to nearly one-half the total number of agrarian households, and the proportion of freeholding peasants decreased from 39 percent to 35 percent (see Table 4). This trend implies not only that new farms were not created on a large scale but also that few new croft leases were arranged. The significant increase in the amount of land under cultivation at the end of the nineteenth century, then, was not linked to the establishment of new crofts, as had previously been the case; rather, the landowner was now ready to cultivate more land personally and to use the farm for commercial dairy farming. Because the number of crofters did not increase, the growth rate of the agrarian proletariat accelerated,[19] and it became largely a 'surplus' population. Accord-

---

19   According to a local study, only 20 percent of the crofters' children in the county of Häme

ing to one estimate, in 1880, 50–60 percent of the then-current labour force would have been sufficient to maintain the prevailing level of agricultural production.[20]

A study made in the most densely populated and prosperous region of the country, the south-west, where the leasehold system was the most widespread and industrial growth the strongest, illustrates the development in the relationship between the landowners and the agrarian workers. Changes in agriculture and the rise in forest prices led to stricter leaseholds. Moreover, landowners divided part of their land into a number of small plots with high rents instead of creating traditional leasehold farms. Thus there emerged a new class of farm workers who lived by temporary work and lacked the relative independence of the crofters. As the population grew, the growth was channelled primarily into this new group, leading finally to an increase in emigration at the end of the century.[21]

In other words, especially those groups that remained outside the traditional peasant community increased. To be a full member of the community, it was necessary to have a certain rough minimum amount of land. The process of modernisation considerably increased the number of those who held less than this minimum;[22] indeed, this growing stratum had even less access to the land than did the crofters. As the landless population expanded without being effectively absorbed into industry, it remained in the countryside, producing a large number of agricultural workers. In 1910 there were 2.3 agricultural workers and 0.5 crofters and other tenant farmers for every landowner, and in the south-west the proportion was much higher, with 4.6 agricultural workers to every landowner.[23]

There is no doubt, then, that the commercialisation of agriculture considerably widened the gap between the landowners and the agrarian labourers. But although the latter became sharply differentiated from the freeholders, it would be erroneous to consider them badly hurt by the transformation. The rise of forestry not only benefited the owners of larger farms, but it also eased the conditions of the agrarian workers. Hence, 'the "breakdown" of old economic forms' in the 1860s and thereafter did not cause them grave economic problems. In fact, their wages actually increased toward the end of the cen-

---

became crofters in the 1870s, whereas 42 percent became agrarian workers (Haapala 1982, p. 58).
20 Kaukiainen 1981, p. 55.
21 Gylling 1907, pp. 168–70.
22 Cf. Moore 1966, pp. 474–5.
23 *Population de la Finlande au 31 décembre 1910* 1915, 2:62, 66.

tury owing both to the work available in logging and floating and to the rise in agricultural productivity.[24] On the one hand, then, the forestry-based capitalist transformation made large groups of the landless a definite and increasingly distinct agrarian lower class, but on the other hand this change caused them no real distress. Both these aspects are significant for understanding the character of the agrarian workers' political mobilisation in the first decades of the twentieth century (see Chapter 6).

3   The Link between Industrial and Agrarian Workers

The nature of capitalist development influenced the make-up not only of the non-landowning agrarian population (both workers and crofters) but also of the industrial working class. Industrial expansion took place largely in rural areas, as evidenced by the fact that the industrial population grew more rapidly than the urban population in the late 1800s. New plants such as sawmills, pulp mills, and paper factories spread throughout the countryside, and in 1910 nearly half the industrial workers lived there, with the sawmill industry alone employing one-quarter, and the wood industry as a whole one-third, of the total industrial labour force. The maximum sawing period per year is estimated to have been only about 190 days in 1880, 220 in 1900; thus, seasonal fluctuation was substantial. Moreover, as just stated, labour-intensive logging and floating provided significant employment for the landless.[25]

Internal migration increased toward the end of the nineteenth century. Set in motion partly by logging and floating jobs, people were gradually pulled toward industrial communities. Migration was facilitated by the fact that many industrial plants, particularly sawmills, pulp and paper factories, and iron works, employed a large number of unskilled workers. Also, many cities grew in the latter years of the nineteenth century as a result of the influx of the landless. In 1870 a narrow majority of the young workers in Tampere, Finland's first and leading large-scale industrial centre, had come from non-landowning rural families, with an additional 20 percent from the freeholding peasantry. Thereafter self-recruitment increased, but in 1910 the proportion of the children of crofters and the landless was still more than one-third.[26] Likewise, at the turn

---

24   Heikkinen et al. 1983, pp. 24–36, 88 (quotation); Soininen 1981, pp. 97–111; Ahvenainen 1984, pp. 303–4.
25   Heikkinen and Hoffman 1982, p. 55; Peltonen 1982, p. 85; Hjerppe and Heikkinen 1978, p. 22; Hoffman 1981, p. 118.
26   Haapala 1982, pp. 56–60, 197, 308. In 1910, fewer than 40 percent of the young workers

of the century nearly two-thirds of the 100,000 inhabitants of the capital, Helsinki, had been born elsewhere. Over half of those who moved to Helsinki toward the end of the century had previously been part of the landless rural proletariat.[27]

All in all, owing to Finland's late industrialisation and the close linkage between the industrial and agricultural transformations, the industrial and agrarian proletariat developed simultaneously and were linked together. For the great majority of the proletariat – that is, the agrarian workers – the connection with the emerging industrial working class was fairly close, for several reasons. First, capitalist development changed the relationship of the growing landless population and the landowners. Through liberal reforms, which enabled the landless to move and sell their labour power, and industrialisation, which contributed directly to the commercialisation process in agriculture, the landless became an increasingly distinct class vis-à-vis the landed. Second, at the same time that the agrarian transformation occurred, an industrial working class emerged that had close connections with the agrarian proletariat. Indeed, the borderline between these two groups was rather hazy, thanks to the marked rural expansion of the sawmills and the wood-processing industry and to seasonal floating and logging. Finally, an overwhelming majority of the industrial workers had been recruited directly from the agrarian population. In the first decades of the twentieth century the Finnish industrial working class was rooted firmly in the countryside.

4   Crofters

The crofters occupied a position different from that of the agrarian workers. The former were small leaseholders who obtained their main livelihood from farming. Usually they worked a minimum of three hectares (1.2 acres), sometimes much more, and kept a couple of cows. Rent was paid mainly by working a certain number of days for the landowner and, to a lesser extent, by payments in kind or money. In the early 1800s the position of the leaseholder was often rather similar to that of the freeholding peasant. The situation changed decisively only toward the end of the century.

The first political protests in late nineteenth-century Finland were by the crofters. Their collective actions against the landowners – mainly demonstra-

---

in Tampere were second-generation urban workers who were born there (Haapala 1982, p. 191).

27   Waris 1932, pp. 298, 300.

tions and petitions – received much attention during the 1880s, and by the turn of the century the so-called leasehold question had become a major political problem for the dominant groups.[28]

It may be argued that the leasehold question resulted from pressures caused by the capitalist development to a pre-capitalist tenancy system. Agreements concerning rents, rights of occupancy, and length of tenancy were usually oral and fairly unambiguous – customary and mutually understood – in the period when the landowner's connection with the market was limited. With the commercialisation of agriculture, however, the role of the croft in the landowner's household changed. Market requirements strained the relationship between the landowner and the leaseholder; consequently, the oral agreements were interpreted in conflicting ways and became a subject of controversy.

Toward the end of the century it became common for landowners to evict crofters and add the land that they had cleared and cultivated to the main farm, to reduce the crofters' forest rights, to increase rent, and to reduce the length of tenancies. Rents were augmented to the extent that the crofters' incomes grew very slowly, if at all. At the same time, as noted above, the wages of the agricultural labourers were going up discernibly.[29] The number of crofts relative to freehold farms decreased significantly in the second half of the nineteenth century (see Table 4). Also, landowners increasingly alleged laziness on the part of the crofters, a reflection, in part, of the demands of market production.[30] The crofts were losing their significance for the management of the main farm, as indicated by the increasing replacement of work rent by monetary payments after 1900. This practice served to weaken the productive link between the leasehold farm and the main farm. Although day labour remained the main form of rent, the spread of monetary payments shows that hired labour was becoming more advantageous than the crofters' day labour, at least on large farms. A 'free' labour force was widely and cheaply available.[31]

Late industrialisation seems to have aggravated the conflict between the freeholding peasants and the crofters, preventing not only the landless but also the crofters from moving elsewhere. The tenancy system did not fade away gradually and smoothly, as in Sweden. In Finland crofters were forced to remain where they were and to fight for their rights. In Sweden crofts increased in number into the 1860s, after which they then began quickly to decline, dropping by 1900 to two-thirds of the 1860s level. In Finland, in contrast, the number

---

28 See Rasila 1961.
29 Heikkinen et al. 1983, pp. 24–46, 95, 100–1.
30 Rasila 1970, p. 17.
31 Ibid., pp. 34–5; Haatanen 1968, pp. 105, 172.

of crofts was slightly greater in 1900 than in 1860, although their proportion had clearly declined. Monetary payments to landowners were also much more common in Sweden than in Finland.[32]

To conclude, like the agrarian workers, the crofters had grievances against the landowners. But in other respects the situations of the two groups were not similar. The crofters had access to the land, and the principal defence strategy open to them was to try to strengthen this control. Both similarities and differences in the two groups' positions were, naturally enough, to manifest themselves in their political reactions. But the somewhat varying structural positions only set certain minimum conditions for these reactions. The actual fusion or dissociation in the crofters' and the workers' organisation and mobilisation was to be powerfully determined by development of the political scene at the turn of the century and thereafter.

---

32   Rasila 1961, pp. 22, 36–9; Rasila 1970, p. 32; Haatanen 1968, p. 176.

CHAPTER 4

Territorial Integration

'In the Finland of 1809 the Russians ran into a country without a centre'.[1] Before 1809, rather than the various regions being oriented to each other through the regional division of labour, giving Finland the status of a separate economic unit, they were oriented mainly to the core of the Swedish state. Only in the nineteenth century was there an economic reorientation: first, partially, to St. Petersburg; and then, definitely, to a core within the grand duchy, with the concomitant integration of the separate regions into a national whole. The capitalist transformation strengthened the ties among the regions and simultaneously accentuated their differences.

In other words, during the Swedish period the Finnish-speaking regions interacted with an external core. Later on, however, an internal core emerged. Both core-periphery processes influenced the consolidation of regionally differentiated class structures at the end of the nineteenth century.

1   Finnish Regions up to 1809

In the seventeenth century, Sweden was a great power in Europe. It had, according to Eli F. Heckscher, 'a strong state power and presumably the most effective administrative organisation among all countries of that time'; despite economic backwardness, 'politically [it was] an exceptionally solidly-built society, where there was no room for particularism'.[2] The relatively high degree of centralisation may be seen in the relation of the Finnish regions to the state centre. The basic structure remained the same up to the end of the period.

The political and economic centre of Sweden was Stockholm, which developed into a metropolis during the seventeenth century.[3]

All over the kingdom, the peasantry was taxed effectively, especially after the 'reductions' of 1680 had brought back to royal jurisdiction lands previously granted to the nobles. Finland was not a separate fiscal unit. Like the rest of Sweden, it was divided into counties whose administration was reformed dur-

---

1   Klinge 1975, p. 28.
2   Heckscher 1936, p. 367 (cited in Åström 1980a, pp. 295–6).
3   Mead 1981, pp. 86–92.

ing the seventeenth century to better serve the needs of the monarchy.[4] In heraldic contexts, the 'Swedish' and 'Finnish' provinces were not presented separately, but in an order starting from the regions around the core and arriving at the more peripheral regions at various corners of the state.[5] Thus, although staple, tariff, and industrial policies did prevent various Finnish regions from developing in the same way as certain 'Swedish' peripheries,[6] Finland was not, as a whole, in a colonial position.

Economic centralisation, based on the principles of mercantilism, was ensured by the rigid regulation of domestic trade and by the concentration of export trade in Stockholm and the so-called staple towns. In connecting the hinterlands to the capital (and to foreign countries), the coastal cities obviously played a central part. In the Finnish territories the city network was located on the eastern coast of the Gulf of Bothnia and on the northern coast of the Gulf of Finland (see Map 1, p. 21).

Commerce with Stockholm and abroad was along three main routes. The principal way station was Turku, in the south-west of what later became Finland. Because this city was the centre of the region with the longest history of Swedish rule, Turku and its hinterland had, besides exports, other close economic connections with nearby Stockholm. The second centre was Viipuri, farther to the east. Only these two Finnish cities, Turku and Viipuri, had full and effective rights to trade overseas; their position reflected the basic twofold division in the Finnish town system.[7] Another staple town, Helsinki, was located on the southern coast, but its exports remained insignificant. The third trade centre was on the Ostrobothnian coast, Oulu being the most important city. No Ostrobothnian city was a staple town, though, and their goods had to pass through Stockholm or Turku.[8]

Although the volume of trade remained limited and the regional division of labour generally weak, the three trade routes still illustrate the separation of the Finnish regions. What mattered were connections with the various centres of trade, not between the regions themselves. Moreover, Finland had no common front in economic policy. On the contrary, in many conflicts Turku and Viipuri opposed Ostrobothnian demands, and in other cases they followed different courses in alliance with certain 'Swedish' cities.[9] In the eighteenth century,

---

4 Åström 1980a, pp. 302, 310–11.
5 Klinge 1975, p. 26.
6 Åström 1980b.
7 A. Peltonen 1982, p. 97.
8 See Åström 1977a, pp. 145–60.
9 Ranta and Åström 1980, pp. 258, 259, 262.

the decline of Sweden complicated the situation, leading to increased Russian influence and partial domination in the east (see Map 1).

The tripartite division applied not only to trade but also to productive and social structures. The three regions, their origins going back to the Middle Ages, developed as a result of varying natural conditions and differing degrees of penetration by the Swedish state.[10] In fact, the different trade orientations only complete the picture. There were even differences in the ideological sphere: the mobile members of the clergy, for instance, seldom crossed regional borders.[11]

Map 2 shows the three main regions, plus eastern Finland, which was an economic hinterland of Viipuri, and the very sparsely populated northern Finland. This basic division is commonly used in accounts dealing with socioeconomic conditions up to the late nineteenth century.[12] It corresponds roughly with the historical division of the provinces[13] and (rather well) with the early twentieth-century apportionment by county or groups of counties (Map 3), the only major exception being Ostrobothnia. To south-western Finland belong the counties of Uusimaa, Turku and Pori, and Häme, and to eastern Finland the main areas of the counties of Kuopio and Mikkeli. Ostrobothnia is composed of the western parts of the county of Vaasa and of the adjacent coastal areas of the county of Oulu. Northern Finland is coterminous with the bulk of the county of Oulu. The regional statistics used in the subsequent pages exist in most cases only for the counties.

Both geographically and socially, the south-west was closest to the core of the Swedish state, being the region first colonised and subjugated by the Swedes. Thus the term *Finland* referred initially to this area specifically. A considerable Swedish-speaking agrarian and fishing population lived along the coast, and not only the largest trading centre, Turku, but also the majority of the manors in Finland were located in this region. Besides the gentry, the wealthier peasants also began to penetrate the agrarian upper class after enclosures and other reforms in the late 1700s. In the early nineteenth century crofters, and especially landless labourers, increased rapidly in number.

---

10   See Kaukiainen 1980, p. 89.
11   Wirilander 1974, pp. 293–8.
12   E.g., Jutikkala 1963, pp. 371–405; Soininen 1974, p. 19; Sarmela 1969, pp. 251–63.
13   Ostrobothnia is one of the historical provinces. South-western Finland is coterminous with Uusimaa, Finland Proper, Satakunta, and the southern areas of Häme; eastern Finland corresponds roughly to Savo and North Karelia; and northern Finland corresponds roughly to Lapland (see Sømme 1968, pp. 6–7).

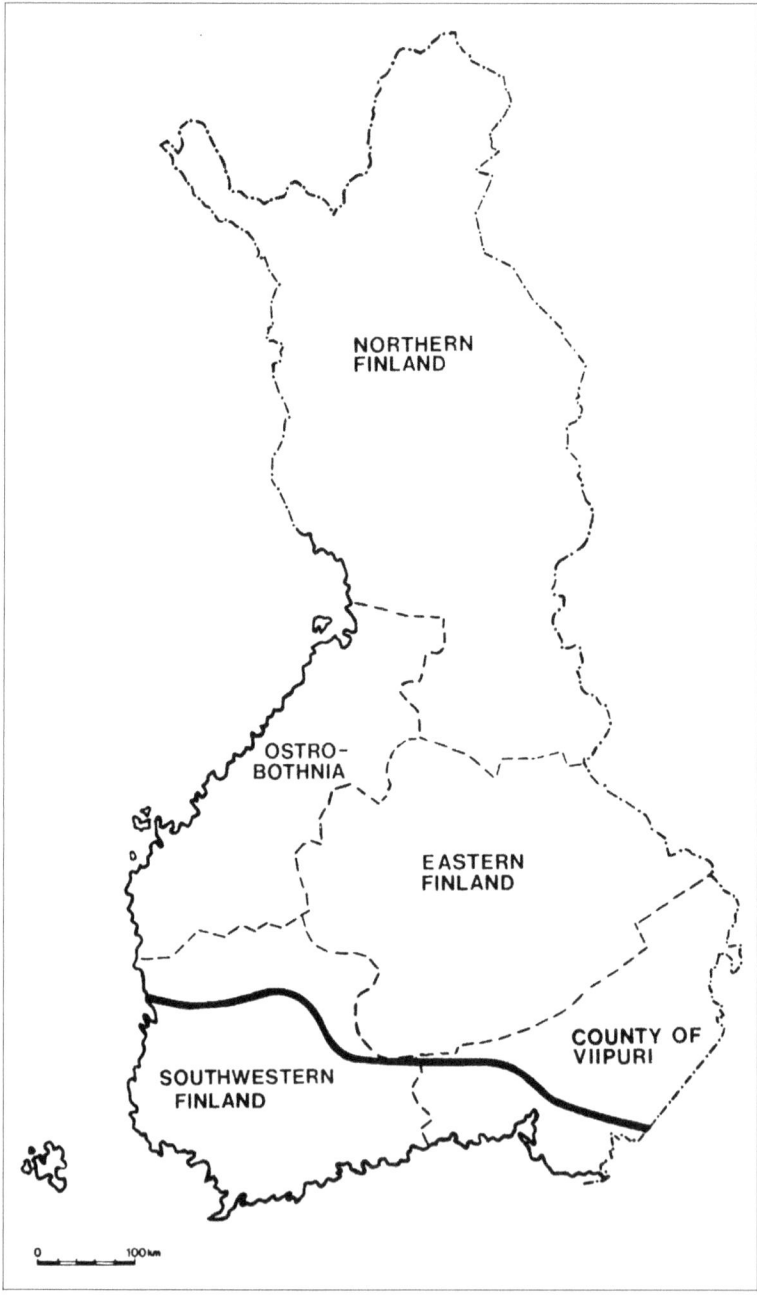

MAP 2 Main Finnish regions and the line between the Reds and the Whites in the revolution of 1918

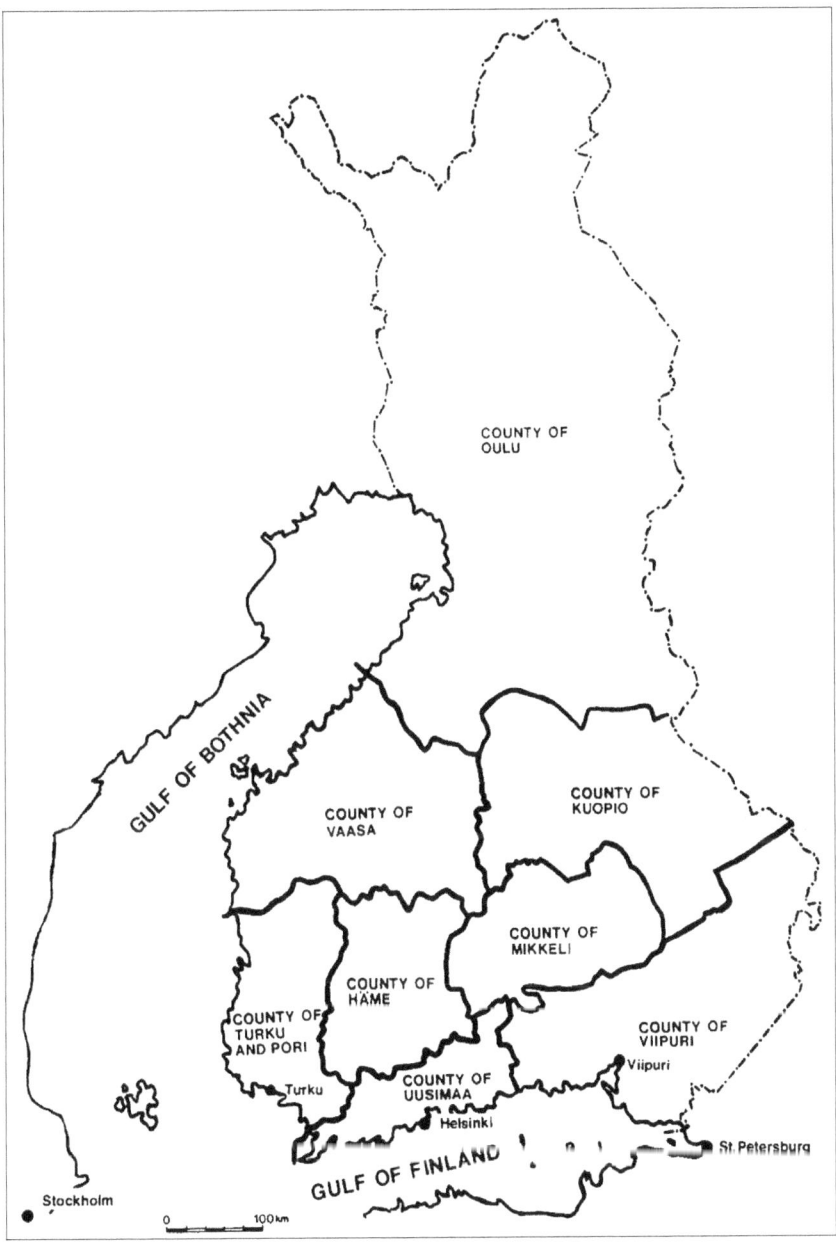

MAP 3   The counties of Finland at the beginning of the twentieth century

The other region with close links to the state core, Ostrobothnia, also had a Swedish-speaking coastal population. An integral part of a larger whole consisting of the lands surrounding the upper end of the Gulf of Bothnia, geographically it displayed 'strong ecological independence',[14] with a ridge separating it from the other Finnish regions, particularly in the south and southeast. Up to the mid-eighteenth century its trade was dominated by Stockholm, with coastal cities serving as way stations between Stockholm and the Ostrobothnian hinterland. The main products traded were tar and ships.

Tar was the second Swedish staple product after iron, and in the seventeenth century the Finnish regions, particularly Ostrobothnia, had become the most important tar-producing area in Europe. Because the Ostrobothnian countryside was dominated by well-to-do independent peasants, the tar-selling peasants evidently had considerable bargaining power in their relations with the merchants in the cities. The villages were compact peasant communities with no manors, and, in contrast with the south-west, the wealth of the peasant upper class was not primarily dependent on the exploitation of crofters' labour power. Rather, the crofters were in a kind of partnership with the landowners, who needed labour for tar production.

Presumably more important still for increasing peasant wealth, however, was the flourishing ship-building industry, which was also based on Ostrobothnian forest reserves. In the seventeenth and eighteenth centuries ship-building was probably the most important branch of the modest industry located in the Finnish regions, and the Ostrobothnian peasants were its main beneficiaries.[15] Moreover, production for the provisioning of Stockholm was quite advanced among Ostrobothnian peasants, who, together with the south-western peasants, enjoyed greater wealth than in the other regions. Wealth was also more evenly divided than in the south-west.[16] This group was capable of acting collectively, as powerfully indicated by the so-called Club War against state encroachments at the end of the sixteenth century. It was the most forcible peasant rebellion ever seen in Finland, and southern Ostrobothnia was its core area.

Developments in the early eighteenth century, when Sweden lost its position as a great power and was forced to surrender the area surrounding the city of Viipuri to Russia, definitely separated and differentiated this region from the south-west. Russian nobles soon dominated large tracts of land, and feudal rela-

---

14   Sarmela 1969, p. 253.
15   Aunola 1967, pp. 336–42, 372, 376; Åström 1977b, p. 103; Virrankoski 1980, p. 244.
16   Jutikkala 1980, p. 228.

tions were introduced in the countryside. At the same time, the proximity of St. Petersburg linked small peasants directly to the market. The small landholding peasants transported their own products to St. Petersburg and performed other transport jobs year-round. In 1800 the Russian capital, with 220,000 inhabitants, was one of the largest cities in Europe, and the number of Finns living there was exceeded only by two Finnish towns.[17]

In the east, or the so-called Savo-Karelian slash-and-burn region, the link with the dominant external centres was tenuous. Until the eighteenth century it remained an economic hinterland of Viipuri. The people were mobile and lived in dispersed settlements; there were no strong exploitative relations within the peasant population and, therefore, no strong peasant upper class. The small local gentry played only a minor role in agricultural production. Up to the eighteenth century the main export product was tar. In contrast to Ostrobothnia, merchant-peasant relations in Savo-Karelia seem to have been exploitative in nature: the merchants were able to squeeze the peasants for their own advantage.[18] After the annexation of Viipuri and its surroundings by Russia in 1721 and 1743, peasant trade with the southern centres declined. Traditional local trade over the Russian border in the east continued, however, now stimulated by the growth of the new centre of St. Petersburg.[19] But the scant grain and tar trade of this area was forced to turn to the Gulf of Bothnia, benefiting the Ostrobothnian economy.

The extremely sparsely populated north of Finland (including Lapland) corresponds roughly to the geographer's 'backwoods Finland' (*Luonnon-Suomi*). During the Swedish period and even later, the north was an area of colonisation. There were also old market connections, based on salmon, furs, and meat, along the rivers running to the upper end of the Gulf of Bothnia. The north-east was involved in the market through Russian centres, across borders that long remained poorly defined.

In 1809, then, the regions of the newly founded Grand Duchy of Finland had a tradition of linkages to several outside centres. The south-west and Ostrobothnia had the closest connections with the core of Sweden; the future county of Viipuri had established close links with St. Petersburg; and in the east the ties with Viipuri had been partly replaced by connections with Ostrobothnia.

---

17   About 3,000 Finns lived in St. Petersburg at that time – as many, incidentally, as lived in Stockholm. The populations of Turku, Oulu, and Helsinki rose to 9,400, 3,500, and 3,000, respectively. The corresponding figure for Viipuri, which then belonged to Russia, was 3,100 (Engman 1983, p. 389).
18   Åström 1977b, pp. 93–5.
19   Engman 1983, pp. 114–16.

The weakest links were between the east and the south-west: even by the mid-nineteenth century, the commercial ties of these areas were 'quite negligible'.[20] Agrarian class relations were most exploitative in the south-west, where the wealthy peasantry and other agrarian upper classes had long been involved in the market through cities and maritime trade. In Ostrobothnia, the traditional peasant society was not severely undermined, and market involvement made the landowning peasants prosper but did not create exploitative relationships comparable to those in the south-west. For the small landholding peasants in the Viipuri region, the St. Petersburg market was growing in importance. And in the east, the independent peasantry, less consolidated than in the south-west or Ostrobothnia, was less involved in the market than elsewhere.

2   Reorientation from Stockholm to St. Petersburg

In the first decades of the autonomous grand duchy, Stockholm was replaced by St. Petersburg in economic importance, although many economic and other connections with Sweden were maintained. With 524,000 inhabitants in 1863, St. Petersburg, the largest city in northern Europe, was a huge centre of consumption.[21] In eastern Finland, peasant trade with the southern coast and with the Russian capital soon recovered, increasing the transportation of goods in the county of Viipuri. Butter became the main export from the east to St. Petersburg, along with timber and some iron from ironworks owned mainly by merchants and industrialists in St. Petersburg. There was considerable seasonal and permanent migration from both Viipuri and eastern Finland to St. Petersburg (Map 4).[22] A significant connection between eastern Finland and the south, and at the same time between eastern Finland and St. Petersburg, was created when the Saimaa Canal from the eastern watercourse to Viipuri was completed in 1856 (Map 5). The railway linking the Finnish centres to St. Petersburg was completed in 1870.

In other words, both regions in the east had close economic connections to the St. Petersburg area. To some extent the same development occurred in other regions as, over the whole country, trade turned increasingly toward Rus-

---

20   Wirilander 1960, pp. 753, 754.
21   Engman 1983, pp. 97–101, 315.
22   For a large number of smallholding peasants, seasonal migration and transport jobs became the primary source of earnings, displacing farming proper (ibid., pp. 138–9, pp. 150–8).

TERRITORIAL INTEGRATION

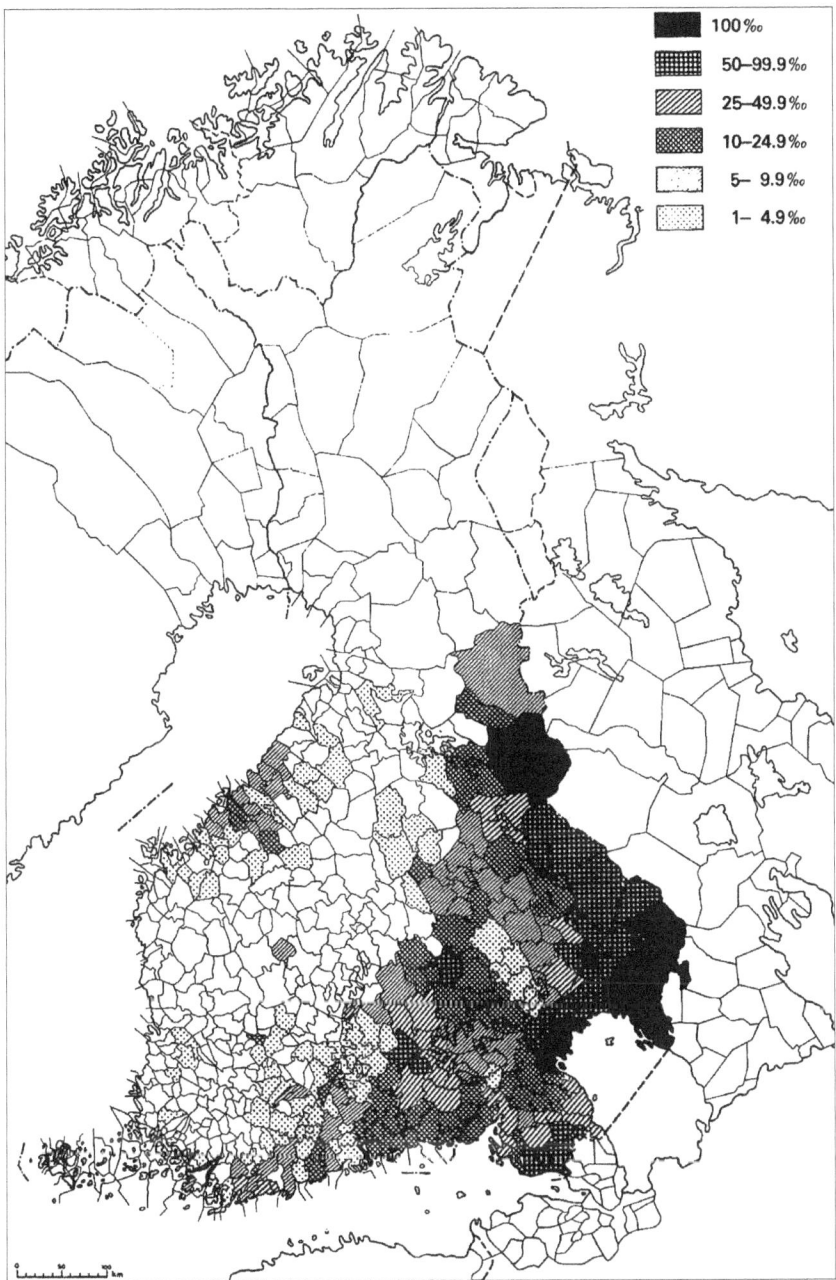

MAP 4   Regional distribution of passport-holding Finns living in Russia in 1881, by domicile in Finland (per thousand of the rural population recorded in the census)
SOURCE: ENGMAN 1978, 169

sia. (An important partial exception was Ostrobothnia, which continuously maintained active trade connections with Sweden).[23] As a target for migration, St. Petersburg totally replaced the other traditional destination, Stockholm: in 1840, the number of St. Petersburg Finns (11,300) nearly equalled the population of Helsinki or Turku (13,300 and 13,200, respectively).[24]

An early indication of efforts on the part of the imperial authorities to weaken the orientation toward Sweden was the establishment, in 1812, of the grand ducal capital in Helsinki and the subsequent consolidation of a Helsinki-oriented town system.[25] Thus Turku, during the Swedish period the most important Finnish centre, where the university, the archbishop's seat, and the court of appeals were situated, and now a border city with both economic and cultural ties to Sweden, was relegated to secondary status, and Helsinki, a small city situated nearer St. Petersburg on the southern coast, was deliberately built up as a prestigious administrative centre for the country. For several decades it was a 'parade capital',[26] with huge and continuous construction works for the central administration, the church, and the university.[27]

3   Territorial Integration in the Late Nineteenth Century

After the middle of the century a development gained momentum which united Finland economically around a domestic core. Capitalist transformation, dealt with above, created a regional division of labour that tied the various regions to one another in a more fundamental sense than ever before and accentuated many regional inequalities. Territorial integration was affected by Finland's dependent position; but above all it was affected by the varying internal characteristics of the regions that had been consolidated earlier. This pattern holds for Western Europe in general: industrial growth in the rise of the capitalist mode of production concentrated in those regions that were initially the more advanced.

The primacy of endogenous over exogenous factors is discernible in the construction of the infrastructure, especially the railways. In the 1850s two plans

---

23   Joustela 1963, pp. 304, 342–3.
24   Engman 1983, p. 389; Engman 1984, pp. 130–1.
25   A. Peltonen 1982, p. 97.
26   Klinge 1975, p. 29.
27   Klinge 1980b, pp. 18–20. Although the university was moved to Helsinki only after a fire devastated Turku in 1827, the decision had presumably been made prior to the destruction.

were conceived for Finland's railways. In one, the key idea was the effective unification of the inland centres with the coasts: a railway system that would spread radially from an inland hub to the coasts. In this plan the railways were supposed to serve internal Finnish trade and traffic specifically. In the competing plan, St. Petersburg was the centre of the railway system, with the main axis running from the south-east to the north-west. At first the former plan held sway (the Russians did not interfere), and the first railway, running from Helsinki to Hämeenlinna, was completed in 1862 (Map 5).[28]

In the long run, however, this plan was modified as a result of the capitalist development that transformed Finland in the latter half of the nineteenth century. In this process, 'Finland's economic face turned from the Gulf of Bothnia to the Gulf of Finland'[29] as the south became the core of the Finnish state: the capital was there, and, being closer to the export markets, it also became the gravitational centre of industrialisation (Maps 6 and 7). By 1894 three parallel south-north railway lines had been constructed, and a connecting east-west railway, running as far as St. Petersburg, went along the southern coast. This infrastructural development not only indicates the consolidation of the south as the core, but it also reflects the division between the two eastern and the two western regions; lines connecting the east and the west were constructed only later.

Territorial integration can be seen in industrialisation as well, as a number of big firms developed into national enterprises. In the sawmill industry, for example, the largest companies soon became 'all-Finnish'. Active in various regions, above all they progressively acquired their raw materials from everywhere in the country, and not only from the local markets as before.[30]

Moreover, in the 1880s migration to St. Petersburg began to stagnate. This situation was partly a result of the city's changing occupational structure, which reduced the relative advantages the Finnish migrants had enjoyed there. But it was also a result of internal Finnish development, as migration became increasingly oriented to southern Finland – another indication of its establishment as the core of the country.[31]

---

28   Jutikkala 1968, pp. 169–73; Tommila 1978, p. 17.
29   Jutikkala 1950, p. 164.
30   Ahvenainen 1984, pp. 274–5, 299.
31   Engman 1983, pp. 289, 334–7, 360, 390–1.

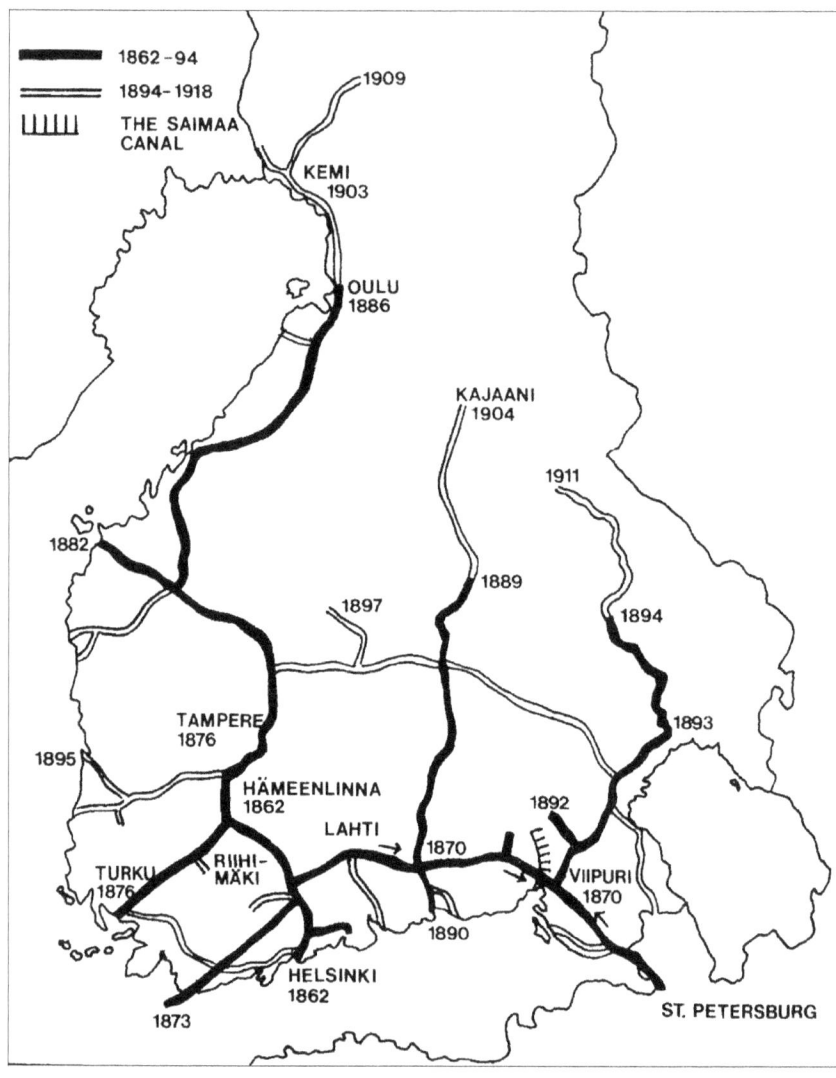

MAP 5   The Finnish railway network by 1918, with the Saimaa Canal
SOURCES: JUTIKKALA 1968, 172; *SUOMEN VALTIONRAUTATIET 1862–1912* 1916, VOL. 2

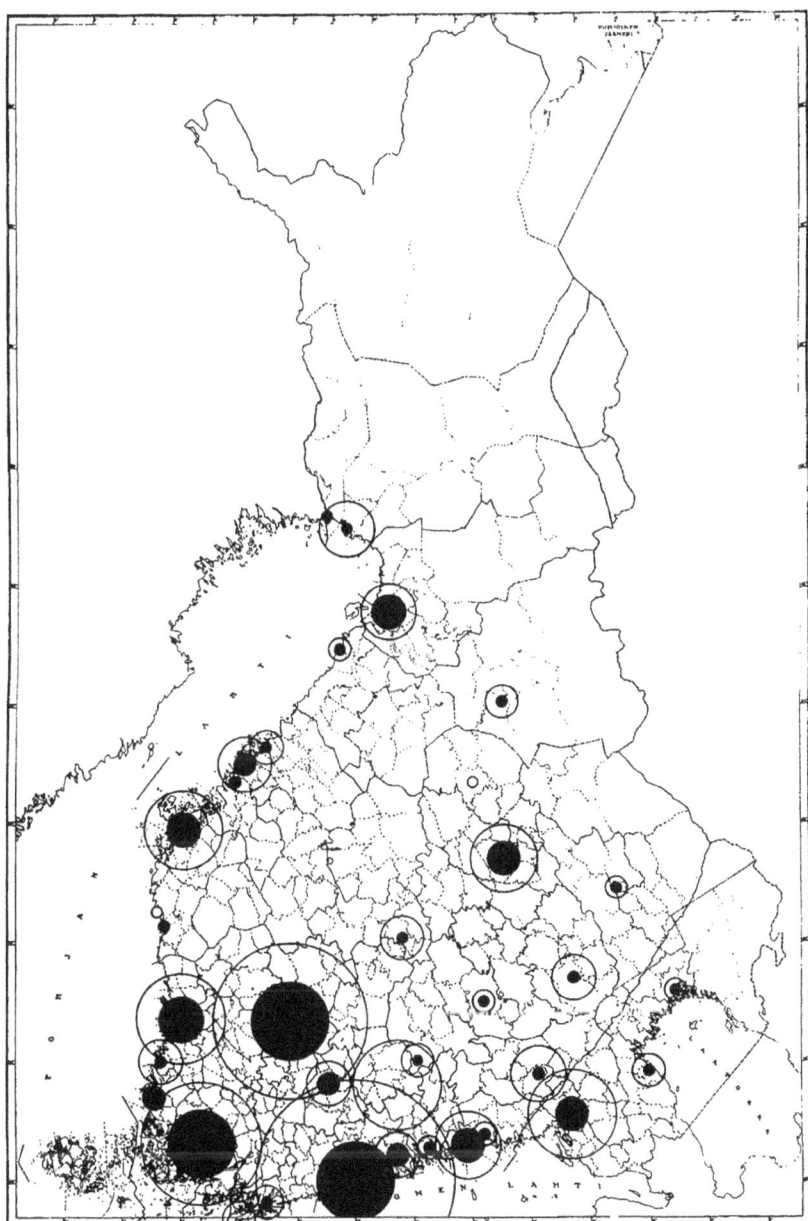

MAP 6   Urban industrial workers, 1884–1885 and 1938
         Note: Darkened circles indicate the number of workers in 1884–5, empty ones
         the number in 1938. The number of industrial workers in Helsinki in 1938, for
         example, was 31,000 (the largest empty circle).
         SOURCE: JUTIKKALA 1959, 61

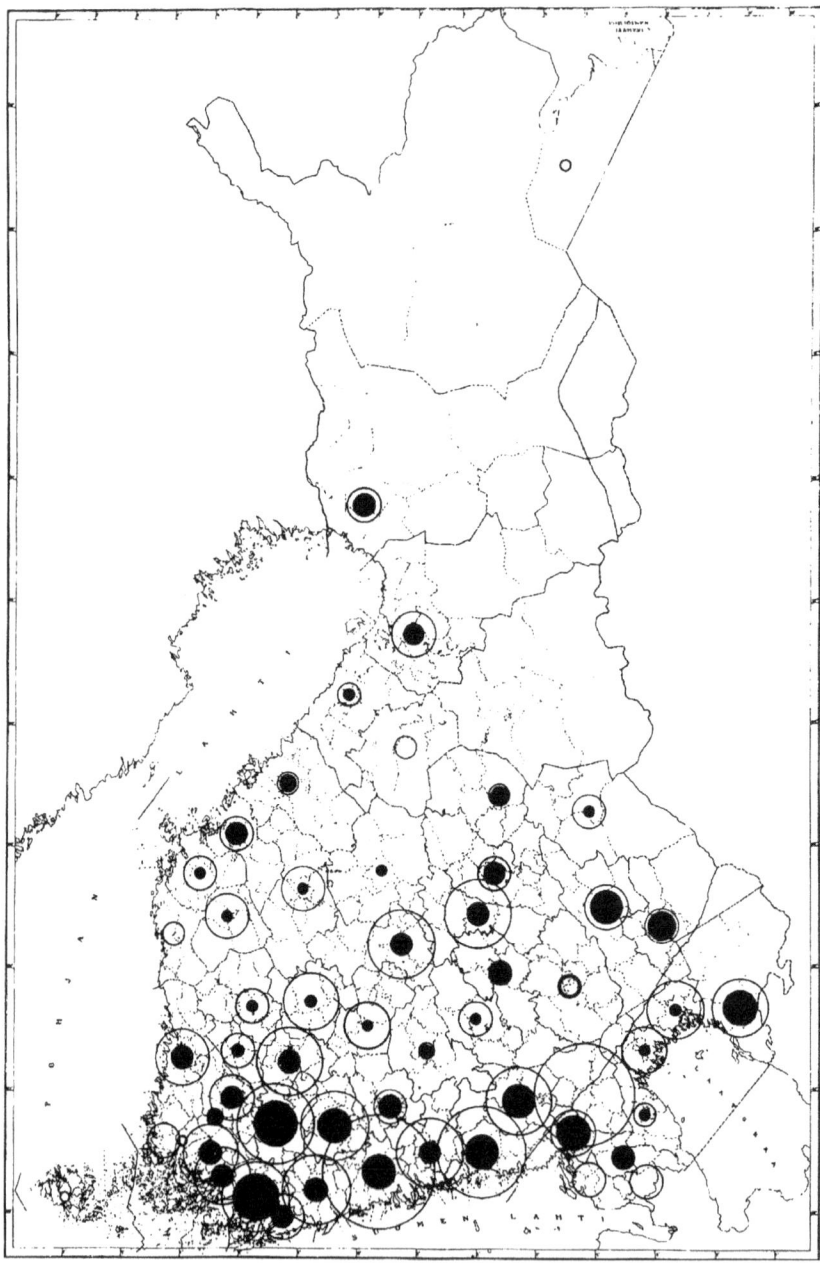

MAP 7   Rural industrial workers, 1884–1885 and 1938
         Note: Darkened circles indicate the number of workers in 1884–1885, empty ones the number in 1938.
         SOURCE: JUTIKKALA 1959, P. 61

4 Core-Periphery Interaction – the County of Viipuri and Eastern Finland

Perhaps the most striking indication of the transformation of regional interconnections was the new linkage between the county of Viipuri, the coastal area of which quickly developed into a part of the core, and eastern Finland, which became a periphery of the emerging Finnish economic entity. In the mid-nineteenth century the sawmill industry was, apart from a modest iron-producing sector, the only industry in the east, which accounted in the 1850s for about two-thirds of Finland's sawn goods. These goods were transported to the coast, where the commercial houses of Viipuri, the least-developed sawmill region in the country, dominated the trade. Simultaneously with the rapid expansion of forestry, however, the location of the sawmill concentration changed completely. By the end of the century, those in the eastern region produced only 12 percent of total output, whereas the county of Viipuri became the main focus of sawmill activity, accounting for about 25 percent of the country's production of sawn goods (Table 5).

The introduction of large steam-operated sawmills played a central role in the redefinition of the regional division of labour. These mills were built at the mouths of rivers on the southern coast, by new domestic and foreign – notably Norwegian – entrepreneurs and by commercial houses in Viipuri and other centres. Most of the timber they required was transported from the eastern region, where the new steam-operated sawmills remained small and the old water-powered sawmills served local needs to a greater extent than before. 'The small firms fell into the hands of the big firms, and the concentration of production in the coastal areas made the former inland centres of industry into mere sites for delivery of raw material'.[32]

In other words, industry in the eastern region stagnated in relation to the south. Not only did the proportion of the industrial labour force living in this region decline at the turn of the century, but its numerical strength also fell temporarily in large areas.[33] The prevalence of agrarian occupations was actually accentuated at this time, as was the lack of an urban population (Table 6).

Perhaps the main indicator of the eastern region's peripheral position, however, is the fact that, beginning in the 1890s, the timber companies purchased large tracts of peasant land almost exclusively in eastern Finland and adja-

---

32 Ahvenainen 1984, pp. 212, 218–30, 250–62, 283–5; Lakio 1975, p. 105 (quotation).
33 Oksa 1978, pp. 72–3.

TABLE 5   Production of sawn goods by county, 1860 and 1900

	1860		1900	
County	Standards (thousands)	Percentage	Standards (thousands)	Percentage
Uusimaa	1.6	4	55.2	9
Turku and Pori	2.1	6	131.0	22
Häme	1.9	5	69.8	12
Viipuri	1.3	3	151.4	25
Kuopio	12.0	31	44.9	8
Mikkeli	13.7	35	24.2	4
Vaasa	1.6	4	50.8	9
Oulu	4.8	12	65.3	11
All counties	39.0	100	592.6	100

SOURCE: HOFFMAN 1980, 193

cent areas to the north. By 1915 the companies had, in large areas of the east, purchased 20 percent or more of the land not owned by the state.[34] In other regions, particularly in the south-west where the timber boom greatly affected the peasants, timber was sold, but not land.

Finally, an important indicator of the intensity and quality of the new interconnection was mass migration to the south (see Map 8). As stated above, whereas St. Petersburg had previously been the main target for migration, toward the end of the 1800s the county of Viipuri took its place. At the same time, the volume of migration greatly increased, apparently accelerated by the completion of railway links in 1889 and 1894.[35] The migrants moved largely to new centres in the county of Viipuri located outside the established towns. Hence the prevalence of the rural in-migration over the rural out-migration for this county (Table 6).

Because migration was more intensive in eastern Finland than in any other region, population increased more slowly there than elsewhere (Table 6). This situation demonstrates the increasing permeability of regional boundaries and also reflects the redefinition of the division of labour between regions.

---

34   Harve 1947, pp. 41–8.
35   Lento 1951, pp. 168–9.

TABLE 6   Population and migration in Finland by county, late nineteenth and early twentieth centuries

County	Population		Percentage growth in population, 1865–1910	Percentage of population engaged in agriculture[a]		Percentage of total population who lived in urban areas		Migrants from rural communes 1891–1900 as percentage of 1891 rural population
	1865 (thousands)	1910 (thousands)		1865	1910	1865	1910	
Uusimaa	172.2	362.9	111	64	43	19	42	3.5
Turku and Pori	327.0	477.1	46	73	63	12	15	4.6
Häme	172.1	334.7	94	80	61	2	16	5.5
Viipuri	279.4	494.1	77	85	65	5	9	−5.1[b]
Mikkeli	163.3	191.9	18	85	82	2	4	5.7
Kuopio	225.9	325.4	44	85	79	3	6	6.4
Vaasa	314.4	439.2	40	84	74	4	8	3.0
Oulu	188.7	296.0	57	78	71	6	8	0.8
All counties	1,843.2	2,921.2	59	79	66	7	14	

a The percentages are systematically too low (cf. Table 1); however, this has little effect on the relative differences between counties.
b I.e., more in-migration than out-migration.
SOURCES: *STATISTICAL YEARBOOK OF FINLAND 1981*, 6; *POPULATION DE LA FINLANDE AU 31 DÉCEMBRE 1865* 1870, PP. 14–15, 20, 36–7; *POPULATION DE LA FINLANDE AU 31 DÉCEMBRE 1910* 1915, PP. 26–8; JUTIKKALA 1963, P. 386

Nearly half the sawmill workers in the county of Viipuri were born elsewhere, mainly in eastern Finland.[36]

The development of the eastern region displays significant parallels with the so-called dependent industrialisation depicted by Michael Hechter.[37] Yet the change may also be portrayed as a move from the dominance of merchant capital to that of industrial capital. During the Swedish period the merchants had dominated the tar-based linkage: they controlled the export of tar, while actual production remained in the hands of the peasants. The same held true for the butter trade. From the late nineteenth century on, however, the owners of capital (still largely merchants from Viipuri) dominated the linkage. Capital was required to construct modern sawmills and buy land; the peasant population

---

36   Snellman 1914, Appendix of tables, p. 35.
37   Hechter 1975, p. 33.

was required mainly as wage labour in felling and floating timber and in the coastal sawmills. In this way the territorial division of labour was redefined, accentuating regional inequalities.

Despite the fact that the capitalist transformation seized the region, it did not enable the growing rural proletariat to move to the towns and industrial centres in the region, as industrialisation in the core had done. It seems that even the intense migration of the late nineteenth century did not reduce the proportion of landless laborers in the east compared to other regions. More important, the structure of the landless population in eastern Finland differed greatly from that elsewhere, for in the east rural poverty was much greater and was presumably on the increase, in relative terms, in the last decades of the 1800s.[38]

It is also significant that in this region the timber boom did not contribute to the creation of a strong peasant upper class. True, the landowning peasants gained by selling timber, but there is no doubt that they were unable to reap the benefits of the boom to the extent that the established peasant upper class in the south-west did. The purchases of peasant land are an eloquent indication of this difference. A crisis in slash-and-burn cultivation in the middle of the century had posed great difficulties for the eastern peasants, and although the butter trade with St. Petersburg eased the situation, paradoxically it also prolonged the crisis, because it was based on pastures created by slash-and-burn practices.[39] By the late nineteenth century many peasants, especially those living in the east and in neighbouring areas to the north, had fallen deeply into debt to merchants, and they were often forced to sell their farms and forests.[40]

5   South-Western Finland as a Core Region

In the transformation, the south-west, along with the southern coast of the county of Viipuri, developed into the core area of Finland.[41] The position of south-western Finland is indicated in Table 6, which gives information on population and urbanisation both before and after industrial take-off. In both 1865 and 1910, Uusimaa had the smallest percentage of population engaged in agriculture, and the greatest percentage living in the cities. (The figures are somewhat distorted by the fact that, particularly in the county of Viipuri, the new

---

38   Haatanen 1968, pp. 142–3.
39   M. Peltonen 1986; Soininen 1974, pp. 384–5.
40   See Hjelt 1893, pp. 15–17.
41   A. Peltonen 1982, pp. 187–9.

POPULATION

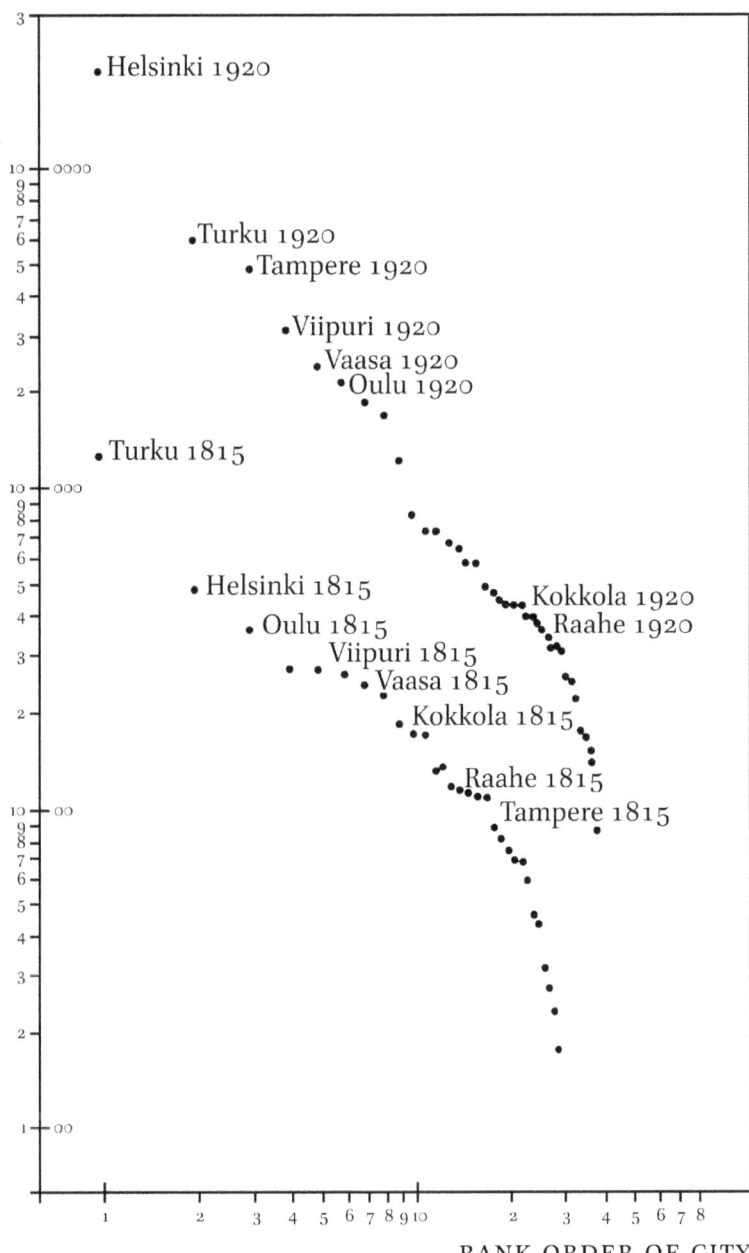

FIGURE 1 Finnish cities, 1815 and 1910, ranked by population
SOURCE: THE FIGURE IS BASED ON *ANNUAIRE STATISTIQUE DE FINLANDE 1922*, TABLE 11

centres were not classified as cities.) But the higher degree of urbanisation in the whole of south-western Finland is much more discernible in 1910 than forty-five years earlier. It was precisely in the three south-western counties (and Viipuri) that urban growth and the decline in the proportion of the agricultural population were greatest. The concentration of industry tells the same story (Maps 6 and 7).

The figures for Uusimaa are highly influenced by the growth of Helsinki. Only in this period did Helsinki become the capital of Finland, not merely administratively and culturally but also economically. During the last third of the nineteenth century Helsinki grew rapidly, and by 1920 it was the dominant city, as may be seen from the ranking of cities by size in the figure on page 67.[42]

This change was initiated and given momentum largely by the construction of the railways. The first two railways, one from Helsinki to Hämeenlinna (1862) and the other from Riihimäki to Lahti (1870), tied two great inland watercourses with Helsinki (Map 5). After the opening of the railways, then, Helsinki became the leading port for imports, the merchant fleet concentrated there, and various industries developed. Turku lost its former hinterland of Häme, and eastern Finland became connected with the capital. In the process, the inland cities developed at the expense of the coastal cities.[43]

It is indicative that the migration from the east, oriented in the 1800s mainly to St. Petersburg and the county of Viipuri, was oriented increasingly toward Helsinki after the turn of the century. Nevertheless, the majority of the nineteenth-century migrants to Helsinki came from western Finland (Map 8).

For the peasants, and above all for the wealthy peasants, industrialisation and urbanisation created opportunities to participate more fully in the market, especially as sellers of dairy products. Both low-priced imported grain and a definite crisis in traditional grain production had led to great difficulties in farming by the 1870s. In this situation the booming sawmill industry was instrumental in the changeover to commercial stock-raising, allowing landowners to finance the transition in part by selling timber from their forests. Thus the south-west went through the process more rapidly and easily than did the east.

In the south-west an established agrarian upper class had existed before the capitalist transformation. Now the changes in production and in market conditions greatly promoted the commercialisation of the agrarian upper class and the penetration of capitalist exchange relations into the countryside. Class con-

---

42   The sizes are plotted by rank, after George Kingsley Zipf's (1941, p. 11) log-normal model for descending population size.
43   Jutikkala 1968, p. 171; Jutikkala 1977, pp. 96, 100.

TERRITORIAL INTEGRATION 69

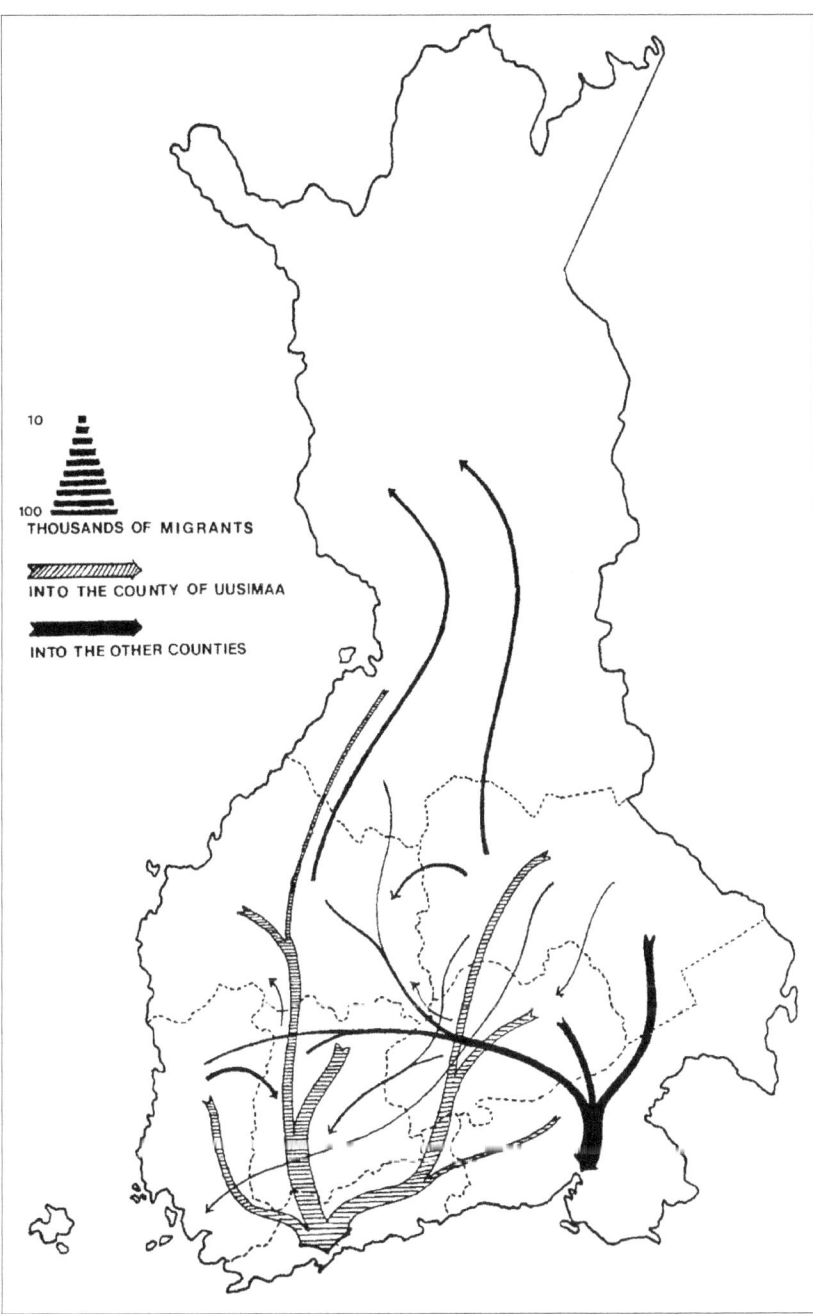

MAP 8   Net internal migration to 1920, by county of birth
SOURCE: LENTO 1951, MAP 8 (APPENDIX)

flict intensified both between the landowners and the crofters and between the landowners and the growing number of agricultural laborers.[44]

6 Declining Ostrobothnia

Perhaps the most important characteristic of the course of events in Ostrobothnia in the nineteenth century is the absence of a sudden capitalist upsurge comparable to that in the south and east, the only exceptions being the region's more northerly towns, which developed into sawmill centres. Relative to the south, this wealthy region declined economically. Moreover, the problems caused by the decline seem to have been distributed more evenly among agrarian groups than was the case in the south with the problems resulting from increasing market involvement.[45] The decline was a result, first, of the cutting off of ties with Sweden. The central areas of Sweden had been the main market for Ostrobothnian grain and butter, which had increasingly replaced tar and ships as the main products of the region after the late 1700s. Sweden remained a central trading partner during the next century, but now sales were crippled by Swedish tariffs. Second, the timber boom, which affected the south-west and the east, failed to affect Ostrobothnia, because the earlier tar-burning and ship-building industries had severely reduced the supply of timber.[46] The Ostrobothnian peasants simply did not have the forest incomes of the wealthy south-western peasants.

The economic decline resulted in the preservation of many traditional traits in the agrarian community, such that its structure did not change drastically during the nineteenth century. Even the very rapid increase in population throughout the century affected the social structure less than might be expected. Part of the increase was channelled into the prevailing structure: in contrast to developments elsewhere, the number of landowning peasants in Ostrobothnia increased, because it was a common practice to divide farms among the heirs of an owner. It was also more common than elsewhere for some of the children to remain on the home farm as crofters paying nominal rent. The increase in population was also channelled outside the region. Emigration from Finland to the United States around the turn of the twentieth century was greatest from Ostrobothnia (Map 9), accounting for nearly

---

44 See Alapuro 1978, pp. 126–8.
45 See Soininen 1974, p. 402.
46 Joustela 1963, pp. 244–9, 304, 342–3; Soininen 1974, pp. 401–2.

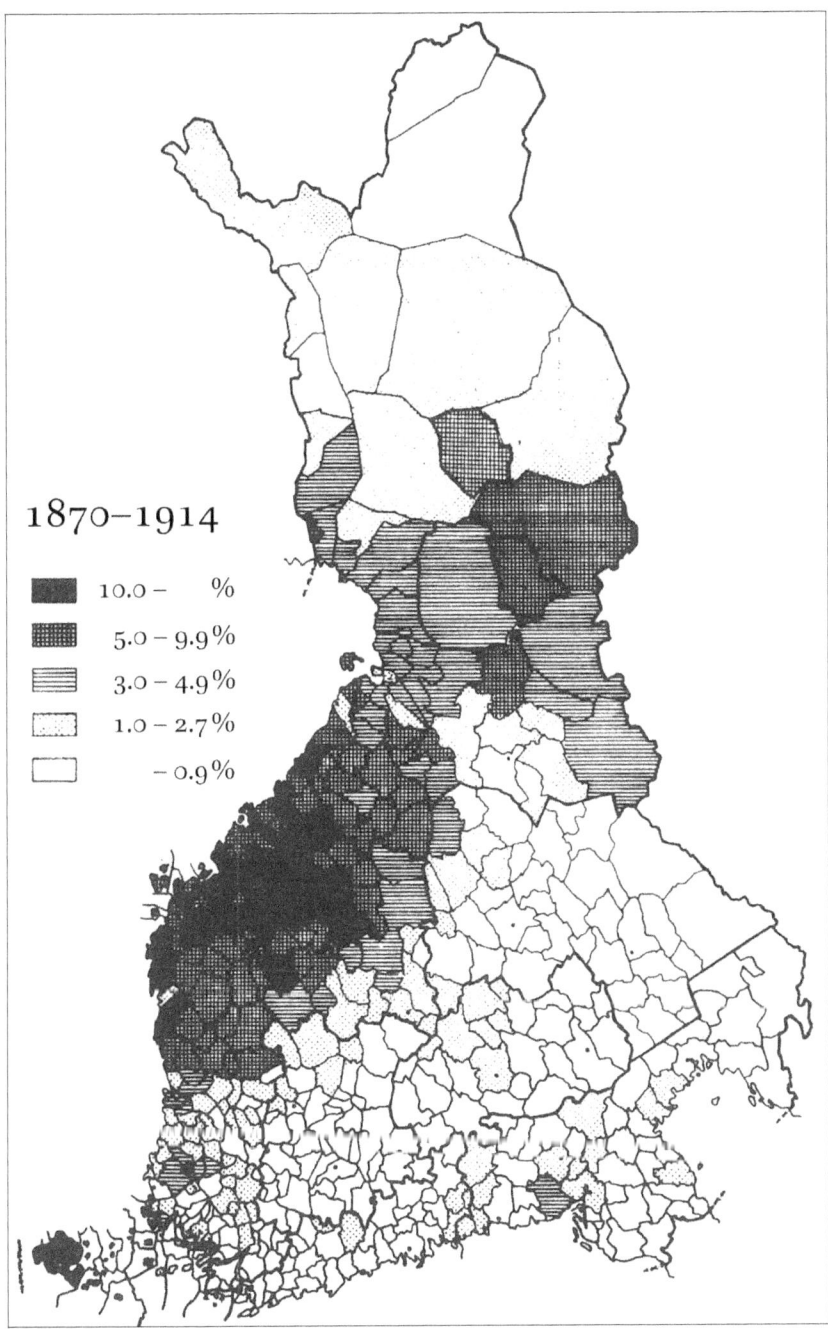

MAP 9   Overseas emigration from Finland, 1870–1914, by commune
SOURCE: KERO 1974, 51

two-thirds of total emigration in 1870–1914 and leading to a decline in Ostrobothnia's share of total Finnish population.[47]

In addition to the economic decline and the persistence of the agrarian community, the region remained isolated economically. In a sense, in the nineteenth century Ostrobothnia still 'did not belong to Finland'.[48] Characteristically, whereas the population increase in other regions during the late nineteenth century led to internal migration, in Ostrobothnia it resulted in increased emigration. Actually, this was not a new phenomenon. In the previous period emigration to Sweden and later to St. Petersburg had made the Ostrobothnian emigration the most extensive in Finland.[49] Emigration to the United States only serves to emphasise the lasting importance of this region's external orientation.

The isolation was, of course, relative. Ostrobothnia was linked to the south by the railways in the 1880s, and many Ostrobothnians migrated to Helsinki in the last decades of the century. But this connection came about very late, given the wealthy past of the province. Moreover, the construction of the railways had considerable adverse effects. The lines' south-north orientation broke old ties that reached from the coast to the inland areas, and it harmed business and industry in the coastal cities. At the same time, the once-thriving ship-building industry declined and ultimately was largely transferred to south-western cities.[50] Apart from Vaasa, the largest Ostrobothnian towns (Oulu, Kokkola, and Raahe) lost their former position in the ranking of Finnish cities by size (see figure, page 67).

The Ostrobothnian experience is in some respects reminiscent of the industrialisation of the periphery portrayed by Sidney Tarrow in his assessment of the theories of 'peripheral marginality'. In the earliest stage of industrialisation, isolated factories and mines grew up wherever there were sources of raw materials. In the second stage, emphasis was on seeking out agglomerations of consumers and services; the industrial core developed in other regions, leaving the periphery in relative isolation and decline. In the third stage, industrialisation occurred again in the isolated region, but this time as a dependent phenomenon.[51]

---

47   Kero 1974, pp. 50–2; Valkonen 1980, p. 184. The proportion calculated by Kero covers an area slightly larger than Ostrobothnia 'proper'.
48   Kaila 1931, p. 360.
49   De Geer and Wester 1976, pp. 30–44.
50   Tommila 1978, p. 26; Rasila 1982c, pp. 114–18.
51   Tarrow 1977, pp. 23–4.

In Ostrobothnia early prosperity was based on the exploitation of forests – on tar-burning and ship-building. These activities later declined just when the Finnish core was consolidated in the south. In the third phase, during the 1900s, Ostrobothnia industrialised, but its industrialisation was secondary to that in the south (and, after World War II, in Sweden). The relative decline of Ostrobothnia and its subsequent linkage to the core of Finland are crucial factors in the analysis of the nature of the religious and political mobilisation in the region (Chapter 7).

7 Division of Labour and State Penetration in Northern Finland

In the north the connection with the Ostrobothnian cities was redefined and strengthened in the late nineteenth and early twentieth centuries, and the region became more closely tied to the integrating state. Yet long distances and sparse population remained of lasting importance. At the beginning of the twentieth century the region accounted for 42 percent of Finland's total area but only five percent of its population. Landholding was rather evenly distributed, and small farms predominated. A regional division of labour arose which resembled that between Viipuri and eastern Finland. The northern Ostrobothnian cities, especially Oulu, developed into centres for the sawmill industry, with the richly forested inland areas in northern Finland serving as sources of raw materials, particularly along the two rivers flowing west to the towns of Oulu and Kemi. Timber companies obtained more forest land here than in any region except eastern Finland.[52]

Before the timber boom the peasants in the Kainuu region, surrounding the town of Kajaani (Map 5), were exploited by the merchants and tar producers of Oulu,[53] as the peasants in eastern Finland had once been exploited by the merchants of Viipuri. Similarly, after the growth of the sawmill industry, a large number of indebted peasants in Kainuu were also forced to sell their lands to the merchants and ultimately to the timber companies; thus – again as in eastern Finland – was created a landless population which then migrated to the coastal centres to work in the sawmill industry.[54]

---

52   Ahvenainen 1984, pp. 236–40, 270–3; Isohookana-Asunmaa 1980, pp. 32–3.
53   See Hautala 1956, pp. 228–39.
54   Kyllönen 1975, pp. 122–3, 131. Kainuu was adjacent to eastern Finland, but because of the direction of the waterways its historical connections were with the Gulf of Bothnia, not with the south.

The sawmill industry, then, tied the northern inland to the coast; but at the same time connections with the south of Finland were also improved. The railway reached Oulu in 1886, and it was extended farther north after 1900; another railway line was extended to Kajaani from the south-east in 1904. The railway broke the monopoly of the Oulu merchants in that area[55] and somewhat eased the miserable conditions of the agrarian population. Another factor connecting the north with other regions was the importance of seasonal logging and floating. After 1900 logging provided work for as many as 10,000 men every winter, with the workforce recruited not only from the north but also from other regions, especially eastern Finland.

There is one further indicator of integration with the south. The enclosures, which elsewhere had been carried out mainly in the decades around the turn of the nineteenth century, were postponed to the late nineteenth and even to the present century. Unlike elsewhere, the boundary between state and private peasant-owned land became a matter of major controversy, only to be aggravated by the rise of forestry. The local peasants considered the reform a violation by the state of the peasants' rights. This was especially the attitude in the eastern areas, where 'people for a longer time than elsewhere had been allowed to live free from societal "bonds"'.[56] In northern Finland the state was widely regarded as an intruder in local life, particularly as it became (again, unlike other regions) the principal forest owner: here both the state and private companies owned large tracts of land.[57] Only in the northernmost areas did the Lapps and others continue to raise reindeer and to trade with centres along the Gulf of Bothnia, although to be sure, their traditional sources of livelihood were disturbed by continuing colonisation.[58]

8   Summary

In the nineteenth century, then, economic integration and state consolidation caused the class structure to develop in regionally different ways (Table 7). South-western Finland, with two-fifths of the total population in 1910, developed into the core, and there the class conflict was heightened both between the prospering landowners and the crofters and between the landowners and the growing number of agricultural laborers. The industrial working class,

---

55   Hautala 1956, pp. 247–9.
56   Kyllönen 1975, p. 279.
57   Isohookana-Asunmaa 1980, pp. 32–3.
58   See Massa 1983, pp. 28–32, 71.

moreover, was more numerous there than elsewhere. The coastal area of Viipuri was another area that developed into the core. Outside the industrial centres, the majority of the population consisted of smallholding peasants who were dependent on the market both as producers and as workers. Eastern Finland and large areas of the north were forced to accept the role of the periphery. There the conflict between the wealthier landowning peasants and the landless was accompanied and partly confounded by conflicts between the landless and private companies, and between the small landholders (both owners and crofters) and these companies. Ostrobothnia stagnated and remained relatively isolated from the other regions. Many traditional traits of the homogeneous agrarian community persisted in Ostrobothnia throughout the nineteenth century.

TABLE 7   Finnish regions in terms of core-periphery position and class relations

Region	Core-periphery position at beginning of twentieth century	Community structure in early nineteenth century	Class relations at beginning of twentieth century
Southwestern Finland	Core	Well-established hierarchical structure; stable involvement in the market through manors and wealthy peasant farms	Traditional community structure undermined by commercial farming and the rise of forestry: sharp class division between an established freeholding class and growing nonlandowning groups; formation of an industrial working class
County of Viipuri	(Core)[a]	Peasant involvement in the market as smallholders and seasonal workers	Peasant involvement in the market as smallholders and seasonal workers; formation of an industrial working class in the coastal zone
Ostrobothnia	Separate region	Well-integrated compact peasant communities with a wealthy upper layer involved in the market through cities	Traditional community structure not severely undermined

TABLE 7   Finnish regions in terms of core-periphery position and class relations (*cont.*)

Region	Core-periphery position at beginning of twentieth century	Community structure in early nineteenth century	Class relations at beginning of twentieth century
Eastern Finland	Periphery	Dispersed settlements with tenuous ties to the market	A rapid market penetration through forestry at the end of the nineteenth century: a weakly established freeholding class and a very poor landless population
Northern Finland	Periphery	Dispersed settlements with tenuous ties to the market; area of colonisation	Penetration by the market (largely through forestry) and by the state: a recently settled and poor landholding class and a poor landless population

a   Only the southern area of the county of Viipuri developed into a part of the core.

Whereas regional variation was exhibited in the agrarian class structure, in industry the situation was somewhat different. Despite marked concentration in the south, industrialisation was creating a modern class of wageworkers all over the country,[59] and by the 1890s the industrial working class had taken shape on a national scale, yet another indication of the advance of territorial integration.

Links between the agrarian and industrial proletariat were naturally closest where logging and floating played an important role. But more significant for the eventual linkage of the two groups is the fact that the growth of the industrial proletariat so closely paralleled the change in agrarian class relations, with the great majority of industrial workers coming from agriculture.

---

59   Regional differences in the wage levels of the agrarian workers decreased in the late 1800s as well, and at the turn of the century a national market for the agrarian labor force began to take shape (Heikkinen et al. 1983, p. 91).

PART 2

National Integration and Class Integration

CHAPTER 5

Finnish Nationalism

By international standards, national consolidation advanced calmly and steadily in nineteenth-century Finland. The changes were accompanied by rather little conflict.¹ What seems essential, and to a certain degree exceptional, is that in Finland not only the middle class but also the upper class had strong incentives for nationalist mobilisation. In explaining this development, the nature of both Finnish state-making and Finnish class structure – or, basically, the development of Finnish nationalism in the interface between Sweden and Russia – seems crucial.

1   The Dual Nature of Nationalism in Nineteenth-Century Europe

In an influential essay, Ernest Gellner portrayed nationalism as 'a phenomenon connected not so much with industrialisation or modernisation as such, but with its uneven diffusion'.² The tidal wave of modernisation has struck various parts of the world in succession, mobilising the latecomers in nationalistic defence against those territories already modernised and bringing about struggles for independence in the territories defined by nationalist criteria. In the nineteenth century, this wave moved from the west to the marchlands of Europe.³

In this view, nationalism is inherent in the process of modernisation. In an industrialising society that is increasingly centralised, specialised, and occupationally mobile, literacy and education acquire an importance greater than ever before. Near-universal education becomes essential to social mobility, which requires communication. There is an objective social need for a cultural homogeneity. From the individual's point of view, full citizenship presupposes access to a common language and culture. Consequently, the language acquires a new and crucial role in defining social boundaries. If the friction that inhibits mobility is not overcome, or is overcome only partially, new 'national' boundaries may be born. This is likely to happen, for example, in a situation in which *one* of the languages in a state – often the language of the old heartland of an empire –

---

1   Klinge 1975, p. 54; Thaden 1981a, p. 6.
2   Gellner 1964, p. 166.
3   Gellner, pp. 164–72.

becomes *the* language of the modern organisations and the new industrial, governmental, and educational institutions.[4] A hierarchical cultural division of labour may arise, as Michael Hechter has called the division of labour in which ethnic groups are differentially stratified.[5]

Gellner's definition of nationalism applies to movements of national self-assertion and liberation, particularly those not linked to an existing or even historically remembered polity (the 'unhistoric nations'), where nationalism is not the awakening of nations to self-consciousness but rather the inventing of nations that never existed. Nationalism arose with the introduction of mass education in those latecomer regions where language or other ethnic differentiae provided a strong incentive as well as a means for the backward population to think of itself as a separate 'nation' and to seek independence – liberation from second-class citizenship. Several nationalist movements in the nineteenth-century multinational empires are good examples.[6]

Besides being a mode of confronting the consequences of later modernisation, however, nationalism has another aspect, which is also implied in Gellner's definition. Nationalism is, to cite E.J. Hobsbawm, a 'civic religion' for the modern territorially centralised state. A territorial state that functions through a direct linkage between the individual citizens and a strong centre must develop a set of motivations in the citizens that gives them a primary and overriding sense of obligation toward the state and eliminates the various other obligations they feel toward other groups and centres within or outside the territory. In the era of capitalist economic development and mass participation in politics, nationalism has functioned as the ideology by which the population has established a sense of identity with the modern state.[7]

The two sides of the phenomenon – or, rather, the two phenomena – are historically linked, at least in the sense that nationalism has functioned as the 'civic religion' of the new state after a successful national liberation struggle.[8]

---

4   The most detailed presentation of this argument is Gellner 1983. See also Gellner 1964, pp. 158–64. The idea is implicit in some of Karl W. Deutsch's formulations of the importance of language for social mobility in the age of industrialisation; see Deutsch 1953, pp. 75–7, 153–4, 162.
5   Hechter 1978, p. 312.
6   Gellner's own term for this variety of nationalism is 'the classical Habsburg (and points south and east) form of nationalism' (1983, 97). See also Hobsbawm 1972, pp. 395–401; Chlebowczyk 1980, pp. 123–6; *Osvoboditel'nye dvizheniia* 1981, pp. 361–6.
7   Hobsbawm 1972, pp. 392, 404; Gellner 1983, pp. 55–8. On the various aspects of the direct relation of the citizen to the sovereign authority in the modern nation-state, see, e.g., Bendix 1964, pp. 89–126.
8   Hobsbawm 1972, p. 404; Kiernan 1976, pp. 115–16.

In nineteenth-century Europe, however, the importance of these two aspects differed in different parts of the continent, as has been explicitly suggested by Tom Nairn.[9] In the established Western European states, the ascendancy of the dominant nationality was maximised during the nineteenth century, whereas in East-Central Europe nationalism arose as a protest of underdeveloped peoples. For the latter, nationalism became the way of mobilising and trying to catch up with the already industrialised areas in the West.

Nairn links the nationalism of the late developers of East-Central Europe to the uneven development of capitalism.[10] It was, in essence, a forced reaction to the spread of capitalism. The majority of the better-off groups saw themselves excluded from the material progress of the advanced lands and mobilised against this 'progress'. In the process of mobilisation, a militant, interclass community was consciously formed and made strongly, though mythically, aware of its separate identity vis-à-vis outside forces of domination. A nationalist mobilisation against 'progress' was the only way for the backward, dominated lands – or, more precisely, for certain social strata in these regions – to seek access to this progress.[11] As Iván T. Berend and György Ránki put it, the Eastern European peripheries had to modernise in their own way in order to protect themselves from the West and to successfully respond to the Western challenge. This process presupposed a struggle for nationhood and national self-determination.[12]

In other words, in the earlier phase of state-making nationalism generally developed only after the strong states had been formed, as a consequence of conscious efforts by the central power. But in the Eastern European latecomer states, the process was reversed: ethnic similarities led to national consciousness before the formation or re-establishment of a state. In this 'autonomist nationalism',[13] common culture preceded political structure and provided a basis for it.

Nairn's analysis demonstrates the close relationship between the two nationalist phenomena. Also essential in nationalism as the protest of underdeveloped peoples (though in an embryonic form) is mobilisation across class boundaries, the creation of an interclass community.

---

9 Nairn 1977, pp. 177–8, 184. Cf. Orridge 1981, pp. 42–7.
10 Nairn 1977, pp. 153–4, 339–40.
11 Yet another formulation of the 'diffusion' of nationalism is that of A.D. Smith (1978, pp. 240, 243). He takes, not modernisation or the uneven development of capitalism, but rather the centralising reform in the ruling bureaucracy and the concomitant demand for a new type of trained personnel, the secular intellectuals, to be crucial in explaining the rise of a nationalist movement against domination.
12 Berend and Ránki 1982, pp. 27, 28, 39–40, 63.
13 Orridge and Williams 1982, pp. 20–1.

Citing Miroslav Hroch's study of nineteenth-century nationalist groups, Nairn states that nationalism as a reaction to underdevelopment normally involved first the intelligentsia, then wider strata of the middle classes, and finally the masses.[14] Hroch's study is a unique piece of comparative research on the structure of 'patriotic' groups in the phase immediately preceding nationalist mass mobilisation among seven small European nationalities: Czechs, Lithuanians, Estonians, Finns, Norwegians, Flemings, and Slovaks. Besides being small nationalities they are, for Hroch, 'repressed peoples', repression meaning an unequal cultural and political position in a larger political unit.[15]

The overwhelming importance of such intellectual groups as university graduates, teachers, and priests was, understandably enough, typical of nationalism in these cases. Moreover, petty officials – in contrast to higher bureaucrats – and small merchants and artisans – in contrast to entrepreneurs and large merchants – tended to provide activists and supporters to the nationalist movements in this early phase. The 'patriots' studied were predominantly upwardly mobile, the sons of parents from the lower ranks, who had risen just as far as was possible for persons of such parentage.[16]

In Hroch's study the Eastern European cases in particular displayed these traits, which fits in well with the suggestions by Gellner and Nairn that nationalism is a reaction to underdevelopment. At the same time, the social structure in these cases bore strong marks of the feudal past. The activists were recruited not only from outside the nobility and high bureaucracy or from outside the ruling class of feudal society (which largely identified itself with the repressing culture), but also from outside the new rising bourgeoisie, which was likewise culturally alien to the nationalist groups. It was these activists who were instrumental in spreading the nationalist ideas to the masses and in mobilising them in the next phase.[17] In the core capitalist areas of Western Europe, in contrast, the main bearers of nationalism were intellectual groups linked to the bourgeois ruling classes. There the key was nationalism as a 'civic religion', the need for a unifying ideology that would overcome the destabilising effects of class conflict.[18]

---

14   Hroch 1968; Nairn 1977, p. 117.
15   Hroch 1968, p. 16.
16   Ibid., pp. 125–37; also Plakans 1974; Chlebowczyk 1980, pp. 95–105; Koralka 1971, pp. 57–8, 62–7; Portal 1971, pp. 97, 100.
17   Hroch 1968, pp. 16–17, 32–3.
18   Kiernan 1976, pp. 111–12. The idea of a nation had gradually evolved in the dominant classes of big absolutist states – notably England, France, and Spain – from the sixteenth century on, linked to such factors as state consolidation and mercantilism. See Vilar 1981, pp. 54–8; and Kiernan 1965, pp. 32–6.

2 Finland in a European Perspective

At first glance, the position of Finland – or, to be precise, that of its large Finnish-speaking majority – in this twofold division of nationalist phenomena seems fairly clear: Finland was one of the 'unhistoric nations'. The Finns were also one of the ethnically distinct minority groups of the multinational empires of the time, in all of which there arose national movements – or, more specifically, an autonomist nationalism that claimed institutional recognition within a larger state.[19] Karl W. Deutsch presents the Finnish development as an example of national conflict against the predominant language or culture. In Hroch's study, the Finnish case appears as an example of national self-assertion by a repressed people, being more reminiscent of the Eastern than the Western cases. For Hugh Seton-Watson, the Finnish national movement closely resembles the national movements that arose in Central and Eastern Europe and the Balkans. The same holds for Andrew W. Orridge and Colin H. Williams's list of Eastern European cases of autonomist nationalism.[20]

In all these respects Finland was certainly one of the late developers of the East. Yet it is not quite correct to picture Finland as a colonial territory or as an Eastern European periphery struggling through nationalism to free itself from the dilemma of uneven development. It may be hypothesised that the Finnish 'deviations' from this pattern, which resulted from its interstitial position and are linked to both state structures and class relations, go a long way in explaining the steady advance of national consolidation and nationalism in Finland.

First, political dependence was comparatively limited. A Finnish polity was founded decades before the politicisation of ethnic differentiae, that is, before the rise of nationalism. In a more fundamental sense than was true for any of the other small nationalities in Hroch's study except Norway, Finland was an autonomous unit, with its own administrative apparatus. This was so especially in the second half of the nineteenth century. The necessity of fighting for a separate status, which faced nationalist movements elsewhere, was not a primary problem in Finland. Moreover, as indicated above, the formation of a national economy had advanced very far by the end of the last century, to the point of Finland being economically 'overdeveloped' relative to Russia. Whereas the linguistic and religious distinctiveness vis-à-vis the metropolitan country was

---

19 Orridge and Williams 1982, pp. 20–1.
20 Deutsch 1953, pp. 102–7; Hroch 1968, p. 16; Seton-Watson 1977, pp. 72, 430; Orridge and Williams 1982, p. 21; Orridge 1981, p. 46.

similar to that of many other minor nationalities, institutional and economic distinctiveness was unusually marked in the Finnish case.[21]

Second, Finnish class structure was peculiar in two respects. Although ultimate control was exercised in St. Petersburg, domination within the country – political, economic, and cultural – was in the hands not of the Russians but of the Swedish-speaking upper class. Thus, although linguistic, social, and educational barriers coincided within Finland, the local elite was not an extension of the metropolitan elite. This situation was not common in Eastern Europe, where the aristocratic upper classes often identified themselves both politically and culturally with the metropolitan power: in a number of areas, for instance, German or Magyar landlords confronted Slav peasantries speaking a different, strictly local language.[22]

True, some cases did resemble Finland: German nobles in the Baltic Provinces and Polish landlords in Lithuania were, like Swedish upper classes in Finland, culturally distinct both from the dominant power and from the subjugated population. Yet another feature of the class structure sets Finland apart even from these cases. During the Swedish period, a non-feudal class structure with a large and strong indigenous peasantry had consolidated itself in Finland. Consequently, the authority of the upper class rested on an exceptionally fragile foundation. This is perhaps the most important divergence in the Finnish situation. Elsewhere, the power of the upper classes lay on a seemingly solid basis, thanks not only to the guarantees of the metropolitan power but also to the prolongation of feudal class domination. In Finland, however, the upper classes had no solid basis in landownership; rather, their position was based almost exclusively on the central role they played in the administration of the emerging state.

To recapitulate, in both types of nationalism mobilisation across class boundaries or the creation of an interclass community was of central importance. The function of this mobilisation – whether as a civic religion for the state or as the protest of underdeveloped peoples – was closely connected with the position of the country or region in the international state system. In the established Western states, which were also core areas of capitalism, nationalism was closely linked to the ruling class; in the periphery, it was linked mainly to middle-class groups seeking popular support against alien economic and political domination.

---

21 See Orridge and Williams's analysis (1982, pp. 22–5) on the structural preconditions for autonomist nationalism.
22 Orridge and Williams 1982, pp. 24, 29, 32; Kann 1964, pp. 50–6; Brass 1980, pp. 14–19.

The early phases of the Finnish case resemble the latter type. During the Swedish period, there arose a hierarchical cultural division of labour, with a Swedish-speaking upper class. At the same time, most of the Finnish-speaking regions were backward in comparison both to the core of Sweden and to Western Europe in general. Immediately before the rise of nationalism, however, this picture was radically altered. Finland was established as a polity, which soon began the process of economic integration. It became dependent on an empire that separated the thin Swedish-speaking upper class from the former Swedish core and endowed this local class in Finland with the central role in the administration of the new political unit, the grand duchy. These conditions point to the possible importance of nationalism as a 'civic religion'.[23]

3   The Consolidation of a National Culture

All these factors combined to create a nationalism in which *both aspects* – nationalism as protest of underdeveloped peoples *and* as civic religion – seem to have intertwined exceptionally closely. Nationalism in Finland did not play the role of a liberating force in the typical Eastern European way; practically from the beginning it served strong elements of a 'civic religion' for the territorially centralised state as well. The upper classes in Finland, with their Swedish culture, found exceptionally strong incentives to adopt or accept the language and culture of the large majority of the people, both because of the country's political dependence on a great autocratic state, Russia, and because of their own need, as state bureaucrats, to establish a sense of obligation to the Finnish polity. As a consequence, a rather unified national culture grew up.

This suggestion implies that in Finland, unlike elsewhere in Eastern Europe,[24] strong incentives for nationalist mobilisation existed not only among the middle classes, the majority of freeholding peasants included, but also among the upper classes. This hypothesis is supported by Hroch's findings. He focused on the development of nationalist movements in the phase when a

---

23 It is true that economic 'overdevelopment' vis-à-vis an empire contains varying elements. Nairn (1977, pp. 185–7) cites such overdevelopment as causing nationalist movements for liberation and self-assertion. But if viewed as a factor in the consolidation of the emerging state, as in late nineteenth-century Finland, it may also strengthen the inculcation of a sense of obligation to the state. Which aspect predominates depends on how tight or loose political dependence is and the extent to which this dependence limits economic freedom of action. In Finland the economic limitations were few.
24 Cf. Molnár 1971, pp. 221–227; Chlebowczyk 1980, pp. 94–5; Eley 1981.

group of 'patriots' had already attempted systematically to spread 'the national idea' but had not as yet penetrated the masses to any extent. In Finland this phase occurred in the 1840s and 1850s, at the same time as economic and social reforms were initiated at the administrative level. During these decades the nationalist movement, or Fennomania, which originated within the Swedish-speaking upper class, began to take on a clearly sociopolitical character under the leadership of J.V. Snellman. According to Hroch, upper-class representation among the nationalist activists of the period was larger than among corresponding activist groups elsewhere in Eastern Europe. The proportion of nobles and high bureaucrats was particularly high. This picture is completed by the pattern of recruitment of activists in Finland, where recruits were less often sons of parents from the lower ranks and less often geographically mobile than elsewhere.[25]

Hroch's results are highly suggestive, even though the role of bureaucrats seems a bit exaggerated. He treats as patriots all members of the Finnish Literary Society, which brought together many high bureaucrats in the 1830s. At that time the society played a role in government efforts to promote the Finnish language and thus weaken traditional ties with Sweden, in accordance with a 'bureaucratic-patriotic idea of Finland' adopted by the leading stratum during the first decades of autonomy.[26] Actually, in the 1840s and 1850s the nationalist activists in the intellectual community came into open conflict with the domestic administration by redefining the language question in explicitly social terms. Institutional tensions between the academic community and the high bureaucracy (see Chapter 2) appear to have played a significant part in the rise of Fennomania in this period.

This qualification should not be taken as casting doubt on the upper-class character of the activists. Hroch's conclusion is supported by an analysis of the leading Fennomans associated with the editorial boards of Helsinki's newspapers. Unlike the 'Old' Fennomans of the 1850s, who in many cases had been upwardly mobile and to whom the Finnish language was familiar from childhood, the so-called Young Fennomans of the late nineteenth century were definitely of upper-class origin. They became spokesmen for Fennomania in the new political phase, after 1863. 'It was the younger men of solid gentry background, with Swedish as their initial language, who laid the basis for conscious

---

25   Hroch 1968, pp. 83–167 *passim*; also Klinge 1969, pp. 189–98. Hroch's results for Norway (1968, pp. 95–100) are largely similar to those for Finland, but because Hroch focuses on the whole Storting (the Norwegian Diet) membership in the decades after 1814, the results for Norway are not fully comparable to the other analyses in the study.
26   Korhonen 1963, pp. 207–14, 218.

political organization and took the initiative in defining an exclusive party program opposed to that of the Liberals'.[27]

Snellman's aim was to establish national unity on a Finnish cultural foundation. He urged Finns with university training to adopt Finnish as a working language and to create cultivated literature that was both popular and patriotic. Over a longer period, national unity and patriotic indoctrination were to be achieved through revision of the school system. A Finland united in language, culture, and loyalty might resist the dangers resulting from the country's dependent position and might also develop further. The concept of the nation as the natural unit of human achievement in history, the identity of nationality and language, and the belief in the power of national culture and consciousness to determine national evolution received definite expression in Snellman's writings. His philosophy of nationality was refined and extended, but not basically altered, by later Fennomans. Complementing Snellman's ideas was the publication in 1835 (enlarged edition, 1849) of the *Kalevala*, a compilation by Elias Lönnrot of ancient folk poems, which was immediately to consolidate itself as the Finnish national epic.[28]

Concrete demands were mainly cultural in nature. The emphasis on culture is reflected in attitudes toward popular groups, which in the Fennoman ideology were equivalent to the independent peasantry. As discussed in Chapter 2, church and university intellectuals, together with the independent peasantry, formed the backbone of the movement. Leaders were typically from the church and university, which had been undermined by economic development in the late nineteenth century: a shift away from the corporate distribution of power tended to put the clerical groups at a disadvantage relative to new commercial and industrial groups. In these circumstances the nationalist activists turned more or less consciously to the independent peasantry. The connection of this group with the (lower) clergy was manifest in the vigorous revivalist movements which, in contrast to the situation in Sweden, were soon accepted by the church.[29] For Snellman, the peasantry constituted the core of the nation, and the landowning peasants had a central place in the Fennoman programme. The goal that they be activated and brought into public life was realised in part in 1863, when their participation in the Diet was revived. But other modalities were also needed: the adoption of Finnish as an administrative language, the establishment of public elementary schools in rural districts, and the development of local parish government. All these contributed to the civic education

---

27   Selleck 1961, pp. 166–8 (quotation from p. 168); Lundin 1981, pp. 400–1.
28   Selleck 1961, pp. 131, 144.
29   Juva 1962, pp. 192–3; Selleck 1961, p. 170; Suolinna 1975, pp. 18–19.

of the freeholding peasants, making them aware of the needs of the nation and their patriotic duties, which transcended the narrow interests of any particular parish or class.[30]

This programme did not include any substantial demands for structural change, however. The new measures were intended to increase the political consciousness of the peasantry without altering the group's agrarian character. The Fennomans' aim was the linguistic conversion of the existing gentry, to be completed, it is true, by men of peasant origin, who would then be personally assimilated into the gentry. The new gentry was to differ only on the vital point of language. A Finland united in language and culture was to establish itself not by dismantling the traditional structure of power, but by subjecting it to guidance by a patriotic intelligentsia.[31] As one student of the phenomenon puts it: 'The fact that the Finnicisation movement was directed against the exclusively privileged Swedish-speaking upper class of that time did not imply that the upper class should have been eliminated in order to found a democratically organised society, but that the upper class speaking Swedish and oriented to the Swedish culture should have been replaced by an upper class speaking Finnish and oriented to the Finnish culture'.[32]

The above elements of the Fennoman programme provide further support for the view that the two aspects of nationalism were closely intertwined in Finland. On the one hand, Fennomania clearly worked for national self-assertion and liberation from Swedish cultural dominance and against the dangers arising from political dependence on an external power. In this respect the Fennomans' advocacy of both the adoption of Finnish as an administrative language and the establishment of public elementary schools in rural districts was essential, for it allowed the cultural emancipation of the independent peasants. Upward social mobility from the peasantry to the educated class was not insignificant either, although it became important only in the recruitment of the clergy. Another group that benefited directly from the reform of the school system was the small but rapidly growing Finnish-speaking middle class.[33] The Fennomans also created the first Finnish mass organisation, the temperance movement, from the 1880s (see Chapter 6). All in all, by urging linguistic reform and the broadening of the social basis for school attendance, the Fennoman movement contributed to the emancipation of new groups and to their recruitment into the upper class in the latter half of the nineteenth cen-

---

30   Selleck 1961, pp. 173–4.
31   Ibid., pp. 147, 173–7, 184, 189, 204; Lundin 1981, pp. 400–1.
32   Wuorinen 1935, p. 273.
33   Ojala 1962; Waris 1947, pp. 242–3; Alapuro 1973a, p. 9.

tury. The movement also acted for the consolidation of the country vis-à-vis Russia. It is true that preference for linguistic over institutional reforms led the Fennomans to ally themselves tactically with imperial interests and to display a loyalty that was quite pronounced when compared with that of the liberals. At a more fundamental level, however, it was linguistic and cultural unity that, in the Fennoman view, enabled the country to resist Russian dominance. The thin and culturally isolated upper layers of society were far too weak to perform this task alone.

On the other hand, the movement strove to create an integrating ideology for the state. The linguistic conversion of the gentry was necessary in order to establish a sentiment of solidarity with the large Finnish-speaking masses, which in turn would help to make the people accept the prevailing relations of power and authority. For all their populism, the Fennomans revealed a strong tendency toward social conservatism, and their view of society was essentially paternalistic. For them, the state had a central role to play, and the long-range goal of linguistic development took precedence over the short-range aim in institutionally guaranteed freedoms. The movement was highly critical of the more volatile urban and industrial groups, which seemed to threaten the traditional structure of society, which was based on corporate representation.[34] In the last decades of the century the Fennoman movement provided an agrarian and religious ideological alternative for the emerging state.

The calm and steady pace of national consolidation characterised the attitude of the liberals, who from the 1860s on constituted the main group opposing the Fennomans. (In the 1860s a Swedish nationalist movement also arose, leaning ideologically on the Swedish-speaking agrarian and fishing population in the coastal areas; its significance remained limited, however.) The liberals derived their support from the rising bourgeois groups, and even from the bureaucracy, the interconnections between which were consolidated during the late nineteenth century (see Chapter 2). Thus the changeover from a 'bureaucratic-conservative' upper-class ideology to a 'bourgeois-liberal' one proceeded in Finland with little tension, and many elements of the bureaucratic culture were transferred to the liberal one.[35]

Although mainly Swedish speakers, the liberals did not focus their main opposition on the cultural aspirations of the Fennoman movement. They opposed the creation of a unilingual Finnish national culture, but for them constitutional legality – that is, the preservation of existing political institutions –

---

34 Klinge 1968, pp. 74, 114; Selleck 1961, pp. 147, 177, 184, 189, 204.
35 Klinge 1980b, p. 40.

and the continuity of the cultural heritage of the Swedish period were more important than language.[36] Consequently, they were prone to stress Finland's position as a separate political unit more sharply than the Fennomans did. It was particularly in liberal circles that the use of some central national symbols, such as the so-called Maiden of Finland, was proposed. They also preferred a national flag that would have been definitely more un-Russian than the one suggested by the Fennomans.[37] Moreover, dominant tendencies in the nationally oriented cultural life fit poorly in the strictly political division. To take only one example, the central artistic movement toward the end of the century, the national-romantic Karelianism, was politically mixed – or, rather, the openly political front lines were irrelevant to it.[38]

In these circumstances, both the Fennoman and the liberal nineteenth-century upper-class cultures shared certain central elements. Structural cleavages remained limited, moreover, notably between the prospering Finnish-speaking peasant landowners and the rising, largely Swedish-speaking industrial and commercial class (see Chapter 2). Finally, the continuing advance of the Finnish language soon began to reduce tensions between the dominant groups. By the end of the century, Finnish had achieved a strong or even predominant position in the central institutional spheres of society. The aim, crystallised in the Fennoman movement, of creating an upper class culturally united with the majority of the people, largely by linguistic conversion, was materialising rapidly.[39] As has been pointed out, there was some upward mobility into the elites, but in the main the old upper stratum, consisting of established noble, burgher, and, in particular, clerical families, was to remain in charge up to independence in 1917 and far beyond.[40]

In the long run all these factors led, despite the linguistic division, to the emergence of a comparatively united nationalistic culture among the upper classes and such middle-class groups as teachers and lower civil servants. The three main party groupings belonged to this culture, and in the 1880s and 1890s the (Old) Finnish party of the Fennomans, the Young Finnish party of 'Finnish-minded' liberals, and the Swedish party consisting of liberal, aristocratic, and Swedish nationalist elements were consolidated.

---

36   Klinge 1975, p. 20.
37   Reitala 1983, pp. 61–85; Klinge 1981, pp. 41–8.
38   Sihvo 1973, pp. 252–60, 286–8.
39   Klinge 1968, pp. 331–2.
40   Klinge 1975, p. 17.

4   Conclusion

> In the 'small' nations ... the dissolution of feudalism was accompanied by the predominance of a bourgeoisie whose culture evidently diverged from that of the 'people'. Such 'small' nations had a very distinctive make-up: they lacked a native aristocracy and were subject to a landed class with an alien language and an already-formed nationality; they lacked a claim to historic statehood or political independence; they had no strong or continuous tradition of high culture in the native language; and they frequently lacked a strong native bourgeoisie. In these circumstances the nationalist movement necessarily drew on a familiar popular coalition: a new secular intelligentsia ... eventually mobilizing large numbers of the petty bourgeoisie and peasantry.[41]

This summary of Hroch's central findings allow us to sketch the similarities and differences between Finland and other small nations in which autonomist nationalism arose.[42] Like the others, Finland lacked a native aristocracy; the tradition of high culture in Finnish was weak; and for a long time the Finns had no strong native bourgeoisie. But unlike the others, there was a distinct political unit (though one without any claim to historical statehood); the 'denationalised' aristocracy was weak as a landed class; and the central landed class consisted of native freeholding peasants.

Eventually the gentry's weakness as a landed class and their position in the state structures led them to adopt Finnish as their own language. This development was exceptional among the small nations: the gentry was nationalised without coercion. Indeed, it promoted the process. The fact that central parts of the Finnish dominant class actively sought an interclass community and national integration on a common cultural basis with popular groups is in line with Barrington Moore's hint that the degree to which a dominant class resists popular demands depends on the extent to which its own livelihood is based on the incentives and opportunities it has to use political power – or state structures – to subordinate labour. In Finland both the incentives and the opportunities were modest compared with Eastern Europe. First, few of the gentry ran large agricultural establishments dependent on disciplined wage

---

41   Eley 1981, p. 103.
42   Orridge and Williams (1982, p. 21) consider most of the Balkan states, Czechoslovakia (especially Bohemia), Hungary, Lithuania, Latvia, Estonia, and Finland to be Eastern European examples of countries displaying autonomist nationalism that achieved independence permanently or temporarily.

labour, and even fewer ran large manufacturing establishments. Second, they had an interest, as state bureaucrats, in generating tax revenues that were likely to increase with peasant commercial activity. And third, they needed, as managers of a vulnerable state apparatus, allies against Russian domination.[43] In this perspective it seems clear that the dominant class in Finland had no strong incentives to attempt the subordination of the peasants or the workers with repressive political methods, but rather had good reason to promote the attachment of the popular groups – notably the freeholding peasantry – to the emerging state. As will be seen in Chapter 6, the relatively tolerant approach of the Finnish dominant class was to manifest itself more clearly a little later, in reaction to incipient mass organisation at the turn of the century.

In the Finnish context it is understandable that linguistic and political radicalism long remained separate. Early Fennomania was grounded in tensions within the upper classes. On the whole, the church and the large peasantry supported the movement, while the industrial and commercial class stayed apart or opposed it. Fennomania greatly contributed to the rise of an independent peasantry and of a Finnish-speaking middle class, but it was also a movement of traditional intellectuals who felt their position threatened by the emerging coalition of bourgeois, technical, and aristocratic interests associated with liberalism. The liberal programme of constitutionalism and of increasing economic freedom meant a reduction in the influence of traditional intellectuals and the corporations they represented. The language issue was employed both to forestall this change and to seek countervailing support from the independent peasantry. Understandably enough, it was the gentry, and not the peasantry, that initially required new language skills. As Roberta Selleck concludes in analysing the pre-1863 situation:

> By identifying linguistic division as the basic source of social tension, and prescribing linguistic reform as a corrective, the Fennocists were able to maintain two important positions. On the one hand, they carried on a contest with the bureaucracy for the exercise of political power through traditional institutions. On the other hand, they were able to resist Liberal attempts to alter these institutions. The linguistic issue concentrated attention upon the cultural identity of persons exercising power, but minimized the importance of governmental structures regulating power.

---

43   Cf. Moore 1966, pp. 433–5, 438, 444. I am grateful to Charles Tilly for suggesting the significance of the specifically economic aspects in the gentry's attitude. Obviously the decline in the role of the land tax toward the end of the century, indicated above, is no evidence against the second proposition.

Thus, the Fennocist party, by 1863, was in effect attacking the bureaucrats while implicitly defending the administrative system of government.[44]

Only with the rise of the Finnish language to a predominant position toward the end of the century did Finnish political liberalism find its expression in a party grouping – the Young Finnish party. In a sense, then, Fennomania was a cultural response to the challenge of modernity: it used cultural means to defend the traditional agrarian and corporate societal structure against the threats of industrialisation. The conflict never reached great dimensions. By the early years of the twentieth century, with the advancement of the Finnish language in the upper classes, with the increase in Russian pressure, and with the organisation and mobilisation of the working class, linguistic conflicts receded into the background.

44 Selleck 1961, p. 203.

CHAPTER 6

Before the Revolution: Organisation, Mobilisation, and the Role of Russia

The Social Democratic working-class movement and its relation to bourgeois organisation and mobilisation were crucial for the process of national and class integration in the early twentieth century. The workers' party, founded in 1899, developed within six years into a huge, markedly agrarian mass movement in which purely political activity nearly eclipsed collective action in the trade unions. In the first parliamentary elections based on universal suffrage, in 1907, the Social Democrats gained 80 of the 200 seats, and their position stabilised during the following decade.

The movement will be analysed in terms of four factors. We will look first at the process of large-scale organisation that occurred at the end of the last century and the beginning of the present. Second, the split among powerholders, both domestic and Russian, that facilitated the movement's initial organisation will be considered. Third, structural and cultural preconditions conducive to strong agrarian socialism will be analysed. And fourth, the part the Russian revolution of 1905 played in determining the role and character of the movement in the process of national and class integration prior to 1917 will be discussed.

1 Early Mass Organisation

In Finland the right to organise into associations, including trade unions that initiated strikes, never became a matter of serious controversy. Mass organisations were formed relatively freely during the late nineteenth century, before the right to establish them was formally acknowledged in 1906. This tolerance was unusual even in comparison with Scandinavia, where the basic trend was nevertheless similar.[1] But it was totally different from developments in Western Europe, where industrialisation had occurred earlier. There the idea that anybody, including the propertyless, could organise freely and on formally equal terms to promote common interests in voluntary associations outside the dir-

---

1 Stenius 1980, p. 198.

ect control of the state and church was accepted only after a hard struggle, notably in the economic and political spheres. In Britain and several other countries it was principally the trade unions that won, through strikes, recognition of the principle of mass organisation. In nineteenth-century Europe the struggle for the right to organise freely was marked by demonstrations, strikes, and violent encounters with the police and the military. Most Western governments finally made strikes legal between 1860 and 1900, under pressure from organised workers and their parliamentary allies.[2]

In Finland the organisation into voluntary associations was preceded, and partly paralleled, by the revivalist movements of the 1830s and 1840s and then again in the 1880s and 1890s. These movements emphatically avoided the registration of their adherents – that is, organisation in the sense of formally constituted associations – but nevertheless, they gathered tens of thousands of people, mainly independent peasants and their offspring, into regular devotional meetings, creating a common identity and unifying structure among the followers. In other words, they organised them.[3] Because their organisation was based on a direct linkage between individuals and religious leaders, these movements undermined the traditional, corporate relationship that linked the members of an agrarian household to the church through the head of the household or through the village community. They contributed to a process which, according to Reinhard Bendix, is central to the creation of the modern nation-state. When activating members as individuals, they inculcated a sense of solidarity that disregarded traditional intermediate agencies of corporate society, thereby playing a pioneering role in the process of national integration – all the more so as they transcended narrow local boundaries and soon spread over the country (see Chapter 7).[4]

These movements were an expression of the growing self-awareness of the freeholding peasants, whose position and relationship with the gentry and other agrarian groups were changing fundamentally but whose political influence remained small until the Diet resumed meeting in 1863.[5] As stated in Chapter 5, this group allied itself closely with the clergy toward the end of the

---

2 Bendix 1964, pp. 98–9; Abendroth 1965, pp. 51–62; Tilly 1978, p. 147; Stenius 1977, pp. 80–2; Stenius 1980, p. 197.
3 Tilly 1978, p. 54.
4 Sulkunen 1983, pp. 2, 12–13; Suolinna 1975, pp. 7–11. On the direct linkage of citizens with the state centre as a characteristic of the modern nation-state, see Bendix 1964, pp. 96–122.
5 Ylikangas 1979, pp. 275–92.

century; one indication is that the church soon accepted all revivalist movements. This alliance of course means that the peasantry remained under the church's control, but it also means that religious solidarity toward the church was to be more of an individual matter than before.[6]

The second phase, accompanying the continuing dissolution of the corporate societal system, extended organisation to popular groups other than the independent peasants. The first voluntary organisations grew up in the towns, where fire brigades were founded after the post-Crimean War period of social and economic reforms. The dissolution of the legal bonds of the guild system and the resumption of parliamentary activity had made urban liberals amenable to volunteer fire brigades, for they propagated the new ideal of a respectable and industrious worker and recruited members mainly from artisanal and other lower-middle-class occupations.[7]

On a larger scale, however, mass organisation gained momentum somewhat later, in the 1880s and 1890s. After the reform of municipal self-government in the countryside (1865) and towns (1873), the local administration represented civil society more adequately than the national political system did. The former was based unambiguously on personal wealth, whereas the latter was based on traditional corporate representation. For the freeholding peasants, the new power in local affairs was accompanied by rapid economic and professional organisation through savings banks, cooperative dairies, and farmers' societies. Elementary schools grew rapidly in the 1890s as well, as did the industrial working class. At the turn of the century nearly half the children of school age attended elementary school.[8]

The first voluntary mass organisation at the national level was the temperance movement, founded in 1883; it remained the largest such group up to the mid-1890s, when it had about 8,500 registered members in towns and in the countryside, mainly workers and artisans. It was then overtaken by the youth associations, made up mainly of sons and daughters of the independent peasantry.[9]

Only in 1905 did the Social Democratic party recruit more members than the youth associations or the temperance movement. Moreover, the party, not the trade unions, dominated the working-class movement. 'Unionization and strikes came in the wake of the political organisation of workers', even in

---

6   Cf. Sulkunen 1986, pp. 277–8.
7   Stenius 1980, pp. 203–4, 211–14.
8   Halila 1980, p. 185.
9   Sulkunen 1977, pp. 53, 73–5, 80–8; Sulkunen 1981, p. 100.

Tampere, the country's principal industrial centre.[10] The first serious strikes had occurred late, in 1896, and during the next ten years trade union activity was concentrated in traditional artisanal and skilled construction occupations. The national organisation was founded only in 1907, after the first Russian revolution.[11]

The membership figures for the three main organisations were not very large even in 1905. In 1902, for example, there were 20,000 members in the temperance movement, 30,000 in the Finnish youth associations, and 8,000 in the Social Democratic party. Trade union activity brought 5,000 to 8,000 adherents, who were largely members of occupation-based sections of party branches.[12] The importance of these organisations was nonetheless considerable: they represented the advance guard of opposition to the principles of corporate society. In all of them the common people enjoyed formal equality with members of higher strata. This was true even for the trade unions, which included employers until the late 1890s.[13] In the temperance and youth organisations, positive values linked to God, the fatherland, the emperor, the family, and cultural and material progress dominated.[14] These groups inculcated a sense of solidarity based on a direct linkage between individual citizens and the national whole, and for their part promoted national integration.

Collective claims gained in importance in the 1890s. In the temperance movement this could already be seen in the 1880s, when the movement vehemently attacked the manufacture and sale of alcohol and made drink a central political issue at the local level.

The three movements became increasingly militant, and although this activism was particularly evident in the emerging working-class movement, it could also be seen in other organisations as well. Of great importance was that the emergence of the working-class movement was not followed by a split between it and earlier mass organisations. What mattered most was the conflict between the defenders of the freedom to organise and their opponents, mainly in the bureaucracy: this was the main division. 'The working-class movement did not remain alone in its stand. In concrete situations – strikes, prohibition, the franchise reform, the politics of tsarism in Finland – the youth association

---

10   Haapala 1982, p. 235. See also Ala-Kapee and Valkonen 1982, pp. 68–70, 115–27.
11   Mattila 1969, pp. 85–8, 118–61, 166–9; Sulkunen 1981, p. 100; Ala-Kapee and Valkonen 1982, pp. 94–6, 114, 128–9.
12   Sulkunen 1981, p. 100; Mattila 1969, p. 104. The figure for trade unions represents the situation at the turn of the century.
13   Mansner 1981, pp. 32–3; Ala-Kapee and Valkonen 1982, pp. 79–87.
14   Stenius 1977, p. 85.

movement, for example, went largely along the same lines'.[15] All principal mass organisations asserted proactive claims, to use Charles Tilly's terminology.[16]

In this controversy influential and even dominant sections of the upper classes defended the right to organise freely. Employers' attitudes toward strikes at the turn of the century were characteristic of the economic elite, who largely accepted the trade union organisation. Although there are parallels with the history of mass organisation in Sweden, Finnish employers tried to restrict the workers' organisation far less than did their Swedish counterparts. Similarly, the Fennoman press opposed attempts to restrict the workers' right to form trade unions.[17] 'Thanks to the parallel efforts of the government, society, and the industrial workers themselves, the worker question has not taken on here as sharp and gloomy a character as in other countries', said Alexandra Kollontay in her 1903 work on the living conditions of the Finnish workers.[18]

Why did the Finnish upper classes so easily accept the right to organise, even among the workers? Employer discussions of trade unions at the turn of the century provide a clue. Not only was the importance of regulation admitted in labour relations, but also an influential body of bourgeois opinion considered free organisation by workers to be one way to reduce conflicts, believing that mass organisations could eventually help in educating the working class and making it more responsible. Related ideas were cherished among university intellectuals.[19]

This amounts to saying that there existed a belief in the ultimate solidarity of the people, a belief that, before 1905, had not been seriously challenged. Two fundamental facts seem to have contributed to this belief: late industrialisation and the social predominance of an independent peasantry. Only in the 1890s did an industrial working class begin to emerge in urban centres; thus, the main occupations responsible for strikes before the end of the century were artisanal. Second, because the strong freeholding peasantry was a central structural buttress for social calm in nineteenth-century Finland, the mass organisations were not seen as a serious threat.

---

15   Ibid., 89. According to Hannu Soikkanen (1961, p. 23), 'especially in the countryside the distinction between a worker association and a youth association remained vague [in the 1890s]'. See also Vattula 1976, pp. 49–51, 54, 58, 86, 95. On the links of religious associations with the other early mass organisation in this period, see Heikkilä 1979, pp. 63–84.
16   Tilly, Tilly and Tilly 1975, pp. 51–4.
17   Mattila 1969, pp. 179–83, 190–1; Stenius 1977, pp. 91–2. Cf. Ala-Kapee and Valkonen 1982, pp. 142, 146, 148.
18   Kollontay 1903, p. 4.
19   Mattila 1969, pp. 190–1; Stenius 1977, pp. 91–2; Mansner 1981, pp. 40–6; Klinge 1968, pp. 196, 201–2, 206–7; Viikari 1984, p. 38.

This latter feature may be formulated in more positive terms. The belief in the ultimate solidarity of the people was reinforced by the development of the national movement in the preceding decades. There was a strong faith in the 'peasant folk', those who had given rise to the revivalist movements and were now organising both professionally and economically. This faith undoubtedly facilitated more popular organisation as well, as Francis G. Castles says happened in Scandinavia during this period. There, the emergence of the nascent popular organisations (Castles speaks specifically of the labour movement) coincided with the achievement of influence by the peasantry, which also lent popular legitimacy to the former.[20] In Finland, with the strong peasant-based national movement, the conditions for mass organisation seem to have been at least as favourable in this respect.

On a more fundamental level, the position and character of the Finnish gentry seems to have been of great importance. As suggested in the previous chapter, the gentry's position not as a landed upper class but as bureaucrats of a dependent state made for a considerable tolerance of demands by other segments of the population for organisation and, finally, even for a popular say in national politics. This tolerance and its linkage to the dominant class's state-making efforts are demonstrated by the relation of the popular organisation to the state. The Finnish mass organisations became strikingly centralised and stable, and only in a few cases did they split into competing organisations. There was no notable tendency toward organisational fragmentation as there was, for example, in Sweden. An important part of the explanation seems to lie in the efforts made from the very beginning by the Finnish elite to tie the organisations to the state. The Fennomans, especially, had an integration strategy that aimed to eliminate all 'sectarian' tendencies in the name of national unity and, at the same time, to establish closer connections between 'Finnish' civil servants and the 'Finnish' people.[21]

The state orientation of the process of popular organisation is another dimension of the main proposition advanced in Chapter 5 – that Finnish nationalism was both a movement for national self-assertion and liberation *and* a civic religion for the state, and that (somewhat of an exception in small European politics) both middle- *and* upper-class groups were active in the national movement. The upper classes were attempting to build the state and the nation, and the Fennomans in particular felt it was imperative to do this by linking the emerging civil society to the state. Characteristically, in the old national state, Sweden, the popular organisations were not nearly as close to

---

20   Castles 1978, p. 14; Alestalo and Kuhnle 1987, pp. 10–11, 21.
21   Stenius 1983.

the state as in Finland.[22] The Fennoman attitude may be seen in the rise of the temperance movement. Its expansion was the work of the Fennoman elite, who seized a largely spontaneous activity and attempted to use it to achieve national integration of the workers. Links between the state and the movement were thus deliberately forged. The founders of the local branches included a number of wealthy peasants, but above all included ministers and elementary school teachers, that is, officials of the state church and civil servants. Most of the adherents were artisans and workers.[23] Also, the first modern mass movement, revivalism, was soon integrated into the church; indeed, several leading figures were ministers.

As stated above, the Fennomans were not the only group active in the process of popular organisation. Connections also developed between other important political organisations and various mass movements.[24] It was no accident that the temperance movement and other mass organisations were created in the 1880s, the decade in which linguistically based party formation took place within the upper classes.

Besides internal Finnish factors, there was perhaps an external one. In the Western countries that industrialised earlier, strikes and the right to organise had been largely legalised by the time the elites in Finland became aware of the need to regulate relations with the popular masses. Using existing models was natural in a situation in which no serious social conflict seemed imminent: the workers' challenge in Western Europe was known, but it seemed avoidable in Finland.[25]

For all these reasons it is understandable that the mass organisation principle was accepted without extensive agitation by the workers. Yet conditions were different from those not only in Western Europe but also in other Eastern European regions. There, the expansion of similar organisations began later than in Finland. In the Baltic Provinces, for example, they grew up only in the opening decades of the twentieth century (see Chapter 11). In East-Central Europe the obstacles were still greater than in the Baltic Provinces, where the level of popular education was comparatively high. Political organisation of workers was opposed or strictly controlled. As suggested in the preceding chapter, in the East the authority rested more on repressive feudal class domination as such, and the upper classes felt less need to develop national solidarity.

---

22 Stenius 1983, pp. 112–16, 118–23.
23 Sulkunen 1981, pp. 105–6; Stenius 1981, pp. 52–3.
24 Sulkunen 1981; Stenius 1981, pp. 48–58.
25 Soikkanen 1961, pp. 22, 27, 33–4, 37; Alapuro and Alestalo 1973, pp. 88–9, 102. Cf. Sulkunen 1980, p. 39.

In short, then, in Finland – and to a lesser degree in Scandinavia[26] – the working-class movement came to be closely linked to other early mass organisations, emerging from an essentially cultural process of organisation. Where the workers were forced to struggle for their right to organise (that is, in Western Europe), they did so in the context of production, where their common interests crystallised and where they had resources to act collectively. But when large-scale organisation was initiated by the upper classes, as was the case in Finland, it began in the cultural sphere. The open challenge to the political and economic system emerged later, strongly influenced by the early cultural organisation. A third pattern is discernible in other Eastern European countries, where up to World War I all political mass organisation remained under strict control.

Most striking is the linkage between the Social Democratic party and the temperance movement, 'the first mass organisation of the Finnish workers'.[27] The working-class associations in the 1880s were started under the paternalistic supervision of the employers. By the end of the century, however, the linkage of the working-class movement, which was now gathering momentum, to the temperance movement proved to be organisationally at least as important as that with the paternalistic working-class associations. The openly political arm of the worker movement developed largely from within the temperance movement, which at the beginning of the twentieth century still had a far larger mass base than the party. In the 1880s and 1890s, the temperance movement energetically attacked the production and distribution of drink, and during the last years of the century anti-capitalism became a stronger theme in its collective activism. Political reorientation took place in both the temperance movement and the working-class associations in 1896. In 1898, that is, before the foundation of a nationwide party, the social democratic leaders organised within the temperance movement a so-called strike for temperance, which was supported by about 70,000 people. The aim was to get the masses to support not only prohibition but also the social democratic demand for equal and universal suffrage. For the leading organisers the 'strike' constituted a means to promote the creation of a working-class party,[28] and this party, which was 'far from socialist',[29] was founded the following year, at first mainly in towns and industrial centres. Even after the turn of the century the boundary between the party and the temperance movement remained quite vague among party adherents.

---

26   See Lundkvist 1980; Svåsand 1980; Wåhlin 1980; also Castles 1978, p. 13.
27   Sulkunen 1980, p. 39.
28   Sulkunen 1980.
29   Kirby 1971, p. 19.

There was a marked evangelical tinge to the speeches of party agitators, with socialism often called the 'evangel of labor'.[30] In the mass meetings held in connection with the general strike of 1905, suffrage and prohibition were often the two central popular demands. The party's prohibition programme was the most radical among the European labour parties, and in 1907, after the introduction of universal suffrage, the party played a decisive role in the passage of prohibition legislation (which came into force only after Finland became independent, however, because the emperor vetoed it).[31]

The temperance movement was not the only mass organisation that facilitated or otherwise marked political organisation by the workers. Often the volunteer fire brigades had the same role as the temperance associations.[32] Workers also participated actively in the consumer cooperatives that expanded rapidly in the first years of the twentieth century. In 1910 the cooperatives had 87,000 members, of whom a number were landowning peasants but most were agrarian and industrial workers and crofters. Together with local officials and wealthy peasants, worker representatives often had seats on the governing bodies.[33] Sports organisations among Finnish workers were also closely connected with the political worker movement – arguably even more closely than elsewhere in Europe – but significantly, the workers' sports clubs were part of a bourgeois central organisation until 1917. In addition, sports were often a key part of the activities of worker associations, very much as in the temperance movement, the youth associations, and the volunteer fire brigades.[34]

In sum, then, by 1905 the working-class movement had only recently and partially separated itself from cultural and economic mass organisations. Ideologically the movement remained vague even after the new party adopted, in 1903, the Social Democratic label and a definite socialist programme, which was an amalgam of the moderate principles in the 1901 programme of the Austrian Social Democratic party, on the one hand, and the concrete demands in the 1891 Erfurt programme of Karl Kautsky, on the other.[35] An element of 'left Fennomania' could also be observed in the movement. In the expansion beyond the early core – the industrial working class and the artisans – this orientation was to prove important.

---

30   Kirby 1971, pp. 23–4.
31   Sulkunen 1986, pp. 253–4; Sulkunen 1981, pp. 98–9, 114.
32   Unfortunately, no systematic study exists on the degree of this interconnection, but many local examples can be easily found.
33   Suonoja 1968, pp. 75–7, 136–47.
34   Laine 1983, pp. 379, 484–485, 493–509, 519; Hentilä 1982, pp. 31, 39–44, 48–63.
35   Borg 1965, pp. 63–8.

2 The Finno-Russian Conflict

Another factor that facilitated the emergence of the working-class movement was the conflict between the imperial authorities and the dominant groups in Finland. The 'administrative Russification' at the turn of the century was mild in comparison with what occurred elsewhere, but to the Finnish political class it seemed utterly outrageous and unjustifiable because Finland had enjoyed exceptional economic and cultural florescence and an exceptional degree of internal autonomy.[36]

Toward the end of the nineteenth century both the Finnish state and the nation had become increasingly consolidated. Finland had developed most of the characteristics of a self-governing state, with an integrated economy and a high degree of national self-awareness in its upper strata. Not surprisingly, politically active Finns considered their country to be a separate state and were eager to limit the scope of general imperial legislation in Finland. A doctrine was developed and generally accepted which held that in 1809 the Finns had acquired irrevocable constitutional guarantees for the country's autonomy.[37] At the same time, Russia was slowly modernising and striving to create a more uniform administration. In the 1890s Finland was the only remnant of the areas conquered by Alexander I with a specific status, 'a uniquely privileged position in the Russian Empire'.[38] Centrifugal forces were considered particularly dangerous in view of Germany's rise in Central Europe. It became increasingly clear to the imperial government that Finnish autonomy was incompatible with Russian autocracy and that, for reasons of security in the St. Petersburg and Baltic regions, Russia was obliged to defend her national interests in Finland without compromise. After all, the south-eastern border of Finland lay only about twenty miles from the Russian capital.[39]

In 1890 the Finnish postal system was incorporated into that of the empire without the consent of the Finnish estates. The conflict really broke out, however, in 1899 with the integration of Finland into the empire's general system of military service. In order to force this plan through, the emperor reserved for himself, in the February Manifesto of 1899, the right to determine the final form of all legislation for Finland in matters of 'general Imperial concern', while the

---

36 Thaden 1981a, pp. 7–8; Thaden 1981c, p. 462; Polvinen 1984, pp. 342–4.
37 Jussila 1979a; Jussila 1984, pp. 98–9; Schweitzer 1978, pp. 4–5, 18–30; Thaden 1984, pp. 91, 211–12, 229–30.
38 Pipes 1964, p. 4.
39 Polvinen 1984, pp. 52–7; Jussila 1979b, pp. 31, 35; Lundin 1981, pp. 357–8, 373; Thaden 1981b, p. 76.

Finnish Diet only had the right to give its opinion.[40] From a strictly legal point of view the manifesto did not greatly change the character of Finno-Russian relations. But the flexibility of the earlier period had made the Finns overconfident about the separate status of their country, and consequently the manifesto was unanimously felt to be a glaring injustice. The estates were 'brought back to earth'.[41]

Several measures integrating Finland more closely into the Russian Empire were carried out by 1905. In 1900 the Language Manifesto extended the use of the Russian language in the administration, particularly at the expense of Swedish. The Russian system of conscription was extended to Finland in 1901; it was followed by passive resistance. The actual consequences for the great majority of the people were minimal, thanks partly to the effectiveness of the 'army strikes', whereby conscription into the Imperial Army was dodged. But the extension of the scope of general imperial legislation remained highly offensive to the Finnish political class.[42]

The Finnish upper classes reacted immediately, in 1899, by looking – for the first time – for popular support to counter the Russian demands. Several petitions were collected, the largest of which, the so-called Great Address, contained 522,000 names, representing more than one-fifth of the total population in 1899. The first Finnish reaction was unanimous, but soon the bourgeois groups adopted different attitudes toward the Russian demands. The Finnish party of the Fennomans (or the Old Finns, as they were generally called), in line with its earlier policy, followed a course of compliance or appeasement, whereas the Swedish party and the liberal Young Finns adopted a policy of passive resistance, forming the constitutionalist bloc. A coalition across the language boundary emerged, and party strife became increasingly tense, connected directly to cooperation or non-cooperation with the imperial authorities.[43]

The constitutionalist Young Finns now sought the support of the working-class movement, in which they had been active during the 1890s: now the Young Finnish Left unconditionally backed the right to strike and in certain cases also supported universal suffrage, the first and foremost goal of the working-class movement. At the same time a strong faction within the workers' party itself sought cooperation with the Young Finns. The introduction to the 1899 party programme specifically stated that the preservation and protection of Finland's national independence was an essential condition for gaining economic and

---

40   Thaden 1981b, p. 82; Polvinen 1984, pp. 108–9.
41   Jussila 1979b, pp. 37–8. See also Polvinen 1984, pp. 110–11.
42   Jussila 1980; Lundin 1981, pp. 439–40.
43   Paasivirta 1981, pp. 176–7; Thaden 1981c, p. 460.

social liberties. The party considered itself 'patriotic and national, but not chauvinist'. In many worker associations in both the countryside and small towns, these early years were marked by a struggle for control between the socialists and the remaining bourgeois radicals, and relations with other parties were relatively close. Some of the Social Democratic leaders and many workers even actively resisted the Russians under the leadership of bourgeois radical groups that had split off from the constitutionalist bloc in 1904.[44]

The working-class movement was treated with sympathy by the opponents of the Young Finns as well. In 1904–6 the Old Finnish Left approached and to a certain extent joined with the Social Democrats. The Fennoman 'love of masses' was revived even before the Russian crisis finally spread to Finland in the autumn of 1905. In June of that year, the Old Finnish party accepted the principle of universal suffrage, though not the need for a unicameral assembly.[45]

The Russian pressure on the bourgeois parties and their deep internal divisions evidently provided some leeway for the working-class movement, which was able to press for its central demands more forcefully and to differentiate itself from the bourgeois parties more sharply than before. The working classes increasingly felt that the resistance was being engineered by the Finnish ruling classes as a means of protecting their own interests. The effects of Russification were felt most keenly by the professional and educated classes, whereas the workers were not so directly affected. Although passive resistance promised franchise reform once the threat to Finnish liberties had been averted, the working-class movement increasingly rejected this order of priorities.[46] This considerable freedom of activity vis-à-vis the bourgeois parties soon made the party's line more independent and tenacious, though by no means revolutionary.

Not surprisingly, the imperial authorities were favourable to the rather small labour party, considering it less dangerous than the more restive bourgeois groups and even hoping to use it against them. The Russians also tried to drive a wedge between the Finns by proposing social reforms, which they thought would strengthen popular allegiance to the empire.[47]

To conclude, the various interests, both Finnish and Russian, having a share in the Finnish government came into conflict. The cleavage led different groups

---

44 Paasivirta 1981, p. 189; Jussila 1979b, p. 25 (quotation), pp. 50–1; Kirby 1971, pp. 19, 21, 25.
45 Stenius 1981, p. 63; Paasivirta 1981, pp. 189–90.
46 Kirby 1971, pp. 29–30. Cf. Paasivirta 1981, p. 182.
47 Polvinen 1984, pp. 287–301; Jussila 1979b, pp. 24, 39–40, 49, 171–2. Cf. Rasila 1961, p. 193; Lundin 1981, pp. 429–33.

of powerholders to seek the support of the emerging working-class movement, or at least to accept it. The situation is familiar: when a split develops among the dominant groups, some of them seek support from popular groups. This pattern has frequently preceded revolutionary situations (for more detail, see Chapter 8), but it has also paved the way for the non-revolutionary extension of political rights. Developments in Finland prior to 1905 point clearly to the latter situation. The workers' party took shape, consolidated its position easily, and remained moderate.

There was one potentially dangerous development for the indigenous dominant groups, however. Heretofore the empire had remained the ultimate guarantor of overall stability in the grand duchy. In addition, the Finnish powerholders controlled a national armed force. In the new situation, however, not only did imperial support become uncertain, but also, in consequence of the new system of military service, the domestic troops were disbanded. In 1901–5 all Finnish units were gradually dissolved, and the Finnish state was left without a coercive apparatus of its own other than the police.

3 The General Strike of 1905, Parliamentary Reform, and the Rise of Agrarian Socialism

The revolutionary situation in Russia extended into Finland in October 1905. Earlier that year demonstrations and other protests were limited to the towns, and no violent events comparable to those in the Baltic Provinces, for example, took place.[48] Even the Russian general strike of October reached Finland only after ten days, despite the proximity of St. Petersburg. But when it finally spread to the grand duchy, it led to substantial mobilisation in both towns and countryside. The strike in Finland began in a national and patriotic spirit, with the constitutionalists and the Social Democrats working together in many towns. As the strike progressed, however, the differences between the two factions grew. Both agreed on the need to reverse the Russian integration policy, but the bourgeois groups and the imperial authorities opposed the Social Democrats' demand for universal suffrage and a unicameral assembly.[49]

The situation was revolutionary in important respects. During a short but decisive period, the government, which had previously been under the control of a single polity, became the object of effective, competing, and mutually

---

48   Jussila 1979b, pp. 58–60.
49   Jussila 1979b, pp. 74–86; Kirby 1971, pp. 49, 58.

exclusive claims by two distinct polities – to use Charles Tilly's definition of a revolutionary situation.[50] The Social Democrats were able to push through their demands for universal suffrage and a one-chamber legislature because the state was paralysed, first by the inability of the autocracy to call on the police and the armed forces, and later by the necessity to fight other enemies within the empire. The crisis resulted in the working-class movement being able to access the polity. The creation of an unofficial armed militia in the first few days of the strike also indicates the state's paralysis. Both the bourgeois civil guards and the Red Guards, which were linked with the worker movement, evolved from the militia. Some of the guards remained in existence well into 1907.[51]

The emperor authorised the transformation of the political system on 4 November 1905, together with the suspension of the February Manifesto, the conscription law, and other integration measures. The new political system was confirmed the following year by the estates, under pressure from the socialists. The estates were replaced by a unicameral assembly based on universal and equal suffrage for both men and women. Finland thus experienced 'Europe's most radical parliamentary reform', in which 'Europe's most conservative estate-based Parliament' was superseded by 'the most democratic' system in the whole Continent.[52] The great leap from the corporate conception of representation to one based on the individual was made all at once, whereas elsewhere this fundamental change took at least several decades.[53] True, there was an essential constraint: the final decision on legislation remained in the hands of the emperor. In the old system only a few thousand persons had had a voice in choosing representatives to the noble and clerical estates, and the latter was the last of its kind in Europe. In the two other estates, those of the burghers and the freeholding peasants, the electoral basis was much larger, but still the reform multiplied tenfold the number of qualified voters from 126,000 to 1,273,000.

The Russian autocracy had guaranteed the quasi-immutability of an antiquated system of corporate representation. Its temporary collapse led in one stroke to a fully democratic electoral system. This sudden extreme leap was intimately bound up with fluctuations in the strength of the imperial authority.

---

50 Tilly 1978, p. 191.
51 On the guards, see Jussila 1979b, pp. 116–39; and Salkola 1985, 1: 45–7.
52 Quotations are from, respectively, Jutikkala and Pirinen 1962, p. 242 (cf. Rokkan 1970, pp. 84–5); Wirilander 1974, p. 21; and Lundin 1981, p. 445. See also Allardt 1981a, pp. 62–3.
53 Bendix 1964, pp. 112–22.

TABLE 8   Distribution of seats in Parliament won in Finnish general elections, 1907, 1916, and 1917

Parties	1907	1916	1917
Social Democratic party	80	103	92
Agrarian Union	9	19	26
Finnish party	59	33	32
Young Finnish party	26	23	24
Swedish People's party	24	21	21
Others	2	1	5
Total	200	200	200
National turnout	70.7%	55.5%	69.2%

SOURCE: *ÉLECTIONS POUR LA DIÈTE EN 1917* 1919, 13, 41–2

In the first general elections, in 1907, the turnout was 71 percent – a figure not surpassed until 1945 – and the Social Democrats gained more than one-third of the vote. With 80 of the 200 seats in Parliament, they became the largest socialist party in Europe (Tables 8 and 9). In agrarian Finland this achievement necessarily required enormous rural support, and indeed, the party received almost nine-tenths of its votes from the countryside. Rural voters were in the majority even in relative terms: the Social Democrats received 34 percent of the urban vote and 38 percent of the rural vote. The success was spectacular, exceeding to some degree even the party's own expectations.[54] Among the bourgeois parties, the Old Finnish party gained a much larger vote than the Young Finns. The former was supported mainly by the independent peasants and the Finnish-speaking educated class, the latter by middle-class groups in both towns and countryside (see Chapter 7). The Swedish party (now the Swedish People's party) received nearly all the Swedish-speaking vote in the coastal areas. Unlike the other parties, the populist Agrarian Union emerged only after suffrage reform in 1906. It was markedly more radical than the other bourgeois parties and was supported above all by the smallholders. Like the Social Democratic party, the Agrarian Union was able to rest on earlier mass organisations – the youth associations and, in some regions, the professional farmers' societies. At first, however, it grew only slowly.

54   Soikkanen 1961, p. 363.

TABLE 9   Rural and urban party support in Finnish general elections, 1907, 1916, and 1917

	Countryside			Cities		
Parties	1907	1916	1917	1907	1916	1917
Social Democratic party	38%	48%	45%	34%	44%	45%
Agrarian Union	7	11	15	0	0	0
Finnish party	29	18	32[a]	20	14	34[a]
Young Finnish party	14	12		13	14	
Swedish People's party	11	10	7	26	25	19
Others	1	1	1	7	3	2
Total	100%	100%	100%	100%	100%	100%
N (thousands)	770	690	840	121	111	158
National turnout	69.6%	56.8%	69.5%	72.7%	49.0%	67.9%

a   Because of party alliance between the Finnish party and the Young Finnish party, their respective votes cannot be distinguished in the 1917 elections.
SOURCES: *ÉLECTIONS POUR LA DIÈTE EN 1907 ET 1908* 1909, 8; *ÉLECTIONS POUR LA DIÈTE EN 1916* 1917, PP. 42–9; *ÉLECTIONS POUR LA DIÈTE EN 1917* 1919, 16, PP. 38–9

The most important and unique feature of the enormous mobilisation in 1905–7 was the rise of agrarian socialism. True, there were certain similarities with the Baltic Provinces in 1905, as will be seen in Chapter 11. Comparisons with some rural regions in Italy and France can also be made.[55] But as an organised phenomenon that spread throughout the entire country, Finnish agrarian socialism is unique. How can the strong agrarian base of the Social Democratic movement be explained, and how did it affect the movement's overall character?

As to the first problem, a number of significant structural factors can be identified. Obviously the agrarian response was linked to the fact that the landless population, forced to remain outside the traditional agrarian community, had grown rapidly at the end of the nineteenth century. At the same time, the leasehold question also emerged, with crofters trying to defend themselves against the increasingly market-oriented landowners (see Chapter 3). These two developments created a foundation for the rise of agrarian socialism. Yet they alone are insufficient to explain either the strength of the movement or its relatively high level of organisation. Eric Wolf has emphasised that the success of peas-

---

55   Linz 1976, pp. 388–92, 402–12, 421–2.

ant movements depends not merely, or even primarily, on the grievances of the participants, but on the connections between the agrarian groups and other, non-agrarian groups. 'Poor peasants and landless laborers ... are unlikely to pursue the course of rebellion, *unless* they are able to rely on some external power to challenge the power which constrains them'.[56] It may be argued that in Finland such an external power existed and that it was made up of, to an exceptionally high degree, the industrial proletariat, or, rather, its party, the Social Democrats. As discussed earlier, the capitalist transformation in Finland took place simultaneously in industry and agriculture. Hence, both the industrial and the agrarian proletariat increased at roughly the same time. Moreover, an exceptionally close link seems to have developed between the two groups, because the industries were mostly located in the countryside, seasonal work was common, and the overwhelming majority of the industrial workers had come directly from agrarian occupations.

It has been argued, to be sure, that the prevailing conditions hampered, rather than helped, the political organisation of the working class. It was difficult, so the argument runs, for the new ideas advanced in the workers' associations to percolate into isolated rural communities. In addition, industry itself was young, and because the workers had been in industrial employment for only a short time, they were still influenced by traditional agrarian values. Finally, because employment was seasonal and the level of skill required generally low, a sense of solidarity was difficult to create.[57]

This argument, however, focuses exclusively on the industrial workers. From the perspective of agrarian workers, the situation appears very different. After all, there is nothing peculiar in the radicalisation and organisation of the industrial working class. The process in Finland followed much the same pattern observed in several other European countries, even though the dispersion of Finland's main industries throughout the countryside may have retarded it. The real point is that Finnish conditions *facilitated*, to an exceptionally large extent, the *radicalisation of the agrarian workers*, and therefore of the great majority of the working class. The situation furthered the rise of class consciousness in the agrarian proletariat, making it easier for the industrial and agrarian workers to forge an alliance.

Moreover, these conditions apparently facilitated the incipient radicalisation of the crofters as well, or at least tended to shape the political form their already manifest but not yet crystallised grievances were to take. Crofters had

---

56   Wolf 1969, p. 290.
57   Soikkanen 1961, p. 5.

been the first to express their discontent in the countryside (Chapter 3), and their strikes multiplied in the years immediately preceding the general strike of 1905. Likewise, they were the only group that indisputably dissociated itself from the bourgeois-led national protests against the Russian integration measures at the turn of the century. Crofters were reluctant to sign the Great Address in 1899, and they took part in the 'army strikes' only passively.[58]

The previous institutional, organisational, and cultural connections between town and country also seem to have played a part in forging the political alliance between them. The most important links were provided by the expansion of the elementary school system and the earlier process of mass organisation. Of the members of the temperance movement, which originated in the towns, one-half lived in the countryside at the end of the last century, and subsequently the proportion of rural members increased considerably. The proportions in the volunteer fire brigades were more or less similar.[59] Common organisational frames presumably facilitated the passage from common interests to explicit political organisation encompassing both towns and countryside – especially because the industrial working class was still weakly structured and therefore without a strong working-class culture.[60] Various cultural activities – theatrical and musical performances, social evenings, athletic events, and so forth – played a central role in the working-class associations, as they did in the temperance movement and the volunteer fire brigades. Indicative of the link or, rather, the continuity is also the fact that the temperance movement began to lose members rapidly as the Social Democratic party expanded after 1905.[61] This cultural connection helped to link the rural and urban poles in the worker movement, all the more so as the face-to-face relationship between agrarian workers and crofters on the one hand and their employers on the other bore little resemblance to the collective conflict between worker and employer in the industrial centres.

In these respects Finland differed from other Eastern European countries. First, although Eastern Europe too had a large landless proletariat, no sectors other than minor groups in the intelligentsia allied themselves with it. There, it was not until the upheavals of World War I that the rural proletariat was

---

58 Ibid., pp. 345–8; Tommila 1967, pp. 150–60; Jutikkala 1970.
59 On the temperance movement, see Sulkunen 1986, p. 106. In the 1880s the number of rural volunteer fire brigades already exceeded that of urban brigades (Stenius 1981, p. 23), even though the number of urban firefighters was presumably greater at that time. Later, moreover, the number of rural brigades grew many times over.
60 Alestalo 1977, pp. 109–10.
61 Sulkunen 1981, p. 114.

radicalised. As feudal relationships between the landless and the landlords disintegrated, they were only slowly replaced by new class relationships. Landless and poor peasants may have been freed from the old, but they were not integrated into the new. Consequently, the peasant movements were mainly outbursts lacking clear political organisation.[62] Second, no popular organisational network covering both town and country existed in Eastern Europe prior to the emergence of the worker movement.

Structural and institutional factors appear to have created conditions favourable to the Finnish Social Democrats. But the nature of the crisis of 1905 – that is, immense mobilisation and subsequent parliamentary reform – was decisive. The Social Democratic party was the only political movement with an organised mass base when the general strike extended into Finland. The previous stability of the political system had meant that other political groupings were formed almost completely within the dominant groups. In 1905 different grievances were suddenly fused within the organisational framework of the Social Democratic party. A link was forged between the early adherents in urban centres and new adherents in the countryside, and also between a number of intellectuals who joined the party and the great agrarian mass. Now an originally urban and industrial-based organisation could directly mobilise large agrarian masses, a fact which Joel S. Migdal, Theda Skocpol, and others maintain is crucial in explaining the rise of political movements among peasants. As in a number of Third World countries, a political movement gaining extensive peasant support was created in Finland as the result of an impetus originating outside the peasantry.[63] But in Finland the factors discussed above contributed to the fact that the urban-rural alliance took shape very rapidly and on an exceptionally large scale.

The spread of worker associations at the beginning of the century indicates both the leading position of the industrial proletariat and the link between town and country. The associations were first established in big towns, then in smaller towns and industrial and commercial centres in the countryside, and finally in the countryside itself. Rural associations were first set up in key villages in the communes and near sawmills and railway stations. With the general strike the focus of the labour movement shifted away from the towns to the industrial centres in the countryside and an agrarian setting.[64]

Agrarian workers joined the party in large numbers. In this atmosphere the Social Democrats were able to attract support from the crofters as well, indeed

62 Galaj 1974, pp. 322–6; Chirot and Ragin 1975; Erényi 1975, pp. 57–61.
63 Migdal 1974, pp. 231–6; Skocpol 1982, pp. 361–7.
64 Soikkanen 1961, pp. 183, 202, 340.

becoming the only party able to create a noteworthy crofter organisation.[65] Party membership went from 16,000 to 45,000 in 1905, and to 85,000 by the end of 1906. In October of 1906 membership rose to 107,000, but after that it began to decline; in 1910 membership stood at 52,000. In 1906 the Social Democratic party was the strongest socialist party in the world in relative terms, and 69 percent of its members were from the countryside. Between 1904 and 1906, moreover, the number of worker associations increased tenfold, from about 100 to nearly 1,000.[66]

All in all, the Finnish situation obviously provides support for Eric Wolf's contention about peasant revolutionary activity: 'It is probably not so much the growth of an industrial proletariat as such which produces revolutionary activity, as the development of an industrial work force still closely geared to life in the villages'.[67] In Finland conditions were favourable for common mobilisation and collective action by the agrarian and industrial working class. But a short-term factor, the Russian revolution of 1905, activated them.

How did the large agrarian response affect the overall character of the movement? First, and understandably enough, the huge rural majority in the party based much of its action on local traditions. The worker movement became distinct from the other popular organisations, but generally the relations with these latter remained reasonably good or even close. The sites for cultural and political activity were the workers' halls, constructed jointly by the members – and arguably the most peculiarly Finnish phenomenon in the whole movement.[68] In this period 'the working-class movement was to a large extent a cultural movement, with the workers' halls as its centres'.[69] They were a major factor behind the cohesiveness of the movement: the party functioned above all 'as the organisational, political, and ideological bond linking the network of workers' halls'.[70] The number of halls rose from 47 in 1905 to 683 in 1910, and to 940 in 1916, with social evenings, various performances, and contests occupying a central place in their utilisation. Although the working-class movement now increasingly distinguished itself from other mass organisations, its internal division of labour was modest. Actually – and again, understandably – political, economic, and cultural aspects were not really differentiated.[71] Seen

---

65   Rasila 1961, pp. 309–11, 412.
66   Soikkanen 1961, pp. 338, 340; Soikkanen 1978, p. 354.
67   Wolf 1969, p. 292.
68   Hentilä 1982, p. 48.
69   Hako 1974, p. 143 (quotation); Hentilä 1982, pp. 47–8. Cf. Alestalo 1977, pp. 98–106.
70   Kettunen 1984, p. 39.
71   Ibid.; Hentilä 1982, pp. 47–8.

from this perspective, William C. Martin's conclusion seems only a little exaggerated: 'The educational activities of the Workers' Party carried the ideas of nationalism outside the literate classes and effectively created a national consciousness among urban workers and landless rural workers'.[72] It is evident that the large agrarian response that assured the labour movement's penetration into the polity influenced the movement in a reformist direction. This is certainly not unique as such,[73] but the scale of agrarian support was without parallel, and so too was its overall impact on the worker movement. In 1913 J.K. Paasikivi, a leading Old Finnish politician and later a president of Finland, thought that, with time, the Social Democrats presumably would develop into a 'radical progressive party'.[74]

Second, rapid and powerful penetration into the polity made the Finnish working-class movement focus on the state rather than on direct confrontation with the capitalist class.[75] Before 1905 both the political movement and the trade union movement were undeveloped in comparison with Western Europe. The first Russian revolution brought about a complete and easy victory in the *political* sphere, but the relations between workers and employers in such an agrarian country as Finland were not greatly affected. Unlike Sweden in 1902, for example, Finland's strike for the franchise was not a manifestation of the power of organised labour. That is, rather than being an internal encounter based on resources arising directly from organisation within the production process,[76] it was a direct result of the country's political dependence.

Strike activity increased temporarily between 1905 and 1908; in other words, it took a political crisis to bring about expansion of the trade union movement. In 1907 both the national trade union organisation and the national employers organisation were founded, but these played only a limited role. The employers did not really recognise the right of organised labour to bargain, and the trade union movement soon adopted the role of a sort of mediator, viewing labour conflicts in a narrow economic perspective.[77] From 1907 to 1916 the membership figures of the national trade union organisation varied between 30 and 60 percent of the Social Democratic party's membership; in the Western countries, in contrast, the ratio was usually the inverse, with the trade unions

---

72 Martin 1970, p. 320. See also Hamalainen 1978, pp. 30–1.
73 Take France, for example; see Gallie 1982, pp. 169–72.
74 Paasikivi 1957, p. 180.
75 See Kettunen 1979, pp. 71–98; Alestalo 1977, pp. 103–6; Hodgson 1974a, p. 30.
76 Hentilä 1979, pp. 127–36; Kettunen 1979, p. 79.
77 Kettunen 1979, pp. 92–3; Mansner 1981, pp. 80–2, 101–16; Ala-Kapee and Valkonen 1982, pp. 273–80, 322–5, 337–40.

serving as the backbone of the labour movement. Even among the industrial proletariat, trade union organisation lagged behind political organisation.[78] Therefore, although it is true that the political and economic spheres were not really differentiated, nonetheless, the political was much more in evidence. Characteristically, in the countryside trade union activity was normally incorporated into the activities of the worker associations, sometimes in separate occupation-based sections.[79]

The relationship between politics and trade union activity resembles in some respects what Edward Shorter and Charles Tilly have, in their analysis of strikes in France, called 'sparkplug unionism'.[80] In new industries and semi-skilled worker occupations that entirely lacked collective traditions and habits, activity was directed at the central forum of national politics as much as at local problems, which, for their part, were above all economic bread-and-butter issues. At the local level a weak union organisation was run by 'sparkplug' militants, an organised nucleus that sparked strike activity. At the national level union activity was in the hands of radical political parties and industrial federations. The solidarity born of sparkplug unionism was usually short-lived: the participants in collective disputes quickly lost interest and drifted back to work. In Finland, workers who were active in unions and strikes lacked traditions of collective action; the entire industrial working class had only recently come from an agrarian base, and the just-created unions owed their expansion to a great political crisis. (In France, sparkplug unionism exploded in 1936, after the stunning electoral victory of the parties of the Left.) Locally, economic demands predominated, and strikes were organised by militants who often acted quite independent of the central organisation.[81] What mattered nationally was politics, if only because at that level the working-class movement really had a say, whereas at the local level it had none.

If the class experience is seen as determined by productive relations, and if class consciousness is the way in which these experiences are handled in cultural terms,[82] the two display rather loose links in the Finnish case. In Finland the 'political' class struggle was not based on the 'economic' one.[83] This situation resulted, however, more from the extraordinary extensiveness of the political organisation than from the weakness of the trade unions. As a matter

---

78 Kettunen 1979, pp. 71–6; Ala-Kapee and Valkonen 1982, pp. 230–8.
79 Ala-Kapee and Valkonen 1982, pp. 111, 124, 243–51.
80 Shorter and Tilly 1974, pp. 127–37, 181, 217.
81 Ala-Kapee and Valkonen 1982, pp. 200–8, 260–9, 301–37.
82 The formulation is E.P. Thompson's (1963, pp. 9–10).
83 Kettunen 1980b, p. 6.

of fact, the trade unions recruited as many workers as could be expected in a country with so few industrial centres.[84] Internal factors – the degree and character of industrialisation – set an upper limit on the trade union organisation, but they did not restrict political organisation, the upper limit of which was determined by Finno-Russian relations.

This specific opportunity structure resulted in collective action different from that in the major Western countries and in Scandinavia. The trade unions were above all auxiliary instruments of the party. The movement's strength lay in its electoral success, not in its capacity for concerted mass action, notably strikes. The party's whole organisation was geared to secure votes in elections, and the typical voters were by no means actual or even potential trade union members: they were agrarian workers or crofters whose relations with their employers were largely traditional and whose political activities were concentrated in the local workers' hall. The only way for them to voice their opinion was to vote in national elections; the local administration remained as before.

In practice the movement grew into a large parliamentary party, with some intellectual leaders, mainly Old Finns who had joined the party in 1905–6; with over a dozen local newspapers; and with a large number of functionaries who concentrated entirely on the electoral work. The Red Guard, which had been formed during and after the general strike of 1905, was disbanded by the party leadership prior to the first elections, in compliance with the Finnish government's suspension order.[85] The parliamentary orientation was certainly not weakened by the fact that the Finnish Social Democratic party was the first and only socialist party in the world to attain an absolute majority before the Russian revolution of 1917. Typically, very few official contacts existed between the Finnish party and the Russian revolutionaries.[86]

In theory the party was revolutionary, awaiting the struggle foreshadowed by the events of 1905 and building up its strength. It paid little attention, however, to how the revolution was to be achieved and what its substance was to be. It was generally believed that a revolution in Russia would produce a bourgeois democracy and that the immediate task of the Finnish Social Democrats would then be to press for a more democratic form of government. Consequently, the socialists came to visualise their party more and more as the leading protagonist in the struggle for democracy, and the meaning of revolution remained extremely vague.[87]

---

84   Cf. Kettunen 1986, pp. 73–81.
85   Salkola 1985, 1:47; Soikkanen 1961, pp. 246–8.
86   Kirby 1970.
87   Kirby 1971, p. 125; Jussila 1979b, pp. 170–1; Hodgson 1974b, pp. 22–4.

Aware that their chances to act were fundamentally dependent on developments in Russia, the Social Democrats came to accept a role of 'class-conscious revolutionary passivity'.[88] The party combined revolutionary rhetoric and reformist practice much as the German Social Democrats did, and Kautsky was indeed the master theoretician for Finnish socialists as well. In contrast with the German movement, however, the backbone of the Finnish movement lay less in the collective organisation of the workers and more in the individual voting behaviour of the party's followers, the great majority of whom were engaged in agriculture. For them the idea of revolution certainly remained much more vague than for party activists.

To conclude, the working-class movement became a powerful instrument for both class and national integration. True, the events of 1905 had bred some familiarity with a revolutionary situation and a diffuse belief in the coming of revolution. But the class conflict was limited, as is reflected in the primacy of parliamentary activity and the rooting of the movement in the general process of mass organisation. In addition, the movement had a pronounced cultural and even national orientation, most obviously at the local level: the worker associations were part and parcel of the rapidly expanding local organisational network, which contributed to a vision of Finland as a political and cultural entity. At this level the labour movement was basically a way of linking the workers with the emerging civil society. Even the great strike of 1905 was important in this respect: as a powerful catalyst in the 'nationalisation' of political life.[89]

The imperial authorities in Finland never seriously doubted the reformist character of the movement. In 1907 administrative Russification was reintroduced, but unlike in the Baltic Provinces there was no repression, and the actual impact had scarcely gone beyond its initial stages by 1914.[90] Even after the Social Democrats' spectacular success in the elections, the Russians were much more alarmed by small bourgeois groups thought to be advocating separatism than by the Social Democrats.[91] Still, the restrictions the imperial authorities imposed enhanced the national orientation of the labour movement. In the Social Democratic opposition to Russian autocracy, national and class aspects were necessarily linked.[92]

---

88   Kirby 1971, p. 129 (quotation); Kettunen 1980b, p. 13.
89   Cf. Tilly, Tilly and Tilly 1975, 53–4.
90   Thaden 1981a, 11; Thaden 1981c, 459.
91   Jussila 1979b, 171–80.
92   Esp. Jussila 1979b, 226–9, 240.

CHAPTER 7

Regional Consolidation of Party Support

The character of the territorial integration (see Chapter 4) explains much of the basic variation in Finnish political ecology. It created crucial preconditions for the national and class integration consolidated after the political mobilisation of 1905.

1   Regions as Loci of Party Systems

Interpretations of regional variations in political mobilisation commonly start with mobilisation itself. They begin by looking at geographic voting patterns, for example, and then compare them with other distributions – the proportion of the rural proletariat, or the areas of small, medium, and large farms, and so forth. If the fit between the two maps is good, the latter structural variables serve to explain the distribution of the vote.[1]

In Finland, explanations given for the main regional variation in party support are based, naturally enough, on differences in the social structure of the agrarian population in various regions. It has been shown that the areas of greatest Social Democratic support were those with the largest proportion of crofters, industrial and agrarian workers, and people without permanent occupations,[2] making up a zone running from the south-west to the north-east and extending into the far north. Similarly, the fact that the Agrarian Union (and before it the Young Finns) received greater support in the zone running from the south-east to the north-west, and also extending into the far north, than in the country as a whole has been explained by reference to the large number of medium-sized and small farms in this zone. And finally, the existence of Finnish party strongholds in the west has been explained by the prevalence of large landholdings in this area.[3] As the Finnish historian Eino Jutikkala sums it up, 'In order to explain the geographical distribution of party support it is necessary to determine the largest common factor from which different attitudes [to fundamental political issues] may be derived'.[4]

---

1   See 'Editorial Essay' in the first issue of *Political Geography Quarterly* (1981, 8).
2   Soikkanen 1961, pp. 368–89.
3   Von Bonsdorff 1954, pp. 54–5, 131–2, 175–80; Salokangas 1975, pp. 175–8.
4   Jutikkala 1974, 143.

The problem is that a similarity of causes is inferred from a similarity of final outcomes. Logically, however, this situation does not necessarily hold. The inference is unjustified if the same outcome can be derived from different starting points. This variability is exactly what the state-making approach to political mobilisation maintains. National political integration is closely linked to state-making, which amounts to the hypothesis that in the process of political integration locally defined conflicts are fused together on an emerging national level. 'Indeed', Charles Tilly has pointed out, 'the process of urbanization facilitates the reforming of persistent local rivalries along lines that have some significance throughout the society'.[5]

This approach suggests that *one and the same party* may have been supported in various regions for somewhat *different reasons*. In the mobilisation process different local issues took on a uniform national form. For example, in one area the vote was divided between the Social Democrats and the Finnish party, and in another between the Social Democrats and the Agrarian Union. The Social Democrats may have gained support in both areas, but their backing was basically linked to two different local conflicts. An approach that focuses on territorial integration makes one aware of the possible regional character of political mobilisation institutionalised in the party system. This does not imply that structural explanations of the type cited above should be abandoned, but if one is interested in the formative phase of a particular political ecology, it is desirable to look at the parties within the framework of the established regions rather than that of the state as a whole. The state-making perspective suggests a common framework for analysing both the consolidation of various regions and regional variations in political mobilisation.

Table 10 shows the combination of party support in the countryside in five regions. As stated above, these regions had different roles in the national division of labour, and this situation was reflected in differences in class structures. At the same time, the capitalist transformation increasingly generalised the industrial class conflict (see Chapter 4). Various regional conflicts were soon fused at the emerging national level – as indicated by the small number of nationally important parties – but they displayed their importance by forming regionally different combinations of party support. The initial regional differences in the strength of the various parties have persisted largely unchanged. It is to be noted, however, that in the 1920s, after the abortive revolution and the foundation in 1918 of the Communist party, support from the worker movement was split between the Social Democrats and the Communists. Also, the

---

5　Tilly 1964, p. 64.

TABLE 10 Regional variations in political mobilisation in the Finnish countryside, 1907–1932

Region	Political parties supported	Role in abortive revolution of 1918	Role in Lapua movement of 1930–2
South-western Finland	Social Democrats and Finnish party	Actively revolutionary	Active
County of Viipuri	Agrarian Union	Passively anti-revolutionary	
Ostrobothnia	Finnish party and Agrarian Union	Actively anti-revolutionary	Active
Eastern Finland	Social Democrats and Agrarian Union	Passive	
Northern Finland	Agrarian Union and Social Democrats	Passive	

Agrarian Union did not succeed in making itself into a national party – at the expense of the liberal Young Finnish party (the Progress party), especially in eastern and northern Finland – until the 1910s and 1920s.

The areas where the Swedish party was strongest (omitted from Table 10) were contiguous with the boundaries of the Swedish-speaking regions on the western and southern coasts. The party even attracted the vote of Swedish-speaking workers. For this linguistic minority, then, the relevant conflict was determined not regionally, but rather relative to the Finnish-speaking majority.[6]

2 The South-Western Core Region

In the south-west both the industrial and the agrarian proletariat were numerous. Together with the crofters, they brought the Social Democrats 43 percent of the vote in 1907. More than anywhere else, the socialist challenge was here organised both in population centres and in the countryside, as indicated by the great number of rural worker associations. Barrington Moore's discussion of radical or rebellious solidarity among peasants seems applicable here.[7] To create this solidarity, institutional arrangements must be such as to spread grievances throughout the peasant community and turn it into a solidarity group

---

6 See Allardt and Miemois 1982, pp. 266–7, 276–8.
7 Moore 1966, pp. 475–7.

hostile to the overlord. This may happen if property arrangements require a minimum amount of property, usually land, in order to be a full member of the village. As Moore points out, the process of modernisation may considerably increase the number of those below this minimum, creating a radical potential. In the south-west, with the increase in the population this number did steadily grow, making the struggle for land more acute than elsewhere and presumably increasing the radical potential. Land prices rose not only as a result of the timber boom but also as a result of attempts by crofters and smallholders to buy land.[8]

Both crofters and landless labourers generally supported the Social Democrats in the elections. Despite their common hunger for land, however, no close alignment into a solidarity group was effected: after the first wave of mobilisation few crofters were active in the rural worker associations.[9] This circumstance may be accounted for by the fact that the crofters were still able to maintain de facto control of the land they cultivated, whereas the landless were forced to compete for this asset.[10]

The Finnish party, that is, the Old Finns, gained 25 percent of the total vote in the south-west and soon developed into a distinctly conservative party, receiving its main support from independent peasant landowners, who, along with the clergy and the Ostrobothnian peasants, had earlier constituted the core for Fennomania. Indeed, the prosperous peasants of the south-west especially helped to delineate the agrarian and religious ideology of the late nineteenth century. When the modern capitalist class conflict emerged in this core region, not only in industry but also in agriculture, the conflict soon reproduced itself in the division between the socialist and the conservative parties.

The religious character of the Finnish party is understandable. It is not uncommon for the agrarian upper classes to defend their position in religious and other moral terms during large-scale political transformations accompanying the rise of capitalism.[11] But here religion was characteristically not as revivalist as in most other regions. Whereas religion had traditionally been essential in the south-western countryside for the maintenance of hierarch-

---

8   Kivialho 1927, pp. 181–6.
9   This situation is striking for the agrarian commune of Huittinen, which is representative of crofter areas in the south-west (Alapuro, unfinished study [appeared in 1994: Risto Alapuro, *Suomen synty paikallisena ilmiönä*, Helsinki: Hanki ja Jää]). The crofters' meagre participation in the Social Democratic organisation for the tenant farmers is well known (Soikkanen 1975, pp. 114, 119, 152).
10 Cf. Soininen 1974, p. 398.
11 Moore 1966, pp. 490–3.

ical relationships in peasant society,[12] now, as class conflict became open, it acquired new importance in the form of 'church religiosity'. It became part of the new ideological equipment of the agrarian upper class.

3   The County of Viipuri

The strength of the Agrarian Union in the county of Viipuri seems to result from the fact that the peasants, as small producers and sellers of their labour power who worked in transportation and different seasonal jobs, were dependent on the market.[13] The proximity of St. Petersburg remained important, but between 1867 and 1891 the domination of large areas by Russian nobles was eliminated as their lands were purchased by the Finnish state and allotted to the peasants. This process freed a large number of peasants from feudal relations.

The Agrarian Union was anti-capitalist and very hostile to bourgeois society, which was seen as dominated by urban elements. As the party's ideological founder expressed it, 'Towns have become fortresses for bourgeois society, from which the surrounding countryside is dominated'; large-scale industry and big business had endowed the towns with power and influence. The first party groupings emerged on a local basis in Ostrobothnia and the county of Viipuri immediately after the parliamentary reform and quickly gained a large share of the vote.[14] The generalisation in Table 10 is less valid for the county's western areas than for its eastern areas, where the Agrarian Union gained 24 percent of the rural vote in 1907 and 54 percent in 1919. In the industrial centres of the western areas, the Social Democrats had several strongholds.

4   Ostrobothnia

Michael Hechter insists that relative isolation only rarely gives rise to a regionally distinctive culture that defines itself in active opposition to the culture of the core. He describes this exceptional case: 'Hypothesized conditions for the emergence of territorial counter-cultures include: the peripheral group must have a territory which facilitates intercollectivity communication; the peri-

---

12   Schmidt 1956b, pp. 25–6; Schmidt 1956a, pp. 86–7.
13   On the peasants' dependence on the market, see Engman 1983, pp. 149–58, 162.
14   Arter 1978, pp. 7–9, 48–58, 63–5. The leader cited is the Ostrobothnian Santeri Alkio (1919, p. 151).

phery must be culturally and economically isolated from the national core, and oriented to some extra-national center; and the periphery must not engage in extensive trade, or other economic transactions, with the core'.[15]

Each of these conditions was met in nineteenth-century Ostrobothnia. It was a territory where intercollective communication was relatively easy because of its geographically separate plain areas. It became increasingly isolated culturally because it remained outside the sudden transformation affecting other regions and therefore preserved its traditional communities. During the Swedish period it had been economically oriented toward Stockholm, and in the nineteenth century its main trading partner was still Sweden. Lastly, the network of railway lines developing from the south failed to provide Ostrobothnia with new trade connections before the 1880s.

Relative stagnation and isolation preserved the self-conscious spirit of enterprise characteristic of Ostrobothnian peasants. The tradition remained unbroken throughout the capitalist transformation,[16] persisting in the rather homogeneous social structure. The stagnation seems to have been conducive to the preservation of the agrarian community as an effective frame for collective action, or to the rise of what Barrington Moore has called conservative solidarity among peasants, whereby those who have actual or potential grievances are tied into the prevailing social structure through a division of labour that provides a legitimate, though lowly, status for persons with little or no property.[17] Something like conservative solidarity seems to have arisen in Ostrobothnia, where much of the growth in population was either channelled to areas outside the region via emigration or else tied to the prevailing structure by dividing the farm among the heirs or leasing a part of it to some of them at a nominal rent. Obtaining the wherewithal to buy a farm was often one of the most central motives for emigration, moreover, and a great many among the one-third who returned realised this wish.[18]

In Ostrobothnia, both strong parties – the Finnish party and the Agrarian Union – defended the agrarian way of life. In 1907 they gained two-thirds of the total vote in the Finnish-speaking areas. The Finnish party, which first predominated, received much support from the larger farms, whereas the Agrarian Union found backing among the smaller farms.[19] Both displayed a very marked

---

15   Hechter 1975, p. 231 (italics deleted). Hechter derives these conditions from Lipset and Rokkan 1967, p. 42.
16   Cf. Ylikangas 1981.
17   Moore 1966, pp. 475–9.
18   Toivonen 1963, pp. 26, 84–6, 189.
19   In the elections of 1907 the Finnish party received 52 percent and the Agrarian Union 12

local colour, and the proudly provincial character of political mobilisation in this region was further accentuated by the strength of revivalism, which was stronger here than anywhere else at the end of the nineteenth century. Revivalism was connected with Finnish party support, and it was rooted in a viable traditional society. Typically, members of the clergy were central in both Ostrobothnian agrarian society and the revivalist movement. Youth associations, an advance guard of early mass organisation, were also more strongly represented here, particularly in the south, than anywhere else in the country.

The same point may be made in a slightly different fashion. In Ostrobothnia it was not essential to defend one's position and way of life in a situation of accentuated class conflict within the community, as was the case in the southwest. Rather, it was essential to defend the Ostrobothnian community and way of life inside Finland as a whole. Both the self-conscious provincial spirit and the moral indignation discernible in Ostrobothnian politics and revivalism may be attributed to the fact that the agrarian cultural pattern they represented was being irrevocably supplanted by the antagonisms and ways of life of capitalist society, which was advancing the integration of the rest of Finland.

5   Eastern Finland

In the first general elections the Social Democrats became the largest party in eastern Finland, gaining 49 and 44 percent of the vote in the counties of Kuopio and Mikkeli, respectively. Since then the support for the left has remained strong in this region.

In the county of Kuopio and in some neighbouring communes in the county of Vaasa, the liberal Young Finns became the second largest party, and together these two parties collected four-fifths of the vote. Elsewhere in the country this constellation was virtually unknown. In the late 1910s and early 1920s the province of Mikkeli definitely followed this pattern. Support for the Young Finns was not to be sustained to the same extent as that for the Social Democrats, however, and it was largely replaced by support for the Agrarian Union, which gained ground more slowly than in the county of Viipuri, Ostrobothnia, and the north. In the county of Kuopio the Young Finns lost ground to the Agrarian Union around 1920; in the county of Mikkeli this happened only in 1927, when the Agrarian Union was also advancing elsewhere.

---

percent of the total vote in the Finnish-speaking areas of Ostrobothnia 'proper'. On the social structure of the supporters of the respective parties, see Salokangas 1975.

By and large, the Social Democrats, followed by the Young Finns and then by the Agrarian Union, were dominant in eastern Finland, and particularly in the county of Kuopio. During the formative period of the party system, this pattern was limited almost exclusively to this region. As in the south-west, support for the Social Democrats indicates the sharpness of class conflict. In the core region, class conflict became manifest especially in relations between agrarian groups, and support for the Social Democrats was accompanied by support for the conservatives. In eastern Finland the class conflict was affected by dependent industrialisation, making the region a periphery in the emerging territorial division of labour: Social Democrat support was accompanied, with a certain delay, by support for the Agrarian Union with its populist ideology. In both political tendencies a strong anti-capitalist feeling was evident; besides being socialist, anti-capitalism also had a peasantist base.

As in Ostrobothnia, the east experienced a revivalist movement, especially in the 1830s and 1840s, simultaneously with a distinct crisis in traditional slash-and-burn cultivation. At the end of the century the movement was still alive but weaker than in Ostrobothnia, and the religious and political mobilisations were not as closely connected as in Ostrobothnia. Here isolated or scattered farmsteads predominated, and the agrarian society was undergoing fundamental change as the previous structure was undermined without being satisfactorily replaced. Hence, the eastern agrarian community seems to have had little potential for functioning as an effective frame for collective action.[20]

6   Northern Finland

The northern party division grew to resemble the eastern one in important respects, except that the Agrarian Union was stronger than the Social Democrats. As early as 1907 the Agrarian Union collected one-fourth of the vote, and in 1919 it gained an absolute majority. The Social Democrats' share in 1907 was 22 percent.

In this region there was, not surprisingly, distinct anti-state mobilisation, which during the general strike of 1905 became manifest in violence against and removal of state officials.[21] Also, the parties had different ties with the social structure than elsewhere – which is one indication of the regional nature of party support. Here the crofters' vote was not as clearly linked to the Social

---

20   Cf. Moore 1966, p. 475.
21   Kyllönen 1975, pp. 147–8.

Democrats as in other regions but was divided among the main parties. The Agrarian Union, especially, had a strong regional character, having in its early days a distinctively northern colour, owing mainly to its strength in northern Ostrobothnia and neighbouring areas in the north.[22] An anti-state tendency has been identified also in the strong revivalist movement, Laestadionism, that obtained a strong foothold in the last decades of the nineteenth century both in northern Sweden and northern Finland. Politically, Laestadionism came to be linked mainly with the Agrarian Union.[23] Finally, voter turnout remained the lowest here: in 1907 it ranged between 30 percent (in Lapland) and 63 percent, whereas in the country as a whole it was 71 percent.

7 Conclusions

In his study of the role of internal colonialism in British national development, Michael Hechter has distinguished two types of sectionalism: peripheral and functional. Peripheral sectionalism applies to situations in which a region's political distinctiveness results from cultural factors. In this case, the cause of political differences results from what is socially defined as the specific culture of the region. All political actors, whatever their class or occupational position, tend to unite behind the common elements of a regional culture, such as a distinctive language or religion.[24] Functional sectionalism, in contrast, results from variations in the social-structural composition of a territory. In this case, class or occupational position determines the actor's political alignment, but certain strata – peasants, or industrial workers, for instance – are disproportionately located in particular regions. Hechter's evidence supports the view that the class-based party division gains strength following industrialisation in culturally homogeneous regions, regardless of whether these regions are advantaged or disadvantaged.[25]

In Finland it was functional sectionalism that became predominant following the capitalist transformation. Only the political distinctiveness of the Swedish-speaking regions can be attributed to cultural factors, and even here it is doubtful whether peripheral sectionalism applies. All this notwithstanding, it is nevertheless reasonable to view Finnish party formation in a regional perspective. The regional perspective seems reasonable, first, because, as indic-

---

22   Isohookana-Asunmaa 1980, pp. 51, 59, 227, and *passim*; Arter 1978, pp. 7–9.
23   Suolinna 1977; Kyllönen 1975, p. 161.
24   Hechter 1975, pp. 208–12.
25   Ibid., pp. 208–12, 331–40.

ated above, it helps us see that the formation of an all-encompassing party structure was simply the way in which national integration was realised in the political sphere. The somewhat differing regional conflicts were reconstituted so that they could be dealt with in the framework of a single national system. Second, this perspective may enhance awareness of the parties' persistent regional peculiarities and the local conflicts that still exist. Both aspects, the advancement of national integration and the simultaneous preservation of certain regional traits, are discernible in the revivalist movements, in early mass organisations, and in party support.

One revivalist movement was active both in eastern Finland and in southern and central Ostrobothnia and was able to cross the cultural line traditionally separating these two regions.[26] This was one of the first important signs of national integration among the peasants.[27] Yet the movement's role in the two regions was different. Characteristically, in Ostrobothnia the leading figures were churchmen, who traditionally had a central role in the local community, whereas in eastern Finland the leaders were mainly laymen. In southern Ostrobothnia revivalism was linked to support for the Finnish party, in eastern Finland to support for the Agrarian Union. Similarly, Laestadionism had a distinctly regional character in the north, but it also expanded into central Ostrobothnia.

The early mass organisations spread throughout the country, but they had regional strongholds and different linkages in various regions. The tenacity of the underlying regional structure is perhaps most clearly discernible in the case of Ostrobothnia. There, all central mass organisations – the temperance movement, the youth associations, the farmers' societies – had a strong foothold. Local society organised itself into several mutually supporting organisations and into two main parties, each of which had a consciously provincial character. Both parties reflected peasant resentment against the upper gentry (although the gentry was more visible nationally than in Ostrobothnia). The provincial tone may even be seen in the consumer cooperatives.[28] Furthermore, contacts between different organisations were not unknown: unlike youth and worker associations in the southwest, those in Ostrobothnia were able to cooperate long after 1905.[29]

In the peripheral north the dominant party, the Agrarian Union, took a more anti-urban and anti-bureaucratic stand than elsewhere, and the early party

---

26 Ylikangas 1979, pp. 201–8.
27 Suolinna 1975, pp. 7–11.
28 Suonoja 1968, p. 94.
29 Ylikangas 1981, p. 231.

programme was confined mainly to local problems.[30] In its other stronghold, the county of Viipuri, the party was firmly rooted in the local structure as well. There, too, it arose in close connection with other mass organisations, notably the youth associations. And because of the county's smallholder basis, the party advocated the cause of small farmers more distinctly than in other regions, a situation that created some tension in the first years of the party's unification.[31]

In the south-west and in eastern Finland, the regional characteristics of political organisation were less obvious. In the south-western core class-based functional sectionalism was more evident than elsewhere. Conditions in the east illustrate how local conflicts can be moulded along nationally significant lines. There, the average farm was nearer the size of farms in western Finland than of the smallholdings in the county of Viipuri.[32] Still, the eastern peasants were to vote mainly for the Agrarian Union. This may well be explained by the adverse effects of capitalist penetration in this region, but it is significant that the party's advance was slower there than in other Agrarian strongholds. The party was able to attract the support of the eastern farmers only after it had consolidated itself at the national level. One indication of the region's dependent position vis-à-vis the core of the country perhaps lies in the fact that only in the county of Kuopio can no correlation be found between support for the Social Democrats in 1907 and the proportion of households owning land.[33] Landownership, in other words, did not necessarily lead to an anti-socialist stand.

30   Isohookana-Asunmaa 1980, pp. 51, 233.
31   Mylly 1975, p. 100; Arter 1978, pp. 37, 57–8.
32   Mylly 1975, p. 95. In contrast to the south-west, however, a distinct class of wealthy peasants did not exist in the east.
33   Soikkanen 1961, pp. 366, 368, 385.

PART 3

The Abortive Revolution

∵

CHAPTER 8

On Preconditions for Revolutionary Situations

In 1917–18 Finland experienced a revolutionary situation, with the worker movement being the main challenger to the established order. I will argue that the response of the movement to the revolutionary opportunity – which was initiated by the sudden collapse of Imperial Russia – followed rather directly from the process of mobilisation described in the preceding pages.

In Chapter 9 the coming of revolution itself will be analysed in the light of the process of Finnish state-making and nation-building. Both long-term and short-term developments are important. On the one hand, the relative weight of structural and institutional preconditions for the revolutionary process must be assessed. The characters of, first, the polity and the class structure and, second, the national movement and the working-class movement, all of which affected the preconditions for collective action in 1917–18, were shaped in the nineteenth and early twentieth centuries. On the other hand, the intricacies of World War I must also be taken into account. The two groups of factors interacted and induced the relatively well entrenched and non-revolutionary working-class movement to a revolution. Chapter 10 will examine the impact of the failed revolution on the existing state structures and on the processes of national and class integration. In short, Part III will delineate the impact of certain structural preconditions on an event, the Finnish revolution, and the repercussions of this event back on those structures.

Of use here is Charles Tilly's model of the proximate causes of revolutionary situations,[1] which is linked to his conception of organisation, mobilisation, and collective action, employed earlier. In deliberately focusing on revolutionary situations in general, not only on successful revolutions, his model suggests comparisons between all cases of serious revolutionary activity, irrespective of their outcome. This is particularly important in the analysis of small polities such as Finland. Although international factors have played a part in nearly all revolutions,[2] only in the small polities has the final success or failure most evidently depended on fluctuations in international power constellations. In other words, it is specifically the *rise* of revolutions that is of interest here.

---

1   Tilly 1978, pp. 200–2.
2   See Dunn 1972, 1977; Skocpol 1979.

In Tilly's view revolutions involve the seizure of control over a governmental apparatus by one class, group, or, more likely, a coalition of several groups. The revolutionary situation itself is defined by what Lenin and Trotsky called 'dual power' and Tilly terms 'multiple sovereignty': the fragmentation of governmental authority into two or more centres, each of which claims exclusive legitimacy. Multiple sovereignty has often emerged when the polity – consisting of the collective action of those groups routinely making successful claims on the exercise of government in their interest – splits into conflicting factions. Such a fragmentation of the ruling establishment, moreover, may provide challengers from below with tactical opportunities to press their demands.[3] By definition, there are three proximate causes of multiple sovereignty:

1. the appearance of contenders, or coalitions of contenders, advancing exclusive alternative claims to the control over the government which is currently exerted by the members of the polity;
2. commitment to those claims by a significant segment of the subject population (especially when those commitments are not simply acknowledged in principle, but activated in the face of prohibitions or contrary directives from the government);
3. incapacity or unwillingness of the agents of the government to suppress the alternative coalition and/or the commitment to its claims.[4]

The causes in Tilly's model are largely consecutive. They form the beginning of 'an idealized revolutionary sequence': first, gradual mobilisation of contenders; then, rapid increase in the number of people accepting those claims or rapid expansion of the alternative coalition; and finally, unsuccessful efforts by the government to suppress the alternative coalition.[5]

This 'idealised sequence', simple as it is, provides a helpful framework for analysing the Finnish case. It helps to relate existing forms of organisation and mobilisation to the opportunities created by the intricacies of World War I. Because the revolutionary situation was, in a sense, a conjunction of internal structural factors and short-term external factors (that is, the crisis in Russia), the framework also helps in assessing the relative importance of domestic and

---

3   Tilly 1978, pp. 190–3. The formulation here is based on Rod Aya's summary (1979, p. 44).
4   Tilly 1978, p. 200.
5   Ibid., pp. 216–17.

foreign developments. It will be suggested, for example, that the third proximate cause, the incapacity of the government to suppress the emerging polity, was particularly important in Finland.

In a more general perspective the specific features of the Finnish case may be clarified by Barrington Moore's discussion of the preconditions for 'major' revolutions.[6] Moore concentrates on three preconditions in the dominant classes. The first is the decay of legitimacy: the whole intellectual and emotional structure that makes the prevailing order seem natural, legitimate, and inevitable begins to crumble in the face of embarrassing questions for which the prevailing orthodoxies gradually cease to provide satisfactory answers; in other words, an intellectual challenge arises for which conventional categories and explanations increasingly fail to make sense. Second, sharp conflicts of interest develop within the dominant classes. These appear as insoluble financial problems but are basically acute disagreements about how to resolve problems arising from new social relationships and, more specifically, about which social groups should pay the costs of these new arrangements. The third precondition is, however, decisive: the loss of unified control over the instruments of violence, that is, over the army and the police. They may refuse to obey, or a section of the dominant classes may break off and take with it a part of the armed forces, or a mixture of the two processes may occur.

Clearly this list is reminiscent of Tilly's.[7] Particularly similar are the loss of unified control over the army and the government's incapacity to suppress commitment to alternative claims. But Moore's time perspective is longer, and he obviously delineates the central preconditions for so-called Great Revolutions – those of France, Russia, and China. In France, an intellectual structure fundamentally critical of the prevailing order developed well before 1789: the revolution was, in essence, a realisation of the intellectual vision of the Enlightenment, which swept through French culture in the late 1700s. Moreover, disagreements between the absolutist Bourbon monarchy and the aristocratic upper classes mounted during the decades preceding the revolution and finally led to a sharp conflict between the government and the Estates General. Third, in 1789 the monarchy lost control of the instruments of violence; it was unable to use the armed forces to impose its will.

The Russian sequence resembles the French one. 'Artists and intellectuals ... had long [before 1917] sung the coming of the revolution' is the way Marc Ferro expresses the first precondition.[8] Also, the imperial state had started a

---

6 Moore 1972, pp. 170–5.
7 Cf. Tilly 1978, p. 201.
8 Ferro 1967–76, 1: 143.

process of industrialisation that furthered the disintegration of old roles in various segments of society and displaced the gentry.[9] Nonetheless, the ensuing conflicts among the dominant groups certainly were not as bitter as in France. World War I dealt the death blow to the autocracy, contributing especially to the dissolution of the army; after the devastating losses in war, the armed forces refused to obey.

The initial phases of the Chinese revolution are comparable to the other cases. The May Fourth Movement of 1919, a mass movement of intellectuals, was 'a kind of Chinese Enlightenment … [that] foreshadowed and paved the way for 1949 just as Voltaire had for 1789'.[10] Besides, discontent among the privileged was rife before the onset of the revolutionary process, that is, before 1911. Many of the members of the revolutionary organisations were from the privileged classes. Soon the new republic crumbled, and rival warlords took over parts of the old armed forces and created their own private armies.

The three preconditions, pertinent as they are for the analysis of the two established European states and China, are less relevant for the revolutionary situations in Finland and other European latecomer states. In Finland, for one thing, the whole intellectual structure legitimising the prevailing order had only recently been constructed, and at the beginning of the twentieth century there was unanimity among all intellectual groups about the basic character of national integration. National identification was clear in the new working-class movement as well; it has even been seen as an outgrowth of the national tradition that originated with Snellman.[11] Moreover, only a handful of intellectuals were active in the Social Democratic movement, and most of them had joined the party between 1904 and 1906. Second, no major conflicts of interest existed within the dominant classes. Indeed, the rise of the working-class movement caused them to close ranks in the decade following the general strike of 1905.[12]

In these two respects the situation in the Eastern European polities was not too different. To be sure, certain countries, such as Hungary and Romania, had dissident intellectual groups, but it seems fair to say that conflicts within the dominant groups remained limited. With respect to national minorities, the preconditions do not really apply. True, national movements struggled for

---

9   Skocpol 1979, pp. 91–2.
10 Bianco 1971, pp. 27–8.
11 Palmgren 1948, pp. 184–204. Cf. Hamalainen 1978, pp. 30–3 and *passim*; and Hodgson 1967, pp. 7–8. One indication of the national identification in the worker movement is the active participation of certain socialist leaders in the nationalist organisation *Suomalaisuuden liitto* (League for the Finnish Culture) after 1906 (Hamalainen 1978, p. 135).
12 This tendency was particularly clear in the cultural sphere. See Murtorinne 1967, pp. 90–104, 222, 229, 231.

self-assertion and liberation, and consequently came into conflict with dominant local groups that identified with the metropolitan country, but minority regions were not usually polities to the extent that Finland was. These movements strove more for the creation of new polities than for power in an already existing one, and severe conflicts remained rare within minority groups until World War I.

The third precondition, however, was absolutely crucial for revolutionary situations in all the latecomer states and dependent regions. The collapse of the two multinational empires in World War I led to the disintegration of the armed forces not only in the core areas of Russia and Austria-Hungary but also in their minority regions. The same was true, at least for brief periods, in Romania, Bulgaria, and Serbia.[13] Opportunities to act collectively were thus thrust upon only modestly organised and mobilised nationalities.

The three preconditions highlight the differences between the established and the new European states delineated in Chapter 1. In the early cases, as exemplified by the French and Russian revolutions, long-term internal processes that prepared the ground for revolution may be discerned, involving not only conflicts within the dominant classes or between the elites and the central governments but also structural preconditions conducive to collective action among peasants and workers. The two processes – state/elite conflicts and popular uprisings – coincided in the revolutions.[14] To cite Barrington Moore, a certain social process 'worked itself out' in these cases.[15] This view is also in line with Theda Skocpol's analysis,[16] although she systematically incorporates the international environment in the analysis of the three Great Revolutions. Actually, Skocpol studies long-term *internal* processes – that is, how domestic class structures and political institutions ultimately made it impossible for the imperial states to cope successfully with competition or intrusions from abroad. The decomposition of the armed forces under international pressure should be viewed against the background of these long-term internal processes.

In Eastern European latecomer polities, opportunities changed quite independently of the strength of domestic collective action. In these cases a short-term external event, World War I, was crucial for the rise of revolutionary activity.

---

13   Steiner 1967, pp. 183, 189; Nagy 1967, p. 162; Moore 1978, pp. 291–309; Schärf 1967, pp. 200, 223–4.
14   See Goldstone 1982, pp. 194–200.
15   Moore 1966, p. xii.
16   Skocpol 1979, esp. pp. 112–17.

The situation of these countries also seems to be systematically different from that of the small non-European polities that have experienced serious revolutionary activity in the twentieth century (that is, the colonial countries). These revolutionary situations have usually emerged after a hard, painful, and often slow process of organisation and mobilisation – accompanied, it is true, by repeated disruptions in colonial control. In typical cases a revolutionary situation was created only after decades or at least many years of 'patient institution-building'.[17] In this comparison too, then, the small European polities emerge as unique cases in which the rapid dissolution of the armed forces played a central role, while the other two preconditions and possibly even anteceding popular organisation were relatively unimportant.

The collapse of the most powerful continental states in 1917–18 created an exceptional opportunity for local forms of organisation and mobilisation to develop with a minimum of hindrance. It should be stressed that local attempts at revolution were genuinely internal: they took place within a polity, and the main contenders were indigenous groups. But there was no long-term 'preparation' for revolution comparable to that preceding the Great Revolutions or the anticolonial revolutions, and thus, in the Finnish case at least, this implies that there were few intellectual instruments for coping with the revolutionary attempt in the post-1918 culture. This qualification helps to relate the previous process of national and class integration not only to the revolution 1917–18 but also to the period following it.

In the next chapter the interplay of internal and external factors leading up to the revolutionary situation will be examined. The central task is to consider how the special characteristics of the internal revolutionary processes in Finland resulted from the country's external dependencies, given the long-term structural and institutional background presented above.

---

17 Migdal 1974, pp. 229–56, 265 (quotation). For an illuminating example of the slow process of revolutionary institution-building, see Popkin 1979, pp. 223–42.

CHAPTER 9

The Abortive Revolution of 1917–1918

1   Socialists within the Polity

The working-class movement penetrated into the polity easily as a result of the 1905 revolution in Russia. It considered itself the leading protagonist of the extension of democracy, its conception of revolution was extremely vague, and it was dominated by a party – the largest in parliament – that devoted its energies to parliamentary activity. But although the party had access to government-controlled resources, this access was not routine, as it was for the other members of the polity. Much like its smaller Scandinavian sister parties, it was not (yet) a full member.[1] The working-class movement had not secured a position for itself in the upper echelons of either the government or the administration, much less civil society, and consequently the party was largely isolated.

The February 1917 revolution in Russia was a great relief for all Finnish political groups, and the ensuing reactivation of the political system was especially important for the Social Democrats. One week after its formation, the Provisional Government in Russia issued a manifesto restoring full constitutional rights to Finland. In the parliamentary elections of 1916, the Social Democrats had gained an absolute majority, 103 seats out of 200, but parliament had not been allowed to convene. Now the party's foremost goal became not only the guarantee of rights gained in 1905 but also their extension. The party wanted full internal autonomy for Finland, leaving only foreign and military policy and mutual relations between Finland and Russia to the Provisional Government. The party programme also included several legal reforms championed unsuccessfully in the previous decade, particularly the eight-hour workday, the democratisation of local government (which had not been reformed in the countryside since 1865 and in the towns since 1873), and the enfranchisement of the crofters and other tenant farmers.

The party entered the government (the Economic Department of the Senate), in which it had six ministers (senators) out of twelve, including the prime minister – the first time in any country that a socialist had become the head

---

1   Tilly 1978, p. 52; Elvander 1980, pp. 33, 35–47; Castles 1978, pp. 17–22.

of a government.² (The other ministers came from the large bourgeois parties.) The Social Democratic party was now clearly a member of the polity, and its demands for reforms certainly did not constitute 'exclusive alternative claims to the control over the government'.³ Cooperation between socialist and bourgeois ministers remained good well into the summer.⁴

The socialists had begun to share political power in a bourgeois state at a difficult moment. The economic and social situation was becoming worse. Grain imports from Russia were drying up, foreshadowing a shortage of food; the cutback in the Russians' fortification and military procurement programmes in Finland contributed to mass unemployment; and inflation accelerated. These short-term problems aggravated a more profound, institutional problem, which the Social Democrats had to face. The prevailing conditions made effective execution of political decisions necessary, but there could be no guarantee that the existing administrative apparatus would prove to be a pliable instrument for Social Democratic policy. The Social Democrats led the government and had a parliamentary majority, but the apparatus they were supposed to work with was solidly bourgeois. Nineteenth-century Finland had been bureaucratically organised, and the bureaucracy remained strong – with the Senate still at the top (see Chapter 2).

Civil society, likewise, had remained highly stable. Unlike much of the rest of Europe, Finland was still institutionally intact in March 1917; economic and social structures had not been undermined by the post-1907 integration measures (as in the Baltic Provinces, for example) or by the war, even though short-term problems were inevitable. Thanks to the suspension of conscription in 1905, the Finns were not called to arms to defend the empire.

If this had been all, the Social Democrats would have shared political power under conditions rather similar to those in many Western European countries, such as Sweden in 1917, for example. But the Finnish state had suffered damage in one essential respect as a result of the February revolution: it was left without control of the principal concentrated means of coercion.⁵ After the dissolution of the domestic troops from 1901 to 1905, the only armed forces the state could rely on in a possible crisis were, in the last analysis, the imperial troops stationed in the country – and the Russian revolution largely paralysed this force. The Finnish police also disintegrated. In the years following the revolution of 1905 the police had been largely 'Russified', that is, reorganised to comply with

---

2   Ketola 1981, p. 29.
3   Tilly 1978, p. 200.
4   Upton 1980, p. 35.
5   Cf. Weber 1948, p. 78; and Tilly 1978, p. 52.

imperial policy. Immediately after the February revolution policemen and rural police officials were again forced to resign, much as they had been in 1905. Until the end of 1917 Finland was not to have a police force strictly constituted according to prevailing legal stipulations.[6] The reorganisation of the police force was to obscure the borderline not only between the state and the working-class movement but also between parliamentary and extra-parliamentary activity in the labour movement.

Symptomatic of the relationship between the state apparatus and the working-class movement was the replacement of the police by the militia in March and April. As in 1905, workers participated actively in the militia. Initially, however, they were far from alone. The democratic maintenance of order was a generally supported goal after the dismissal of the 'Russified' police.[7] At the same time, specific worker militias were founded in a few urban centres. These were often rudimentary and transient in character, organised largely to maintain order among the workers themselves. In several cases they overlapped partly or wholly with the communal militias, or else the latter were supervised by committees in which the Social Democrats were represented through the worker councils that had been founded in many towns in the spring. Hence, the distinction between public and private maintenance of order was not clear immediately after the February revolution.[8]

At first the bourgeois groups did not oppose the setting up of communal militias,[9] because they considered them necessary in the short run and, in any case, provisional. Soon, however, they began to call for a return to 'normalcy', and in the spring all bourgeois parties agreed on this demand.[10] In the towns the militias were partly disbanded in early summer. The bourgeois minister for the interior, without consulting his Social Democratic colleagues, sent a circular calling on local authorities to appoint chiefs of police who would cooperate with local militia committees to get the police back 'on a regular footing'. Because these efforts were not supported by the Social Democrats and because the workers were generally not well represented in local government, it is no wonder the workers were usually not ready to disband the militias.[11] The line between public maintenance of order and the workers' own

---

6   Salkola 1975, pp. 30, 54–5, 145; Piilonen 1982, p. 65; Kirby 1971, pp. 203–4, 206–7; Soikkanen 1975, p. 229; Lindman 1968, p. 123.
7   Salkola 1985, 1: 45, 73–7; Soikkanen 1975, pp. 228–9.
8   Salkola 1985, 1: 53, 64, 74–80, 95–6, 185, 188, 377–80; Kirby 1971, pp. 206–9.
9   Piilonen 1982, pp. 65, 73; Salkola 1985, 1: 77, 131.
10 Salkola 1975, pp. 147–8.
11 See Piilonen 1982, pp. 66–7; Salkola 1985, 1: 77–78, 199; Upton 1980, p. 60.

initiative remained vague: militias continued to be worker-controlled, but they were often paid by the local authorities.[12]

In other words, from the winter of 1917 on, the agents of government would have been incapable of suppressing an alternative coalition – if there had been one. The dominant Finnish groups had lost the ultimate protection which control of the armed forces gives, at the very moment that the Russian autocracy collapsed. And they were unable to rebuild the instruments of violence without the consent of the socialist parvenus. Contrary to the 'idealised sequence', the decomposition of the armed forces and the dismissal of the domestic police had not been the last stage in the movement toward multiple sovereignty. The means of coercion collapsed because of events outside the Finnish polity, and no contender presenting exclusive alternative claims existed. The Social Democrats had penetrated into a polity unable to resort to force but still rooted in a solid bourgeois institutional structure. In the long run, the absence of the instruments of coercion, together with shared control of the provisional arrangements for maintaining order, was an asset for the Social Democrats, a potential weapon for exercising pressure on the state power.

The militias, however, which were official, semi-official, or private to varying degrees, were of value to the party only if they could be kept under control – that is, only if the movement, headed by the parliamentary party, could control extra-parliamentary activity. In the spring this did not appear too difficult: the party was well organised, most militia members were also members of the party, and the overall number of distinct worker militias remained small.[13] But serious problems were in sight. Unemployment was increasing and the food situation deteriorating. As a result of the revolution in Russia, wartime regulations were repealed and strikes were again permitted. All this contributed to an enormous wave of organisation and mobilisation, which had already started in 1916. At that time the party's adherents had grown in number from 52,000 to 73,000; by the end of 1917 this number was to rise to between 120,000 and 130,000. The growth in the trade union movement was faster still: in 1916 membership figures increased from 30,000 to 42,000, and by December 1917 they had climbed to 165,000, a fourfold increase. For the first time in Finland trade union membership exceeded that of the Social Democratic party.[14] In the spring and summer the figures were still far from their peak, but the balance between the established leaders and older members on the one hand and the new

---

12   Salkola 1985, 1: 74–76, 80–1; Piilonen 1982, p. 72.
13   Piilonen 1982, pp. 65–9, 73; Salkola 1985, 1: 148–149, 201–5, 377–80.
14   Soikkanen 1975, pp. 193–5, 260–2; Ala-Kapee and Valkonen 1982, pp. 406–10.

adherents on the other was becoming delicate within both the party and the working-class movement as a whole.

The party did not – and possibly could not – take a clear-cut stand when the rapidly mobilised masses presented the state with their demands. The party had not consolidated itself in the polity; therefore it needed the support of the masses. Characteristic of the ambiguous situation is the fact that the Social Democratic ministers were not leading figures and that the party did not form the government alone, although it could have in March. Thus the government did not have the whole-hearted support of the movement.

The party's ability to solve the short-term problems and carry through the reforms it considered central was extremely important. Party objectives could be achieved only if life continued in an orderly fashion, and achieving these objectives would make it easier to maintain order. At first everything seemed quite satisfactory, even though some untoward incidents occurred.

The eight-hour workday, local government reform, and the enfranchisement act were presented to Parliament, and their consideration proceeded rapidly. In April, however, just as the eight-hour-day legislation was being considered, strikes spread in industry, and soon employers in a number of industries were forced to accept the workers' demands. In early May the strikes spread into agriculture, continuing into early June. The Social Democrats were surprised and disturbed by the farm strikes. The main party paper urged the agrarian labourers not to waste their energies in strikes but to build up solid trade unions, and the government, which had become a 'mediator in labour disputes', issued a statement urging the strikers not to intensify their action and to come to terms with the landowners.[15] But strikes broke out again at the end of June and continued here and there until August; they had, however, practically no effect on the harvest.[16] The workers also exerted pressure on local government, which was dominated by the urban bourgeoisie or wealthy landowners. In these cases, too, the party tried both directly and indirectly, through the government, to control the movement.[17]

In the spring the government took up the impending food crisis. Finland had escaped the war, and the scarcity of food was not comparable to that in the countries devastated by battle. Modest measures of rationing had been initiated only at the end of 1916, and even in spring 1917 grain, the main staple,

---

15 Ketola 1981, p. 59 (quotation); Upton 1980, pp. 58–9; Ala-Kapee and Valkonen 1982, pp. 393–403.
16 Kirby 1971, pp. 226–7.
17 Piilonen 1982, pp. 44, 48–56, 64; Upton 1980, pp. 60–2.

was not rationed.[18] But when grain imports from Russia began to dry up, the situation deteriorated. In June a food law was enacted which regulated consumption, controlled prices, and made the expropriation of food possible. The government announced that all grain reserved for home consumption was to be confiscated and began to organise its distribution. The problem of assuring support of inventory-taking and rationing on the part of producers and consumers alike was solved by co-opting the various 'social forces' into the organisation responsible for rationing. This system was controlled by the government, which urged the formation of local food committees 'according to the local social structure'. On the whole, the strategy proved successful: the inventory appears to have provided fairly accurate statistics, even though the farmers supplied the information on their own. In other words, despite the farm strikes in May and June, the grain confiscations and the rationing of consumption were tacitly approved. The rationing worked moderately well: grain and other foodstuffs were available, and there was no real shortage in the summer, even in the towns.[19]

All in all, no serious disorders occurred in the spring or summer. The Social Democratic party strove to maintain calm, and by and large it succeeded. In this the worker militias, based on party cadres, played no small role. Their principal task was to prevent possible disturbances in strikes and demonstrations held in support of the new communal law and the eight-hour workday.[20] In June the party ignored demands – which were few – to call a general strike.[21] As Anthony F. Upton sums it up, 'Until August 1917 the situation in Finland, in spite of the revolution and the disorders it had occasioned, was still recognizably normal. A legitimate Finnish government and parliament governed the country, however unsatisfactorily, within the bounds of the constitution and the law'.[22]

Nevertheless, it is no wonder that by the summer maintenance of order had become the major problem confronting the bourgeois groups. The dismissal of the police had deprived the state of the only apparatus that truly safeguarded individual and property rights, and interventions by the mobilised workers, few as they were, seemed to constitute a great potential threat. But in the situation that prevailed there was no legal recourse to 'traditional repression to deal with disorders'. When in June the bourgeois minister for the interior was asked about legalising the bourgeois counter-militias or setting up a paramil-

---

18   Rantatupa 1979, pp. 54–62, 69.
19   Rantatupa 1979, pp. 71–87.
20   Salkola 1985, 1: 197, 203, 206.
21   Piilonen 1982, p. 44; Upton 1980, pp. 52–3.
22   Upton 1980, p. 102.

itary police force, he rejected both ideas: the bourgeois militias would be an incitement to civil war, and the Russians would not permit the raising of a paramilitary police.[23]

These impediments notwithstanding, there were grounds for a bourgeois paramilitary organisation, whose rise would eventually accentuate the private character of the worker-controlled militias. Even if it had had an official or semi-official status, a militia could not have avoided a choice when confronted with mass demonstrations for the eight-hour day, the democratisation of local government, the control of prices, the confiscation of grain stocks, or communal relief work for the unemployed. The problem was aggravated by the fact that the bourgeoisie continued to exercise power at the local level, as Parliament had not yet passed the new communal law. Often the situation was inherently ambiguous. For example, the government's injunction to set up the food committees in line with the numerical strength of local social groups was only a recommendation. If the local powerholders did not comply, disagreements and conflicts between the landowners and the organised workers were imminent, whatever the status of the local militia. Also, the reorganisation of the urban police, mentioned above, incited the workers to set up militias of their own, or at least not to disperse the existing ones.[24]

Because the working-class movement had a share in political decision-making at the top of the polity and in the maintenance of order, every bourgeois attempt to restore the pre-March situation was bound to lead to private organisation – that is, outside the governmental apparatus. Civil society was in good shape, so this kind of organisation was easy. A telling example is the Farmers Congress in Helsinki at the end of May, during the first wave of farm strikes. The farmers were contemptuous of the government and its measures, which they said were leading to the breakdown of law and order; the congress therefore asked the farmers to organise their own defence. For the most part, however, 'anti-hooliganism' organisations existed only on paper until August, in all regions except south-western Finland. There the farmers established 'fire brigades' and 'security corps' in answer to the farm strikes.[25]

Another factor contributed to the establishment of a bourgeois force. A group of 'Activists' had worked for Finnish independence since 1915. Until the spring of 1917 the most nationally oriented Social Democrats were numbered among their supporters.[26] The Activists looked to Germany for help. In 1915

---

23   Upton 1980, pp. 51 (quotation), 60.
24   Salkola 1975, pp. 53–70, 133–58, 277–8; Salkola 1985, 1: 377–80.
25   Salkola 1985, 1: 246–259, 290–310; Upton 1980, pp. 59, 62.
26   Ketola 1981, pp. 254–4; Hodgson 1967, pp. 21–2.

and 1916 Germany had created a *Jäger* battalion consisting of 1,500 Finnish volunteers, which fought on Germany's eastern front and was, given opportune conditions, supposed to act to separate Finland from Russia, with German help, using an organisation to be set up in Finland. The Activists considered their principal enemy to be the Russians stationed in Finland, who at the beginning of 1917 numbered 40,000 and by August had reached a peak of 100,000 men. In the summer of 1917, however, the Activists received only limited support; some anti-Russian security guards were created by August, mainly in Ostrobothnia, a region with many Russian troops. Although Finnish independence was the Activists' objective, the fact remains that they envisioned an armed bourgeois organisation. Therefore their efforts were potentially linked with more popular bourgeois efforts to 'restore internal order': both had as their ultimate goal the protection and fortification of the bourgeois state and civil society.

The working-class movement's position in the polity was put to an explicit, even decisive, test when Parliament took a stand on Finnish independence and the way in which exercise of the imperial prerogative should be transferred to the Finnish government after the February revolution. This event was to be the single most important step toward multiple sovereignty.

In the grand duchy the laws passed by Parliament needed the emperor's confirmation. The government, moreover, was not a sovereign executive: it was rather a committee of departmental heads, appointed by and answerable to the emperor, whose representative, the governor general, could preside over its meetings. After the February revolution these rights of supervision and approval were transferred to the Provisional Government.

The Social Democrats aimed at the extension of autonomy and, if possible, full independence. This as such would have enhanced their room for manoeuvre. The party was also willing to raise Parliament to a politically dominant position, which would have strengthened the socialists' institutional hold on the state, although the state would have remained unquestionably bourgeois. National orientation in the party was now accompanied by increasing nationalist fervour among the masses. In the working-class movement, orientation toward independence and the goal of extending political democracy were seen to be intimately connected.[27]

The party worked for independence both in government and outside, ignoring the negative attitude of the Provisional Government. After having made contacts with various political groups in Russia, the party finally pushed

---

27 Soikkanen 1975, pp. 208–18; Ketola 1981, pp. 93, 118–19, 276–8; Salkola 1985, 1: 49–50; Ferro 1967–1976, 2: 171–5.

through a so-called law on authority (*valtalaki*) on 17 and 18 July.[28] This law proclaimed the full internal autonomy of Finland and the transfer of imperial prerogatives to Parliament. Only foreign policy and military affairs were left under the jurisdiction of the Provisional Government.

There were protagonists of independence in the bourgeois parties as well. Disorder in Russia led many people to strive for at least an extension of internal autonomy, if not full independence. The Activists and some other supporters of independence at first backed the Social Democrats' efforts. But the bourgeois groups generally opposed the *valtalaki*, notably because it would have increased the socialists' grip on the state, but also because the Provisional Government could have used the armed forces to suppress it. When the decisive votes were cast, though, most bourgeois representatives backed the law: they followed a course they believed was massively supported by the population.[29]

The socialists had envisioned the formation of a purely Social Democratic government after the approval of the *valtalaki*. Once the Provisional Government had endured the so-called July Days, however, it refused to approve the law, dissolved Parliament, and ordered new elections. It was of utmost importance that all bourgeois groups sided with the Provisional Government. Many bourgeois proponents of the *valtalaki* dissociated themselves from it, and opponents of the law actively cooperated with the Provisional Government in order to make sure that it was rejected and new elections ordered.[30] By the same token, the eight-hour workday and local government acts, which had already gone through Parliament, were left unconfirmed.

In a sense, the *valtalaki* led to a bourgeois coup d'état. For besides the problem of law and order in 1917 Finland, there was the relationship with Russia, and the bourgeois groups utilised this second ambiguity to their advantage. The Social Democrats' position in the polity was challenged in a manner unacceptable to all tendencies in the socialist movement. Thus, because the *valtalaki* had been passed by Parliament in accordance with regular procedures, and because it rejected the authority of the Provisional Government, the Social Democrats were never to regard the new elections and the subsequent developments as legal.[31]

Just what was and was not legal in that spring and summer is of secondary importance here. What is essential is that both the socialists and the bourgeois groups utilised the state's prevailing ambiguities and weaknesses in their

---

28   Upton 1980, pp. 86–92.
29   Ibid., p. 92; Lindman 1968, p. 83.
30   Polvinen 1967, pp. 91–3; Upton 1980, pp. 94–6.
31   Cf. Lindman 1978, p. xix. For one exception, see Lindman 1968, pp. 136–8.

struggle to gain control. After the February revolution in Russia the state had been damaged and was incapable of guaranteeing some of the basic conditions of the prevailing order. Now the conflict with the Provisional Government broke its fragile structure, and the way was paved for the struggle between the social classes to grow. In the late summer and the autumn, two polities began to take shape. And both had troops which sought arms.

2 The Rise of Multiple Sovereignty

In practice, the socialists had to confront the fact that the *valtalaki* had been rejected and Parliament dissolved. The bourgeois groups sided unanimously with the Provisional Government, which presumably would also have been able to resort to force. No open conflict occurred, however.

First the socialist ministers left the government. Only the bourgeois ministers stayed, and their first objective became 'achieving a powerful security force for the country'. The government was willing to dissolve the militias and re-establish the regular police, but because the ministers feared that the radicalised Russian soldiers would intervene, it did not do so. And certainly the militias themselves would not have disbanded voluntarily. Therefore, the government resorted to semi-secret operations. In August it was decided to raise a clandestine police force in Helsinki, and in September the government initiated the training of a mounted police force. The latter plan was official, but the socialists learned about it only afterward. It met with difficulties mainly because the Russians did not deliver arms.[32]

Links were soon forged between the government and the Activists. An Activist entered the government, replacing the former socialist minister for food, and the government set up a committee composed of Activists 'for establishing our own domestic armed force'. The secret police force in Helsinki was placed under its jurisdiction, and these police were to be integrated into the proposed armed force.[33] In addition, Activists attempted to create a nationwide organisation, but really succeeded only in Ostrobothnia. On 31 October the first noticeable shipment of arms from Germany arrived in Ostrobothnia.

Other efforts specifically intended to restore internal order also gained momentum after the collapse of the *valtalaki*, and the distinction between these attempts and Activist efforts to achieve independence nearly disappeared: both were aimed at fortifying the prevailing societal system, including

---

32 Upton 1980, pp. 107–8 (quotation from p. 107).
33 Upton 1980, p. 112 (quotation from the same page).

its constellation of political power. The economic elite and other groups supported both types of activity, but they saw the Activists as struggling against 'hooliganism' within the country. The organisation for restoring internal order gained the upper hand and soon mushroomed: by the end of September there were considerably more bourgeois guards than worker militias or guards.[34]

The bourgeois parties' main theme in the electoral campaign preceding the October elections was law and order. The largest bourgeois parties agreed to support a common ticket and concentrated all their efforts on achieving a bourgeois majority. The Social Democrats, for their part, campaigned on the *valtalaki* – that is, on independence – and did not say much about their social objectives. They thought that they would succeed simply as proponents of independence.[35]

The socialist party was defeated, however. It lost eleven seats, and the bourgeois parties won a majority. The defeat made the party confront the problem that the leadership had been well aware of since the failure of the *valtalaki*: how to control the rising revolutionary mood of the masses. Above all, the Social Democrats feared that the 'attempted bourgeois coup' would reverse the gains that the workers had made since March.[36] Many leaders had been wary about withdrawing from the government in August because they saw participation as a means of holding off the masses. The same idea was expressed during the electoral campaign. O.W. Kuusinen, one of the leading figures of the party, saw the implications of losing in this way: 'What will happen if we are defeated in the elections? Then a revolution could be sparked off amongst the people. But there is no knowing how such a revolution would end. It could bring disaster to the whole labour movement, and that is one reason why we should endeavour to win victory in the elections'. After the elections were over, but before the results were known, Kuusinen said that 'a general rising of the people must be held off until the election is declared'.[37]

---

34   Fol 1977, pp. 220–1; Upton 1980, pp. 109–10; Salkola 1985, 2: 164. According to Marja-Leena Salkola, by that time bourgeois guards had been set up at the most in 271 of the 509 communes, and workers' militias or guards in 29. The comparison gives only a rough idea of the relative strength of the organisation on both sides, because the available sources for the bourgeois guards seem to exaggerate their number. Another form of workers' organisation, more widespread but normally much looser and largely transient, consisted of picket marshals, whose principal duty was to maintain order during strikes. If these marshals are included, the number of communes in which the problem of maintaining order had led to organised activity by workers by the end of September rises to 202 (Salkola 1985, 1: 243–4, 298–9).

35   Soikkanen 1975, pp. 236–7; Upton 1980, p. 122.

36   Upton 1980, pp. 130, 137; Salkola 1985, 1: 52.

37   Cited in Kirby 1971, p. 248; and in Upton 1980, p. 126, respectively.

Less than a fortnight after the results were announced, a national Worker Security Guard was established. There were, of course, worker militias, and in Helsinki some members of the 1905 Red Guard had attempted to revive that organisation. But, despite popular pressure, the party had been able to prevent the establishment of militant guards. In the early fall, however, after the suppression of the *valtalaki*, and particularly with the proliferation of the bourgeois guards in August and September, conditions began to change. Organisation started from the grassroots: militant security guards, willing to acquire their own arms, tended to form within the existing militias and other groups. They were conceived as protecting workers, mainly against the bourgeois guards but also against the state (often seen as synonymous with these guards). In early September the formation of a nationwide armed workers' organisation was proposed, and the party began to acquiesce, mainly because a central organisation seemed the only way of controlling the swelling movement. The decision was made before the movement got off the ground outside the biggest centres: by 20 October, when the decision was published as a statement of the trade union organisation, only Helsinki, Tampere, and Turku had substantial security guards.[38]

According to the rules, the worker security guards were to be disciplined, and the traditional working-class movement was to have complete control over them. Actually, the party's authority in the movement was on the decline. Sometimes, notably in the largest population centres, the guards were started by militias or other groups with only loose connections to the party. But this decline was by no means a *loss* of authority. Despite radicalisation and rapid expansion of other branches of the movement, the party was not overwhelmed. Even though its authority was questioned, it was able to maintain a central position. Defence of the rights won after the February revolution remained the main task of the national Worker Security Guard, the core, probably even the majority, of which consisted locally, the sudden expansion notwithstanding, of established members of the party and trade union branches.[39] The party's dominant role in the working-class movement and its central role in the nation's political life could not be eliminated overnight.

The worsening food shortage played a central role in radicalising the masses. In late September the party leaders stated that the masses were getting restless

---

[38] Salkola 1979, pp. 352–3; Salkola 1985, 1:320, 335–45, 365–6, 373, 484–8, 2:31; Upton 1980, pp. 114–18. By 20 October, worker security guards or militias existed in 37 of the 509 communes (Salkola 1985, 1:122).

[39] Salkola 1985, 1: 350–2, 375, 2: 41, 68–76, 82–93, 142; Klemettilä 1976, pp. 40–1, 130, 141, 162–6, 177–8, 189, 196–7.

about the food situation, and a few days before the foundation of the national security guard organisation, party and trade union leaders unanimously agreed that the workers could not be held back if the government did not take action on food. Thus the call of 20 October for the workers to join the security guards was accompanied by an ultimatum concerning food.[40]

Toward autumn, grain imports from Russia declined even from the low level of the preceding months, but conditions did not yet appear critical to the authorities. (For example, rations of grain products were increased in August.)[41] At the same time, however, the whole system of rationing began to break down. After the *valtalaki* had been rejected and parliament was dissolved, mass meetings and demonstrations against the food supply policy became common. Social Democratic members began to resign from the local food committees, which were accused of rationing food in a perfunctory manner and raising prices without reason. In early August the first food riots occurred in Turku and Helsinki. Yet it was not a food shortage, and especially not a shortage of grain, that caused the disorders. In Turku no butter had been distributed for a week, and the rioters believed it had been hidden in the hope that the price would rise. In the same month several mass meetings demanded a reduction in controlled prices and an end to speculation and urged that 'representatives elected by the consumers' find and distribute food. As a consequence, the organisation in charge of butter distribution ceased operating, and the central committee on food, which was subordinate to the ministry for food, resigned.[42] On this note the Social Democrats also began their withdrawal from the government as the socialist minister for food resigned – one week before the party decided to leave the government altogether.

It was more difficult to take an inventory of the harvest in the autumn than in the spring; because the shortage was expected to worsen, causing prices to rise, considerably more grain was hoarded. Statistics based on the inventory amount to only about 60 percent of the grain shown by the official statistics collected with more reliable methods.[43] In towns, serious fears about scarcity began to arise. The rural food committees delivered grain only reluctantly, and the central organisation was unable to rectify the situation. Moreover, the new Activist minister for food felt that his foremost task was to make preparations for 'the future military operations',[44] and the steps he took to augment the food

---

40   Upton 1980, pp. 117, 131–2.
41   Rantatupa 1979, p. 94.
42   Rantatupa 1979, pp. 88–90, 92.
43   Rantatupa 1979, pp. 96–7, 99.
44   Rantatupa 1979, p. 98.

stocks in the towns only increased disorder. Prices continued to rise, and farmers delayed their sales in the hope that prices would rise even more.[45]

But although the situation was alarming, it was far from catastrophic. Despite all the problems, the food committees were able to administer the distribution of grain even in the towns,[46] and the shortage was by no means out of control. Rather than being ruthlessly present, scarcity was stealthily lurking around the corner.

The last step preceding the beginning of the revolutionary situation was taken on 1 November, when the Social Democrats issued a programme called 'We Demand'. It stated that the dissolution of parliament had resulted from a conspiracy between the Finnish bourgeoisie and Russian reactionaries and that the old parliament was still the only legal one. The central demands included the election of a constituent assembly, immediate action on food and employment, implementation of the reforms passed by the previous parliament, and the dissolution of the bourgeois civil guards. The party was fully aware of the strong pressure from below; thus, the programme was issued above all in order to relieve this pressure and find an escape from the situation – as a last chance for the bourgeoisie to avert a revolution.[47] It did not constitute a challenge to the basic structure of capitalist society but rather appears to have been a genuine attempt to settle the political crisis,[48] motivated by the party's desire to stave off the revolution. As a leader pessimistically prophesied a few days before the program was issued: 'We cannot avoid the revolution for very long ... Faith in the value of peaceful activity is lost and the working class is beginning to trust only in its own strength ... If we are mistaken about the rapid approach of revolution, I would be delighted'.[49]

But, understandably enough, the bourgeois groups had no intention of giving in to the central demands. Notably, they were not ready to dissolve the civil guards, to admit the illegality of the new parliament, or to have a constituent assembly elected.

In a word, multiple sovereignty had begun to emerge. In one polity the active role was played by the bourgeoisie and the peasant landowners, who had regained control of a state that still suffered from the lack of an armed force. The other polity was composed of the various parts of the working-class movement. It had originated in the period when the Social Democrats had particip-

---

45 Rantatupa 1979, pp. 98–100, 106.
46 Rantatupa 1979, p. 105.
47 Upton 1980, pp. 134–5.
48 Upton 1980, p. 135; Salkola 1985, 2: 144–5.
49 This leader was Kullervo Manner; cited in Upton 1980, p. 133.

ated in the government owing to the necessity of establishing a (temporary) force for maintaining order. This polity began to take shape rapidly after the socialists were debarred from political power and after the bourgeois organisations promoting law and order had proliferated. It had three constituent elements: the party, the trade unions, and the Worker Security Guard. The role of the party and the trade unions was clear: to consistently hamper the guards from advancing exclusive alternative claims to control over the government. Although they succeeded in this effort for several months, in early November their position became critical.

Developments in Russia played a part in the Finnish situation in three main respects. First, the Social Democrats' penetration into the polity had been facilitated by the state's lack of a monopoly on physical force. Second, the bourgeois groups had forced the socialists out of the polity with the help of the Provisional Government. And third, Russian troops were in the country. Their number rose to about 100,000 by August 1917 and then began to decline rapidly. The Activists believed that considerable German support was needed to rid Finland of these troops and achieve independence, and they were actually ready to reduce the country to the status of a German protectorate.[50] The majority of the bourgeoisie, however, saw the Russian soldiers as only another element contributing to the mounting disorder. In the autumn of 1917 there were only a few effective military units; often the soldiers confiscated food or caused other disruptions. Especially irksome was the socialists' alleged fraternisation with them – a claim that carried some truth: Russian soldiers often took part in the workers' mass meetings and demonstrations, and they even raided a bourgeois security force stronghold on behalf of the Social Democrats. Some worker guards or militias succeeded in obtaining a few Russian rifles. Party representatives made similar attempts but met with no success.[51] Conditions were so chaotic, however, that the Russians also sold arms to bourgeois purchasers and were often not trusted by the working-class movement. Frequently, fear of Russian soldiers, the desire to prevent the soldiers' possible interference in the maintenance of order, and the socialists' wish to promote the national cause were among the main reasons why the worker militias were set up. In fact, this last, national, motive was one reason why more militias emerged in localities where there were Russian troops than in those where there were none.[52]

---

50 Upton 1980, p. 113.
51 Kirby 1971, pp. 212–14; Salkola 1985, 1: 363–4, 2: 61–7, 147–50, 161–3; Upton 1980, 47–8, 60–1, 108–9, 118, 131–2; Ketola 1981, pp. 85–9, 92–103.
52 Tanskanen 1978, pp. 105–9; Upton 1980, pp. 111, 211; Salkola 1985, 1: 225–32, 238–40, 270–84, 384. In this light it is no wonder that in a number of communes the worker guards and

On the whole, though, direct intervention in Finnish affairs by the Russians remained very limited – which is not to say that their presence was not strongly felt, notably by the bourgeois groups. Another important factor was the Social Democrats' connections with the Bolsheviks, who, alone among the Russian political groupings, supported the socialists' demand for Finnish independence. Thanks to this attitude, the Bolsheviks were, paradoxically, able to press the 'social-patriotic' Finnish party to join the radical Zimmerwald International in the summer of 1917. But otherwise they had little effect on the Finnish worker movement.[53] Among the Russian troops in Finland the Bolsheviks gained a majority in late September.

3 The Revolutionary Situation

The general strike in November sparked off the revolutionary situation. Although it was not until one and a half months later that hostilities broke out, the revolutionary situation was imminent from the general strike on as the government became the object of effective, competing, mutually exclusive claims by two distinct polities. True, the effectiveness of the contenders' claims might be questioned before late January, but placing the starting point in November focuses attention on an important feature of the Finnish revolution: no one date or single event marks its beginning. The country drifted into revolution, and from early November it became virtually impossible to avert.

The new Parliament convened at the beginning of November. The party and trade union leaderships had decided to urge acceptance of the 'We Demand' programme, a programme for recapturing the party's hold on the government. The Bolshevik revolution had just taken place in Petrograd, and there was no fear that the Russians would intervene to suppress the separatist claims of the *valtalaki*, or any other analogous demands. Pressure from below was still increasing, and the only real alternative envisioned by party and trade union leaders was that 'the organized workers would take power into their own hands'.[54] But at the same time there was 'no clear idea of what to do with the power'.[55]

---

the bourgeois guards were seen as parallel organisations and were even able to cooperate well into the autumn (Salkola 1985, 1: 291–6).
53 Ketola 1981, pp. 283–91, 292, 300 (quotation); Upton 1980, pp. 85–6, 126–7, and *passim*.
54 Cited in Upton 1980, pp. 140–1. See also Wiik 1978, pp. 23, 25–31.
55 Written in the diary of one of the Social Democratic leaders, 10 November 1917 (Wiik 1978, p. 29).

Because the bourgeois parties stood firm against the socialists' demands, the party leadership was forced to consent to a general strike. The strike call, containing largely the same points as the 'We Demand' programme, was published on 14 November. Now the party leadership had to face the problem of the seizure of power. Many trade union leaders had urged such a course in the meeting that preceded the strike, and the militant worker guards in Helsinki and other centres backed their proposal.[56] The party, which was still in command of the movement despite all the opposition, was now forced to make a decision.

Insofar as the control of everyday activities was concerned, the strike was enormously successful. Revolutionary councils were set up in most areas, particularly in population centres, to oversee the orderly execution of the strike, to maintain calm, and to control the local worker guards. The bourgeoisie was unprepared, disorganised, and poorly armed, and as a result the guards usually gained control. In some cases the Russians were willing to lend – but only lend – rifles to the guards, but on the whole the Russians, the only real armed force in the country, were reluctant to get involved, and their basic attitude toward the worker guards was one of 'benevolent neutrality'. The strike was also effective in that the local government bill was finally passed and the eight-hour workday established by Parliament.[57]

Soon the Social Democratic party took a clear stand: it would do all it could to prevent the strike from turning into a full-scale seizure of power. There is no reason to marvel at this attitude, whether in light of the situation at hand or of the party's earlier history. The Bolsheviks had taken power only one week before the general strike, and for the Finns the events in Petrograd were mainly a nearby struggle, the outcome of which remained unknown.[58] At that moment no one could be sure about the future: 'During the days which preceded the October insurrection, nobody imagined, and certainly not the Bolsheviks, that Lenin's party would seize the power for itself all alone and forever'.[59] One week later the situation had not greatly changed. The Bolshevik revolution had in no way provoked the general strike in Finland, and the two events were not connected, as they were in the Baltic Provinces. Of the World War I revolutionary situations not directly connected with the October revolution, only the Finnish one began at virtually the same time that the Bolsheviks seized power. The Bolshevik takeover did not really figure in the Finnish socialists' calculations, as

---

56 Salkola 1985, 2: 145–56, 173–6.
57 Upton 1980, pp. 150–1, 152–3 (quotation); Salkola 1985, 2: 158, 165–76.
58 Upton 1980, p. 147; Hodgson 1974a, p. 67; Salkola 1985, 2: 135, 148.
59 Ferro 1967, p. 24.

it was to do a little later in Hungary and Germany, where the revolutionary leaders had witnessed at least the temporary stabilisation of Soviet power. There, only the final collapse in war created the revolutionary situation; in Finland, it was the disappearance of dependence on Russia in the spring, summer, and autumn of 1917 that was critical.

The Finnish Social Democrats could not envision a socialist revolution 'in tiny, underdeveloped Finland in isolation'.[60] If power were seized it would be held only until a constituent assembly could be elected, which would then enact laws in a country that would remain capitalist but in which the rights the workers had gained in 1917 were guaranteed. While an alternative polity was taking shape, a total seizure of power was not feasible: taking care of the administration and of other basic tasks of the state seemed to be beyond the party's capacity. Even the militant worker guards did not envision a social revolution.[61] As one Social Democratic leader put it in his diary during the strike: 'The revolution is preposterous, we cannot force the civil servants to obey when we cannot even force them to go on strike ... As a consequence of our lack of intellectuals, we shall not be able to master the machinery of government'.[62]

This was so because the alternative polity did not result from the fragmentation of the existing polity but from its penetration by the working-class movement at a moment of weakness. The party leaders were compelled to participate in the general strike, but they had no real vision of what should be done with the power they obtained. Thus in a sense, although the objective causes of revolution existed, the subjective causes – the instruments of revolution – were lacking. Favourable as the situation was, no revolution occurred, for want of an organised revolutionary movement armed with a doctrine, long-term objectives, and a clear political strategy – to paraphrase Lucien Bianco's analysis of the Chinese revolution. The contrast is at least as striking if the Finnish Social Democrats are compared with the Bolsheviks.[63] The entire earlier history of the Finnish movement spoke against organised revolutionary action: it could not be created in a few months.

---

60 Cited in Upton 1980, p. 162. Cf. Kirby 1971, pp. 305–6; and Salkola 1985, 1: 49.
61 Upton 1980, pp. 144, 147–8; Salkola 1985, 1: 56, 2: 174–6, 179–80.
62 This leader was K.H. Wiik; cited in Upton 1980, 156. See also Lindman 1978, pp. xxi–xxii.
63 Bianco 1971, p. 203. The difference between the Bolsheviks and the Finnish Social Democrats is graphically reflected in the wide gap between Lenin's *State and Revolution*, written in the early autumn of 1917 (when Lenin was, incidentally, hiding in Helsinki), and O.W. Kuusinen's views in 1917–18, when he was the party's theoretician and apparently the most powerful leader of the Finnish revolution (see Hodgson 1974b, chap. 3). The most eloquent testimony of irresolution among the Social Democratic leaders before the outbreak of the revolution is the detailed diary kept by K.H. Wiik (1978).

Within a couple of days, confronted with disorder and uncertainty about the final goal, the party and trade union leaders tried to stop the strike. Although in most regions the strike was peaceful, the party leaders' fears were justified in a number of cases: sixteen murders were committed during the strike, notably in Helsinki and its surroundings. Fourteen members or supporters of the bourgeois guards and three members of the worker guards died in encounters. Also, as the strike went on, demands for a full-scale seizure of power became increasingly forceful: 'We cannot have two governments', insisted the Tampere worker guard.[64] Of great importance, the strike emphasised for the first time the existence of a few revolutionary Red Guards in Helsinki and elsewhere, as distinct from the party-dominated worker security guards. The division had begun to evolve in September, but only now did the militant – largely anarchic – line openly challenge the authority of the party.[65]

Although the bourgeois groups made no concessions, the strike was called off on the fifth day. The mobilised masses accepted the decision, but with great resentment and bitterness.[66] The general strike showed that an alternative polity really existed, but it also showed this polity's limits.

The strike closed the ranks of the bourgeoisie more effectively than anything else: the government began to work firmly and resolutely, and civil society considerably increased its material and other support for the maintenance of order; moreover, the two efforts were united. Only a week after the end of the strike a coalition government of all bourgeois parties was formed, with the Activists well represented. The most important tasks were identified as 'the securing of Finland's political independence' and the establishment of a strong force for the maintenance of order.

The issue of independence was brought to the fore by the October revolution, which caused utter dismay among the Finnish non-socialist politicians. By mid-November, when parliament assumed the exercise of sovereign powers in the country, independence was supported also by all bourgeois parties, for which, however, this question was inseparable from the problem of internal order. The bourgeois leaders wanted to exploit Germany's and the Entente's anti-Bolshevik feelings in order to win independence. For them, Germany's

---

64 Salkola 1985, 2: 186–8; Upton 1980, p. 155 (quotation).
65 Salkola 1985, 2: 178–81. To be sure, the terminological distinction between the worker security guard and the Red Guard, although corresponding to an increasingly discernible division, was not systematically made in the autumn of 1917. Officially, after 1905–7 the term *Red Guard* was first used only when the Helsinki worker security guard declared its independence from the party in early January 1918 (Salkola 1985, 2: 346–54).
66 Kirby 1971, p. 308.

attitude was crucial. In early January 1918 the Germans were secretly asked to provide arms and to send the Finnish *Jägers* home. The bourgeois leaders wished to mobilise Germany in order to compel the Bolsheviks to recognise Finnish independence and withdraw the Russian troops from Finland. Only then would they be free to restore internal order.[67]

Independence was proclaimed on 6 December and recognised by the Bolshevik government, at the Finns' request, three weeks later. It was decided to form the force for maintaining order from the civil guards, which had grown considerably after the general strike and were now increasingly supported by businessmen and local authorities. (In this respect it was helpful that the Activist leadership had close links with the country's economic elite.)[68] Training was provided by former domestic army officers and by *Jäger*s who returned home before the main body of troops. Their impact has been considered incalculably important.[69] By the end of January they were able to train a cadre having military skills their opponents lacked.

On 9 January 1918 the government, despite fierce opposition by the Social Democrats, sought, and a few days later received, authorisation from parliament for the creation of a strong security force. Civil society again provided abundant support, especially in the form of rapid financial aid.[70] The last step was taken on 25 January when the civil guards were officially declared the troops of the government. On the morning of 28 January their supreme commander, a former general of the Imperial Russian Army, C.G.E. Mannerheim, began to disarm Russian garrisons in Ostrobothnia. Thus began the revolutionary war on the White side.

By this action the state apparatus, put on the defensive in a revolutionary situation, co-opted one of the two class-based organisations that had taken shape in civil society during the summer and autumn. On the one hand, it was perfectly clear that in the long run the country could not 'have two governments', and after the general strike the bourgeoisie was fully prepared to restore its monopoly on physical force by invoking the civil guards, that is, to exercise a kind of coup d'état. On the other hand, it was just as clear that the working-class movement would not voluntarily comply and dissolve the alternative polity. During December and January the socialist leaders repeatedly spoke about bourgeois aggression and the intended seizure of power by government.

---

67   Upton 1980, pp. 140, 170, 183; Hodgson 1967, p. 33; Fol 1977, pp. 236–7.
68   Upton 1980, pp. 170, 210; Fol 1977, pp. 216, 218, 220–1, 327–30, 885, 908–9; Salkola 1985, 2: 271.
69   Upton 1980, pp. 210–11.
70   Fol 1977, pp. 353, 355; Upton 1980, p. 237; Mannerheim 1953, pp. 135–6.

The rules of the worker guards, confirmed in late December, stated that their purpose was the defence of the working class from armed attack, a formulation imposed by the party. In practice, however, a more militant view stressing the guards' active role in opposing the bourgeoisie rapidly gained ground.[71] Raiding parties searched for food and arms or exerted pressure on local bourgeois authorities. More important, revolutionary tendencies were gaining ground in the worker guards, and in mid-January they came to predominate when the government received authorisation to create a strong security force.[72] Even the party leadership could not ignore the government's intention to put down the worker security guards as soon as it felt strong enough. After encounters with the bourgeois guards in several localities, and after the civil guards gained official status as governmental troops, it was decided, with great reluctance, to launch the revolution on 27 January. Not surprisingly, it was described as having 'a defensive character'.[73] Revolutionary spirits ran generally low among the party leaders, but despite misgivings and opposition in previous months, few felt that they could distance themselves from the attempt.[74]

But the Red Guards – as all guards were now called[75] – were far from ready to wage war. On the contrary, they were very much in disarray. The central organisation was inchoate, and the local branches often had not the slightest idea of the most elementary rules of military conduct. Unlike the Whites, the Red Guards had no military cadre. The first commander in chief was an ex-lieutenant from the Imperial Army, the only former Finnish officer among the Red troops, who, however, was demoted at the beginning of the hostilities. Initially the Red Guards had no military plans. Also, arms were in short supply – to a considerable degree they were obtained only after the war had broken out, and then thanks to Russian deliveries.[76] Otherwise the Russians' contribution was minimal: they confined themselves mainly to giving advice and exhortation. For them, getting their own disorganised troops home was a demanding enough task. Their primary concern lay in Petrograd and the situation there.[77]

The revolution began right in the core of Finland. It was declared at the Helsinki headquarters of the Social Democratic party, and in a couple of weeks the southern core regions of the country were established as the revolutionary

---

71 Lappalainen 1981, 1: 18–21; Upton 1980, pp. 219–22.
72 Lappalainen 1981, 1: 20; Salkola 1979, p. 361.
73 Upton 1980, p. 265. See also Salomaa 1983, p. 183; Salkola 1985, 1: 57–9, 2: 372–381.
74 Salkola 1985, 2: 374, 377; Rinta-Tassi 1972, pp. 66–72. Cf. Wiik 1978, pp. 118–37.
75 Salkola 1985, 2: 388–9.
76 Lappalainen 1981, 1: 29–48, 52–8, 155, 205–28; Upton 1980, p. 267.
77 Upton 1980, pp. 187–9.

stronghold (see Map 2, p. 55). The Whites' stronghold was Ostrobothnia, particularly southern Ostrobothnia, the largest city of which, Vaasa (Vasa), became 'the capital of the White Finland'.

At first the two armies had roughly the same number of men, although later the Red Guards had a slight edge. In the beginning the revolutionaries had 12,000–15,000 troops, by the end of February 40,000, and in late March 76,500. Frontline troops, however, numbered far fewer: 35,000 in mid-March, for example, but even these could not be used effectively because of poor organisation and a shortage of weapons. Although arms were obtained by mid-February, the command's poor performance was not rectified, and it became the most fateful problem for the revolutionary army.[78]

Under these conditions, the help that some Russian officers offered the 'amateur Red army' had only a modest impact.[79] Russian soldiers played a minor role in the battles: at its highest their number at the front was only about 2,000 troops, just a few percent of the total Red Guard strength; after early March the number declined to less than 1,500. In addition, the Russians continued to send their troops home throughout the war: after one month of armed conflict, which at first was fairly mild, only 6,000 Russian troops were still in the country. Russian arms deliveries – received both from Petrograd and from the troops stationed in Finland – were, however, critical.[80]

One indication of the revolution's defensive character is the passivity of the military operations. After Helsinki and southern Finland were in their control, the socialist leaders considered the revolution more or less over: they thought the situation was similar to the one in November at the time of the general strike. The socialists, unlike the Whites, therefore devoted considerable attention to consolidating the administration at the expense of military development. To be sure, to a certain extent this task was necessary. Practically the entire central administration had deserted, and the Social Democrats had to work hard to keep it running[81] – another indication that the revolutionary polity did not result from the fragmentation of the old polity but that power was being seized by another polity whose members had been only marginally involved in the old one.[82]

Also, the goals of the revolution are expressive of its character: they were not very ambitious. Governmental organs were established largely following

---

78 Lappalainen 1981, 1: 173–6, 205–28.
79 Tanskanen 1978, p. 207 (quotation); Lappalainen 1981, 1: 150–3.
80 Lappalainen 1981, 1: 167–8, 2: 259; Tanskanen 1978, pp. 39–42, 206; Hodgson 1967, pp. 74–80.
81 Rinta-Tassi 1972, pp. 90–3; Piilonen 1982, pp. 114–19.
82 Cf. Rinta-Tassi 1972, pp. 75–86, 160–71.

the organisational principles of the earlier government and the parliament.[83] Civilian and military functions were separated, and after the revolution Finland was to become a democratic, parliamentary republic with a controlled capitalist economy. In line with these plans (and because of the revolutionaries' need to secure allies), tenant farmers were enfranchised and became independent smallholders. The constitution – worked out mainly by O.W. Kuusinen and proposed by the revolutionary government (called the People's Deputation) – envisaged a political system modelled on the Swiss one.[84] In the short run, existing practices were maintained. Despite the war, legal principles were usually respected, even to the extent that the 'repression of the internal enemy by the Red regime was suicidally lenient'.[85] Each local takeover was to be decided case by case and was always considered a temporary necessity made inevitable by the war. The worker movement captured full power in only three of every five communes in the region dominated by revolutionary forces. In a number of communes local elections were held in which bourgeois candidates ran, and often the bourgeois chairman of the communal board kept his post.[86] Consolidation was attempted without the usual instruments of revolutionary dictatorship, such as a powerful police force or monopoly over the diffusion of ideas.[87] All in all, life went on fairly normally for most of the bourgeois citizens.[88]

Of course, this does not necessarily imply that only limited changes would have followed if the revolution had really been successful. Revolutions have often concluded with results not intended or foreseen by their principal makers, and radical designs for thorough change have often been as much the products as the precursors of revolutionary upheaval.[89] This line only shows that in the winter of 1918 the revolutionary polity followed the course that the Social Democratic party had adopted in the previous decade.

Undoubtedly, the maintenance of legality was motivated in part by the hope to win allies outside the working class. This feature, too, is distinctive of the Finnish situation. The building of a new socialist economic and political order

---

83 Salomaa 1983, pp. 184, 188.
84 Rinta-Tassi 1972, pp. 58–66; Martin 1970, 389–94, 466–77; Lappalainen 1981, 1: 122–7; Soikkanen 1975, pp. 273–75, 279–81; Salomaa 1983, pp. 188–92; Upton 1980, pp. 303–4; Hodgson 1974b, p. 51.
85 Upton 1980, p. 381. Cf. Fol 1977, pp. 403–4; and Piilonen 1982, pp. 119–24, 207–8.
86 Piilonen 1982, pp. 44–5, 82–4, 124–8, 135–8, 160, 167–73.
87 See Barrington Moore's discussion of this problem (1978, pp. 291–9); and Salomaa 1983, pp. 185–8, 194–6.
88 Upton 1980, p. 382.
89 Aya 1979, pp. 46–7.

was not envisioned; rather, the leaders of the revolution clung to the views they had adopted in previous years and advocated during the general strike. The Finnish revolution was really a defensive revolution that strove more to secure the advantages gained in 1917 than to create a fundamentally new society.

The governmental troops were also poorly prepared for war. At the end of January the new security forces were not yet ready for action, and the government had tried to postpone armed confrontation for as long as possible. In the early phases of the war, the White army was roughly as strong as the Red, with about 12,000 to 15,000 men.[90] But because society had not been seriously damaged during the earlier revolutionary process, White Finland remained superior in resources and organisation. Most important, the upper echelons of the White army consisted of professional soldiers – former Imperial Army officers, Swedish officers who had volunteered, and, especially, the 1,200 *Jägers* who had returned home in late February. Weapons were acquired first from disarmed local Russian troops, but above all from Germany. In late February general conscription was enforced, and at the beginning of May White troops numbered about 70,000.[91]

Germany contributed decisively to the Whites' warfare. Not only did it deliver arms and send home the *Jägers* who had been trained in Germany, but it also intervened in the war. In February the Activists presented a request for intervention and then made the politicians approve an agreement reducing Finland to the status of a German vassal.[92] At the beginning of April, German troops landed on the southern coast and marched into Helsinki; at nearly the same time, the Finnish Whites won their first decisive victory by taking Tampere. In a couple of weeks the revolutionary troops collapsed, and by early May the entire country was in White and German hands.

4   The Aftermath

During the war neither the Reds nor the Whites were able to prevent a number of terrorist acts. Despite repeated and unequivocal condemnation of terrorism by the People's Deputation, about a thousand White sympathisers had been killed outside the battles by mid-April; with the collapse of discipline in the last two weeks of the war and early May, 600 to 650 more murders were commit-

---

90   Upton 1980, pp. 242, 263; Lappalainen 1981, 1: 176.
91   Upton 1980, pp. 325–30, 335–6, 342–3; Fol 1977, pp. 388–90, 438, 444, 554; Lappalainen 1981, 1: 176 (70,000 is the maximum figure).
92   Upton 1980, pp. 336–42; Fol 1977, pp. 448, 452–3, 459.

ted.[93] Wartime terror perpetrated by the Whites was somewhat more regular and more extensive, the number of killings rising to at least 1,200–1,300 by mid-April,[94] when the Reds were in chaotic retreat. Then, at and following the end of the war, a large-scale reign of White terror broke out. During the first week after the war the Whites executed on average 200 people a day, and the total number of Reds executed in the last weeks of the war and immediately thereafter rose to about 5,600. In addition, roughly 12,500 persons died in prison camps, in which the victors incarcerated about 82,000 people.[95] In a country of 3.1 million people, the executions and camp deaths were so extensive that they exceeded, both relatively and absolutely, the contemporaneous ones in Hungary.[96]

In the short run, the attempt at revolution was followed by a distinct counterrevolution. The Social Democratic party was prevented from participating in the political system, and the Communist party of Finland, founded by emigrants in Moscow, was declared illegal. During the war the White supreme commander, General Mannerheim, had assumed nearly dictatorial powers because the bourgeois political leadership, partly in Vaasa and partly hiding in Helsinki, had been unable to act jointly. For example, the prime minister, Svinhufvud, managed to escape from Helsinki and arrive in Vaasa only in March. But the arrival of the German troops and the end of the war changed the balance of power in favour of Svinhufvud, who worked to create a monarchy dependent on Germany. In autumn 1918, a German-born prince was preliminarily elected king. After Germany's defeat, however, the Entente-oriented Mannerheim became head of state in Svinhufvud's place. Democratic general elections – one of the Entente's conditions for the recognition of Finnish independence[97] – were held in 1919, with reasonable Social Democratic success and great advances by the Agrarian Union (see Table 11, p. 206). In the same year, a republican constitution was confirmed, and a Liberal was elected president, supported by the Social Democrats.

Just as the international power constellation had decisively contributed to the revolutionary situation, so too did it influence the post-war political system in Finland. When the revolution was crushed, the counterrevolutionary forces (which, it is true, had no deep roots in the social structure) were the first to

---

93 Paavolainen 1966–7, 1: 94–5, 271–313. Because of Paavolainen's rough periodisation, the figures are only approximations. Cf. Rinta-Tassi 1972, pp. 211–14; Piilonen 1982, pp. 207–8; Upton 1980, pp. 376–82.
94 Paavolainen 1966–7, 2: 192–3; Upton 1980, pp. 314–18; Fol 1977, pp. 428–31, 472–4.
95 Paavolainen 1966–7, 2: 192–3; Paavolainen 1971, p. 332. The total number of victims of the White terror rose to 8,380.
96 See Barta et al. 1971, pp. 454–7.
97 Fol 1977, pp. 687–8, 692, 795–6, 817.

gain the upper hand. But then, thanks to the Entente victory, the protagonists of the republican constitution and political democracy moved to the fore, and soon a part of the elite was forced to surrender the counterrevolutionary gains. Both Svinhufvud and Mannerheim, the two leading figures in putting down the revolution, were compelled to step aside, leaving a significant potential for discontent within the dominant groups. In 1919 Mannerheim and an influential rightist group had a plan not only for an attack against Petrograd but even for a coup d'état in Finland. The opponents of the new political system were mainly former Activists who had key positions in the national civil guard organisation, established after the war, and, to a lesser extent, in the army and the state police.[98]

5 The Social and Regional Basis for the Revolution

In the parliamentary elections of 1916, the Social Democratic party had won 103 seats out of 200 and 47 percent of the total vote, being backed mainly by industrial workers, agrarian workers, and crofters. Yet what effectiveness did this coalition of interests have in the revolution itself? Both weak and strong organisation may produce electoral success, but presumably only strong organisation can provide a basis for effective action in a revolutionary situation.

The question is, were all voter groups mobilised in the revolution? The answer is clear: the industrial working class and many agrarian workers backed the revolution, but the crofters were rather passive; and typically, the intellectuals provided no support.

A crucial indicator of revolutionary mobilisation is the social composition of the Red troops: here, the industrial and agrarian proletariat dominated.[99] These two groups' grievances were fused to a large extent after the 1905 revolution, as the spread of the worker associations indicated. There were also important institutional and cultural linkages between town and country (see Chapter 6). In the countryside, the worker associations presumably consisted much more of agrarian workers than of crofters, not only absolutely but also relatively. The

---

98 Ahti 1982, pp. 175–80; Ahti 1984a, p. 240.
99 Rasila 1968, pp. 32–3; Lappalainen 1981, 1: 168–73; Soikkanen 1975, p. 299. Various groups of rural workers made up 21 percent of the revolutionary dead, but the proportion of 'workers' without more specific description was 48 percent, most of whom lived in the countryside and were largely sons of crofters and other workers closely involved with agrarian life. The proportion of industrial workers, craftsmen, and artisans among the dead was 12 percent (Rasila 1968, pp. 34–48).

worker security guards in 1917 and the Red Guards during the war appear to have recruited their troops notably from among the members of the worker associations and other Social Democratic organisations.[100] And, as had been the case when the worker associations were set up, the towns and other industrial centres took the lead, with the countryside soon following.[101] The character of the revolutionary sequence, moreover, probably helped to maintain links between various worker groups. Because the mass mobilisation of late 1917 and the rise and culmination of the revolutionary situation were largely defensive, there was little room for serious cleavages among the core supporters, the industrial and agrarian workers. It may be hypothesised that an active *seizure* of power might have divided various elements of the working-class movement but that a defensive revolution instead caused them to close their ranks.[102] This situation may be clearly seen in the attitude of the leadership. Despite serious disagreements before the war, virtually every top leader took part in the revolution once it broke out; some stepped aside, but nobody worked against it.[103] Also, local government was built using experienced party cadres.[104]

The crofters, however, remained 'passive', not even reacting to their enfranchisement at the beginning of the war. Their attitude – that is, strong electoral support for the Social Democrats on the one hand and relatively weak political organisation and limited mobilisation during the revolution on the other – may be explained by viewing the crofters as a pre-capitalist group suffering from the intrusions of capitalism.

Eric Wolf has observed that the middle peasants have played a central role in most important revolutionary wars of the twentieth century, as the stratum 'most instrumental in dynamiting the peasant social order'.[105] Paradoxically, at first sight, the Finnish crofters had many characteristics of the middle peasants, as Wolf defines them. For him, middle peasants are those who have secure access to land of their own and who cultivate it with family labour, as well as many of those whose holdings lie within the power domain of a superior. These cultivators are able to protest because they possess the 'minimum tactical freedom required to challenge their overlord'.[106] But even somewhat poorer groups may be in a similar position: 'The same ... holds for a peasantry, poor or "middle",

---

100   Klemettilä 1976, pp. 40–1, 130, 141, 162–6, 177–8, 189, 196–7; Lappalainen 1981, 1: 157–64; Soikkanen 1975, pp. 299–300; Salkola 1985, vol. 1, chaps. 3–5 *passim*.
101   Salkola 1985, 1: 121–2; Lappalainen 1967, p. 86. Cf. Klemettilä 1976, p. 241.
102   Cf. Rinta-Tassi 1972, pp. 72–4; and Salkola 1985, 1: 173–4.
103   Rinta-Tassi 1972, pp. 66–72; Soikkanen 1975, pp. 270–2.
104   Piilonen 1982, pp. 322–5.
105   Wolf 1969, p. 292.
106   Wolf 1969, p. 291.

whose settlements are only under marginal control from the outside. Here landholdings may be insufficient for the support of the peasant household; but subsidiary activities such as casual labor, smuggling, livestock raising – not under the direct constraint of an external power domain – supplement land in sufficient quantity to grant the peasantry some latitude of movement'.[107] Peasants of this kind have more resources than the landless, but their interests do not tie them to the prevailing economic and political system, as is the case with the wealthier peasants. At the same time, the economic position of these middle peasants is based on pre-capitalist relations of production, and their social relations remain encased within the traditional design. They therefore tend to be quite vulnerable to the economic changes wrought by commercialisation. Their 'balance is continuously threatened by population growth; by the encroachment of rival landlords; by the loss of rights to grazing, forest, and water; by falling prices and unfavorable conditions of market; by interest payments and foreclosures'.[108]

During the twentieth century middle peasants in Third World countries particularly have been hurt by capitalist development and have been able to react collectively. By protesting, they have tried to regain their lost rights. 'Thus it is the very attempt of the middle ... peasant to remain traditional which makes him revolutionary'.[109] This was true in revolutionary Russia as well: the Bolsheviks were supported not only by the industrial proletariat but also by the peasantry, all except the upper strata. The peasants fought against the restoration of the landowners' repression, not for a socialist society.[110]

Wolf's description throws light on the leasehold question in Finland. The Finnish crofters were poor or 'middle' peasants whose holdings were subject to the power of a superior. Significantly, the first indication that agrarian conflicts were worsening lay in the reaction of the crofters (not the agrarian workers) from the 1880s onward. Leasehold was made an issue by a group whose position was based on pre-capitalist relations of production, a group especially vulnerable to the economic changes brought about by commercialisation. At the same time, the crofters had more resources and capacity for collective action than the landless population.

Unlike the countries in Wolf's analysis, however, Finland was not in a colonial position, nor was it as dependent on 'North Atlantic' capitalism.[111] Finland

---

107　Ibid.
108　Wolf 1969, p. 292.
109　Ibid.
110　Wolf 1969, pp. 88–99; Ferro 1967–76, 2: 211–29.
111　Wolf 1969, p. 276.

was developing into a capitalist country; the peasants were becoming farmers, that is, commercial producers. The crofters' demands did not stand in real contradiction to this development. By the early years of the twentieth century, the crofters were becoming progressively bound to the market as small producers, all the limitations notwithstanding.[112]

The crofters wanted to strengthen their access to the land – to improve the conditions of leasehold or to become landowners. In the countryside, socialism was often understood to involve the redistribution of land.[113] This objective was not inconceivable for the bourgeoisie in the 1910s, a significant part of which supported, at least in principle, the conversion of the crofts into the property of the leaseholders. The Social Democrats also had to concede to the crofters' demands. The party strove to strengthen the crofters' position and, at one moment in the 1910s, proposed that the crofters should in practice become landowners. The crofters' political strength can be seen in the fact that up to 1918 their position was safeguarded by various measures. Most important, their leases were prolonged for seven years from 1909, and extended again in 1915 until the legislation defining the crofters' position had been prepared and approved. By January 1918 a law had been prepared that would have allowed the crofters to become the owners of the land they cultivated.[114]

This perspective explains both the importance of the leasehold question at the turn of the century and the crofters' passivity during the revolution, or, put another way, both the electoral support the crofters gave the Social Democrats and the minor role they played in the war of 1918. Their problems never became so serious that they would have become 'instrumental in dynamiting the peasant social order'. If the working-class movement had actively attempted to seize power, the crofters might well have dissociated themselves still more from the revolution.

But it is not only the crofters' passivity that is important. In a larger perspective their reaction meant that the 'middle' and 'poor' peasants did not join forces in Finland: the two groups proved unable to engage in concerted collective action in the revolutionary situation. The Finnish revolutionary challenger, the Social Democratic party, could not create a common front of various peasant groups. As many commentators have pointed out, an appeal to *different* peasant strata has been paramount in all successful revolutionary movements, the central role of the middle peasants notwithstanding. In these cases the

---

112   M. Peltonen 1985, pp. 7–9.
113   Soikkanen 1978, p. 354.
114   See Rasila 1970, pp. 21–2, 122–4, 209–12, 230–2, 390.

revolutionary parties have been able to stimulate demand for, and then supply, tangible *collective* benefits at the local level, such as local political power or redistributed land, thereby uniting different kinds of cultivator and landless groups. In the next phase the parties have profited from the peasants' willingness to act together in defence of the collective benefits they have gained.[115] In Finland the alliance between the party and the peasants was different because of the non-revolutionary character of the party as well as the limited scale of agrarian class conflicts. On the one hand, the Social Democrats advocated proletarian policies for the workers, but on the other, they were forced to take into account the crofters' aspirations for their own farms. Even if some of the benefits proposed to the two subgroups, the landless and the crofters, were collective (such as the democratisation of local government), others were not (such as the strengthening of the crofters' position, which was not accompanied by a corresponding demand that land be redistributed to the landless).[116] Besides, even in 1917 the party was only just starting its work: it had not yet supplied collective benefits; it had merely been stimulating demand for them. Finally, these attempts had taken place notably at the national level, in the Parliament, and were by 1917 little based on direct collective action at the local level, within the agrarian communities themselves.

On the bourgeois side, the independent peasantry provided the backbone of the army, which was rightly called a 'White peasant army'; there were many crofter and worker recruits as well, especially after the introduction of general conscription.[117] The upper and middle classes, including the intellectuals, were also in the White camp. There had been no long-term loss of legitimacy among the Finnish intellectuals who had created and consolidated the national culture only a few decades earlier, nor had sharp conflicts of interest

---

115 Skocpol 1982, pp. 364–6; Goldstone 1982, p. 198. A case in point are the Vietnamese Communists; see Popkin 1979, pp. 223–42.
116 See Rasila 1970, pp. 95–105, 120–5.
117 Workers numbered less than one-sixth, and crofters and other tenant farmers a little more than one-tenth, of the total number of the White troops (Rasila, Jutikkala, and Kulha 1976, p. 87). Ohto Manninen, in his study on the White conscripts, does not explicitly deal with the impact of conscription on the social composition of the White troops, but obviously those who were most unwilling to be conscripted – who tried to avoid or resist military service – came overwhelmingly from the popular groups (O. Manninen 1974, esp. chaps. 6 and 7). Manninen's conclusion that the 'White army was not a class army in its aims, nor was it in its composition' (1978, 239) seems grossly misleading. Conscription was started in late February, as Manninen is well aware. Barrington Moore's remark about a Latin American country whose army is made up mostly of peasant conscripts is relevant here: the fact that casualties on both sides of a revolution are mainly peasants is certainly no indication of the absence of class conflict (Moore 1966, p. 518).

developed within the dominant classes. A telling example is the role of the university students, who have been conspicuous in several revolutions. According to one study, in Finland only two students were among the revolutionary dead, whereas on the bourgeois side the corresponding figure was 251. The entire Red local government, moreover, recruited only a dozen people who had passed the university entry examination,[118] and only one major writer rallied to the revolution.[119]

The main regional variations dealt with in Chapters 4 and 7 were reflected in the consolidation of Red and White Finland. The revolution was declared in Helsinki, and the revolutionaries seized the entire core of the country (see Map 2, p. 55), where a certain radical solidarity among agrarian workers seems to have developed in the late nineteenth and early twentieth centuries. Eastern Finland, although it strongly supported the Social Democrats in the elections, was, with only few local exceptions, immediately dominated by the Whites.[120] As was stated above, the dissolution of the agrarian community appears to have provided little basis for collective action in the east, and the Social Democrats' rural organisation remained weaker than in the south-west. The region also lagged behind the core in industrialisation. The Whites' real stronghold, however, was in Ostrobothnia. In that region the local peasant capacity for collective action had already manifested itself, notably in the great peasant rebellion of the late 1500s, in powerful revivalist movements, and in other processes of popular organisation in the late 1800s and early 1900s. Now the peasants' conservative solidarity led them to play a prominent role in the 'White peasant army' and also to influence the White side ideologically.[121]

Regional variations in both organisation and the nature of solidarity can be seen in the spread of the worker militias and security guards and the civil guards in 1917. The worker militias were first set up in the largest towns and other centres in the south. The rural worker militias, for their part, were strongest in the three south-western counties, where the farm strikes had been concentrated. The White organisation grew most rapidly in Ostrobothnia: in the summer of 1917 this province had far more civil guards than did other regions; in central and southern Finland they gained ground only later, the most important exceptions being localities where bourgeois 'security corps' were formed after the farm strikes.[122]

---

118 Rasila 1968, 34–35; Piilonen 1982, pp. 316–18.
119 This writer was Algot Untola; see M.-L. Kunnas 1976, pp. 25–37.
120 O. Manninen 1975, pp. 433–9.
121 E.g., Ylikangas 1981, pp. 232–4.
122 Salkola 1985, 1: 246, 480–1, 520–7; Piilonen 1982, pp. 65–74.

Finally, the same pattern may be seen in the regionally varying conceptions of the nature of the revolution. In the core the war was, naturally enough, conceived of in class terms. But in Ostrobothnia, where the strong, conservative solidarity of the peasant community had been preserved and where more Russian troops were stationed than elsewhere, it was defined in different terms. During the fighting the Ostrobothnian newspapers depicted the war above all as a 'struggle for liberation', whereas in other White Finnish regions it was often called a civil or internal war.[123] For the Ostrobothnian peasants, it was a war of liberation against the Russian troops still in the country; the revolutionaries were traitors to the nation. Moral indignation was directed against disruptive class antagonism in the south and against the increasing indifference to religion that accompanied it. Characteristically, 'for the revivalists, this war was a holy war'; 'one made his way to the liberation war as to a prayer meeting: the war was also a war against the devil and the godless'.[124]

6   On the Character of the Finnish Revolution

The Finnish revolution may be viewed as the outcome of the long-term factors dealt with in Parts I and II of this study and the short-term factors laid out in this section. It was an encounter, on the one hand, of the class relations institutionalised in the state and, on the other, of the domestic consequences of Russia's collapse.

As to the long-run developments, it was argued above that the nature of class relations, the strength of the domestic state structures, and the character of national and class-based political organisation at their intersection encompass the main processes in Finnish state-making and nation-building by the early twentieth century. What, then, was their role in the abortive revolution of 1917–18?

It is helpful first to look at colonial peripheries, where these three factors seem to have been paramount in giving momentum to the development of revolutionary challenges and situations. Theda Skocpol has pointed out that the two major consequences of globally expanding capitalism for peasant-based revolutions have been shifts in (agrarian) class relations and disintegration of the metropoles' controlling capacity. The capitalist expansion has caused market economics to impinge on agrarian strata, arousing peasants to

---

123   T. Manninen 1982, pp. 135–51.
124   Rosenqvist 1952, p. 45; Vilkuna 1950, p. 172.

defensive revolts or creating new social strata prone to revolution. It has also created interstate rivalries, which have loosened the grip of large powers on smaller ones.[125]

It is in this twin context that the third long-term factor, the role of the organised challenger in the rise of revolutionary situations, should be assessed. The first two long-term factors have placed constraints on challengers in their political struggle to bridge the gap between peasants and the national state or a nationally distinct but dependent region. Success in the countryside has depended on the specific features of local class and institutional arrangements among the peasantry and on the degree of political control faced by the native challengers. Both local class relations and state controls have played their part in determining what strategies have been feasible in the mobilisation of the peasantry – whether challengers have been in a position to successfully offer collective benefits for various strata of the peasants and thereby actively mobilise them to a revolution, or whether the challengers have been well advised to offer more modest, economic benefits to particular subgroups within the peasantry.[126]

Viewed in this triple perspective of class relations, state structures, and political organisation, the Finnish revolution seems a very unlikely event. Peasants in colonial states have been hurt by capitalist commercialisation to a much greater degree than peasants in Finland. Preconditions for forming a revolutionary alliance between peasants and political parties were therefore from the outset much more favourable in the colonial cases. Increased market participation by peasants – stemming from economic crises and accompanied by corruption, monopoly, and the lack of viable, well-regulated institutions – has enabled revolutionary organisations to absorb peasants and thereby expand power. Just these conditions have made not only the middle peasants but also various other segments of poorer peasants amenable to revolutionary mobilisation.[127]

Finland is peculiar in that a revolution occurred *without* either similar threats from capitalist penetration or a comparable revolutionary party. In Finland the worker movement was obviously advised to offer economic benefits to various subgroups in the peasantry – that is, it was ready to improve the conditions of the landless and to strengthen the position of crofters even up to the

---

125 Skocpol 1982, pp. 367–73.
126 Ibid., pp. 361–7; Migdal 1974, pp. 231–6.
127 Migdal 1974, pp. 230–2, 247; Popkin 1979, chap. 5; Skocpol 1982, pp. 364–6; Goldstone 1982, pp. 197–9.

point of supporting de facto landownership. This course was reasonable not only because of the crofters' incipient changeover to commercial production but also because of rather loose political control – in other words, because of the opportunities offered by the political system after 1905.

The revolution's hesitancy, even defensiveness, is very much a result of these conditions. No revolutionary alliance existed between the peasantry and an organised revolutionary movement headed by intellectuals, simply because few peasants were amenable to revolutionary mobilisation and because there was no truly revolutionary party. The problem was recognised by the two foremost leaders of the revolution, who later concluded that its failure could be traced to weak support by the 'toiling peasantry' and to the reformist character of the party.[128]

But, paradoxically, the same set of factors is important in explaining why the revolution broke out. The extensive but 'reformist' mobilisation in the countryside helped the Social Democratic party secure a comparatively solid position in the polity by 1917. At that time the simple fact that they had access to political power proved paramount in producing the revolutionary situation.

What having sudden access to political power in 1917 implies, however, is that in the end a fourth factor was decisive for the outbreak of the Finnish revolution: the mode and timing of the final collapse of the metropolitan power. This feature – together with the simultaneous disintegration of the apparatus of coercion in the small polities themselves – differentiates all the European revolutionary challenges from the mainstream of the Third World situations. The breakdown of three European empires in the world war, combined with direct pressure the war exerted on local structures of dominance, was so thorough and abrupt that it is hardly equalled by any other favourable situation faced by revolutionaries in smaller countries seeking liberation from political dependence. Also unlike many colonial countries, the collapse took place *before* any widely organised *revolutionary* challenger had emerged in the Eastern European countryside (see Chapter 11). Although, to be sure, defeats in wars and international military interventions have often created favourable situations in colonial countries as well, generally the revolutionary organisations have grown up earlier, with recurrent disruptions in metropolitan control. When the favourable situation has finally come, the organised challengers have been ready to exploit the situation. Unlike several colonial cases, the local challengers among the smaller European nationalities were generally poorly

---

128   Kullervo Manner (1924, pp. 3–6) discusses both problems, O.W. Kuusinen (1919, pp. 1–14) the latter one.

organised or concentrated in urban areas and played no role whatsoever in the sudden disappearance of external control.

With this fourth factor added to the character of class relations, state structures, and political organisation, the specificity of the Finnish case becomes obvious. With the abrupt end of the Russian Empire and the sudden disappearance of state control, the reluctant but strong Social Democrats were finally pushed to revolution. Yet the whole nature of the alliance between the party and the peasantry made the attempt hollow, or at best half-hearted. Its tragedy was that it was so hopelessly ambivalent.

The specific character of the Finnish revolution may also be formulated in terms of both Moore's view of the preconditions for major revolutions and Tilly's model of the proximate causes of revolutionary situations. A revolution was attempted despite the fact that the country had long avoided war, with its accompanying threat to the integrity of both the polity and civil society, and the fact that the Social Democratic party did all it could to prevent the revolution. Nor was the Finnish revolution preceded by a decay of the prevailing system's legitimacy among the intellectuals. With few exceptions, the Finnish educated class unanimously shared the categories and explanations developed in the national culture during the previous seventy or eighty years. No insurmountable contradictions existed between the educated class and the tiny socialist intelligentsia, or, for that matter, within the dominant classes, which were basically united. Moreover, the developments leading up to the revolutionary situation did not begin with the gradual mobilisation of contenders making exclusive claims to governmental control, followed by a rapid increase in the number of people accepting these claims, and finally by the incapacity or unwillingness of the agents of the government to suppress the alternative coalition.

What initiated the process in Finland was governmental incapacity, which was followed only slowly and painfully by mobilisation and an increase in the number of people accepting exclusive alternative claims. Of crucial importance was that the Social Democrats happened to enter into government just when the state lost the instruments of coercion. The essential precondition for the onset of the whole process was the existence in 1917 of a worker movement that was well organised and comparatively well entrenched in the political system. The February revolution in Russia led to this movement's acquiring a central political role, corresponding to its electoral strength. Multiple sovereignty resulted only when the movement was deprived of institutionalised political power. In the summer of 1917 all the Provisional Government and the Finnish bourgeois parties could do was expel the socialists from power: they could not eliminate or control them. This expulsion united and consolidated the alternative socialist coalition, and dual power accordingly emerged. The revolutionary determination that existed – and there was not much – mattered little. What did matter was, first, the labour movement's strong grip on state power, which had no coercive apparatus of its own, and, second, the contested loss of this control.

The Finnish revolutionary sequence, then, did not fully follow the 'idealised sequence' depicted by Tilly, and the third proximate cause played a far more central part than the first two. According to Barrington Moore's perspective, then, the loss of unified control over the instruments of violence proved to be decisive. This framework helps us see how the specific features of *internal* revolutionary developments resulted from Finland's *external* dependence. The process was genuinely internal in that it took place within the Finnish polity and the main contenders were Finnish groups; it was initiated, however, by the collapse of imperial authority, on which the maintenance of internal order ultimately depended.

7 Breakdown of Society or Contest for State Power?

The treatment of the revolution in the historical literature may be commented upon briefly using the above perspective. Conceptions of the prime reasons for the revolutionary situation, the role of the Social Democratic party, and the social basis for the revolution are crucial to an overall assessment.

Understandably, all students of the revolution have portrayed it as a coincidence of both the crisis in Russia and domestic factors. In this view a critical role was played, first, by long-term internal strains, which the Russian collapse allowed to come to the surface: 'The Russian revolution with its consequences had released the forces pent up in Finnish society, giving them a chance to burst out'.[129] Reference has been made to the grave problems of the industrial and agrarian workers and of the crofters; the political stagnation resulting from the reintroduction of Russification and the state of emergency during World War I, which had stopped social and economic reforms; the weakening of social and cultural restraints on violence because of the continued struggle against Russia; and the example and memory of mass action in 1905.[130]

---

129 Paasivirta 1957, p. 59.
130 Kirby 1971, pp. 382–4; Paavolainen 1966–7, 1: 23–9; Paasivirta 1957, p. 59; C.J. Smith 1958, pp. 6–7; Soikkanen 1975, pp. 191–3, 220; Rasila, Jutikkala, and Kulha 1976, pp. 76–8; Martin and Hopkins 1980; Martin 1970, chaps. 2–5, esp. 117–22, 237–9, 324–32.

Usually, however, attention has focused on short-term problems. In full accordance with the opinion of the contemporary Social Democratic leaders, the food shortage has been seen to be decisive, as the primary factor responsible for the establishment of the worker security guards. More generally, the fear of starvation, accompanied by the increasing unemployment and inflation, has been thought to be the single most important factor behind the popular unrest and, ultimately, the revolution.[131] Because of the food shortage and the Bolshevik revolution, 'the party was rolling down tracks, like a heavy train, and the leaders had only to avoid being crushed'.[132] In this view the main causal chain begins with the collapse in Russia (which led to the drying up of the Russian grain supplies, mass unemployment because of the stopping of the Russian fortification works and military procurement programmes, problems in the maintenance of order, disturbances caused by undisciplined Russian troops, and general economic dislocation) and runs to the fear of starvation, to large-scale unrest, to the organisation of the militant Red Guards, and finally to the outbreak of the war.[133]

Essential to this perspective is the idea that the food shortage and related problems brought existing social strains to the surface. As Viljo Rasila concludes his study of the social background of the war: 'Only the events linked to the two successive revolutions in Russia, particularly the unemployment and starvation prevalent in the most industrialized areas, could aggravate [the long-term internal tension] to such an extent that it broke out as Civil War'.[134] Studies based on this perspective vary only in the relative weight given to the long-term preconditions and the short-term aggravation of the economic and social situation.

This approach seems to have one fundamental problem: it does not take seriously the fact that the arena of a revolution is the *state* – the state understood in Weber's sense, that is, as the institution that claims a monopoly on the legitimate use of physical force within a given territory.[135] Revolutions are contests for state power. Significantly, the upheaval is commonly called the *Civil War* in the

---

131 Soikkanen 1975, p. 224; Salkola 1985, 2: 432; Paavolainen 1966–7, 1: 31–54; Kirby 1971, p. 384; Rinta-Tassi 1972, pp. 6–8; Fol 1977, pp. 87–8, 127–8, 184–6, 225–6; Upton 1980, pp. 18, 64–5, 66–7, 123–4, 222–3; Holodkovski 1978, pp. 12–18, 132–8; Lappalainen 1967, pp. 55–8; Paasivirta 1957, pp. 59–60; Polvinen 1980, pp. 117, 118; Rasila, Jutikkala, and Kulha 1976, pp. 80–1; Jokipii 1981, p. 41; Hamalainen 1978, pp. 7–9, 115.
132 Hodgson 1967, p. 32, referring to Matti Turkia, the party secretary.
133 This sequence is implicit or very incomplete in a number of studies because they focus predominantly on the narration of political events.
134 Rasila 1968, p. 153; also Rasila 1982b, p. 165.
135 Weber 1948, p. 78.

Finnish scholarly literature and practically never, in the strict sense of the word, the *revolution*.[136] The state has not been totally ignored, of course, but over the long run it figures mainly through Russification and legislative dependence on Russia (the emperor's veto stopped several political reforms). And in the short run, the disintegration of order as a consequence of Russia's collapse figures only as one more factor responsible for general social disruption.

Basically, the long-run argument as it is presented above states only that the contenders on opposite sides in 1917–18 were largely from different social classes and that therefore (long-term) strains related to the social structure must have existed. In this view it appears self-evident that the pre-1917 Social Democratic party adopted a 'radical line' focusing on the 'class struggle' – that is, that it was 'revolutionary'.[137] The assertion, however, is retrospective: the strength of previous conflicts is simply deduced from the social basis of the revolution. Actually, the nature of earlier conflicts should be assessed independently of the revolution itself, and in particular they should be related to the state, which determined the preconditions for collective action on the part of the working classes in nineteenth- and early twentieth-century Europe. In Chapter 6 it was argued that although the class conflict was pervasive, in the sense that the structural preconditions for collective action were favourable, the easy penetration of the working class into the polity in 1905–7, aided by those very same structural factors, led to its increasing integration into the state by 1917. In a comparative perspective this tendency seems much more characteristic of the pre-revolutionary period than an existence of acute tensions (see Chapter 11).

Similarly, the state should be taken into account in analysing short-term problems. There is considerable evidence that starvation has not been a central factor leading up to revolutionary situations.[138] Starvation has afflicted much of humankind for centuries, often in conjunction with more general disorder, but a revolution is something very exceptional. In Finland the disastrous famine of 1867–8 led to the decimation of eight percent of the population without provoking the slightest sign of revolt. The same goes for the *fear* of starvation: it can be seen as a prime reason for revolution, or even revolutionary unrest, only if an extremely narrow perspective is used. The state, however, provides the necessary context for an analysis of the fear of starvation and related problems. The food shortage played an important role, but only because

---

136   It is a revolution especially for Holodkovski (1978) and Upton (1980). See also Martin 1970 and C.J. Smith 1971. The term also figures in the title of Piilonen's study (1982).
137   Soikkanen 1967, pp. 190, 196–8; Lipset 1983, p. 15.
138   E.g., Aya 1979.

of developments in the state, that is, only because of the government's inability to suppress alternative claims. Governmental inactivity became clear in early August. At that time, the scarcity of food itself was not critical, but the decomposition of the system for rationing was. The system could not work because the governmental apparatus was disintegrating, and it was disintegrating because the government's capacity to act effectively depended entirely on the Social Democrats' continued presence in the government. This dependence, furthermore, resulted from the working-class movement's share in the maintenance of order or, ultimately, from the absence of the established instruments of coercion. By the early autumn a rudimentary alternative polity had grown up, partly outside the state and partly under its protection, owing to the Social Democrats' position in the state. When the party was ejected from the established polity, an alternative polity gradually consolidated itself, gaining strength from the fear of starvation. In these institutional conditions, rumours of food scarcity and starvation easily spread. Basically, though, it was the emerging multiple sovereignty or dual power that mattered, and the food shortage (which was not actually critical in 1917)[139] only acted as tinder. Indeed, it is highly significant that the only exhaustive local study of the worker security guards in existence accords the food shortage and related factors only a very minor role.[140]

The character of the revolutionary process has a considerable bearing on the Social Democratic party's position in the alternative polity. Students of the revolution have generally portrayed the party as being unable to resist the militant Red Guards, and consequently as being largely responsible for the war.[141] In this view, the party gradually crumbled and finally capitulated to the guards in the period running from the general strike to the end of January 1918. In a larger perspective, however, exactly the opposite seems true: *the party was able to postpone* the outbreak of the revolution until long after the beginning of the revolutionary situation. True, it could not confine the guards strictly within the rules, but it was able to neutralise their militancy until the government had definitively decided to restore order and had energetically begun to make preparations for doing so – up to the point, that is, when the government decided

---

139   Rantatupa 1979, pp. 106, 108, 114–15.
140   Klemettilä 1976, pp. 171–2, 175–7.
141   Paasivirta 1957, pp. 65–71; Lappalainen 1967, 86–8; Rinta-Tassi 1972, pp. 21–41; Rasila, Jutikkala, and Kulha 1976, pp. 80–5; also Hodgson 1967, pp. 39–50, 53, 67. D.G. Kirby (1978, pp. 32–5) and V.M. Holodkovski (1978, pp. 55–82) stress the inability of the party to pursue a revolutionary course. So does Anthony F. Upton (1980, pp. 160–1 and *passim*), but in the last analysis he portrays the party as gradually capitulating (1980, pp. 206–8, 232–3).

to make the bourgeois paramilitary organisation the core of its armed forces. The worker guards did not launch a revolution in November, when the working-class movement was playing an active role, but only in late January when it was forced to react to the bourgeois initiative (as O.W. Kuusinen noted in a sharp-sighted comment written in the summer of 1918).[142] The Finnish abhorrence of fragmentation in popular organisations, the early development of the working-class movement in a more general process of organisation, its easy penetration into the polity in 1905–7, its strength based on extended agrarian electoral support, its focus on the state and on reforms in the framework of the prevailing political system – all these factors make it perfectly understandable that the core of the movement, the party, was able to postpone the revolution for so long. Ultimately the working-class movement was drawn into it. The Finnish situation is radically different from what took place in Estonia and Hungary. There, the working-class movement became linked with a new militant grouping and was rapidly and rather easily overwhelmed.

The Social Democrats' role raises a more general question about the character of the Finnish revolution. Practically all scholarly studies see the development leading up to the revolution as a breakdown or a sudden release of dark forces. Many of the above citations testify to this view.[143] The image is 'hydraulic', as Charles Tilly has called it: 'hardship increases, pressure builds up, the vessel bursts'.[144] Rod Aya has termed this view the 'volcanic' model: 'The onrush of uncontrolled changes in the structure of society begets multiplex tensions which, if unrelieved, erupt into mass violence where and when social controls relax or weaken'.[145]

In the study of revolutions and collective violence, the 'hydraulic' or 'volcanic' approach involves many insurmountable empirical and other difficulties. The most serious problems arise from concentration on states of mind, impulses, strains, and other ultimately psychological factors and the corresponding neglect of structural and institutional factors.[146] The present study holds that the conditions that lead to violent protest are similar to those that lead to other kinds of collective action in the pursuit of common interests.[147] This approach suggests, for example, that the revolutionary crowds were recruited from groups that were well integrated into the working-class movement

---

142   Kuusinen 1919.
143   The only clear-cut exceptions are Holodkovski 1978 and Salkola 1985, vol. 2.
144   Tilly 1975a, p. 390.
145   Aya 1979, p. 51.
146   See, e.g., Aya 1979.
147   See Tilly, Tilly, and Tilly 1975, pp. 2–13, 239–45; and Aya 1979.

rather than from the marginal, floating population in the towns and countryside. Recent findings seem to support this view,[148] but the implications have not yet been completely worked out.

One qualification, however, is needed. The disappearance of the army and the police in the wake of the Russian collapse was more essential for the Finnish revolution than were other factors. Like other Eastern European latecomers in 1917–19, Finland was suddenly presented with the opportunity for collective action. This makes comprehensible the Social Democratic leaders' fear that they would not be able to restrain the masses. It would be groundless to deny the existence of 'impulses and their release' in the summer and autumn of 1917. But the 'release of tensions' should be put in an institutional context in order to make it understandable.

The favourable opportunity for collective action is also reflected in the social basis of the revolution. The Red troops and the entire revolutionary organisation were predominantly proletarian. The Finnish revolution has even been called 'perhaps Europe's most clear-cut class war in the twentieth century'.[149] Of the more than 3,500 Reds killed in battle, 78 percent were workers. More than 90 percent of the worker security guard of Tampere, admittedly an industrial town, were from the working class.[150] And the most serious problem in battle was the nearly total absence of trained leadership.

This situation contrasts strikingly with several other revolutions. As Rod Aya puts it, 'Popular movements have been led, staffed, and supported by, not the altogether downtrodden and oppressed segments of society, but groups that, while having plenty to fight for and against, had something to fight with'. The 'masses' in various revolutionary upheavals 'were people of local standing and substance, however modest – small proprietors, mostly, peasant landowners, shopkeepers, artisans, journeymen, and snugly entwined in community networks'.[151] Besides grievances, then, *tactical power* was necessary, as Eric Wolf has pointed out in analysing the middle peasants' prominent role in various revolutions.[152]

Reasons were given above to explain why the support of Finnish 'middle peasants' for the revolution was so limited. The revolution had a strong proletarian character, which of course did not prevent the industrial workers, par-

---

148   Klemettilä 1976; Salkola 1985.
149   Martin 1970, p. 412.
150   Rasila 1968, pp. 34–5, 41; Klemettilä 1976, pp. 154–5. On the largely similar composition of the revolutionary local government, see Piilonen 1982, pp. 309–14.
151   Aya 1979, p. 74.
152   Wolf 1969, p. 290.

ticularly the most resourceful groups among them, from taking the lead.[153] The proletarian character may be seen as resulting from the linkage to Russia. Thanks to fluctuations in imperial authority, the labour movement was able to gain access to the polity in 1905–7 and subsequently to tighten its grip in early 1917 with relative ease – and *without assistance from allies within the polity*. This is significantly different from Scandinavia, for example, where the early struggle to extend democracy was a joint enterprise of the working-class movement and the Liberals.

In late 1917 and early 1918 the working-class movement tried basically to *maintain* the power and advantages it had gained in 1917, not to seize power. As such, this attempt is not unique. 'Revolutions commonly commence with efforts at conservative restoration', Rod Aya states. And when in certain revolutions the workers 'took up arms and marched under radical banners, it was to defend recent reformist gains against reactionary violence'.[154] But in Finland the defence of recently gained advantages was linked with a high degree of class integration manifest in the working-class movement, an absence of a coalition partner for the Social Democrats among the established members of the polity, a revolutionary sequence starting from the governmental incapacity to make use of the means of coercion, and finally an irresolution of the revolutionaries after they had gained power. In this combination lies the specificity of the Finnish revolutionary situation.

---

153 The central role of the most resourceful industrial workers is evident in Klemettilä's exhaustive study on the worker guard of Tampere (1976, pp. 153–7).
154 Aya 1979, pp. 46–47, 73.

CHAPTER 10

State and Nation after the Failed Revolution

Chapter 9 examined how certain structures (and the intricacies of World War I) affected an event, the Finnish revolution. In this chapter the opposite question will be considered: that is, what effect this failed revolution had on certain structures. To answer this question the revolution will be viewed as part of a long-term development going beyond the event itself. The question is, what was the role of the abortive revolution in converting the grand duchy into an independent republic, and in particular what was its impact on the existing state structures and the process of national and class integration? The Russian revolution had provided the opportunity, the Finnish working-class movement had initiated a revolution that failed, and then the earlier nationally oriented culture provided the instruments for defining and analysing, in the White Finland of the 1920s and 1930s, what had taken place in 1917–18. How did the attempt at revolution modify the conditions governing national and class integration? What was to be the role of the entire national heritage in the newly independent country?

An answer to these questions requires both a state-making perspective and a conception of the specificity of the revolutionary situation in Finland. It also requires an analysis of Finnish fascism. Finland's interface position meant that a country with a Scandinavian social structure had confronted the collapse of a multinational empire, a situation unique in post-world-war history.[1] A largely Eastern European fear of disorder and revolution was present, but dissimilarities in the social structure and state-making made it appear and function differently.

1   The Failed Revolution and the Nation

During the abortive revolution, a conception of the struggle emerged and was immediately consolidated in the dominant culture, where it took root and flourished well beyond World War II. The conflict was defined above all as a war for freedom or liberation (*vapaussota*), implying that it had primarily been a struggle for the liberation of Finland from Russian imperialism, which took

---

[1]   The closest case is Czechoslovakia, which, however, did not go through a revolution.

the form of Bolshevism after the autumn of 1917. In this light, Finnish revolutionaries were seen to be traitors who had conspired with the Russians to undo the newly won independence of their fatherland. The war thus acquired a certain internal character too, becoming, secondarily, a civil war (*kansalaissota*).[2]

In many ways this conception is understandable. The administrative Russification in the previous years had generated resentment, and fear of undisciplined Russian troops had grown among the bourgeois groups in 1917. A revolutionary Finland could hardly have escaped some sort of dependence on Soviet Russia. Also, when the Communist party of Finland was founded in Moscow in 1918, it was run by leaders of the failed revolution. But far more important were, first, the character and role of the national culture and, second, the specifically Finnish characteristics of the revolutionary situation.

As stated above, no signs of dissolution were discernible within the dominant classes prior to the outbreak of the revolution. No major conflicts of interest existed, and a far-reaching consensus about national integration prevailed. Only a few decades earlier, the intellectuals had formulated somewhat varying versions of nationalism as a civic religion for the emerging Finnish state, and the fundamentals of this nationalism were accepted fairly unanimously. Also, the Finnish educated class had become a bureaucratic intelligentsia: it participated actively in the construction of the state, and the university elite played a central role in politics and the bureaucracy.[3] This distinguishes Finnish intellectuals radically from, say, their French counterparts under the *ancien régime* or the unemployed intellectuals in various pre-independence colonial countries.[4] In Finland, because no powerful section of the elite was decisively outside the state bureaucracy, the variety of intra-elite conflicts that is apparently a key precondition for the emergence of a revolutionary situation did not exist.[5] As to the socialist intellectuals, they were a tiny group, their revolutionary conceptions were quite vague, and they were nationalists who had actively propounded political democracy and Finnish independence since the spring of 1917.

A tradition that provided few means for handling class conflict thus prevailed in the intellectual culture. It was this intellectual and emotional struc-

---

2   An example, as well as a prominent codification, of this view can be found in *The Memoirs of Marshal Mannerheim* (1953, chaps. 6 and 7). See also Ketonen 1983, pp. 23–4, 30–4.
3   Rommi 1964, pp. 129–30; Klinge 1970, p. 26.
4   These intellectuals were not only critical of the prevailing order but also isolated from political decision making. The classical analysis of France is Tocqueville's *The Old Regime and the French Revolution*.
5   Goldstone 1982, pp. 194–7.

ture that, in 1917–18, was suddenly and without premonition forced to react to and try to comprehend a revolutionary situation. The revolution was a horrible and nearly total surprise for the entire intellectual culture – as it was a surprise for the great majority of the revolutionaries themselves. A revolution occurred which was not preceded by long-term fissures within the dominant classes or by deterioration of the social and economic fabric in the world war, but which was a result largely of Finland's dependence on Russia for the maintenance of order. The solidarity of the people with the 'national' educated class, one of the basic tenets of the national ideology, seemed to break down all at once, and in a manner that could not have been reasonably expected given the nature of the previous Social Democratic challenge.[6]

The 'catastrophe' was interpreted, naturally enough, within the framework of the national ideology. Although the White military and political leaders as well as the White press were fully aware of the domestic character of the war from the outset,[7] this conception did not take root. Immediately after the war broke out, a notion emerged that portrayed it as a struggle for the 'fatherland', for 'freedom', and for the 'whole Finnish people', against 'dark forces', 'criminal bands', and 'chaos'.[8] The Russians fit into this perspective admirably. The existing distrust toward them grew to totally new – racialist – proportions. The Finnish challenge to state authority was seen as resulting from the 'Russian plague' that had 'infected' the revolutionaries.[9] Soon this conception evolved into the idea of a 'war for freedom' against Bolshevik Russia. Although initially formulated in the Activist propaganda meant for both the foreign and the domestic audience,[10] the conception corresponded first and foremost to long-run trends in the prevailing culture, and not merely to the short-run character of the revolutionary situation. This notion explained in the simplest possible way the seemingly inconceivable revolt of a part of the people 'against itself'. In the nationalist perspective, seeing the armed conflict as a war for freedom certainly made more sense than any alternative interpretation: it preserved the idea of a single national entity, precious for the national ideology, by projecting

---

[6] There were exceptions, mainly in the Swedish-speaking intelligentsia. Some of its representatives had adopted racial ideas from Western Europe or even had visions, in the prerevolutionary years, of a socialist holocaust. See Hyvämäki 1971, pp. 33–49, 58–9; and Klinge 1972, pp. 51–3, 96, 105–8. Another matter concerned the fissures left by the 1905 revolution in the idealised conception of the people. See below, n. 12.

[7] T. Manninen 1982, pp. 30–2, 73–5, 83–8, 141–7. The Ostrobothnian newspapers were a partial exception (ibid., pp. 135–40).

[8] Ibid., pp. 154–64; M.-L. Kunnas 1976, p. 52. See also Paavolainen 1966–7, 2: 27–39.

[9] T. Manninen 1982, pp. 164–79; Upton 1980, pp. 311–13; Kena 1979, pp. 83–9.

[10] T. Manninen 1982, pp. 95–7.

the cause of revolution outside the nation. It minimised Finnish participation in the conflict, thus concealing its class character.

In this perspective the Finnish Reds are seen as 'misled' – misled by the Russians or, more commonly, by their own leaders who were infected by the Bolsheviks.[11] A related view asserts that they were easily misled because of a specific purported national character. In this view, Finns are sullen and suspicious but, if angered, totally uncontrollable, insidious, and ready to stab their compatriots in the back. The view had older roots, notably in the fissures left in the idealised conception of the people by the 1905 revolution. But now it seemed enormously more persuasive than ever before.[12] It was as if Russian incitement had released the dark forces hiding in the Finnish soul, causing some Finns to join forces with the foreign enemy.

This is obviously a specifically Finnish version of the volcanic model of revolution – which, as Rod Aya says, is apparently the most persistent (and persistently misleading) way of seeing the revolutionary process.[13] But although the conception does not adequately explain the Finnish revolution, seeing the revolutionaries as misled may still catch something important. F.E. Sillanpää's masterly novel *Meek Heritage* expresses this beautifully. Written in the summer and fall of 1918 and published in 1919, this book was profoundly sympathetic to the defeated, whom it portrayed as being at the mercy of greater forces. The leading character is a cottager executed by the victorious Whites. This naive and passive man, having no idea of the political implications of his modest services to the local administration, is finally shot due to a misunderstanding, and thus is 'drawn into the swelling turmoil of the times'.[14] He is an 'unconscious' victim of a revolutionary process that is totally beyond his comprehension. Certainly there are people like him in all major uprisings, but the characterisation captures something essential in the Finnish revolution. The revolutionaries were really *drawn into* revolution, and when it began they had no clear idea what to do with the power they obtained. Among the masses, the confusion, lack of enthusiasm, and irresolution were at least as grave as among the leaders. In a word, the Finnish revolution was *underdetermined*: there were no deep endemic grievances among the masses that would have made them complete the destruction of the old order spontaneously.[15] Sillanpää's novel may be seen

---

11 See ibid., pp. 178–9; M.-L. Kunnas 1976, p. 171.
12 Klinge 1972, pp. 105, 108–10; M.-L. Kunnas 1976, pp. 65, 102, 108–9; Hamalainen 1978, pp. 95–97, 121–2; Sarajas 1962, pp. 135–80.
13 Aya 1979, p. 50.
14 Sillanpää 1938, p. 222.
15 Certainly the action of the Finnish masses was very far from the spontaneous and autono-

as characterising a revolution whose participants were seriously at a loss about how to use the power they had.

In accounting for the White terror, the character of the revolutionary situation and of the dominant culture also appear important. It is true, of course, that bloody repression has frequently accompanied the crushing of revolutions and other upheavals. But the fact that the revolutionary challenge remained incomprehensible and even insulting to the victors may explain some of the large-scale and summary killing (and also the continuous massacre of captured Russians).[16] Ilmari Kianto, the author of a famous novel dealing with the 1906–1907 political mobilisation in the eastern backwoods (see p. 213), was not alone when he wrote toward the end of the war: 'Is it not prejudice or downright short-sightedness to leave unpunished precisely those who, simply by adding to their families, strengthen the enemy force? Would it not be a correct tactic to take some stated percentage of the second sex of the enemy?' He went on to say that those who carried out such a work would be 'creating a great new Finland, the vigilant representatives of the fatherland and high idealism'.[17]

2   The Persistence of the Volcanic Model of the Finnish Revolution

The process of disengagement from the original 'volcanic' model of the Finnish revolution has been slow and painful, reflecting the continuing difficulty of the dominant culture to come to grips with the conflict. Today, although the original model has practically no advocates, its long shadow may still be discerned in the historiography (see p. 176).[18] For decades the academic community was incapable of dealing with the encounter, and it is thus perhaps no wonder that literary works have been instrumental in reinterpreting the revolution and making it comprehensible for the dominant culture.[19] Sillanpää's novel caught

---

mous violence James C. Scott argues is characteristic of the peasant movements that have instigated rebellions or contributed to the rise of revolutionary situations. See Scott 1976, pp. 193–203; and Scott 1977, p. 243.

16   See Upton 1980, pp. 311–13.

17   Cited in Upton 1980, p. 314. See also T. Manninen 1982, pp. 157–61.

18   The conception of the war as a combination of an outburst, an insurrection of the misled against the legal government, and a war for liberation from Russia was widely accepted among historians as late as the early 1960s (see Stormbom 1963, pp. 207–15). Today historians still may portray the revolution, in the last analysis, as a challenge to 'legal government' (Jokipii 1981, p. 48) or to 'lawfully elected government' (O. Manninen 1975, p. 471; see also O. Manninen 1978, p. 229). This perspective is understandable given that the challengers lost, but it does not seem helpful in analysing a social conflict.

19   This is perhaps particularly true of the period before the 1950s, when the most percept-

something essential long before any serious professional study.[20] It also exerted some influence, even though it could not really breach the bourgeois hegemony of the time.[21] Significantly, the definite fall of the original volcanic model was effected – four decades later – by another literary work, the second volume of Väinö Linna's great three-volume novel *Here Underneath the North Star* (1960). In this fresco of the year 1918 in a south-western agrarian community with a large crofter population, the conflict is crystallised in the vicissitudes of a crofter's son, who is an active member of the local workers' association, a Red Guard leader, and finally one of the tens of thousands of prisoners in the White camps.

This work so changed the atmosphere that the academic historians of the 1960s and the 1970s were encouraged to study seriously various aspects of the conflict. Linna's book was well grounded in historical fact and consciously 'sociological'.[22] Most important was his portrayal of the revolutionaries, not as misled or misbehaved, but as sensible and responsible people acting reasonably in their own interest. In the novel this characterisation added forcefully to the tragedy of the conflict and served as a distinct departure from the mainstream of earlier thinking. But Linna also saw the outbreak of the revolution as a reaction to unbearable circumstances, a release, made possible by the two subsequent revolutions in Russia, of the forces that had been blocked during the previous period.[23] This perspective seems quite natural in a novel that details the behaviour and motives of individual human beings in a social microcosm. And indeed, there were grievances among the landless and the crofters, grievances that certainly came into the open in the revolution. But as noted above, this view, when seen from a larger historical perspective, fails to take into account the institutional context and therefore does not permit an adequate assessment of the overall significance of the 'release of tensions'. In the absence of an army and a police force, even comparatively minor grievances may eventually grow into overpowering claims. Consequently, Linna's interpretation, powerful as it was, did not cause historians and other students to question the very foundations of the volcanic view of the Finnish revolution.

ive analyses of the societal conflicts in twentieth-century Finland were made by writers rather than historians or social scientists. Sillanpää is only one example.
20   The first serious historical study came out in 1957 (Paasivirta 1957).
21   Rajala 1983, pp. 207–9, 212–14; Paavolainen 1966–1967, 2: 396–7.
22   Stormbom 1963, pp. 230, 271–2.
23   See also ibid., pp. 196, 204.

3 On the State, the Nation, and Class Balance

After the revolution was crushed, the class balance in the country changed radically. The Communist party was, naturally enough, declared illegal, and there was no question of the Social Democratic movement acting in a framework similar to the one that prevailed between 1907 and 1917. The most eloquent indication of bourgeois domination was the position of the Civil Guard, which after the war was instituted as a nationwide organisation and maintained over and above the regular army, allegedly to secure the country against external and internal threats,[24] and from which the Social Democrats were excluded.

Nevertheless, Finland experienced greater institutional continuity in state structures than practically any other inter-war Eastern or East-Central European state. A new independent state, it had a constitution and a political party system closely linked with pre-World War I developments, even though its preservation had been guaranteed by Entente pressure. The republican constitution, confirmed in 1919, had been prepared for the most part in late 1917 in keeping with the constitutional tradition, and it helped to fulfil the bourgeois objective of a 'strong governmental power'. The highest executive, the president, had substantially more prerogatives than in most other contemporary parliamentary political systems.[25] Nothing strange was seen in linking the Civil Guard with the state machinery and in giving it considerable autonomy in internal matters.

In the inter-war bourgeois perspective, the war was only a tragic interlude in the unfolding of the nation. It was from this perspective that the victors attempted to reconstruct the broken national integration, to re-create an inter-class community bringing all the Finns together.

Efforts to create a strong national *Gemeinschaft* predominated on the right. The inspiration came from Fennomania, which was modified in light of prevailing conditions. Peasant values were revived, and a Finland united in culture – a 'national entity' – was to be built up and fortified against internal and external threats. Much more than ever before, Fennoman ideas were used to inculcate a civic religion for the state, and now strict ideological conformity was required. For example, the ideal world revealed in native folk poetry (particularly the *Ka-levala*), so central for the national ideology, was reinterpreted to correspond to

---

24 See Tervasmäki 1964, pp. 61–71. On the intertwining of internal and external threats in the postwar period, see Ahti 1984b.
25 Lindman 1968, pp. 331–43, 369–72; Jyränki 1978, pp. 19–21, 24–47. There was a marked resemblance between the Finnish and the new German constitution.

the claim for a rigorous martial unity, both outward and inward.[26] As in other upper classes threatened by political upheavals, moral regeneration and the inculcation of moral virtues were seen to be central, and the church gained much in importance among the Whites.[27] Politically the conception was represented by the National Coalition party, formed in 1919 from the monarchist majority of the (Old) Finnish party and the monarchist minority of the Young Finns, and largely supported by the Finnish-speaking wealthy landowners, the industrial and commercial elite, the higher bureaucracy, the military, and the clergy. In the 1920s, this party was the staunchest opponent of the 'unnational' working-class movement.

But another view of national integration emerged, stressing a certain degree of conciliation with the working class. Politically its proponents belonged to the liberal Progressive party, made up mainly of former Young Finns, and to the Agrarian Union, which in 1919 became a large party. The sixteen parliamentary seats the Agrarians had in 1916 grew in 1919 to forty-two, and in the 1920s they became the largest bourgeois party (Table 11). During the early populist period after 1905, the Agrarians, feeling affinity for the nineteenth-century national movement, had considered it their task to be the revival and further development of that movement's democratic traditions. In the post-1918 situation, then, they presented the agrarian-national ideology, with the peasants as its foundation, as the only programme capable of reconciling the two main challengers of the war. A far-reaching agrarian reform, making landowners of the crofters and many cottagers, was implemented, largely because of pressure from the Agrarians. Plans for land reform had been prepared before the outbreak of the revolution, but now it was explicitly presented as a way of fortifying the nation and protecting it from further upheavals. For rehabilitating the rebels the Agrarians and the Progressivists envisioned amnesties and sociopolitical reforms.[28]

The distinction between the two views of national integration is reminiscent of the difference between the conservative ideology prevalent among the agrarian upper classes of Central and East-Central Europe and the populist or peasantist agrarian ideology found in the same areas. In the inter-war period there was a corresponding difference between the authoritarian and fascist ideologies.[29] But although this distinction may be reasonably applied to Finland, it was of less importance there than elsewhere. What seems char-

---

26 See the detailed study of William A. Wilson (1976, esp. pp. 103, 107–11, 115–72).
27 Kena 1979, pp. 66–73; Alapuro 1973a, pp. 37–8.
28 For more detail, see Alapuro 1973a, pp. 24–6, 39–40; Kettunen 1979, pp. 284–94.
29 Ionescu 1969, pp. 99–19; Moore 1966, pp. 448–52; Fischer-Galati 1980.

TABLE 11 Distribution of seats in Parliament won in selected Finnish general elections, 1919–1933

Parties	1919	1927	1929	1930	1933
Social Democratic party	80	60	59	66	78
Socialist Workers' party[a]	–	20	23	–	–
Agrarian Union	42	52	60	59	53
National Coalition party	28	34	28	42	18
People's Patriotic Movement	–	–	–	–	14
National Progress party	26	10	7	11	11
Swedish People's party	22	24	23	21	21
Others	2	0	0	1	5
Total	200	200	200	200	200
National turnout	67.1%	55.8%	55.6%	65.9%	62.2%

a Communists and left-wing socialists.
SOURCES: *ÉLECTIONS POUR LA DIÈTE EN 1919* 1920, 27; *ÉLECTIONS POUR LA DIÈTE EN 1929* 1930, 25; *ÉLECTIONS AU PARLEMENT DE FINLANDE EN 1933* 1934, 7, 28

acteristic, rather, is a more-or-less united political culture – arguably a more unified bourgeois hegemony than in other countries influenced by the collapse of a multinational empire. A relatively united nationalistic culture had arisen by the first decades of the twentieth century, and it was solidified by the revolutionary experience and concomitant fear of a new Soviet state. The character of the landed class provided a solid basis for such unity. No clear-cut lines differentiated the wealthy peasants from the less prosperous ones, and when the Agrarians won over conservative-voting farmers in the 1920s, the party's populist image was obliterated, showing that no wide gap separated the two nationalist programmes. Both exalted the independent peasantry and peasant virtues.

The most revealing sign of the bourgeois consensus is certainly the Civil Guard. Unlike other bourgeois paramilitary organisations in inter-war Europe, the Guard was unanimously supported by *all* bourgeois parties, whether Finnish or Swedish. Its potential in a crisis can be seen from the fact that between 80,000 and 100,000 armed men served in the Civil Guard, as compared with some 25,000 to 30,000 in the army.

Another feature of the consensus is the overwhelming domination of a single organisation, the nationalist Academic Karelia Society (AKS), among the Finnish-speaking students. No other student movement could seriously compete with this group, and both nationalist views on integration, with some degree of tension between them, flourished in the AKS. True, the students campaigned against the use of Swedish by the upper strata and thereby irritated the bourgeois front, but in this effort they gradually became isolated. Even the Agrarians followed them only half-heartedly, not to speak of the Coalition party.[30] Moreover, the position of the Swedish language was guaranteed in both the constitution and language acts in a manner satisfactory to the Swedish-speakers.

Equally important for the political atmosphere was the attitude of the working-class movement. The Social Democrats were allowed to act, but within limits set by the dominant bourgeoisie. The very existence of the Civil Guard defined what was 'reasonable' political activity. The Social Democrats accepted these basic conditions and backed the centrist line, avoiding any encounters that would have brought the Centre closer to the right. They defended and worked for the consolidation of representative political structures, following a consistent policy of 'class peace'. Significantly, in 1919 the constitution of the new, and independent, republic had granted the Social Democrats access to the polity, and not only at the national level but now also at the local level.[31]

Social Democratic compliance may be seen most concretely in the party's overwhelming concentration on *political* activity. This was, of course, consistent with the movement's earlier orientation, and therefore it is no surprise that the Social Democrats suffered a loss of key trade union positions to the Communists, who for their part had great difficulties in the political arena (see Table 11). Basically, however, the limits to the Socialists' trade union activity were imposed by the existing order. In inter-war Finland employers had no need to accept collective agreements in the labour market, and they never did. A strike-breaking organisation was active and effective throughout the 1920s. Individual voting acts were recognised, but collective action in the labour market was not. The Social Democrats' role in labour struggles thus remained minor, and ultimately, in 1929–30, they founded a new, purely Social Democratic trade union organisations.[32]

---

30 Rintala 1972; Alapuro 1973b, pp. 116–19, 124–7.
31 Kettunen 1979, pp. 328–51; Rintala 1969, pp. 55–6, 63–4 (the term *class peace* is from Rintala); Kettunen 1980a, pp. 131–43.
32 Kettunen 1979, pp. 154–6, 203–17, 279, 353–75, 412–13, 465–85. The Social Democrats formed a minority government in 1926. Its policies were far from socialist, and the Communists found no difficulty in attacking it. Interestingly, however, it was widely supported by the workers; what counted were not real achievements or the lack of them but the apparent recognition of a certain *decency* in the working class, reflected in the fact that its party had been accepted as a governmental party (Kettunen 1979, pp. 323–6, 343).

The party's active involvement in parliamentary action by no means precluded the emergence of a 'camp mentality' among the workers: political and economic second-class citizenship was accompanied by cultural isolation. This isolation was reflected in an organisational network parallel to the bourgeois one. In the 1920s the workers not only voted for their own parties, but they also played, read, sung, participated in sports, shopped, and deposited their savings primarily in their own organisations and enterprises. The deep and pervasive concentration of popular activities around the workers' halls on the one hand and the civil guard halls on the other, so characteristic of local life in this period, reflects this polarisation better than anything else. The workers also definitely drew away from the church's sphere of influence.[33]

All in all, despite the revolution and its suppression, Finland had preserved the political system instituted in 1906, fortified now with a domestic president and a government. The Social Democrats could act, and were willing to act, within the prevailing system, and on the bourgeois side the only distinctively anti-parliamentary group, with roots in the counterrevolution of 1918–19, was quite small. Political consensus on fundamental questions ran from the Agrarians all the way through most of the right. In other words, the reactionary tendency was of little importance. This unanimity meant, however, that the entire bourgeois front was strongly anti-socialist – thanks to the fact that its ideological point of departure was a national heritage from which the working class was cut off and into which the traumatic experience of 1917–18 had been incorporated.

4   The Lapua Movement, 1930–2

The post-revolutionary quest for national integration climaxed in a Finnish variant of fascism, which, as in many other European countries, gained a real foothold during the Great Depression. The so-called Lapua movement greatly affected politics and nearly dominated the country in 1930, more than a decade after the abortive revolution. It was nationalist and anti-Russian in the extreme, held the party-based political system in contempt, succeeded in having all public activities by Communists – understood in a very diffuse sense – banned, and watched over the final disintegration of the trade union movement. After crushing the Communists, the movement attacked the Social Democrats, envi-

---

33   Suonoja 1968, pp. 59–60; Kena 1979, pp. 103–4, 121–3; Hentilä 1982, pp. 68, 70, 81, 83; Seppänen 1972, pp. 165–7, 171; Kettunen 1984, p. 38.

sioning a reduction of political rights that would guarantee bourgeois supremacy in politics. At times, a seizure of power was not out of the question; the most serious threat appears to have been in the summer of 1930.[34] In 1932, the movement attempted a coup d'état. Its failure led to the foundation of a political party, the People's Patriotic Movement, which held from eight to fourteen parliamentary seats from 1933 until World War II (see Table 11).

The Communists had succeeded in maintaining a presence in parliament and local politics under various labels throughout most of the 1920s (Table 11), and in the late 1920s real and putative Communist activity led to a number of strikes. Meanwhile, the bourgeois parties were able to form only weak minority governments, demonstrating the deficiencies of the parliamentary system. In these ominous conditions, reminiscent of other pre-fascist situations, the Lapua movement emerged at the end of 1929, with anti-communist riots serving as its starting signal.[35] The movement received its strongest immediate support from the Coalition party, but it found considerable sympathy in the political centre as well. From the end of 1929, the government, composed mainly of Agrarians, gave in to the Lapua movement constantly. Communists and those considered to be Communists were denied the freedom to form associations, and the government suppressed their publications after riots and other forms of pressure. In the summer and early autumn a fairly organised wave of terrorist acts, notably abductions, was undertaken, in which the police connived. The terrorists were civil guards, but as an organisation the Civil Guard itself stood aloof. Three people were killed. The total number of abductions and assaults rose to 254, with four-fifths of the victims being Communists (actual or alleged), the rest being Social Democrats. Among those abducted were members of local government bodies, party branches, public agencies, trade unions, newspaper staffs, candidates for and members of Parliament (including the deputy speaker), and even the country's first president.[36]

Through abductions and other pressure, the movement forced the replacement of the centrist government by a definitely rightist one in early July 1930, backing Svinhufvud as the new prime minister. Although he had been compelled to step aside in 1918, Svinhufvud nonetheless had enormous prestige as a symbol of victorious White Finland. He offered representatives of the Lapua movement portfolios in the government, but because of internal dissension its members refused. The cabinet arranged for the arrest of the Communist

---

34   Hyvämäki 1977, p. 135; Siltala 1985, p. 498.
35   Actually, at that time the Communist party was nearly paralysed.
36   Siltala 1985, pt. 1, and pp. 319–33, 357–67; Rintala 1962, pp. 167, 174–5.

deputies, and all organised activity considered to be Communist was systematically put down. These measures were later confirmed with anti-Communist laws, which were effected by ensuring a sufficiently large non-socialist majority in Parliament through new elections, held under heavy pressure from the Lapua movement. Communists and related groups were hindered in running for office.[37]

The culmination of this activity was reached in the pre-election period. In July 1930, 12,000 Lapua movement members, mainly farmers, marched on the capital with their demands, recalling the Whites' victory parade in 1918.[38] The Peasants' March, as it was called, was carried out under the auspices of the Civil Guard, and Mannerheim as well as Prime Minister Svinhufvud and the president, the Agrarian Relander, were present at the main demonstration.

After the elections and confirmation of the anti-Communist laws, conservative support for the movement began to decline. The movement turned against the Social Democrats, calling for the extermination of every form of 'Marxism' in Finland. Although the movement had elevated Svinhufvud to the premiership as its own man, friction arose almost immediately after he assumed office. More distinct differences came to the surface in 1931 when Svinhufvud was elected president as a Coalition party candidate. The movement, to be sure, strongly supported him during the electoral campaign; it is also evident that the Civil Guard exercised pressure on members of the electoral college, and especially on the Agrarian electors, before the final vote.[39]

The differences became irreconcilable, however, at the time of the so-called Mäntsälä revolt, which led to the dissolution of the Lapua movement, at least in its original form. In the spring of 1932 the movement's leadership lent its support to a revolt in Mäntsälä, a community near the capital, attempting to secure the backing of the civil guards there.[40] Among its demands was a call for the government's resignation and the establishment of a new, 'apolitical', 'patriotic' government. The aim was apparently to make Mannerheim head of state and to appoint a conservative industrialist – a former general and a member of the Lapua movement leadership – as prime minister. Numerous Coalition party leaders, a large portion of the Civil Guard leadership, including its commander, and many officers of the armed forces rallied to the movement's cause.

Thanks to resistance personified notably by Svinhufvud and the commander in chief of the army, the Lapua movement failed, however. At the crucial

---

37 Siltala 1985, pp. 112, 144–86.
38 Siltala 1985, p. 122.
39 Rintala 1962, pp. 177, 189; Kalela 1976, p. 117.
40 On the Mäntsälä revolt, see Rintala 1962, pp. 191–4.

moment it could not mobilise the rank and file of the local civil guards, in which rural elements constituted a clear majority; the commercial and industrial elite had withdrawn much of its initial support for the movement; and the non-conservative bourgeois parties and the Social Democrats had, of course, increasingly opposed the movement since late 1930.[41]

The mass following of the movement was centred mainly in the peasantry and certain middle-class groups. From the beginning it was considered to be basically a peasant movement: a rising against a conception of communist doctrine that damned everything the religious and patriotic peasants held sacred. As case studies consistently show, the big and middle-sized farms provided the main rural backing.[42] The conservative Coalition party's strong support for the movement certainly resulted at least in part from the attitude of the large farmers. Among the Agrarians, however, small farmers appear not to have become involved.[43] Ideological features point in the same direction. In defending 'old values'[44] the movement was more conservative than most other fascist groups. Characteristically, the archbishop publicly adopted a favourable attitude to the movement in its initial phase. The absence of anti-capitalist demands in its proclamations, too, is rather exceptional. Although the movement was based on a peasant *Weltanschauung* that was alien to capitalism, it did not focus on the workings or threats of the capitalist system; rather, it stressed almost solely the manifestations of capitalism in class struggle. The Lapua movement felt that its main task was the continuation of the 'war for freedom' against the Communists, Social Democrats, and even the Russians. Its rhetoric repeated the most extreme images of 1918 White propaganda,[45] capped by its two main symbolic figures, Svinhufvud and Mannerheim, the two most prominent White leaders of 1918.

Moreover, although the movement was supported in rural areas nationwide, it had two clear-cut regional strongholds, and these were not small-farmer regions. It was in the southern Ostrobothnian commune of Lapua that the anti-Communist riots took place in 1929. In this province peasantist moral indignation, springing from threats to a way of life, reappeared forcefully. As stated above, there was a marked contrast between the way of life here and in other

---

41 Upton 1968, pp. 209–10; Siltala 1985, pp. 143, 187–97.
42 E.g., Siltala 1984, pp. 22–4; Nieminen 1981, pp. 159–64.
43 Only in the county of Viipuri was there distinct small-farmer Agrarian support for the movement. But there the reaction was both weaker and less extreme than in Ostrobothnia and the south-west. See Siltala 1984, pp. 23–6.
44 Hyvämäki 1977, p. 134.
45 Siltala 1985, pp. 443–9, 455–69.

regions. The provincial character of various revivalist and xenophobic manifestations of the movement is known: it was as if Ostrobothnia wanted to make it clear that when Lapua speaks, all of Finland must listen.[46] The second bastion of support was in the south-west,[47] the most prosperous farming region.

The reasons why agrarian support came mainly from large- and medium-scale farmers can presumably be traced back to the abortive revolution. These groups had provided the backbone of the 'White peasant army'. Moreover, the movement's strongholds corresponded to the two regions where the farmers had been most involved in the war as enemies of the revolution or subject to its rule (see Table 10, p. 120). The completion of the 'war for freedom' was an essential part of the movement's ideology, and the Coalition and Agrarian parties had played a central part in the subsequent national integration. But apparently a third ingredient was needed as well: the Great Depression. This crisis did not merely affect farmers in general, but it also first hit large and middle-sized farms, which experienced a decline in forestry income as early as 1928. Soon grain prices declined, aggravating the problems and leading to a great number of compulsory auctions at the turn of the decade.[48]

There is also evidence that the grievances of the small farmers were not channelled through the Lapua movement during the Depression. This group was hit by economic malaise later than others, for the forest work on which they so heavily depended was not decisively reduced until the early 1930s. Only subsequently were small farms sold at auction in large numbers. It was among these cultivators that the so-called Depression movements erupted in the winter of 1931, concentrated in regions where small farmers had, to a larger extent than elsewhere, cleared land for cultivation, gone into debt, and been forced to give up their farms. In contrast to the Lapua movement, some of these amorphous and dispersed eruptions had distinct anti-capitalist features.[49] In the 1933 elections various small parties linked with Depression movements won five seats in Parliament (Table 11). These movements had helped the Agrarian Union to dissociate itself from the Lapua movement, which consequently came more under the influence of the Coalition party.[50]

Various middle-class groups in liberal professions, commerce, and administration also provided support for the Lapua movement. It is indicative that

---

46 See, e.g., Rintala 1962, pp. 165, 169, 175–176.
47 Siltala 1984, p. 22.
48 P. Kuusterä 1979, pp. 3, 108–13.
49 P. Kuusterä 1979, pp. 4, 19–38, 108, 119, 132–6, Table 13 (appendix); Lackman 1985, pp. 209–25, 284–9.
50 Kalela 1976, p. 120.

not only the Coalition party but also the more definitely middle-class Progress party went along with the Lapua movement in its initial phase. The role of the university-educated was very conspicuous. They were well represented among the organisers and supporters of the abductions, and they dominated the leading organs of the movement. A third of the members of the central council and of the district boards came from professional and governmental groups with higher education; together with people from the managerial and proprietary classes, they constituted a clear majority. It is no wonder, then, that the courts were reluctant to sentence the terrorists.[51] Students and young academics, too, notably the Academic Karelia Society, the dominant organisation among Finnish-speaking students and the young educated class – were important supporters of the Lapua movement.[52]

The attitude of the educated middle classes differed from that of the peasants in one important respect, however. Rural support was based on a deep anti-communism, which was exacerbated by the Depression, and it declined soon after the elimination of the Communists from public life. But after mass support waned – and with Hitler's rise to power – fascism continued to attract the educated middle classes. In this, the permanent quest for national integration appears pivotal. The recovery of national integrity, lost in 1918, had been sought by the AKS throughout the 1920s. The Lapua movement seemed to provide an opportunity to restore solidarity between the people and the national educated class. Correspondingly, the new party, the People's Patriotic Movement (*Isänmaallinen kansanliike*, or IKL), which considered itself to be the heir of the Lapua movement, had a strong academic hue in its upper echelons. Its ideology, moreover, was more overtly fascist than that of the Lapua movement, with minor direct borrowings from German and Italian fascism.[53]

5   The Mass Movement and the Dominant Classes in Finnish Fascism

As I have described it, the Lapua movement was related mainly to the state and the various social classes, which are of the greatest relevance when assessing the role of fascism in Finnish state-making and when comparing it to fascist phenomena in other countries. The crucial problem is the relation of the fascist movement to authoritarian or conservative forces, or, in slightly different

---

51   Siltala 1984, pp. 22, 30; Siltala 1985, pp. 403–19; Alapuro 1973a, p. 223.
52   Alapuro 1973b, pp. 128–9.
53   Alapuro 1973a, pp. 53–4, 125–36, 144–6; Rintala 1963, pp. 308–10; Heinonen 1980, pp. 693–4.

terms, the role of the dominant classes in the mass movement. Commonly, the former exploited the latter, but the two are generally more or less distinct. Fascism was not conservatism so much as 'an attempt to make reaction and conservatism popular and plebeian', as Barrington Moore puts it.[54] Or, in Reinhard Kühnl's words: 'In order for the coup d'état to have a chance to materialize, a supply, i.e., a fascist mass movement created by socio-economic crisis, must be met by a corresponding demand, i.e., the hope by the ruling class for a fascist power system'.[55] Kühnl's remark brings to mind Germany in particular, where the dominant classes came to look on fascism as a potentially valuable ally against the workers only after it had proved its strength, its right to be taken seriously.

In characterisations of this kind, the relative autonomy of the fascist mass movement is stressed. Its specific character may be seen in its ideology, which to some extent differed from the ideology of the dominant classes, even if the two often had common roots.[56] It is also known that the fascist movements drew their main support from the middle classes and, in the countryside, from the small farmers – that is, from outside both the working-class parties and the traditional conservative parties.

What was the relation between the mass movement and the dominant classes in Finland? Although it was supported by middle-sized farmers and to some extent by the middle classes, the Lapua movement was from the very beginning also a movement of the conservatives, including the large farmers. As time passed, the conservative or reactionary character of the movement became increasingly evident. And what is more, the small farmers, the backbone of rural fascism in a number of other countries, remained outside the movement, expressing their dissatisfactions through other channels.

It is characteristic of the phenomenon that the Lapua movement was not a political party and that its leadership remained vague. Rather, it was a loosely organised pressure group or faction within several parties, notably the Coalition party and, to a lesser extent, the Agrarian Union. The Swedish People's party, too, gave the movement considerable support. Differences in the attitudes of the bourgeois parties began to crystallise only in the course of time: in the initial stages acceptance and even enthusiasm were widespread, though not universal, in all of them. Finnish fascism assumed a more distinct middle-class character only after mass support had petered out. The IKL bore the stamp

---

54   Moore 1966, p. 447.
55   Kühnl 1971, p. 103.
56   Kühnl 1971, pp. 84–99; Moore 1966, 448–52.

of the middle class, even if most of its adherents were former conservative voters.[57] It also cooperated closely with the Coalition party up until the latter half of the 1930s.

What all this means is that in Finland, the relation between the fascist mass movement and the dominant classes was intimate *from the very beginning*. In its initial stage the Lapua movement was basically a general bourgeois reaction, though whether the mass movement arose spontaneously or was instigated by the dominant classes has been a subject of controversy.[58] In the present perspective this question is not very relevant. The rise of the mass movement and the dominant classes' need for it were closely interconnected. The view of fascism as an agent called in to restore order only after it had proved its right to be taken seriously is not accurate in the Finnish case.

The connection seems to result from the character of the bourgeois front after the abortive revolution. As stated above, a united, nationalistic political culture existed, despite different national integration strategies. On the one hand this unity implied that there was considerable rightist potential in the bourgeois groups, all prone to react strongly to any threat against central national values. On the other hand, noting the strength and cultural unity of the bourgeois front is merely another way of indicating the absence of strong and salient reactionary forces in the bourgeoisie. In this situation, the emergence of an extensive fascist-type movement was easy, but it was therefore also destined to remain rather shallow, without a distinct profile of its own. It was, as has been said, 'the political extension of the civil guard ethos'.[59]

In the end, no German- or Italian-type basis for a fascist takeover existed in Finland. In Germany and Italy, World War I had left the capitalists in control of the economy but at the same time accorded the working class a share of the political power and the right to organise and agitate for its own ends. In Finland rather the contrary was true: the working class had been defeated in 1918. When the Lapua movement eliminated the Communists in 1930, moreover, it thereby emasculated the trade union movement, which in the 1920s had been fairly active.[60] During the Depression workers' wages fell in Finland more than in Scandinavia, mainly because of trade union weakness: in the mid-1930s, wages

---

57 In the general elections of 1933, the Coalition party and the IKL formed party alliances in almost all constituencies. Small towns were the most typical IKL strongholds (Djupsund and Karvonen 1984, pp. 51–4, 79–81).
58 See Wahlbäck 1967, pp. 107–10.
59 Siltala 1985, p. 497.
60 The final blow against the trade union movement was preceded by a deep internal crisis in 1929, resulting from conflict between the Communists and the Social Democrats. See Kettunen 1979, pp. 309–11, 453–73.

were generally less than half what they were in Sweden or England.[61] Thus the interests of industry were very well taken care of by the existing political and economic system. The export industry in particular maintained its competitiveness, escaping the Depression comparatively unscathed, and economic growth in the inter-war period was very rapid.[62] The conflicts in the economy, with the accompanying turmoil in the labour market and in society as a whole, never polarised the population in Finland as they did in Germany, where the dominant classes felt even more urgently the need to find an agent to restore order.

The stand of the peasantry was at least as important. Although peasants responded enthusiastically to the Lapua movement, they soon began to dissociate themselves from it. For one thing, the early proscription of the Communists satisfied most of the peasants' demands, and the Depression movements caused the Agrarians to withdraw their support. In 1932, too, the Depression began to abate. Finally, the Agrarian Union showed no sympathy for the movement's agitation against the Social Democrats, who, in the centrist view, were to be reintegrated in the national body and who in the 1920s had confirmed their non-radical orientation. In this respect the Finnish Social Democrats differed greatly from certain brother parties, which responded to the rise of fascism with a revolutionary counter-mobilisation.[63] Indeed, the exclusion of the Social Democrats would have unbalanced the political system to the advantage of the right, a development that would have been unacceptable to the centrists.

The solid position of the independent peasantry and their party in the state and society was largely responsible for this pattern of events.[64] To a very large extent, both the rise and fall of the Lapua movement were determined by the peasantry – as the failure of the movement's leadership to mobilise the peasant rank and file of the civil guards during the Mäntsälä revolt indicates: the peasantry, influenced by the preceding Agrarian propaganda, obeyed Svinhufvud's exhortation to stay at home. The fear generated by the attempted revolution, combined with the proximity of the consolidating Soviet state, laid the ground for an extensive fascist-type movement, but the weak position of the working class, the strong role of the executive, a political system that had been firmly anchored in social groups since 1906, and, ultimately, the Scandinavian social structure placed constraints on it.

---

61 Knoellinger 1960, p. 85.
62 Pollard 1981, p. 289; Raumolin 1981, pp. 3–5.
63 Linz 1978, pp. 162–7, 178; Simon 1978, pp. 104–6.
64 Cf. Ahti 1984b, pp. 35–7.

PART 4

*The Finnish State and Revolution
in a European Perspective*

∴

CHAPTER 11

Eastern European Revolutionary Movements

By the time World War I broke out, various political organisations existed in the smaller Eastern European polities and the minority regions, but nowhere had a well-organised revolutionary party emerged in the countryside, as such parties did prior to a number of anti-colonial revolutions. Certainly none of these smaller polities or nationally distinct regions was predestined to social revolution in the following years. But revolutions did occur in some of them between 1917 and 1919, and in nearly all other cases such a conflict seemed possible at one time or another.

In order to determine the factors that account for these challenges, all of the smaller Eastern European polities should, at least in principle, be taken into account. In this chapter, the nature of the conflicts will be discussed in terms of the three-part perspective utilised above: (agrarian) class relations, political dependence, and organised challengers as expressions of national and class integration.

Nearly everywhere a subordinate position in the capitalist world-economy and increased demographic pressure had transformed traditional agrarian class relations and created an incipient industrial proletariat. In some cases local upper classes were closely tied to the metropole culturally or economically; in other cases the ties were looser. Regions also varied markedly in the character of political dependence. A notable transition occurred, of course, in the Ottoman Empire, which was forced to abandon its control by 1914. Moreover, the degree of local autonomy varied considerably within each empire as well. These two conditions shaped the third factor, the character of popular political organisation before the world war.

As in the case of Finland, a fourth, short-term condition should be added: the mode and timing of the collapse of the mother empire, combined with the direct pressure of war on the local structures of power. The three long-term factors determined the nature of the challenge on the eve of the final breakdown of the metropole, whereas the long- and short-term factors together affected both the ability of the challengers to mobilise the masses after 1917 and the way the existing local authority disintegrated.

This perspective makes it easier to identify the major differences between the European cases and the majority of the colonial cases and to situate Finland among the Eastern European dependent nationalities.

Between 1830 and 1918, twelve nationally distinct independent states emerged in Eastern Europe as Russia, Austria-Hungary, and the Ottoman

Empire disintegrated: Finland (1917), Estonia (1918), Latvia (1918), Lithuania (1918), Poland (1918), Czechoslovakia (1918), Hungary (1918), Romania (1878), Bulgaria (1908), Yugoslavia (1918), Albania (1913), and Greece (1830). All these cases cannot be examined here, not even all the so-called successor states, created or re-created at the end of the war. Presumably the most relevant cases for comparison are two other cases of autonomist nationalism in the Russian Empire:[1] the neighbouring Baltic Provinces, soon to be Estonia and Latvia. The rudimentary polities of these regions, too, were directly affected by the revolution of 1905 as well as by the February and October revolutions.

In the Habsburg Empire dismemberment brought about a revolution in Hungary[2] and, together with substantial help from the labour movement, the birth of the Czechoslovak state. In the Balkans the war eliminated the vestiges of the Ottoman period and led to a major territorial expansion in Romania, a kind of peasant revolution in Bulgaria, and the expansion of Serbia in the new state of Yugoslavia. Yet no outright social revolution occurred in the Balkans, despite some critical moments. The same holds for Poland, which had been divided among three empires.

Finally, inter-war fascism in Eastern Europe bears strong marks of local social structures, of problems created by the reformation of political systems after World War I, and of the memories of revolutionary unrest in 1917–20. The rapid re-establishment of traditional elites and economic dependence on the more developed countries of Western Europe appear to be key factors influencing the Eastern variant of fascism.

1 National Movements in the Baltic Provinces

Three conditions that paved the way for the steady advancement of Finnish nationalism were mentioned in Chapter 5. First, Finland was an established, separate political unit, whose distinctiveness was consolidated in the course of the nineteenth century. Second, its upper classes had adopted neither the native Finnish nor the metropolitan Russian culture but rather the Swedish language and culture; therefore, external political domination on the one hand

---

1 Orridge and Williams 1982, p. 21. Despite a revolutionary situation in 1918–19, I decided to omit the other Baltic territories, or the Lithuanian-speaking areas, from this discussion because they were occupied by the Germans in 1915–18. Besides, they did not have a separate political structure even to the degree the Baltic Provinces had.

2 No other revolutionary situations occurred elsewhere in East-Central Europe, except the short-lived Slovak Socialist Republic created by the Hungarian revolution.

and internal cultural and economic domination on the other were not superimposed on one another. Third, because a non-feudal class structure with a large, strong indigenous peasantry had been consolidated during the Swedish period, the dominant position of Finland's upper classes was not based primarily on landownership. Baltic deviations from this pattern seem to explain many of the differences between the Estonian and Latvian national movements and the Finnish movement. In the former, the first and third conditions were not fulfilled; only the second one was. But because the three conditions interacted, even this seeming similarity had different consequences in the two cases.

In the three Baltic Provinces of Estland, Livland, and Kurland, populated by Estonians and Latvians (see Map 10),[3] noble landownership was the most extensive, and capitalist development in agriculture the most intensive, in all of European Russia. At the beginning of the twentieth century the average size of estates in the *gubernii* of Estland and Livland was 2,677 and 3,232 *desiatina*s (one *desiatina* being the equivalent of 2.7 acres), respectively, whereas the corresponding figure for European Russia as a whole was 496 *desiatina*s.[4] Although members of the estate-owning German nobility were less than one percent of the agrarian population, they owned about half the available land.[5] To keep the labour force in place large tracts were leased to the peasantry, especially after internal passport reforms in the 1860s made it easy for peasants to migrate to the cities and to the Russian interior. Money rent predominated, but labour rent and other feudal obligations survived until the early 1900s.[6]

Besides tenant farmers and cottagers, the huge estates needed many agrarian wageworkers. These workers constituted one-quarter of the local labour force, by far the largest proportion of any workforce in European Russia.[7] Thus in the Baltic Provinces the so-called Prussian way to capitalism in agriculture had progressed further than anywhere else in the empire. On one side there was a conservative capitalist Junker-type class, on the other a growing class of agrarian wageworkers. Commercialisation, however, occurred more slowly

---

3   Lettgallia was also a Latvian-speaking region, but the elites were Russian and Polish and the villages were closer to the Russian type than were those in the Baltic Provinces.
4   *Istoriia Estonskoi SSR* 1966, 351–2.
5   In the Estonian-speaking areas, estate owners and their family members accounted for 0.7 percent of the total agrarian population in 1916 (Siilivask 1975, p. 69); according to Koval'chenko and Borodkin (1979, p. 87), noble lands accounted for 49 percent of total lands at the turn of the century. Local Estonian and Latvian historians give somewhat higher percentages, often including state and church properties (Saat and Siilivask 1977, p. 27; *Istoriia Estonskoi SSR* 1966, pp. 351–2; Draudin 1959, p. 21).
6   Anfimov 1969, pp. 175–6; *Istoriia Estonskoi SSR* 1966, pp. 69–80, 352–3, 361; Vilks 1962, pp. 83–7.
7   Koval'chenko and Borodkin 1979, p. 87; Siilivask 1975, p. 65.

MAP 10   The Baltic Provinces (Estland, Livland, Kurland) and the border between Estonia and Latvia after 1917

than in Germany, and traditional methods of exploitation – of squeezing surplus out of the peasantry – lingered, despite the rapid expansion of new, capitalist ones. As production intensified, the Baltic barons sought to maintain their position by continuing to impose various traditional obligations and by using strong political methods to keep the labour force on the land. In a word, 'labour-repressive' trends toward commercial agriculture dominated. These were guaranteed by the Russian state, which was actually, to use Barrington Moore's terminology, an agrarian bureaucracy. The estate owners depended on the central authority for the extraction of the peasant surplus.[8]

---

8 Koval'chenko and Borodkin 1979, pp. 78, 86–91; Anfimov 1969, pp. 175–6, 360–81; Saat and

The Germans came to dominate Baltic society through the agreements they had concluded with representatives of Peter the Great at the beginning of the eighteenth century and which they were able to maintain in essence until 1917. In annexing the former Swedish provinces, the emperor had granted them extensive self-rule, thereby guaranteeing the rights and privileges of the German nobles and burghers – an expedient that assured upper-class cooperation, exactly as it would in Finland one century later with the Swedish-speaking upper classes. The agreements guaranteed the nobles an oligarchic system of government, the German judicial system, the use of German as the official language, and control over the church, which was Evangelical-Lutheran. In each of the Baltic Provinces, the *Landtag*, or the assembly of the province's nobility, functioned as the highest administrative organ. Local government was also in German hands – in the cities through guilds and councils, and in the countryside through parishes led by German pastors. Much like Finland, then, the Baltic Provinces were in the interface between two established states: they had an alien upper class whose position was first guaranteed by the Swedish crown and then by the Russian autocracy.[9]

The German estate owners may have dominated the capitalist transformation,[10] but commercialisation occurred in another form as well, as the landowning peasantry increased in importance. In the 1810s the Baltic serfs had been formally emancipated, and during the 1850s and 1860s the Estonians and the Latvians had obtained the right to purchase land. By 1900 an independent peasant class had grown up, with a small *Grossbauer* stratum at its top. The progress this class made may be seen in the rapid development of a network of economic and professional organisations in the early decades of the twentieth century.[11]

A conflict existed, then, between the German landlords and the large masses of landless labourers and poor tenants. Hunger for land was common among the latter: the Baltic countryside was 'bound by semi-feudal relationships and suffering from the dearth of land'.[12] Additionally, a tension developed between the estate owners and the new indigenous peasant proprietors, who were encumbered with mortgage payments. The peasant landowners felt the weight of the former group's privileges and increasingly challenged its authority. The

---

Siilivask 1977, p. 26; Moore 1966, pp. 420, 434, 459, 473, 478; *Istoriia Estonskoi SSR* 1966, pp. 69–80, 352–3; Draudin 1959, pp. 7, 16–17, 31–5.
9   Haltzel 1981, pp. 112–14. Kurland, however, was taken from Poland (in 1795).
10 See Koval'chenko and Borodkin 1979, p. 89.
11 Kahk 1982, pp. 83–104; Kahk and Vassar 1970; Rosenberg 1985; Loit 1985, pp. 64–7.
12 Saat and Siilivask 1977, p. 26.

prevailing order had lost the support of the upper crust of the peasantry, which was emancipating and organising itself. As Barrington Moore maintains, this is one of the greatest dangers for an *ancien régime*.[13]

The landless and the poor peasants had ties with the growing industrial working class. After a period of very rapid growth at the beginning of the twentieth century, the Baltic Provinces were among the leading industrialised and urbanised regions of the Russian Empire and a central way-station in commerce with Western countries. Thanks to the region's position as an interface between the West and the interior of Russia, much of the empire's modern, foreign-dominated industry, 'implanted ready-made from abroad',[14] was located there, producing for the internal Russian market. The Baltic Provinces were thus part of Russia in a much stricter sense than was Finland, not only politically but also economically.[15] Riga, the capital of Livland, specialised in engineering and metallurgy. With 530,000 inhabitants in 1914, it was the fifth largest city of the Russian Empire, and its industrial proletariat was concentrated in large mills and factories. The situation was analogous in Reval, although on a smaller scale. The Kreenholm cotton mill in Narva was reputedly the largest in the world. The labour force required by the swelling industrial centres was recruited above all from among the landless and poor peasantry. In Reval, for example, two-thirds of the population in 1897 had been born elsewhere, with nearly 40 percent coming from the rest of the *guberniia* of Estland.[16]

In the late nineteenth and early twentieth centuries, an indigenous bourgeoisie emerged, made up of merchants, minor officials, artisans, and a professional middle class of teachers, lawyers, and physicians. The clergy did not figure prominently in the formation of the native middle class owing to the Germans' hold on the church.[17]

All in all, late nineteenth-century capitalist development created various groups of Estonian- or Latvian-speakers who were increasingly opposed to the existing system of (German) domination: in the middle and upper echelons of society, the peasant proprietors, the urban and rural bourgeoisie, and the middle classes were obvious challengers. At the same time, the industrial work-

---

13   *Istoriia Estonskoi SSR* 1966, pp. 71–2, 83, 362–4; Draudin 1959, pp. 16–17, 25; Balevits 1962, pp. 171–3, 177, 196–7; Moore 1966, p. 474.
14   Pollard 1981, p. 240.
15   See Karma and Köörna 1977, pp. 50–62.
16   Vilks 1962; Karma 1963, pp. 110–20, 335–47; Pullat 1976, p. 53; Schram 1957, pp. 55–60; Pollard 1981, pp. 240–1.
17   Kruus 1935, pp. 131, 179–81; Plakans 1981, pp. 248–9; Jansen 1985, pp. 48–9.

ing class, drawn primarily from the lowest strata of the peasantry, grew rapidly and came to be concentrated in a few large centres. And of great importance, all the native groups were highly literate.

The class structure here differed fundamentally from that in Finland. In the nineteenth century both Finnish and Baltic societies were predominantly agrarian, but in Finland the prospering indigenous peasantry was the dominant landowning class. Consequently, the peasant landowners' relationship to the crofters and the landless became the prime source for social conflict in the late nineteenth century. These landowners, together with the increasingly Finnish-speaking upper classes, played a central role in the process of national integration. Together they introduced, in the form of Fennomania, an agrarian 'civic religion' which guided the integration of the state.

In the Baltic Provinces, the independent peasantry remained small and suffered greatly from the dominance of the German landowners. There, the peasant proprietors played a significant role in the national movement for self-assertion and liberation from the 1860s and 1870s on – that is, almost immediately after they had obtained the right to own land. Whereas in Finland during the last decades of the nineteenth century the wealthy peasants were a distinctly conservative force, in the Baltic Provinces they were pivotal in challenging the prevailing order. They came into conflict much more with the dominant German classes than with the working classes because they did not have an established position in the local political and economic structure. The economic and social aspect was very pronounced in their nascent opposition, and the anti-German struggle was considered more important than opposition to administrative Russification from the 1880s to 1905.[18] The emerging indigenous middle classes, too – particularly the teachers, who were often of peasant origins – played a central role. Moreover, the elimination of the prevailing order was certainly in the interest of the poor and landless peasants, and the industrial workers as well.[19]

This is not to say that the various indigenous groups shared common class interests. Rather, it illuminates the point made in Chapter 5 about the preconditions for movements of national self-assertion and liberation, that mobilisation across class boundaries – the creation of an interclass community – is essential. In the early phase, clearing the way for social and national liberation in the

---

18   Kruus 1935, pp. 133, 153; Plakans 1981, pp. 225, 241, 255–7. Toivo U. Raun says (1981, p. 340): 'Before the Revolution of 1905, the great majority of the [Estonian] intelligentsia and the masses regarded the administrative [if not cultural] Russification as an important means to break Baltic German hegemony over local institutions'.

19   Hroch 1968, pp. 72–80; Kruus 1935, pp. 133, 181–7; Plakans 1981, p. 249.

Baltic Provinces fell to the strongest indigenous groups – mainly to the middle classes and the peasant proprietors, as Miroslav Hroch suggests in his study.

What the coalition was to do in the later phases of organisation and mobilisation is, however, quite another question. In the Baltic Provinces, the independent peasantry and the middle classes, by contributing to the challenge against the prevailing order, were actually opening the way for a more radical protest. It was argued above that the temporal conjunction of the rise of the peasantry and the emergence of popular organisations, including the worker movement, lent popular legitimacy to the latter in Finland.[20] In a sense this appears to have been true in the Baltic Provinces as well: the peasant landowners and the indigenous (petty) bourgeoisie took the lead in a movement which nevertheless included, at least in principle, the indigenous working classes.[21] But whereas in Finland this coincidence ultimately served to integrate the popular classes into the state, in the Baltic Provinces it opened the way for a much more thorough challenge, one that grew partly out of the national movement itself.

In the Baltic Provinces the national movement was unambiguously a liberation movement; it was also anti-clerical because of the German dominance of the church. The adoption of a socialist ideology seems to have been easier there than in Finland. Socialist propositions became increasingly popular in the 1890s, notably among the Latvians, as the urban intelligentsia and other middle-class groups grew. By this time, continuing differentiation within the peasantry had created a more discernible proletarian population in agriculture, and an industrial working class was emerging in the big cities. Moreover, the indigenous groups were still excluded from local political institutions. A new, more radical generation of intellectuals was willing to include the proletariat and semi-proletariat in the national movement.[22] Among the Estonians, then, two main groupings gradually emerged, and among the Latvians the entire movement experienced considerable radicalisation.

Among the Estonians, the bourgeois-national movement was based on the bourgeoisie and wealthy peasantry, with the university town of Dorpat serving as its main centre. The movement's aim was to overcome the Germans peacefully and gradually to replace them with an Estonian landowner class and an Estonian bourgeoisie that would dominate local political institutions. But another, more radical centre grew up in the industrial city of Reval. This movement had various tendencies, including social democratic ones inspired by

---

20 This was originally Francis Castles's idea (1978, p. 14); see above, Chapter 6.
21 Kruus 1935, pp. 181–2.
22 Plakans 1981, pp. 254–62; Kruus 1935, pp. 188–91.

German and Russian socialism (the radical currents of Russia being far better known here than in Finland). Unlike the more conservative movement, this grouping of intellectuals attempted to unite the radical petty bourgeoisie and the urban and rural working classes, which all suffered, their very different class interests notwithstanding, from the same political oppression. In 1904 this group, in coalition with local Russians, won control of Reval in the municipal elections.[23] It is important to note that, although Marxist-inspired currents ran through the radical wing, this was not a socialist movement. Nevertheless, the Estonian intellectuals were more susceptible than the Finnish to socialist ideas. Besides the two nationalist tendencies, there was also an unequivocally socialist group of intellectuals in Dorpat, with its own journal.[24] 'The casual circumstance that the social problem is at the same time a national one lends the movement its singular coloring. [The coincidence of these two problems] rendered excellent service to the Social Democrats', a German professor, writing on the Baltic Provinces, bitterly pointed out a little later.[25] In an opposite perspective, this remark means that because of severe oppression along national lines, the radical bourgeoisie was able to attract the Estonian working classes and retard the development of their class consciousness.[26] In any case, a part of the national movement clearly had a radical hue.

Among the Latvians the process went much further. In the 1890s the so-called New Current emerged, attracting the most active representatives of the younger generation and soon becoming the dominant intellectual movement. Ideologically it drew primarily on German social democracy, and the national emphasis was much less evident than in the Estonian movement. In 1904 the Social Democratic party was founded from within the New Current; this party immediately surpassed all other Latvian political groupings, rapidly gaining support from the urban working class.[27]

All in all, then, in the Baltic Provinces both the class structure and the character of the local polities tended to radicalise the national movement. The class

---

23 Kruus 1935, pp. 182–91; Nodel 1963, pp. 123–4, 129, 133–4. The two tendencies were led, respectively, by Jaan Tõnisson and Konstantin Päts.
24 Kruus 1935, pp. 191–2. There had already been a radical national current in the 1880s when socialist ideas were put forth (*Istoriia Estonskoi SSR* 1966, pp. 217–18, 236–8; Nodel 1963, p. 118).
25 The Baltic-born T. Schiemann, writing after the 1905 revolution in Russia (cited in Meiksins 1943, p. 25).
26 *Istoriia Estonskoi SSR* 1966, pp. 405–6.
27 Germanis 1974, pp. 52–3, 149; Ezergailis 1974, p. 114. There was also a more nationalist radical group, which based its ideology on the interests of the Latvian working class, but it remained weak (Germanis 1968, pp. 27–8).

structure bore deep marks of the feudal past, and the weak local polities were much more open to Russian influence than was the case in Finland. Equally important, the indigenous groups here had great difficulty penetrating into established political institutions.

It is in this context that the third condition – the presence of an upper class that was alien but not of metropolitan nationality – played its role. In Finland the Swedish-speaking upper class, first, had no monopoly on the ownership of land but had to reckon with indigenous peasant landowners; and second, it had vested interests in the consolidation of the already existing state. Consequently, it almost willingly nationalised itself, greatly facilitating the process of national integration. In other words, in Finland the combined effect of the two other conditions, agrarian class structure and political autonomy, tended to *neutralise* the effect of the superimposition of national and social boundaries within the country. The Baltic German upper class had no comparable reason to surrender to the indigenous challengers, thanks to its class domination, which was embodied in (weak) local political structures. It therefore seems that in the Baltic Provinces, unlike in Finland, the combined effect of the three conditions served to generate wide opposition to the local upper class and to unite the radical challengers with the anti-tsarist Russian groups. These features became more salient in 1905 and 1917–18.

2   Revolution in the Baltic Provinces, 1905 and 1917–18

In 1905 and 1917–18, although the opportunity for collective action was rather similar in Finland and in the Baltic Provinces, the structural and institutional conditions varied, and with these also the basis for organisation and mobilisation. The question then is, what sort of working-class movement emerged in the Baltic Provinces and under what conditions was it to act in 1905 and in 1917–18?

The 1905 challenge found 'a fully prepared ground'[28] in the Baltic Provinces, where several Estonian and Latvian groups saw it as a chance to alleviate their specific grievances, whether economic, political, or cultural. The unrest began with large-scale strikes in the major cities, immediately after January's so-called Bloody Sunday massacre had provoked a strike in St. Petersburg.[29] The indus-

---

28   Kruus 1935, p. 200.
29   For the sake of conformity, all dates to the end of 1917 are provided according to New Style, although in the Baltic Provinces, unlike Finland, Old Style was used in this period.

trial proletariat took the lead, but thereafter the countryside followed. Tenant farmers wanted the vestigial forms of corvée to be abolished and the tenancy agreements to be revised; the landless demanded better working conditions and better wages. Other peasants, except the uppermost stratum, also participated in the movement.[30] Rural unrest climaxed in the summer and autumn, and in the Baltic Provinces the whole revolutionary movement took on a strong agrarian flavour. Increasingly the poor and landless peasants played the most active role – a feature that differentiated the region from the interior of Russia, where middle-peasant unrest, to use Eric Wolf's terminology, predominated. Lands were confiscated, and the expropriation of all noble, state, and church land was demanded. In the fall jacqueries occurred: nobles were killed, manors burned, records destroyed, churches sacked. The destruction was much more widespread in the Latvian part of the Baltic Provinces, where the German presence was larger. There, 38 percent of the estates were destroyed or damaged, compared to 19 percent in the Estonian countryside.[31]

Among the organised political groups, the Social Democrats and the radical wing of the Estonian nationalist movement gained ground. Demands were made for universal suffrage, the convocation of a constituent assembly in Russia, and the rights of free speech and free assembly. In the autumn the overthrow of the autocracy, the supply of arms to the masses, and the abolition of taxes were added to the other claims. In many districts elementary education in Estonian and Latvian was reintroduced for the first time since its suspension during the cultural Russification of the previous decades.[32] In the Latvian areas the Social Democrats, with their main base in Riga, definitely took the lead. Among the Estonians the corresponding process was slower and less complete, but during the latter part of 1905 both the Estonian Social Democratic party (founded only in this year) and the Estonians associated with the Russian Social Democrats operated quite openly.[33] They alone agitated for the continuation of the revolution, surpassing the radical group of the nationalists, who dominated the city council of Reval. But in the earlier months of 1905 revolutionary demands grew louder among the radical nationalists, too, and their majority envisaged, for national reasons, cooperation with the revolutionary movement in Russia. In the All-Estonian Con-

---

30   Karjahärm and Pullat 1975, pp. 48–58; Kruus 1935, pp. 198–202; Ezergailis 1974, pp. 5–6.
31   Von Pistohlkors 1978, p. 229; Draudin 1959, pp. 7–8, 34, 37–9; 47; Ezergailis 1974, pp. 6–7, 13–14; 23; Karjahärm and Pullat 1975, pp. 117–24; Kruus 1935, pp. 198–202, 208; Raun 1984b, pp. 461–3.
32   Draudin 1959, pp. 44–6; Ezergailis 1974, pp. 6–7, 13–14; Kruus 1935, pp. 200–8.
33   Karjahärm and Pullat 1975, pp. 106–7; Raun 1982, p. 52; Raun 1984a, pp. 132, 137.

gress in December, the major division was between the radical nationalists and the socialists on the one hand, and the more conservative nationalists on the other. Although their economic and social demands differed greatly, the mainstream of all three orientations stressed Estonian cultural and administrative autonomy.[34]

The socialists were supported by urban intellectuals and workers; the latter, who had many connections in the villages, were then instrumental in extending political organisation into the countryside. In the autumn, trade unions, other associations, and even elected committees and popular militias were set up in the cities and the countryside.[35] The agrarian movement seems to have had more of a socialist character in the Baltic Provinces that in most of the other *gubernii*. In Lenin's assessment, the Latvian proletariat and peasantry played a leading role in the whole revolutionary movement of 1905.[36] And G.T. Robinson states in his classic account that the social democrats 'attained their greatest success' in the Baltic Provinces. There, where 'agriculture was organized so largely on a capitalistic basis ... the mass of landless agricultural laborers furnished just the soil that the Social Democrats liked best to cultivate'.[37]

But the devastating agrarian revolt soon expanded beyond the organisational capacities of the social democrats and other radical groupings: their attempts to restrain disorder and pillaging met with little success. In the Estonian areas, urban workers from the largest cities joined the peasants in the jacqueries, or even took the initiative in starting the violence. In the Latvian countryside the destruction of landed estates appears to have occurred independently of urban support; the socialists also disagreed with the peasants who had confiscated land.[38]

A severe repression followed the re-establishment of imperial authority. At least 300 Estonians were murdered or sentenced to death, and the popular organisations were proscribed. Among the Latvians, 2,000–2,500 persons were executed and 5,000 exiled because of their active role in the revolutionary

---

34 Von Pistohlkors 1978, pp. 231–7; Karjahärm and Pullat 1975, pp. 113–16; Kruus 1935, pp. 203–8; Raun 1981, pp. 320, 338–9; Raun 1982, pp. 62–5. As to administrative autonomy, the Bolshevik-oriented Estonian Social Democrats differed from the others in their insistence on an all-Russian, centralist perspective (Raun 1984a, pp. 137–8).
35 Draudin 1959, pp. 39–42; Kruus 1935, pp. 200–2.
36 Germanis 1974, pp. 53–4; Apine 1970, pp. 213–14.
37 Robinson 1932, p. 158.
38 Kruus 1935, p. 208; Nodel 1963, pp. 143, 152–3; Ezergailis 1974, pp. 6–7, 13–14; Raun 1984b, p. 461.

movement. Underground activity continued, especially in Latvia, but the popular organisations, which had grown so rapidly, were liquidated.[39]

In both Finland and the Baltic Provinces, the 1905 revolution launched a mass movement that, although supported initially by the industrial working class, quickly spread to the countryside, involving not only the middle strata of peasants but also – or even especially – the landless. At least part of the explanation for the ability of the poorest rural strata to act on their own behalf lies, in both cases, in the sudden collapse of government and in their strong links with the industrial workers.

But then the differences must be examined. The Baltic reaction was immensely more rapid, more spontaneous, and more powerful than the Finnish: large-scale agrarian capitalism, combined with lingering feudal methods of exploitation, created a strong potential for endemic peasant unrest (as in a number of other *ancien régime* societies). Soon the nationalist bourgeoisie found that they could not control the revolt, and a large proportion of the national bourgeois groups joined the popular challengers (in Estonian areas), or entire middle-class groups were overwhelmed by radical intellectuals from the outset (in Latvian areas) – in both cases, to a much greater extent than in Finland. In the Baltic Provinces, the indigenous bourgeois and middle classes had practically no institutional positions to defend in the local polities. Moreover, the emerging working-class movement did not have effective control over the mass movement. A large-scale socialist organisation was totally unthinkable before 1905, and the notoriously oppressed rural masses could not be organised and disciplined in only a few months. The situation was radically different in Finland, where the Social Democratic agitators' main worry in many areas was how to activate the crofters and landless to vote in the elections of 1907 (a process depicted in Ilmari Kianto's 1909 novel *The Red Line*).[40]

Lastly, in the Baltic Provinces the main non-national target was initially the local German upper class, whereas in Finland it was the Russian autocracy. The intrasocietal aspect with national overtones was more pronounced in the Baltic Provinces than in Finland, where the Swedish-Finnish division was of secondary significance. What counted in Finland was the defence of the Finnish polity and, for the working-class movement, its internal transformation. The Social Democrats' national orientation was strong and authentic. In the Baltic Provinces, in contrast, what counted was the removal of the (German) economic and political oppression, which soon led to demands for radical political

---

39 Karjahärm and Pullat 1975, pp. 150–3; Kruus 1935, pp. 210–11; Germanis 1974, pp. 56, 77–8; Karjahärm, Krastyn', and Tila 1981, pp. 74–6.
40 Cf. Hamalainen 1978, pp. 66–7.

reforms on a pan-Russian scale but only secondarily to a call for the reversal of Russification. Given these ends, connections with Russian revolutionaries were natural.

In early 1917 the popular groups and the radical, notably socialist, challengers were in a situation very similar to the one of twelve years earlier. Again the masses were unorganised and entirely unrepresented in the Baltic political structures, and again the radicals remained scattered, with no established links to popular groups. The Latvian Social Democrats had been forced to go underground. The Estonians, for their part, had made a 'quantum leap' toward much greater political awareness and sophistication after the revolution of 1905,[41] and the most influential current, the radical Young Estonia cultural movement, was clearly socialist in hue. The most marked institutional difference between 1917 and 1905 lay in the position of the national bourgeoisie, and even this distinction was confined primarily to the Estonians. Estonian statemaking and nation-building had progressed from about the mid-1890s on, but they gathered momentum after the first Russian revolution: by 1914 the Estonian nationalists had won control of six of the ten major cities in Estland and northern Livland, thereby obtaining a definite share of political power. But this was just one aspect of how the locus of Estonian public life shifted to the cities. A network of cultural and professional organisations also grew up, and Estonian culture made rapid progress in literature and education as well. At the same time, agricultural societies and cooperatives spread throughout the countryside. In the political sphere, the conservative nationalists' Estonian Progressive People's party, founded in 1905 and the only legal Estonian party until the February revolution, played the main role.[42] A civil society, based on the national bourgeoisie, the independent peasantry, and the middle class, was clearly consolidating itself.

Unlike Finland, the Baltic Provinces were directly affected by the war. Estonian and Latvian conscripts served in the Imperial Army, and, more important still, with the continuation of the war both nationalities acquired their own troops. The Latvian Riflemen's battalions, later renamed regiments, were created in 1915 after the successful German counter-offensive. The same occurred in Estonia, but only after the February revolution, and then on a smaller scale.[43] In any case, during the critical summer and autumn of 1917, both nationalities were to have a domestic apparatus of violence. Also, the German menace was far more real in the Baltic regions than in Finland. By March 1917, half of

41   Raun 1982, p. 65.
42   Kruus 1935, pp. 193–6, 219–20; Raun 1981, pp. 308, 322, 332, 339; Raun 1982, pp. 65–71.
43   Ezergailis 1974, pp. 167–9; Kruus 1935, pp. 236–7.

Kurland was occupied and Riga evacuated; moreover, the German occupation forces were nationally close to the local – German – upper class. Finally, these regions suffered economically much more than Finland. But while the war certainly hurt the Estonians and the Latvians more than the Finns, short-term differences are presumably of secondary importance when explaining variations in the revolutionary process. As Andrew Ezergailis points out in his study of the Latvian revolution, 'The war did not create Latvian radicalism; it was there already in 1905.'[44] Long-term factors conditioned the Baltic developments in 1917 in very essential respects.

Of the two nationalities, closer to the Finns in their political development in 1917 were the Estonians (as they incidentally were in a linguistic and geographical sense, too). Not surprisingly, it was the nationalist Estonian Progressive People's party – the only organised indigenous political force – that took the initiative after the February revolution. Already in April the bourgeois groups succeeded in establishing self-government for the Estonian areas. The Provisional Government of Russia abandoned the local Germans completely and formed a new *guberniia* out of Estland and the Estonian-speaking part of Livland, with its own governmental organ, the Diet. In the elections of early June, the bourgeois parties gained half the seats, the other half being divided between the Estonian Socialist Revolutionaries and the social democratic groupings. Although these parties had originated in earlier years and subsequently developed connections with the revolutionary Russian parties, they were all organised or reorganised only after the February revolution.[45] The Bolsheviks gained just one seat. It is true that the electoral system was based on indirect (if universal) suffrage, that it disfavoured the industrial proletariat in the short run, and that the turnout was low, but this result gives a fairly accurate picture of the parties' relative strength in the spring.[46] In other words, the well-organised bourgeoisie was in the best position to exploit the opportunity created by the war, but in a few months more radical indigenous challengers were able to draw even with it.

Soviets were now being set up, first in towns and then, to a lesser extent, in the countryside, as elsewhere in the empire. The Socialist Revolutionaries dom-

---

44   Ezergailis 1974, p. 204.
45   Raun 1981, pp. 339–40; Raun 1982, pp. 70–2.
46   Arens 1978, pp. 19–23; Kruus 1935, pp. 230–4; Saat and Siilivask 1977, pp. 63, 65, 76–85, 100, 140–6, 163. Urban deputies to the Diet were elected in the late summer and autumn only (see Arens 1978, pp. 23, 26). The Estonian Socialist Revolutionary organisation at first included both Russians and Estonians, but during the summer the Estonian section broke off and became the overwhelmingly stronger faction (Saat and Siilivask 1977, p. 104).

inated all the soviets except one in the spring and summer, as they dominated political activity among the Russian troops that were stationed in Estonia. During this initial phase the Russian soldiers and sailors played a significant role in the principal soviets. The Estonian participants and supporters were mainly factory workers: the soviets were linked to collective action in the towns, action that had begun with the revolution in Petrograd through the form of strikes, demonstrations, and trade union activity. As in 1905, poor peasants, cottagers, and the landless figured among the rural challengers, demanding the confiscation and distribution of noble, state, and church lands, reduction of working hours, and higher wages.[47]

The Estonian polity, established at last, was valued by the non-bourgeois groups, and the other parties gradually came to accept the bourgeois national programme of substantial governmental autonomy in a federal Russia. In the spring and early summer there were no irreconcilable disagreements within the Diet or between it and the majority of the soviets, with the notable exception of Reval.[48] It is indicative of the limited scope of conflicts that a new police force, replacing the tsarist police, was successfully organised in most cities by the town councils and town soviets. In the countryside the police force was administered by the new organs of local government that emerged linked to preparations for the Diet elections.[49]

But, as in many other parts of Russia, a dual power began to take shape. During the summer and autumn the masses were so thoroughly radicalised that the non-bourgeois parties were largely overwhelmed by a more extreme challenge. The Estonian Bolsheviks, starting from modest beginnings in the spring, were able to take over the soviets and organise the masses, first in the cities, but then even in the countryside. Significantly, they gained control of the national troops in September and early October, a couple of months after the troops had been created.[50] In August, Bolshevik membership figures surpassed those of all other parties, thanks largely to the support of urban workers. The Bolsheviks became the largest party in the soviet of Reval in August and gained an absolute majority in September. The same development occurred in soviets in a number of other cities. In the municipal elections, too, the Bolsheviks made increasing

---

47   Saat and Siilivask 1977, pp. 40–57, 63–4, 67, 116–17, 126–31, 178; Arens 1982, 295–301.
48   Saat and Siilivask 1977, pp. 86, 100–4, 340–2. The first serious controversy occurred in early June when the soviet of Reval unsuccessfully attempted to push aside the local Estonian government and to delay the elections to the Diet (Saat and Siilivask 1977, pp. 146–52; Kruus 1935, p. 231).
49   Arens 1978, p. 24.
50   Saat and Siilivask 1977, p. 235; Kruus 1935, p. 239.

progress as the summer wore on and autumn approached.[51] In the elections to the Russian Constituent Assembly, two weeks after the October revolution, the Bolsheviks gained 40 percent of the vote and became by far the largest party in Estonia – a performance equalled or surpassed in very few other *gubernii*. The bourgeois parties won only 29 percent of the vote, with the remaining 31 percent divided among various social democratic parties and the Estonian Socialist Revolutionaries. In all electoral districts but one, the Bolsheviks gained more votes than any other party.[52]

The Bolsheviks gained ground mainly at the expense of the other left-wing parties. In half a year they were able to defeat their competitors not only in the cities but also in the rural areas; indeed, in the Constituent Assembly elections they became the largest party in the countryside.

How did all this happen? Crucial, of course, was the Bolsheviks' ability to capture the soviets – that is, the key loci of popular organisation – and the national Estonian troops. But their success both in the soviets and among the masses would not have been possible had their programme not strongly corresponded to popular grievances. Their consistent anti-government and anti-war line, together with their revolutionary demands, won them large-scale support among the urban workers; and their agrarian programme for expropriating the big properties without indemnification, in accordance with the so-called April theses of Lenin, met with resounding approval among the 'toiling peasantry'. In August they extended the list of agrarian enemies from the nobles, the church, and the state to the wealthy Estonian peasantry. Attacking the landlords more uncompromisingly than any other party brought considerable support for the Bolsheviks, even if their eventual plans to distribute expropriated lands remained vague and at best limited.[53]

When the revolution occurred in Petrograd in early November, the local Bolsheviks took power in Estonia. Unimportant as this move was in terms of the Russian Constituent Assembly elections, in a larger sense it was a watershed. The Estonian Bolsheviks' national programme had been limited, aiming at self-determination and local autonomy with an Estonian administration and school system, whereas the other parties had advocated an autonomous Estonia within a federative Russia.[54] The Bolsheviks' electoral success seems to indicate the secondary role of national considerations. But after the Bolshevik takeover the national question became salient: before its dissolution by the

---

51   Saat and Siilivask 1977, pp. 189–96, 212–16, 228–30; Kruus 1935, pp. 234–5, 239.
52   Saat and Siilivask 1977, pp. 257–60; Radkey 1950, pp. 78–80.
53   See Arens 1982, pp. 303–8; Saat and Siilivask 1977, pp. 182–4, 200, 235–6, 325–6.
54   Saat and Siilivask 1977, pp. 340–2.

Bolsheviks in the end of November, the Estonian Diet declared itself entitled to wield supreme power, and all non-Bolshevik parties included, more or less clearly, Estonian independence in their programmes, thus emphasising their distinctiveness from the Bolsheviks.[55] It was presumably this turn that led to the defeat of the Bolsheviks in the elections to the Estonian Constituent Assembly in January 1918. Also the poor peasants' thirst for land seems to have been detrimental to the Bolsheviks: in December and early January it had become clear that the Bolsheviks intended to preserve the large estates and transform them into collective farms.[56] The turnout rose to 75 percent (from 57 percent in November), but the Bolsheviks' proportion declined, and the elections were stopped. They lost mainly to other leftist parties, especially in the countryside.[57] The tide perhaps began to change, then, following the October revolution. But what remains important to note is the Bolsheviks' phenomenal capacity to supplant the more moderate Left within just a few months in the summer and autumn of 1917.

The Latvians were won over to revolution more easily and more thoroughly. Already in 1905 the Social Democrats had become the most powerful political force, and they maintained this position throughout the later years of clandestine activity. In April 1917 the party, which had earlier joined forces with the Bolsheviks, merged with them more definitely than ever. This Social Democratic party took command immediately after it came above ground in March, and it generally won the majority of both the urban and the rural vote in the various elections held in the summer and the autumn, reflecting weak popular support for the Latvian Mensheviks and the bourgeois parties.[58] As a matter of fact, the Latvian areas were the first in the whole of Russia to be bolshevised, and arguably the party would already have been able to seize power in the summer had there been no Russian troops. Of crucial importance in this respect was the early dominance of the Riflemen's regiments by the Bolsheviks.[59]

Just as the outbreak of revolution in Estonia and Latvia was determined by the international power constellation, so too was the final outcome. In the power vacuum following the February revolution, the local revolutionaries were able to win considerable popular support and then, at the time of the takeover in Petrograd, to seize power. But the German troops drove the local Bolsheviks out in early 1918, and bourgeois organs declared their countries

---

55   Aun 1982; Saat and Siilivask 1977, pp. 374–7; Kruus 1935, pp. 240, 244.
56   Saat and Siilivask 1977, pp. 329–32, 381.
57   Saat and Siilivask 1977, p. 379; Kruus 1935, pp. 242–3.
58   Ezergailis 1974, pp. 192–3; Germanis 1974, p. 248; von Rauch 1977, p. 47.
59   Ezergailis 1974, pp. 134, 179–83, 204, 251; Ezergailis 1982.

independent. After Germany's collapse, the Entente guaranteed the survival of the new, bourgeois republics as a part of their efforts to make the Baltic area 'a barbed wire entanglement'[60] protecting the West from Bolshevik Russia. The German troop withdrawal was delayed until the local bourgeois governments could establish themselves and the Entente and neighbouring Western powers could give material and other assistance. This greatly contributed to local ability to repulse the attacks by Bolshevik troops, which were partly – or, in the Latvian case, overwhelmingly – composed of indigenous groups.[61]

To conclude, the context – the power struggle in Eastern Europe in 1914–20 – was common to Finland, Estonia, and Latvia alike. Decisive for each was the collapse of the two main warring partners, first Imperial Russia, and then Imperial Germany. In every case the revolutionary situation was provoked by the collapse of Russian autocracy, and in every case German troops defeated or at least greatly contributed to the defeat of the revolution. Furthermore, all were saved from German domination by the subsequent defeat of Germany a little later. And finally, the victorious Western powers, in pursuing their own interests, guaranteed the survival of the new states (in the case of Estonia and Latvia) or influenced the orientation of internal politics (in the case of Finland).

The similarity of the international context conceals marked differences in the way the revolutionary process took place, however. The close parallel with pan-Russian revolutionary developments was obvious in the Baltic Provinces. Actually, the revolution in Estonia and Latvia in the autumn of 1917 was a part of the October revolution itself, whereas most of the Russian influences in Finland were mediated indirectly and primarily affected the Finnish state's capacity to maintain order. Also, the Baltic Provinces, like the rest of Russia, had been waging war for three years, with ensuing suffering and economic deterioration.

These differences amount to saying that there was no separate polity in the Baltic Provinces, such as there was in Finland. The corresponding structures were more modest, and the indigenous groups' position in them precarious at best. The radical tendency in the Estonian and Latvian national movements was attributed above to this condition. The Latvians' position in the polity was especially weak, and so national integration never became a key task for them, as it did for the Finnish nationalists. The weakness of local polities also denied the Estonian and Latvian radical parties the opportunity to organise openly; the Social Democrats were under the same repression as in the interior of Russia.

---

60 As Clemenceau put it (cited in Meiksins 1943, p. 172). See also E. Anderson 1977, pp. 340, 350, 363, 376.
61 Schram 1957, pp. 36–49; Kruus 1935, pp. 258–9.

In these circumstances the Estonian – not to speak of the Latvian – Bolsheviks were able to head the mass movement in 1917 by capturing the support not only of the industrial workers but also of the unorganised poor and landless peasants. The other, shallowly rooted left-wing parties were pushed aside rather easily, at least momentarily, when the Bolsheviks turned against the indigenous bourgeoisie and wealthy peasantry. The Latvians and the Estonians followed the 'idealised revolutionary sequence' much more closely than the Finns. True, in all cases the process was launched by the collapse of imperial authority in March. But the consequences were different in Finland, thanks to the distinctiveness of the Finnish polity. The restoration of Finnish autonomy, together with growing self-assertion in the face of the Provisional Government, left the Finnish state totally without control of the concentrated means of coercion within the population. The process was completed by the dismissal of the 'Russified' police. In Estonia and Latvia, the main authority rested instead above all with the Provisional Government, which maintained that authority up to the autumn. The February revolution progressed from gradual mobilisation of contenders, through a rapid increase in the number of people accepting their claims, to the government's incapacity to suppress the alternative coalition. Finally, power was seized by the Bolsheviks.

This development resulted not only from the weakness of the local polities; the Baltic class structure was at least as important. In 1917 the landless and poor peasants, suffering from a mixture of capitalist and semi-feudal methods of exploitation, were again, as in 1905, ready to dynamite the existing order. The industrial working class, moreover, being concentrated in a few big centres, above all in Riga, was in much the same position as the workers in Petrograd and Moscow.

All this places the Finnish situation in 1917 in perspective. First, in the Finnish polity, the socialists shared political power when they started on the road to revolution. Second, in Finland the reformist working-class movement was able to maintain its grip on the masses throughout 1917: the party effectively held the radicalisation in check. The militants took over the worker security guards only after a long struggle – and only after the bourgeois counteroffensive had become evident. In Estonia, in contrast, the local Socialist Revolutionaries and social democrats, who had won the overwhelming majority of the proletarian and semi-proletarian vote in the spring, were rapidly eliminated by a more revolutionary challenger. In Latvia the process was faster and still more complete.

3   Challenges in East-Central Europe

The generalised collapse in 1918 created favourable opportunities for popular collective action in East-Central Europe, the Balkans included. The crucial issues were again the character of the worker movement before World War I on the one hand, and the impact of the war on local power structures on the other. These two factors are presumably central in accounting for the local challengers' ability (or inability) to seize power in a sudden power vacuum.

The Habsburg monarchy provides an illuminating example of the fortunes of a minority region that, at least politically, was far more dependent than Finland: the Czech lands. While these had a strong linkage to a historically remembered polity, the Kingdom of Bohemia, administratively they were divided into three parts: Bohemia, Moravia, and Austrian Silesia. The Czech territory was entirely within the boundaries of the monarchy, making the Czechs a pure example of autonomist nationalism. In terms of class structure, the region bore a certain resemblance to Finland. Bohemia was the most industrialised part in the whole empire, and the Czech lands had an industrial working class, a class of prospering peasants, and a high level of elementary education.[62]

The national movement, notably in Bohemia, was directed against the Germanised nobility and the German bourgeoisie. In the 1870s and 1880s the Czech Social Democrats, a separate section within the Austrian Social Democratic party, had much the same national objectives as the nationalist Young Czechs; then in the 1890s, with the national question generating more and more tension with the Austrian-dominated mother party, they gradually established themselves as a separate party. The national orientation was facilitated by radical tendencies in the nationalist movement, represented particularly by various bourgeois and lower-middle-class groups having their origins in the peasantry.[63] In the 1890s the so-called Progressive movement strove to unite social and national aims, and the Czech National Socialist party, supported by the Young Czechs, was founded to compete with the Social Democrats for the worker vote. Despite growing social differentiation among the Czechs, the national flavour persisted in the working-class movement after the turn of the century. In the first Austrian general elections with universal and equal male suffrage, held in 1907, the Social Democrats gained 38 percent of the Czech vote: they seemed indisputably a central force in a possible Czech – or Czechoslovak – polity. During the war, national fervour spread among the work-

---

62   Pollard 1981, pp. 222–5; Lemberg 1977, p. 323; Orridge and Williams 1982, p. 21.
63   Hroch 1968, pp. 41–61; Koralka 1971, pp. 58–65; Lemberg 1977, p. 324.

ing people, and socialist slogans in strikes and demonstrations were overshadowed by general enthusiasm for national freedom. In the period immediately preceding the foundation of the Czechoslovak state in October 1918, 'the working people became the main force of the Czech national liberation struggle', believing that an independent state would satisfy their social demands.[64]

There are considerable and illuminating differences between the Czech and Finnish experiences, both in long-term political dependence and in the way the collapse of the mother empire affected the national minority. In the Czech case, social and national oppression largely overlapped, and there was no autonomous polity. National oppression was associated with the dominant metropolitan nationality. The Czech experience, moreover, shows how 'relative over-development' can give rise to nationalist movements for liberation and self-assertion.[65] Not surprisingly, although both the Czech and the Finnish labour movements were nationalist, nationalism was more pronounced – and presumably more aggressive – in the Czech Social Democratic party.

In Finland, when the metropolitan power collapsed, a separate polity existed and, significantly, the socialists had an important share of the power. There was no Czech polity in which Czech socialists could act and make their influence felt. What occurred in the Finnish case was a contest for power within an existing polity; in the Czech case the struggle was to create a new polity that would grant the Social Democrats a share of the power and make democratic reforms possible. The first and foremost concern of the Finnish socialists was the preservation and extension of democracy; the first concern of the Czech socialists was the establishment of a polity. Thus, differences in the context – not differences in revolutionary inclinations or attitudes (which, in fact, were quite minor) – led to varying roles for the Czech and Finnish Social Democrats in 1917–18.

Much of what was just said about Czechoslovakia applies to the rebirth of Poland as well, the large political and economic differences notwithstanding. Common to the two cases was a lack of self-administration, which in the Polish regions was exacerbated by partition among three empires. Deep political dependence was combined with an even more vivid remembrance of a historical polity. The dominant wing of the worker movement, the Polish Socialist party, was markedly nationalist. It was unreasonable to expect that the small revolutionary movement, consisting of Rosa Luxemburg's Social Democrats and the socialist Left, would have been able to penetrate peasant masses in

64   Koralka 1971, pp. 57–65, 69–73 (quotation from p. 73); Droz 1971, pp. 75–85, 87–9.
65   Nairn 1977, pp. 185–6.

1917–18 or immediately after. The revolutionaries' inability to co-opt the peasants had been foreshadowed in 1905–7, when the first Russian revolution gave rise to a strong but momentary wave of collective action in the Russian partition. Now for a sizable majority of the organised workers, as well as for a large number of peasants, the rebirth of the Polish state seemed a necessary precondition for all reforms and progress.[66]

Hungary, in contrast, was a country where a powerful challenger armed with a revolutionary doctrine and revolutionary long-term objectives existed in early 1919 in a stricter sense than anywhere else in the region. Of all the successor states, Hungary was the least politically dependent. A formal partnership had prevailed in the empire since the Dualism creating Austria-Hungary in 1867. Economically, Hungary was one of the East-Central European regions where one-sided agrarian progress was the core of the process of capitalist transformation, thanks to demand in the more industrialised parts of Europe. In this case the demand resulted from the western parts of the Dual Monarchy, which as the main purchaser of Hungary's products effected a transformation in its agriculture. The agrarian laws of the mid-1800s assured the predominance of capitalist relations in the countryside, that is, the so-called Prussian pattern of development, with noble latifundia on the one side, and a formally emancipated but downtrodden peasantry providing cheap labor on the other. Only at the end of the century did an industrial working class begin to develop, and then mainly in large centres not directly connected with the agrarian population.[67]

These circumstances left their mark on the Hungarian Social Democratic party, which from its inception in 1890 was a movement of the industrial proletariat, rooted in a few main centres, most notably Budapest. No real attempt was made to mobilise the oppressed rural masses, nor was the organisation involved in their revolts after the turn of the century. The party was merely semi-legal and was harassed incessantly by the authorities. Based on the trade unions, it fought for improvements in working conditions and wage increases and, in the political realm, for universal suffrage: in other words, it was 'reformist' and 'revisionist'. Few intellectuals figured in its leadership. In any case, it was the only Hungarian party with links to popular groups.[68]

---

66   Ajnenkiel 1969, pp. 48–9; Kalabinski and Tych 1962, pp. 204–9, 226–7, 231–2.
67   Berend and Ránki 1974, pp. 31–3, 39–40, 47, 122–9. True, in terms of production there was a connection between the agrarian transformation and industrialisation in that food processing became the leading industry. But at the same time, food processing's share in total employment remained far below its share in production.
68   Erényi 1975, pp. 55–73; Nagy 1967, p. 159; Deák 1968, p. 134; Kenez 1972, pp. 64–5; Király 1977, 407–16.

The party altered its position dramatically in 1917 as social and economic problems worsened and the October revolution erupted in Russia. Workers' councils were set up, and mass demonstrations, strikes, and trade union activity mushroomed, as did revolts and army desertions. But although the radicals gained some ground, the party leaders remained well in control of the swelling movement and maintained the traditional, non-revolutionary line. The decisive change came with the bloodless bourgeois revolution of October 1918. Lacking a clear strategy – they 'responded to the challenge with a sense of shock'[69] – the Social Democrats simply acquiesced and formed a coalition government with the bourgeois liberals and radicals. They accepted a secondary role in the new government, despite being practically the only viable political force in the country, having brought together nearly a million organised workers.[70]

The situation was extremely grave for the new republic. Decay in the economic and social fabric had been accompanied by the disintegration of the army and the return of hundreds of thousands of armed soldiers from the front or from captivity in revolutionary Russia. Together with workers, they played a central role in councils and other organisations demanding rapid and thorough social reforms. Moreover, external pressures added to internal ones. In November the government was obliged to sign an armistice agreement that divested Hungary of about half of her former territory, leaving the country vulnerable to an invasion by Romanian, Czechoslovak, Serbian, and French forces.[71]

While the Social Democrats were, with the bourgeois parties, trying to re-establish the authority of the state, a new, revolutionary challenger emerged. The Hungarian Communist party was founded in November 1918, mainly by a group of former prisoners of war returned from Russia, where they had set up a Hungarian group within the Bolshevik party. Their revolutionary programme gave direction and coherence to the radicalised groups, which were by then disappointed with the socialists' policy. Being able agitators and organisers, the Communists rapidly gained ground in the soldiers' organisations and among the active workers, both employed and unemployed, although their numbers were small compared with those of the Social Democrats.[72]

In a few months the socialists found that the fate of the new republic lay increasingly in their hands. With the gradual weakening of the bourgeois parties, they began to dominate the political scene in December 1918. In January the government was reorganised to the socialists' advantage, and in February

---

69 Vermes 1971, p. 36.
70 Vermes 1971, p. 49; Nagy 1967, pp. 160–1; Tökés 1967, pp. 30–47, 85–7.
71 Tökés 1967, pp. 84–5; Nagy 1967, p. 162.
72 Tökés 1967, pp. 92–122.

the leading Communists were imprisoned. But despite extensive membership and growing power on all levels of central and local administration, the Social Democrats did not succeed in consolidating their position or the authority of the prevailing system (which amounted to the same thing). Internal order was nearing total collapse in February and March.[73]

This situation may be compared with the post-war disintegration in Germany and Austria, where, simultaneously, the social democrats were actually saving the bourgeois states. The Hungarian party, however, lacked the political experience and established membership in the polity that its brother parties had. The Hungarian party was unable to choose between firm action in defence of the prevailing system and adoption of a definitely revolutionary policy; its leaders abhorred the methods of Gustav Noske, but they also rejected the Bolshevik example.[74] In previous years the party had not gained membership in the polity, but at the same time it had not really been persecuted. As a consequence, it had developed a narrow trade-unionist perspective.

From the Communists' point of view, however, the situation resembled the one in Russia after the February revolution. They looked forward to seizing power from the bourgeois-socialist coalition in the same way the Bolsheviks had taken it from the Provisional Government. This opportunity seemed to present itself in March, when internal disintegration culminated, and the Entente issued an ultimatum that would have opened the way for Czech, Romanian, and French troops to occupy the bulk of the country. The prime minister and other bourgeois ministers felt compelled to surrender power to the only remaining organised force, the working-class parties. Béla Kun and other Communist leaders were released from prison, and on 21 March power was transferred to the Social Democrats and Communists. Not only did these two groups then form a common government, but they also merged into a new, unified Hungarian Socialist party. The far smaller but much more resolute Communist faction gained the upper hand, with Béla Kun becoming the leader of the new Hungarian Soviet Republic.[75] Thus Hungary followed the 'idealised revolutionary sequence'.

The national emergency helped the revolutionaries to stabilise the military situation temporarily, and in June the Hungarians even extended the revolution into Slovakia.[76] Four months later, though, the revolution was defeated – a failure in part a result of external pressure, but also of grave errors made by the

---

73 Vermes 1971, pp. 52–4.
74 Vermes 1971, p. 50.
75 Tökés 1967, pp. 129, 132–4.
76 See Toma 1958.

revolutionaries themselves, who antagonised the rural masses by obstinately advocating large collective estates despite the deep-rooted hopes of the poor and landless peasantry for their own farms.[77] In other words, although Hungary did not follow the German social democratic example, it did not follow the Bolshevik example, either.

In both Finland and Hungary the nonrevolutionary social democratic parties were driven to revolution. This development occurred under different conditions, however. First, the Hungarian party had been marginal in the political system; because it had no established position in the polity, it was unable, in the tumultuous conditions of 1918–19, to resist the challenge of a more radical party. Thus the Communists could rapidly gain ground, make the socialists accept the revolution, and finally enlist them in efforts to transform society from bottom to top,[78] a progression reminiscent of the Baltic developments in the summer and autumn of 1917. The Finnish party, in contrast, was deeply rooted in the population and comparatively well entrenched in the political system when the crisis suddenly occurred. It was therefore in a much better position to control the radical but diffuse challenge of the worker guards. It also envisioned a revolution that would extend democracy – but only within the bounds of the capitalist society.

Second, the Hungarian state and society were in a state of dissolution at the time the crisis occurred in October 1918. Hungary had collapsed, and the ruins were left to the socialists simply because no other hope for survival existed. The party had no choice but to take responsibility, first with the bourgeois parties and then, after further deterioration of the situation, with the Communists. It *accepted* power; it did not seize it as the Bolsheviks had done. The statement of the provisional president, Count Károlyi, on 21 March 1919 is symptomatic: he 'transferred the power to the proletariat of the Hungarian peoples'.[79]

The Finnish state, for its part, had one fatal weakness after the February revolution: lack of control over the means of coercion. Otherwise the state remained effective, and civil society, too, was well integrated and strong. After socialists had penetrated into the very heart of the state, then, the bourgeois state and civil society reasserted themselves, causing the socialists to attempt to hold on to what they had gained in 1917. This was the road to revolution in the Finnish case.

Thus, although at one phase both the Hungarian and the Finnish socialists were in coalition with bourgeois parties, after that their paths diverged. In

---

77   Tökés 1967, pp. 185–8.
78   See Eckelt 1971.
79   Cited in Toma 1958, p. 203.

Hungary it was the combination of pressure from the left and fear of internal anarchy and foreign occupation that drove the socialists to revolution; in Finland it was the resolute bourgeois effort to recapture the monopoly on power.

Revolutionary determination on the part of the socialist parties on the eve of the sudden collapse was not of primary importance. There was no such determination in any serious sense in either the Finnish or the Hungarian parties when the Russian and Habsburg empires collapsed. What mattered most was simply the existence of well-organised working-class movements. In both cases a crisis in the state finally drove the challengers to revolution, irrespective of their initial conceptions. Characteristically, in both Finland and Hungary the socialists largely supported the decision about the revolution after it had finally been made: dissenters were few.[80] Only the position of the party and the character of the collapse varied, and therefore also the road to the revolutionary situation.

The significance of the peasants' passivity or hostility for the final failure of the revolution was also similar in the two cases. As stated above, in anticolonial revolutions an alliance between the organised revolutionary party and the peasantry has generally been forged well before the opportunity for revolt has presented itself, and this alliance has been essential for victory. In Hungary, power was instead granted to the revolutionaries without their having formed any such alliance; nor had they any real willingness to do so, either before or after their ascent to power. Indeed, the mere fact that power was *granted* to the revolutionaries made an alliance with the agrarian masses a topic of little moment. In Finland, an alliance did exist, but because a considerable part of the Social Democrats' agrarian following, the crofters, was attracted to the party for economic reasons, when the revolutionary encounter came their support waned. In both Hungary and Finland, the presence of an organised challenger per se was enough to provoke the revolution, but in the longer run the lack of massive agrarian support caused it to be put down or at least greatly contributed to its failure.

In the Balkans, political dependence on the Ottoman Empire made for autonomist nationalism in many cases. Although Romania, Serbia, and Greece achieved independence in the 1800s and Bulgaria in the early 1900s, they remained under the tutelage of the great powers and devoted substantial resources to acquiring ethnically similar or related areas still under Ottoman or Habsburg control. Here, political dependence and the way various regions worked free from it brought about direct economic changes and affected local

---

80   On Hungary, see Deák 1968, p. 135.

class structures. When the Ottoman export controls were abolished in Romania, for example, the country was rapidly integrated into the Western market. Grain trade with the West soon led to a true 'second serfdom' when the powerful Romanian boyar class reimposed servile obligations on the depressed peasantry. In the other cases the consequences were different because Ottoman rule had not left the lands under indigenous landlords but had replaced the local aristocracies with Turkish overlords. The achievement of political independence was automatically accompanied by economic upheaval as the Turkish landlords abandoned their estates to the peasants who had tilled them. No strong domestic landed class sprang up instantly, and independent Bulgaria, Serbia, and Greece became essentially countries of small peasant proprietors. The peasants' economic backwardness and dependence were soon aggravated by increasing overpopulation, divided holdings, and indebtedness. Politically, however, the peasants could not be disregarded permanently.[81] In Bulgaria, most notably, the peasant party, the Bulgarian Agrarian National Union, emerged as the main popular opposition force at the beginning of the twentieth century.[82]

Romania and Bulgaria suffered greatly from the war. Their armies disintegrated in its final phase, and in 1918–19 both countries had a large number of unemployed, armed ex-soldiers, many of whom were influenced by the October revolution in Russia. The same is true to a lesser extent of the South Slav regions. Still, the socialists' plans to seize power were inchoate and ineffective. In Romania and Bulgaria the social democratic parties were founded in the 1890s, and in Serbia during the next decade, but the industrial working classes were small, having hardly emerged from the peasant base, and political pressure and the low level of education made organisation difficult. The crisis of 1917–18 found the social democrats in the peninsula unable, even unwilling, to organise the peasant masses, and also largely unwilling to follow a revolutionary course. The Bulgarians were the strongest and most successful, the Communist party having been founded in 1919, earlier than elsewhere, but in all cases revolution was not feasible, for the extensive peasant unrest remained divorced from socialist guidance. As was mentioned above, the peasant party emerged from the war as the major organised force in Bulgaria; the comparatively weak upper classes were not in the position to control the situation, and the peasants elevated Alexander Stamboliski, the leader of the Agrarian

---

81   P. Anderson 1974, pp. 390–4; Jelavich and Jelavich 1977, pp. 196–221; Bell 1977, pp. 4, 12–13; Berend and Ránki 1974, pp. 49–52.
82   See Bell 1977.

National Union, to power.[83] In Romania the ruling elite had been frightened by the great peasant revolt of 1907, and in 1917–18 it was prepared to concede to land reform and universal suffrage and thereby assure its own existence and a common front against external threats. Also of considerable significance is the fact that Romania emerged from the war as a victorious power, thus doubling its population and territory. The Romanians became enthused with the creation of a Greater Romania.[84]

The Romanian and Bulgarian experiences demonstrate that governmental incapacity to suppress commitment to alternative claims was not enough to bring about revolutionary situations, even in fully formed polities. As in Hungary, the war was not an encounter that would have brought liberation from an earlier political subordination; instead, it seriously undermined the structures of control in the polities themselves. Apart from governmental incapacity, what was important was the presence or absence of a well-organised challenger. The depressed Romanian peasantry had no such challenger before the war, and none was able to emerge in only a few years. One did take power for a moment in Bulgaria, but in this agrarian country it represented the small proprietors; and however land-hungry they were, the land had already been distributed. They were able to elevate the peasant party to political power for a moment, but the party did not envision a new economic and social order.

In the South Slav regions the foundation of Yugoslavia, with Serbia as its nucleus, took precedence over the other objectives of the major political movements. The class struggle and struggle for national liberation were, for the Serbs, Croats, and Slovenes, 'inseparable':[85] not only had social and national oppression been generally superimposed under Ottoman or Habsburg rule,[86] but in a number of South Slav regions the religious division reinforced social and national distinctions.

All in all, in East-Central Europe a revolutionary situation arose only in Hungary, the country where the war had destroyed the state apparatus and damaged the social fabric more thoroughly than anywhere else in the region. Although the worker movement was comparatively well organised, it could acquire power only after a total collapse of state authority – in which lay,

---

83   Bell 1977, pp. 82, 110, 122–53; Rankoff 1977, pp. 466–8, 476–7; Schärf 1967, 195–206.
84   Schärf 1967, pp. 195–9, 218–28; Musat and Zaharia 1980, pp. 44–50; Roberts 1951, pp. 21–32; Chirot 1976, pp. 151, 155–6.
85   Portal 1971, p. 95.
86   Moritsch 1977, pp. 359–63, 366–71, 377–9, 388, 393–4; Portal 1971, p. 94; Kann 1964, pp. 30–56, 243–6. Among the Croats, who had an effective self-administration, a native aristocracy cooperated with Vienna and Budapest.

moreover, a real risk that the whole country would dissolve. In the two other fully formed polities, boyar-dominated Romania and the 'peasant state' of Bulgaria,[87] the worker movements were initially weaker and the pressures of war on the polities themselves more limited than in Hungary.

In the cases in which no states or autonomous polities existed and political dependence was deeper, the first concern of the socialists was to create, or re-create, a (national) state rather than to contest for power in an already existing one. But even after the national revolutions were completed (and, of great importance, the political systems at least formally democratised), the worker movements were not willing or able to convert popular movements into social revolutions. Actually, the weakness or moderation of the locally dominant Polish, Czech, Slovak, and South Slav socialist movements in 1917–19 fits in well with nationalism as a liberation movement (see Chapter 5): social and national aspects were closely intertwined until the twentieth century. Small revolutionary groupings could not harness extensive peasant unrest during the brief period of opportunity at the end of the war.

This situation of course contrasts with that in the Baltic Provinces. The Latvians and the Estonians also lacked established autonomous political structures before World War I, but the revolutionary upsurge proved powerful and culminated in a revolutionary situation. The difference seems to stem from the nature of class structure and political dependence in the Baltic Provinces. The comparatively large industrial working class and the labour-repressive methods used in the commercialisation of agriculture played an important part, but they alone were not enough. What is crucial is that there, and only there, a revolutionary party existed that was based primarily on industrial workers and that at the same time was able to forge an alliance with the peasant masses. The locally dominant challengers, the Latvian and Estonian Bolsheviks, had their mother organisation in Russia.

Why was it so easy for the local counterparts of the metropolitan challenger to gain ground in the Baltic Provinces? The answer seems to be, first, that unlike in the Polish, Czech, Slovak, and South Slav cases, the oppressive local upper class was both alien *and* not of metropolitan nationality. Consequently, the local national movements were not only radical, but they were also willing to develop links with Russian socialist currents. Of no minor importance in this respect was the 'dress rehearsal' of 1905, as Lenin called it, which reinforced contacts with Russian radicals, made evident common interests in the anti-tsarist struggle, and showed that the landless and poor peasants were ready

---

87   The phrase was coined at the end of the nineteenth century; see Sugar 1969, p. 53.

to dynamite the existing order. Whereas in the Polish and Czech cases it was the metropolitan nationalities – that is, the Russians and Germans – who were opposed, in the Baltic regions it was the locally dominant nationality. Opposition to the metropolis was thus largely social in the sense that it was directed against the autocratic system that ultimately guaranteed the indigenous groups' economic and political subordination. Second, the Poles and Czechs had a recollection of a national polity, whereas the Estonians and Latvians had no such memory.

In short, in the Baltic Provinces grievances were widespread among the industrial workers and the exploited peasant masses, national movements were comparatively recent and defined primarily in terms of opposition to a local alien nationality, and opposition to the autocratic system was shared with radical Russian groups. When the revolutionary movement gathered momentum in the metropole itself in 1905 and 1917, the local liberation movements did not, at least in the short run, undertake a determined course of action explicitly intended to create separate national states; rather, they simply opposed the existing social and economic order.[88] The local ethnic and the metropolitan challenges were fused to an extent that was exceptional in Eastern Europe.

4 Fascism in Eastern Europe

A revolution occurred in only a few successor states, and even in these it was defeated. But in most cases the upheavals of the war and the disintegration of the empires led to an extension of political democracy comparable to that experienced in Finland in 1906 (Hungary being an exception).

In this sudden gaining of political rights culminated the specific character of the collective action in the formation of the Eastern European latecomer polities (see Chapter 1). In Western Europe, the working classes had gradually organised and mobilised themselves, first in trade unions and then in political parties, and in this way eventually gained membership in the polity. The parliamentarian political system was basically the form that the balance of power assumed in the state when the dominant groups were forced to acknowledge the popular challenge, or the way 'the entrance of the masses onto the historical stage' was institutionalised in these countries. In the East, corresponding systems did not develop in the same way but were instead copied from

---

[88] In the Latvian areas, where internal oppression by the German upper class was accompanied by an external German threat, the Bolshevik takeover actually advanced more rapidly than in the Russian interior.

the West, achieved when the dominant classes were momentarily weakened but not actually broken by the war. The traditional aristocratic elites, in rough coalition with commercial and manufacturing interests, retained much of their power despite the land reforms, which were carried out merely to forestall new revolutionary upheavals; most of these reforms were limited.[89]

It is in the position of the dominant groups that the basis for Eastern European fascism should first be sought. In all countries of the region, these were to regain much of their political power after a few years. Yet a simple return to the old order was not feasible: not only was it politically inconceivable, but economically the need to mobilise resources was of paramount concern. These countries faced during this period the serious dilemma of all backward countries in the international system, a dilemma that became more serious during the Great Depression, which was far more damaging to Eastern Europe than to Finland. Their economies, both agricultural and industrial, were at the mercy of developments in Western Europe. Economic growth was slow, population increase was faster than in other parts of Europe, and the swelling agrarian proletariat was largely doomed to remain in the countryside. In all the countries of Eastern Europe except Czechoslovakia, the economic structure changed little.[90] Thorough structural reforms, although needed, were unthinkable in the context of a reactionary coalition. The elites and various middle-class groupings recognised the necessity of modernising, but they tried to bring it about without making fundamental changes in social structures. They tried to solve a problem that was inherently insoluble.[91]

Here, then, is the twin basis for Eastern European fascism: the retention by the traditional elites of a substantial share in power in an era of mass politics, together with extreme economic dependence on Western Europe.[92] In a number of East-Central European countries, consequently, the authoritarian regimes developed a sort of symbiotic relationship with the native fascist movements, as the only acceptable way in which the masses could be mobilised and economic and social stagnation overcome. To solve the insoluble, they tried to make the reaction 'popular and plebeian' by promulgating, or at least tacitly approving, the fascist parties or wings: these groups could 'remain in the ruling or local majority parties … they could find a place for themselves in the new parties that the leaders of autocratic dictatorships created to give them-

---

89 In Romania and the Baltic states the land reforms were exceptionally far-reaching. See, e.g., Simunek 1980, 73–4.
90 See Berend and Ránki 1974, pp. 143–257, 285–97.
91 As Barrington Moore (1966, p. 442) puts it.
92 See Moore 1966, pp. 437–8.

selves the appearance of popular backing ... or they could expect the dictators to cooperate with them ... or at least look tolerantly at their activities'.[93]

Relevant examples are Codreanu's Iron Guard in Romania, Gömbös's Party of National Unity and Szálasi's Arrow Cross in Hungary, and Dmowski's movement in Poland. They were distinguishable from the conservative upper classes but linked to them, and in Depression-stricken Hungary the Party of National Unity even had a fleeting taste of power. Gömbös had tried to mobilise the masses in the 1920s, but the miserable conditions that prevailed in the countryside had frustrated his efforts. He therefore focused on fascistisation from within the prevailing system, notably after the Depression had helped him rise to power. Gömbös had a clear vision of the necessity of popular mobilisation for modernisation, a course that, though alien to the conservatives, was of course far preferable to socialist mobilisation.[94] Yet the fascist-xenophobic attempts to raise the country from a state of torpor were as temporary and ephemeral in Hungary as elsewhere. In Poland fascist action was much more limited than in Hungary;[95] and in Romania the authoritarian elites finally put the Iron Guard down, after it had started the march to power in the late 1930s. But everywhere, the same tendency – mobilisation of the masses using a native fascist ideology in the attempt to solve problems of uneven modernisation – was discernible.

Finland's differences vis-à-vis Germany and Italy were mentioned above. In these countries, the fascist seizure of power was made possible by the upper classes' need to restore order after the working class had obtained political influence in the wake of the world war. In Finland, no such need existed. Compared with East-Central Europe, too, the basis for fascism seems to have been rather weak in Finland, where there were no strong landed elites or vestiges of labour-repressive agrarian systems and no common international position. The 'nameless horror'[96] among the upper and middle classes, provoked by revolutionary unrest in 1917–18, was similar in Finland and other countries, but this alone did not provoke a rightist dictatorship or provide the foundation for the fascistisation of the political system.

The situation in the new Baltic states was seemingly different from that in East-Central Europe because the German or Polish aristocratic classes were eliminated and the land distributed to the peasants. The difference, however, is more apparent than real. In these countries, too, there was an incongruity between the political system and the social structure, thanks to the powerful

---

93   Sugar 1971, p. 149.
94   Janos 1982, pp. 244–7, 256–9, 287–9; Simunek 1980, 263–6, 295–302.
95   See Simunek 1980, 236–8, 248, 366–72.
96   Nolte 1968, p. 44.

but transitory mobilisation of the working class. In its national, social democratic versions, the labour movement participated actively in the constituent assemblies, bringing 'ultra-democratic' constitutions to the new states.[97] The political systems functioned ineffectively, however, and soon the strong bureaucratic-military-agrarian coalitions began to usurp the powers of the state. Authoritarian systems emerged in Lithuania in 1926–7, and in Estonia and Latvia in 1934 in the wake of the Depression. In all these cases conservative peasant parties took over initially, but later the systems assumed a more-or-less open fascist character – even in Estonia, where the coup had been justified as a move against a fascist-type threat.[98] The need to reinvigorate the economy and win popular legitimacy was as pressing in the Baltic states as in East-Central Europe. As exporters of agrarian products, in which they almost deliberately specialised (to the detriment of industrial production), the Baltic states were also profoundly dependent on Western Europe.[99] Both in ideology and in reality, then, the peasant landowners became 'the base of the national edifice',[100] though the peasant parties were largely manipulated by their non-peasant leaders and were less autonomous than the Agrarian Union in Finland.

Certain affinities exist, however, between conditions in Finland and in the Baltic countries. Svinhufvud was a conservative peasant leader comparable to Päts in Estonia, Ulmanis in Latvia, and Smetona in Lithuania.[101] The Lapua movement had a pronounced peasantist flavour, and well-to-do peasant parties participated in the Baltic coups. But whereas the Baltic attempts succeeded in fundamentally changing the system and putting their leaders at the head of new dictatorships, in Finland the Lapua movement succeeded only in eliminating the Communists from the political scene and in having Svinhufvud elected president. Indeed, the Finnish attempt to overthrow the existing system was rebuffed by Svinhufvud himself. There is no doubt that the ultra-democratic nature of the Baltic constitutions, as compared with the more conservative Finnish constitution, was one factor contributing to the difference in outcomes,[102] but in a wider perspective even this is just another indication of differences in the entire pre-world war state-making history and, consequently, in the degree of continuity between the pre- and post-war political systems.

---

97   Schram 1957, p. 63; Hyvämäki 1977, 118–21.
98   On the authoritarian takeovers and subsequent fascistisation, see Schram 1957, pp. 63–7; Remeikis 1977, pp. 252–63; Weiss 1977, pp. 211–19; von Hehn 1977, pp. 232–6.
99   Schram 1957, pp. 55–63, 67–70.
100 Cited in Schram 1957, p. 62.
101 Von Rauch 1967, pp. 146, 152–3.
102 Hyvämäki 1977, p. 135.

All in all, the most salient feature in the Finnish case is the fact that fascist intrusions remained limited *despite* the attempt at revolution in 1917–18. Finnish fascism was basically a general bourgeois reaction aimed at the reassertion of the Whites' victory in 1918, which had been partly compromised in 1919 and which seemed threatened by the consolidation of the Soviet Union. As such, it was a culmination of Finnish nationalism – an attempt to regain the long-sought unity that had been lost in the traumatic experience of 1918. The nature of the fascism in Finland resulted from the country's social structure and, notably, from the character of the peasantry. Well organised and mobilised, and with a well-established position in the political system, the Finnish peasantry was totally unlike the Eastern European peasantries, which were frequently exploited by the political elites. Moreover, Finland, again unlike most other successor states, had seen its working class defeated at the very outset of the period. Thus, symbolic adjustments were enough, and increased pressure could be placed on the left without fundamentally altering the prevailing system.

CHAPTER 12

The Formation of Finland in Europe

In the wake of World War I, serious revolutionary challenges emerged on a wide scale in the minority regions that were or had recently been parts of the Russian, Habsburg, and Ottoman empires. In five cases – Finland, Estonia, Latvia, Lithuania, and Hungary – social revolution occurred, and then failed. The war had led to the breakdown or elimination of the vestiges of all three empires and released the minority regions and small polities from their political dependence; but at the same time, it caused destruction and undermined power structures in the dependent regions themselves.

The war occurred at a time when the various nationalities were in widely differing phases of political development. Because of variations in local class relations, distinctiveness of local state structures, and the character of national and class-based organisation, the European latecomers reacted in divergent ways to the common opportunity that arose at the war's end. Finland's reaction was one variant among many.

In this final chapter, rather than simply recapitulating what has been suggested in the previous pages, an attempt will be made to highlight a few key aspects of both phases: Finland's specificity as a 'deviant' Eastern European case before the world war, and its reaction to the common opportunity in the wake of the war. First, the region's economic consolidation, the formation of the Finnish state and nation during the nineteenth century, and the class-based challenge preceding the collapse of the mother empire will be contrasted to developments elsewhere in Eastern Europe or Scandinavia. Then an attempt will be made to delineate Finland's position in a larger constellation of twentieth-century revolutionary situations.

1 Economic Consolidation

The interaction between class relations on the one hand and economic and political dependence on the other laid the foundation for the emergence of an autonomous Finnish economy in the nineteenth century. In attempting to understand the economic consolidation, it is reasonable to start from Finland's position at an interface – that is, from the dominantly exogenous factors. But it is essential to ask why certain exogenous forces were conducive to autonomous development. The crucial question is *how* the exogenous forces – Russian domination and dependence on the capitalist world-market in the West – were *mediated* within Finnish society. Here the crucial endogenous factor, class structure, comes into play.

The problem is reminiscent of Robert Brenner's criticism of Immanuel Wallerstein's work on the rise of the capitalist world-system. Brenner evaluates the role of outside economic incentives and of the indigenous class structure in the development of both the national economy and the state. For Wallerstein, the position of a region or country in the world-market essentially determines its class and state structure. In the fifteenth and sixteenth centuries, for example, the rural Polish nobility was in a position to export grain to the expanding market in the capitalist core areas of north-western Europe by using traditional means to squeeze more surplus from the peasants – that is, by forcing them into a 'second serfdom'. Basically, the market connection determined the strength of the Polish agrarian upper class, the exploitation of the peasants, and the weakness of the indigenous bourgeoisie.[1]

Brenner's argument is just the reverse. He does not deny the importance of market pressures and the like, but he says that the class structure itself tends to shape society's response to economic forces, rather than *being* shaped by these forces.[2] In our Polish example, then, more important than the impact of the capitalist market as such was the previous agrarian class structure, which determined the way market incentives were felt within society and how they affected the course of development. Similar market incentives resulted in different outcomes in Western Europe vis-à-vis Eastern Europe when the price of food rose substantially in the sixteenth century. In short, without an analysis of the endogenous factors, it is impossible to explain how the same economic forces led to different outcomes in different countries. 'It was not the fact of production for export which determined export dependence; it was the class structure through which export production was carried out ... which determined that increasing export production would lead to underdevelopment rather than development', says Brenner, criticising André Gunder Frank.[3]

Brenner's argument provides a starting point for assessing the interplay of exogenous and endogenous factors in the formation of the Finnish national economy. Two factors were crucial: (1) the pulling power of the capitalist world-market that made Finland a raw-material producer for the Western countries, and (2) its role as an exporter of processed products to Russia, made possible by Finland's position as an autonomous grand duchy in the empire.

---

1 Wallerstein 1974, pp. 94–7, 122, 155–6, 304–7, 309–11, 321–4.
2 Brenner 1975, p. 68.
3 Brenner 1977, p. 86.

The critical question is, which groups were best placed to take advantage of this type of market situation? As Brenner suggests, the previous agrarian class structure seems to have been of strategic importance. An independent peasantry existed that had prospered to some extent in the early nineteenth century. But commercialisation and the increase in wealth gained momentum only in the last decades of the century. A transition to dairy farming took place then, aided by the income acquired from the sale of timber. These changes increased the peasants' purchasing power, which in turn spurred domestic industry. The spread of incomes from forestry and dairy farming to a large number of landowners was important in helping Finland escape from the staple trap, that is, from the dominance of a narrow export sector and from external economic dependence.[4]

The Finnish landowning class was not comparable to the one in Poland during the expansion of grain trade to the West; nor was it comparable to the elites in developing Latin American countries today. A situation in which a strong agrarian upper class would have been able to obtain the wealth accruing to exporters and to buy luxury goods rather than invest in domestic industry was totally unthinkable in Finland. The peasant upper class grew stronger, but it was never able to repress the other agrarian classes to the extent that the Polish nobles or, for that matter, the grain-exporting German landowners in the Baltic Provinces of Russia were – just as the freeholding peasantry was in no position to obstruct the emergence of a new industrial and commercial class.

Taken together, it seems reasonable to say that the specific set of class relations that existed in the countryside on the eve of the capitalist transformation had a great impact on the process of autonomous economic development. Brenner's argument appears to apply in the Finnish case. The Finnish class structure contributed greatly to economic consolidation by encouraging the landowning peasants to diversify their activities and by strengthening the home market – which, however, was not a market in luxuries. This process was determined not by the expansion of international trade or by international demand for timber and dairy products as such, but fundamentally by a class structure that brought about the emergence of an internal dynamic of development and at the same time ensured that the commercially induced dynamic from outside would lead to progress, not retrogression.[5]

It is a reflection of Finland's interface position that even such a crucial internal factor as class structure had its origins in an external influence. Its roots

---

4   Hoffman 1980, p. 175; Heikkinen and Hoffman 1982, pp. 65, 84. See also Rasila 1982b, pp. 159–60.
5   Cf. Brenner 1977, p. 71.

go back to the Swedish period, when peasant landownership was consolidated and, concomitantly, economic and cultural conditions rose to levels that, by Russian standards, were quite high.

This relative 'overdevelopment' vis-à-vis Russia, then, provided the second crucial precondition for Finland's economic consolidation. Thanks to it, Finland became not only an exporter of raw materials to the West but also an exporter of processed products to Russia, which stimulated manufacturing and facilitated Finland's autonomous economic development. In a word, the possibilities for taking advantage of market incentives had been created in the earlier, Swedish period. Then came the Russian contribution: the creation of a distinct political unit that served as the framework for this enterprise.

2   The Formation of State and Nation

Economic integration did not remain the only aspect of Finland's consolidation in the nineteenth century. Of all of Russia's western borderlands, only Finland could retain and even strengthen its autonomy in this period. The Baltic Provinces, whose status was largely similar at the beginning of the century,[6] gradually lost the major portion of their institutional specificity. Congress Poland, which initially enjoyed even more autonomy than Finland, was finally incorporated into the Russian administrative structure. And Bessarabia, acquired by Russia in 1812, had lost all autonomy by 1828.

What explains this unique success? In Finland, as in many other minority regions, the Russian government relied on a co-opted local elite to maintain both political order and the prevailing social relations. As Edward C. Thaden has pointed out, the importance of this task explains better than anything else the granting of a political status with special rights and privileges to the elites of the conquered, ethnically distinct borderlands.[7] It is important to note that this task was considerably less problematic for the elite in Finland than in the Baltic Provinces. Because Finland had no heritage of a prolonged feudal class domination, there were no grounds for endemic peasant unrest against the ethnically different upper class as in the Baltic Provinces.[8] Instead, Finland had a free indigenous peasantry that strengthened its position in the course of the nineteenth century, had a stake in the existing system, and successfully masked the growth of the landless groups developing outside the traditional peasant community.

---

6   Jussila 1985, p. 60.
7   Thaden 1984, pp. 4, 231–2.
8   Cf. Thaden 1984, p. 95.

From the Russian point of view, then, the dominant class in Finland performed its principal task well. The Russians never had to intervene in the regulation of relations between the landlords and the peasants, as they had on the southern side of the Gulf of Finland. Moreover, the Finnish elite itself was remarkably loyal to Russia, especially in comparison with the Poles. This is not surprising, given the completely different character of the elites. The Polish elite had been deprived of its traditional independence and had a sophisticated culture and a collective memory of centuries of great statehood. In Finland, rather the contrary was true. After having conquered Sweden's mainly Finnish-speaking regions in 1808–9, the Russian emperor had created out of them a new political unit and thereby elevated the Finnish elite into a position hitherto unknown. Indeed, as was pointed out earlier, the position of the Finnish elite was based primarily on the administration of the new grand duchy.

Thanks to the stability of the internal social order and the loyalty of the local elite – or, ultimately, to the class structure and the newly created state structures – Finland, 'this quiet backwater of the empire and of Europe',[9] was never a primary concern for the Russian government until the end of the nineteenth century. Indeed, Emperor Nicholas I once remarked: 'Leave the Finns in peace. That is the only province of my great realm which has caused me no anxiety or dissatisfaction throughout my reign'.[10] Certainly one reason for the lack of interference by the Russians was Finland's peripheral geographical position, making it strategically less important than the empire's more southern borderlands.[11]

Also, as stated above, the structural relationship between the Swedish-speaking elite and the Finnish-speaking freeholding peasantry made the former exceptionally responsive to the Finnish national movement. As nationalism gained ground within the two groups, a relatively strong foundation for a common culture was created. Nothing comparable happened in the Baltic Provinces, where participation by the German nobles in a national movement was inconceivable. Consequently, the Estonian and Latvian national movements both developed later and remained weaker than the Finnish one. In other words, it simply was not possible to build a common cultural basis for political distinctiveness in those regions, whereas it was in Finland.

Finally, an important further consequence of social tranquillity and of the elite's considerable loyalty in Finland was that national integration could occur

---

9   Ibid., p. 80.
10 Cited in Jussila 1984, pp. 96–7.
11 Paasikivi's reflections, as cited for example in Tanner 1966, pp. 254–69, are enlightening in this respect.

without being noticed by the Russians (or, for that matter, by the Finns themselves, at least in certain respects).[12] The Russians even inadvertently opened the way for nation-building by supporting the increased use of Finnish, which they saw as a means of counterbalancing the influence of Swedish and, ultimately, of Sweden; Finnish was not seriously considered to be a potential language of civilisation and culture. When the Russian government finally realised, in the late nineteenth century, that a state was consolidating itself 'somewhere behind Viipuri',[13] the development could not be easily reversed. The national ideology, including the myth of irrevocably acquired constitutional guarantees for Finnish rights, had become a powerful buttress for institutional consolidation and a common rallying point for the defence of the nascent Finnish state.

3   Political Organisation and Mobilisation before 1917

The above comparisons with Eastern Europe illustrate the importance of a Scandinavian-type class structure for Finland's process of economic and political consolidation. In order to see how this class structure affected the class-based challenge within the country, we must change perspectives. Comparisons with Scandinavia may show how Finland's dependence on the East differentiated it from the political pattern of neighbours to the west and south-west.

Given the Scandinavian class structure, it is not surprising that the party system that emerged in Finland was quite similar to those in Scandinavia. The basic similarity of social structures, level of economic development, and extent of education was reflected in similarities in party systems, as Stein Kuhnle has pointed out. Before 1918 Sweden, Denmark, Norway, and Finland all had four major parties: conservative, liberal, agrarian, and social democratic. The conservative and liberal parties emerged in the late nineteenth century, the social democratic parties a little later, and the agrarian parties were formed after the turn of the century. There were only two major exceptions to this pattern. In Denmark, no purely agrarian party was founded: farmers' interests were represented by the agrarian-liberal Venstre. The other exception was the small Swedish party in Finland.[14]

---

12   This was true notably in the economic sphere. In a number of cases, integration was largely an incidental by-product of narrowly economic reform programmes (Pihkala 1985, pp. 28, 31–32).
13   Cited in Jussila 1984, p. 99.
14   Kuhnle 1975, pp. 25–6; Mylly 1980, pp. 277–89; Elder, Thomas and Arter 1982, pp. 34–42.

But this is not to say that political *mobilisation* and *collective action* were similar in all countries. These were dependent not only on social structures but also on the state-making process, which was different in each of the four countries. This is evident from Kuhnle's comparison: he traces the varying patterns of political participation in the Nordic countries to differences in the level and pace of urbanisation, economic development, and education; to varying institutional heritages; to the presence of mass parties; and to the centre-periphery variation within the countries.[15]

In the Finnish case, the 'institutional heritage' seems particularly significant – that is, the timing of the extension of political rights. Here, dependence on Russia is obviously important. As was suggested in Chapter 1, differing opportunity structures led to a major difference in the preconditions for collective action in the established Western countries on the one hand, and in the latecomers on the other. The distinction is relevant when comparing Finland with the other Nordic countries: Sweden and Denmark were old national states, whereas Norway and Finland were latecomers. Even Norway was in a quasi-independent position from 1815 on, when it had to join a so-called personal union with Sweden. (This included a common monarch – the king of Sweden – but separate political institutions for the two countries.)

Although international crises contributed to the extension of political rights in every case (after all, these were all small countries in nineteenth-century Europe), the international linkage was by far the most dramatic in Finland, and nearly non-existent in Sweden. In Norway and Denmark, international crises provided an initial impetus for democratisation, if only in terms of the rules by which mass political mobilisation was to take place. In Finland, however, the very process of political mobilisation itself was sparked by an international crisis – the 1905 revolution in Russia.[16]

The only conflict that touched Sweden was the Napoleonic Wars. Even though the loss of Finland in 1809 led to the elimination of the Gustavian constitution, representation by estates was maintained until 1866, when it was replaced by a two-chamber system and political rights were extended. The system nevertheless remained conservative, and general male suffrage was achieved only in 1909. Sweden was an established European national

---

15   Kuhnle 1975, p. 69.
16   See, for more detail, Alapuro 1985. On the timing of the extension of political rights and of the mobilisation of the peasantry in Norway and Denmark, see Østerud 1978a, pp. 216–21. Something comparable to the Norwegian and Danish developments took place in Finland in 1863 when Alexander II agreed to the resumption and regularisation of parliamentary sessions after the post-Crimean War crisis in autocracy.

state, even a former great power, and its geographical location was exceptionally secure. Here the working class had to struggle for political rights against domestic powerholders who had been able to formulate the initial rules of the political system and were safeguarded from international pressures. The struggle resembled that in many other Western countries. The Social Democratic party, founded in 1889, was anchored in a strong trade union movement, and the fight for universal suffrage was marked by strikes and demonstrations: the general strike of 1902, for example, was instigated by organised labour. All in all, Sweden, where international crises affected the political system only marginally,[17] had the slowest and most difficult time achieving political democracy, as regards both universal suffrage and the adoption of the principle of parliamentarism.

The workers' struggle was easier in the two other Scandinavian countries, facilitated by the fact that the political systems in the era preceding the period of mass organisation and mobilisation were far more democratic than in Sweden – a result, in turn, of international crises. When Denmark was defeated in the Napoleonic Wars, it lost Norway; and the Norwegians instituted very radical suffrage reforms. About 45 percent of all men more than twenty-five years old became entitled to vote. The new electoral system remained in force during Norway's personal union with Sweden and was considered the most democratic in Europe at the time.[18] Later, in the 1880s, the principle of parliamentarism was forced through rather easily by the Norwegians who opposed the king of Sweden. The Labour party was founded in 1887 and was here, too, based on the trade unions, which, to be sure, were at first dominated by the liberal Venstre. The two parties cooperated in the struggle for suffrage reform (1898) and thereafter until the dissolution of the personal union in 1905.

The Danish labour movement resembled the other Scandinavian movements in that it too originated from and was based on the trade unions. Absolutist rule came to an end after Denmark was defeated in the war with Prussia in 1849, and the new constitution provided for nearly general (but not secret) adult male suffrage in what was at the time one of the most liberal European electoral systems.[19] In these conditions the Labour party (founded as early as 1878) fought for final suffrage reforms and parliamentarism in alliance with the Venstre.

In sum, then, largely internal conflicts conditioned the emergence and expansion of the labour movement in the Scandinavian countries. In Norway and

---

17 See Castles 1973, pp. 314–15, 322; Tilton 1974, pp. 567–70.
18 Kuhnle 1975, p. 17.
19 Ibid.

Denmark the achievement of universal suffrage and the adoption of the principle of parliamentarism were facilitated by comparatively democratic political systems, introduced as a result of international crises. But in all the Scandinavian countries the movement developed through alliances with the liberals, through the painstaking pooling of resources at workplaces, through the foundation of political parties, and through the use of organised labour in the struggle for political rights. In Finland, in contrast, an international crisis led to universal suffrage only a few years after the labour party had been founded and even before a nationwide trade union organisation had been created. The crisis swelled the party's ranks and made it focus on parliamentary work. No assistance was needed from allies within the polity.

The rapid rise of the working-class movement as a consequence of international crisis is reminiscent of certain Eastern European regions. The social structure linked Finland to Scandinavia; the role of sudden changes in the metropolitan country linked it to Eastern Europe. The resemblance to Scandinavia was obviously stronger in the pre-1917 period, all the differences in timing notwithstanding. The Finnish worker movement played a central role in the national integration of the workers and in the process of class integration.

4   Revolutionary Situations in Small European Polities

Most revolutionary outbreaks in formerly colonial countries have been initiated by one dominant challenger combining both national and revolutionary aspirations. In many cases such a situation is self-evident: a revolutionary situation could have arisen in Vietnam, Algeria, or Angola only because a single powerful movement had asserted itself. Only such a challenger was able to break the colonial or neo-colonial bonds, and nationalism was a natural ingredient in the revolutionary struggle. In Eastern Europe on the eve of World War I the situation was very different. Various local challengers existed, many or all of them organised to some degree. Varying shades of national and revolutionary aspirations were represented, and frequently the organised expressions of the two strands stood in opposition to each other. In Romania and Bulgaria, ties to the mother empire (if not to the great powers) had already been severed, and nationalism was increasingly becoming a civic religion for the state. In these countries the local nationalist rulers therefore faced radical opposition primarily within the polity. This was not the case among the Poles and the Czechs, who fought for self-assertion against foreign rulers; but even among them the idea of a national interclass community, implied by the liberation struggle, was not as evident in 1914 as it had been in the previous century, having been confounded, but not overwhelmed, by a socialist challenge. Frequently, middle-class nationalism and various socialist parties existed side by side. Still another, and arguably the most notable, difference between the Eastern European situation and the colonial one was the absence of an alliance between the socialists and the peasant masses – in all areas except the Baltic Provinces and Finland.

These differences between the colonial countries and the small nationalities of Eastern Europe are obviously linked to differences in the nature of political dependence. In the Afro-Asian possessions of the European powers, groups that were distinct both racially and culturally controlled and exploited territories far from their homelands. Imperial expansion within Europe, instead, generally proceeded through the annexation of geographically contiguous areas; thus, cultures as well as economies were likely to be much more similar. In the former cases, the gap between the rulers and the ruled, the colonisers and the colonised, tended to be much greater than in the latter.[20] There is no doubt that clear-cut opposition between nationalist local revolutionaries on the one hand and the metropolitan power with its local representatives and collaborators on the other emerged more easily in the colonial context than in the European.

Furthermore – and most important – there was considerable variation in the way in which the political arena was finally opened. The character of the organised challengers is crucial in this respect. In the colonial cases a sort of dialectical relationship existed between the indigenous challenger and metropolitan repression, with the former contributing actively to the emergence of the revolutionary situation itself. In Eastern Europe the decisive point was how the generalised collapse in 1917–18 was mediated through existing institutional and class structures, and how existing forms of political organisation produced or failed to produce a revolutionary situation. The crucial process was not an interaction between two conflicting partners but rather a *reaction* on the part of domestic challengers to the collapse of the metropole.

In other words, at issue in the peripheries under colonial control was a process of organisation, mobilisation, and collective action in the face of repression. These countries were generally forced to go through a hard, painful, and often slow process before final liberation or revolution; hence the particular relevance of the triple perspective of class relations, the capacity of the metropole to exercise control, and nationalist and socialist political organisation at their intersection. What counted in Eastern Europe was the opportunity, or, more

---

20   See Orridge 1982, p. 45.

precisely, the reaction to an opportunity: what kind of immediate repercussions the opportunity had on organisation, mobilisation, and collective action.

All these rather evident differences point to the importance of *accident* in determining the revolutions among the smaller nationalities of Eastern Europe. Whether or not a revolutionary situation arose was determined by the circumstances that happened to prevail in 1917, 1918, or 1919. A difference of a decade or so in timing could easily have made a great difference in the position of the domestic contenders and hence in their capacity to react immediately to an opportunity. Perhaps the only definite exception is Latvia, where the revolutionaries were easily able to forge a strong alliance with the peasants. But in Finland, for example, domestic troops were still in the country at the beginning of the century, and, despite their modest size, their presence would have radically altered the impact of the metropolitan collapse, had it occurred at that time. In Estonia, national consciousness might have been much more developed ten years later. In Hungary, the labour movement was poorly developed at the turn of the century. And so on. For this reason, then, the sheer existence of an organised challenger may have been more significant than the degree of its revolutionary determination. Whether or not the organisation led to revolution depended not so much on the degree of revolutionary fervour as on the context in which the worker movement acted. In the Czech context the rather non-revolutionary socialist challenger was active in the gaining of independence, whereas in Finland a comparable challenger spearheaded the revolution. In these conditions even the 'idealised revolutionary sequence' was not necessarily followed, as plausible and even self-evident as it may seem. Such a sequence presupposes organisation and mobilisation in the face of governmental control or repression. But in Eastern Europe this development was not true to the same extent as in Western Europe or in former colonies – an idea that has run through this entire book.

5   State and Revolution in Finland

In Finland, the pattern of class relations, state structures, and political organisation differed from that in the other regions between Russia and the rest of Europe. The existence of an autonomous polity within a multinational empire at the outbreak of World War I was unique. The other nationalities either had no comparable polity of their own (the Estonians, Latvians, Lithuanians, Poles, Czechs, Slovaks, Croats, and Slovenes) or had already gained formal independence (the Romanians, Bulgarians, Serbs, and of course, in their specific way, the Hungarians). The Finns were the only nationality to have a largely

Scandinavian type of social structure and political system. The presence of a strong landowning peasantry, together with the attachment of the Swedish-speaking upper class to the state bureaucracy, had led to the easy adoption of the Finnish language and Finnish culture by the latter group and to a rather frictionless national consolidation by the beginning of the twentieth century. The 1905 revolution in Russia brought the Social Democrats into the Finnish polity, but the party's character was determined by the preceding state-making and nation-building. The worker movement developed in close connection with other types of popular organisation: it was national as well as reformist, much like its Scandinavian brother movements, and it focused specifically on the state. Ties between town and country provided it with massive agrarian support, which in 1916 helped it win an absolute majority in Parliament, but there was little potential for violent agrarian unrest.

Being dependent on Russia, this polity, along with the rest of Eastern Europe, faced the opening of the political arena in 1917–18. But the mode and the impact of the collapse had a specific character in the Finnish case. The war had hit the core territories of Russia and Austria-Hungary hard, bringing down an edifice that had long been decaying internally; defeat in war, by eliminating the main instruments of repression, caused the final collapse. Latecomer polities and minority regions, in contrast, were not necessarily exposed to the war's ravages to the same degree. Many of them probably escaped the most severe blows because they were not the main targets, and their social structures and institutions may in any case have been more resistant than those of the metropolitan countries. In a word, fissures in the power structure may well have been initiated from the outside in a much more definite sense than in the mother empires.

It is important to note that this characterisation fits Finland better than any other small polity or minority region in Eastern Europe in 1917–19. The war wrought economic and social damage on all the others *before* the revolutionary situation emerged or revolutionary movements seriously threatened the existing order. This holds for the Baltic Provinces, Lithuania, and the partitions of Poland, various minorities in the Habsburg Empire, and Romania, Bulgaria, and Serbia. Unlike them, Finland was not destroyed or subjected to severe damage by the world war. Although a revolutionary situation did arise in Finland, it was not, as in the Baltic Provinces and Hungary, the result of the disintegration of metropolitan or domestic power. It resulted, rather, from the polity's dependence on Russia for maintaining order, combined with an internal precondition: the exceptionally strong position of the working-class movement in the political system. These factors permitted the Social Democrats to proceed and push through reforms *within* the existing system. Finally, a revolution occurred in which the labour movement attempted to counter the bourgeoisie's effort to recapture political power. The party basically attempted to *retain* the power it had gained after the February revolution. In the Baltic Provinces, instead, the revolutionaries really *seized* power, and in Hungary they *accepted* it – in both cases only after the state machinery had been destroyed in the war.

All this suggests that Finland was a kind of mixed case between West and East. This interstitial position can be seen by relating the Finnish Social Democrats to modern worker movements in both the core and the periphery of the world economy. Melvyn Dubofsky has suggested that the development and fluctuations of a world economy since the 1870s provided the larger context in which regional and national working-class movements have emerged and grown up. Moreover, he maintains that the most decisive shifts in class relations and in the development of worker movements have been associated with war and its impact on domestic politics. And finally, he proposes that a fundamental difference can be identified between patterns in the core and in the periphery: that in the former, worker movements have been gradually but thoroughly integrated into the prevailing system of power relations, whereas in the latter, worker movements have been more closely related to the dynamics of inclusive national movements and have also remained more prone to revolutionary forms of action.[21]

On the whole, Finland fits into this perspective well. Understanding the development of the world economy, mediated through the European state structure, is absolutely necessary for understanding the emergence and development of the Finnish worker movement. Likewise, the wars and their impact on domestic politics decisively influenced class relations and the growth of the Social Democratic working-class movement. And finally, in peripheral Finland the labour movement was bound up with the dynamics of the national movement and proved prone to revolutionary forms of action in 1918.

Interestingly, though, the third point – the only one that includes a hypothesis about the difference between the core and the periphery – raises some problems. Although Finnish workers participated in a revolutionary attempt in 1918, they had been well 'integrated into the prevailing system of relations' in the preceding years – a characteristic, supposedly, of the core. This deviation illuminates the nature of state-making in Finland, or the fact that, in a sense, Finland lies between the European core and its periphery. The Finnish social structure, providing fundamental preconditions for state-making, was similar

---

21   *Newsletter of the Fernand Braudel Center for the Study of Economies, Historical Systems, and Civilizations*, no. 5 (15 August, 1981): 2.

to that in Western Europe. But the control system and the opportunities open to the worker movement were of an Eastern European type: in the early twentieth century opportunities changed rapidly and quite independently of the strength of domestic collective action. Basically, this pattern resulted from the country's interface position between a core state, Sweden,[22] and a peripheral state, Russia. Under the former Finland's social structure was established and the basis for its economic and social development laid; from the latter it attained its ultimate system of control, against which the worker movement was obliged to mobilise, organise, and act collectively. In combination, the two conditions created a worker movement that finally, in 1917–18, was forced to attempt a revolution.

Finland was, then, a special case among the (Eastern) European latecomer polities of the 1800s and early 1900s – which, in turn, were exceptional among other peripheral states. But their opportunities differed not only from those in the peripheries under colonial control but also from those surrounding the post – World War II upheavals in East-Central Europe. In 1918–19, the rapid and coincident disintegration of Russia, Austria-Hungary, and Germany created a power vacuum and opened the way for a contest between domestic social forces that determined the nature of these countries' political systems. While the international system played an important role, direct foreign intervention of the type experienced in the Baltic countries was not the rule – a situation that was only natural, given that all the principal powers in Central and Eastern Europe had collapsed and that the Western powers were forced to exert their influence more indirectly.

Corresponding opportunities did not arise in the wake of World War II. Then, too, the ravages of the war sealed the fate of the old, inter-war systems. But this time the eventual victors not only brought about the ruin of the old systems; they also shaped the new ones, thanks to the division of Europe into zones of influence. Germany collapsed, but the Soviet Union consolidated itself. In this perspective too, then, the opportunities created by the generalised collapse resulting from World War I appear unique.

---

22   Wallerstein (1980, p. 203) argues that, from 1600 to 1750, Sweden was a semi-periphery, but nonetheless one that 'clearly heads the list' of the semi-peripheries.

Postscript to the Second Printing

1   A Personal Note[1]

The origins of this book date to the academic year 1973–4, which I spent at the University of Michigan, Ann Arbor.[2] In Charles Tilly's seminars, I became familiar with the resource mobilisation approach, which was later notably crystallised in his *From Mobilization to Revolution*.[3] Those responsible for the Fulbright program had decided to send me to the Center for Research on Social Organization run by this great scholar whom I knew only by name before visiting Ann Arbor. The most appealing feature of his approach to collective action was the idea that all forms of contention, both crises and politics as usual, are to be understood and analysed in the same basic framework, as struggles defined by the resources at people's disposal; thus, there is no fundamental difference between the forces at play in everyday political activity and in revolts, rebellions, and revolutions. One can make sense of all these varieties of contention by examining the hard facts stemming from people's capacity or incapacity to act on their own behalf. As I saw it, there was a sense of disillusionment in this perspective that added to its strength, a sense of disillusionment that I had found earlier, in a most impressive form, in Barrington Moore's clarity of vision when analysing the social origins of dictatorship and democracy.[4]

Somehow this approach resonated with the sensibilities of someone raised to adulthood in the Finland of the 1960s. One of the big questions of the epoch – and an issue that typified the gap between the generations – was the stand taken on the 'problem of communism', or on the large following enjoyed by the extreme left, which, in Western Europe, was comparable in scale only to the levels of support found in France and Italy. In Finland the emerging attitude toward Communists stressed a 'rational' approach, by accepting them as a legitimate political group. Consequently, in dealings with the Communists the same rules were to be applied as in dealings with other political groups. This integration strategy (which was to prove successful) was propagated by the new social sciences, above all by Erik Allardt.[5] It seemed to represent a

---

1   I thank Rod Aya and the members of the Helsinki Research Group for Political Sociology for their helpful comments and suggestions.
2   I have drawn here on Alapuro 2004, pp. 139–41.
3   Tilly 1978.
4   Moore 1966.
5   See, e.g., Allardt 1962.

cool, analytical approach to the Communists, in contrast to the emotional and irrational anti-communism that had prevailed in Finland since 1918, when a workers' revolution was defeated by the bourgeoisie after a difficult and costly war. The new perspective was like a breath of fresh air compared to the sentimental patriotism and anti-intellectualism of the older generation. Moreover, it was in line with the literary modernism of 1950s Finland, an intellectual current that strove to rid the language of all imprecision and dramatisation, as a part of breaking with pre-World War II patriotism and its calls for rigorous national unity.

Thus, in the 1970s and 1980s, I found in Moore and the resource mobilisation approach (or so it seems in retrospect) the tools for constructing my own sense of the political conflicts in Finland – in my case not the 'problem of communism' as it appeared in the 1960s or the 1970s, but the dramatic initial point from which this problem derived, or appeared to have been derived, namely the civil war of 1918. This conflict was the subject of reappraisal in the 1960s, along with the emerging new attitude towards the Communists, and both phenomena contributed to the erosion of the traditional nationalist culture in Finland. Along with many of my peers, I shared these emerging views, as well as sympathy toward the rebels of 1918. Moreover, of no minor importance to the formation of these views was the notion of revolution present in the imagery of the 1960s in Finland and elsewhere.

The latter phenomenon was central to Eric Wolf's *Peasant Wars of the Twentieth Century*,[6] with which I became familiar at Michigan, along with Tilly's texts. When reading his account of the revolutions that had marked the century in Russia, China, Vietnam and elsewhere, the fervour and depth of the social conflicts in these countries seemed enormously more pronounced than those of early twentieth-century Finland. This impression contradicted the view commonly held by Finnish historians that it was the depth of social cleavages, the grievances of the industrial and agrarian workers, the food shortages and unemployment provoked by the two revolutions in Russia in 1917, and finally the breakdown of social control, that precipitated the Finnish civil war (see below).

In other words, the resource mobilisation view of the political process, cleared of all excessive dramatisation, and the impression I had of the comparative moderation of social conflicts in Finland combined to underpin my dissatisfaction with the prevailing picture. Consequently, both these concep-

---

6   Wolf 1969.

tions placed their stamp on my interpretation of the civil war. I saw the Finnish revolution not as a breakdown or a release of dark forces, but as the result of a political process, of a struggle for state power that Finns were forced to wage under the conditions imposed on them in 1917. Moreover, the Finnish revolutionary movement was far removed from those that seized power in Russia, China or Vietnam, as the latter were self-conscious revolutionary movements with a doctrine and a political strategy.

2 A Recapitulation

Today, a quarter of a century since the dissolution of the Soviet Union, it is customary to state that Finland is part of the West, or that Western Europe is its proper reference group. The argument presented in the book suggests, however, that Finland should be viewed, especially from a long-term perspective, as lying between West and East.

In the nineteenth century, after Sweden ceded Finland to Russia as a by-product of the Napoleonic wars, Finland was, like many Eastern or East-Central European minority regions, dependent on a large empire. Nevertheless it differed in two respects. First, it exhibited many more Western social and institutional structures (which it shared notably with Sweden) than these regions. Moreover, it enjoyed the benefits of an exceptionally autonomous administrative framework; it was a separate unit, a Grand Duchy in the Russian empire. The Finnish combination of Eastern-style dependence and a Western-style society was therefore unique among the regions and polities that were to emerge as so-called successor states in the wake of World War I.

It was Finland's position at the interface of East and West that provided the basic preconditions for the Finnish revolution of 1918. The conflict was unleashed by the paralysis of established means of coercion, due to Eastern dependence, accompanied by the strong presence of a non-revolutionary worker movement, developed on the basis of Western structures and institutions.

During the nineteenth century, an ideology of integration was created for the Finnish polity. Fennoman civil servants and other nationalists in the educated class developed an ideological position based on their cultural proximity to the country's Finnish-speaking majority. Their self-image was founded on the supposed loyalty of the population towards its 'own' educated class. At the turn of the twentieth century, a worker movement emerged as part of a wave of economic, cultural and political popular organisation; it resembled the corresponding movements in Scandinavian countries.

After Russia's February Revolution of 1917, this Social Democratic movement entered a coalition government, and the prime minister was chosen from its ranks, thanks to the movement's parliamentary majority. This occurred at a moment when the Russian crisis had left Finland without any established means of coercion – including the army or even the police. Together, these two circumstances crucially advanced a process that consolidated an alternative power centre in the country. A major step toward dual power was taken when the Social Democrats were removed from government and defeated in subsequent parliamentary elections. The party was removed from power as the result of a controversial conflict in which the Russian Provisional Government refused to transfer imperial prerogatives to the Finnish Parliament and dissolved it with the support of Finnish bourgeois groups. In the autumn of 1917, the conflict escalated to the point where the bourgeois government decided to restore order and disarm the worker guards. The worker movement resisted, and a revolution broke out, which was crushed in three months.

In this interpretation, the Social Democrats were simply attempting to maintain the power and advantages they had gained within the political system by the middle of 1917. Rather than actively seizing power, they were striving to counter the bourgeoisie's attempts to recapture it. What mattered most was, first, the strong grip of the worker movement on state power, which had no coercive apparatus of its own, and then the contested loss of this control.

The revolution was strikingly proletarian: unlike most revolutions, intellectual groups were not involved.[7] In Finland the intelligentsia had developed a national ideology only a few decades earlier, and the entire 'national' educated class was horrified by this breakdown in solidarity among the people. Indeed, it was this shock that triggered Finland's own version of fascism, the Lapua movement. The Lapua movement was no distinct group or specific party, in contrast to many other countries; rather, it was a common bourgeois reaction to the Finnish communist movement, which originated in the harsh suppression of the revolution and which enjoyed remarkably close ties to the new Soviet state.

For such an interpretation I found support, above all, in Charles Tilly's model of the proximate causes of revolutionary situations. Nevertheless, the revolutionary process in Finland failed to follow Tilly's 'Idealised revolutionary sequence', which begins with the gradual mobilisation of contenders and is followed by a rapid increase in support for their claims and, finally, by unsuccessful government efforts to suppress the alternative coalition. By contrast, a peculiarity of the dependent character of the Finnish revolution is that the

---

7   See, e.g., Goldstone 2003; Goldstone 2014.

road to revolution began via the third proximate cause, the incapacity of the government to suppress an eventual revolutionary contender. This contender only appeared gradually, as a result of a laborious process of mobilisation. Thus, Tilly's model is useful not because of its consistency with Finnish developments, but because its three proximate causes and the Finnish deviations from them shed light on the particularity of the Finnish case, allowing comparisons with revolutionary situations in other places and times. What is crucial for understanding the Finnish revolution is an appreciation of the specific interconnection between external and internal factors – the paralysis of the apparatus of coercion as a consequence of the crisis in Russia, on the one hand, and the strong position of the domestic worker movement at the outset of the crisis, on the other.

3 The Reception of the Comparative Perspective

3.1 *Finland Compared*

The goal of the book was comparative in two senses. The intended audience was both non-Finnish social scientists and Finnish historians. For the former, the book was an attempt to place the Finnish case within a larger framework through theories of state-building and revolution, and for the latter it was an attempt to demonstrate that the Finnish case was not as unique as Finnish historians had liked to think. It was an attempt to show that the Finnish experience can contribute to the wider discussion on revolutions and their preconditions and that the wider discussion on revolutions can contribute to understanding of the Finnish case.

The former objective was the subject of comment from several social scientists. For instance, John D. Stephens began his review by asking, '[w]hy should you read a book about a small country that … has no apparent characteristic that makes it a special case worthy of general attention?'[8] His answer was that Finland indeed *has* special characteristics which make it interesting to comparativists, and that the book's theoretical and methodological approach provide an appropriate framework for demonstrating Finland's comparative relevance, as the study is an application of the 'case in comparative perspective' method.[9] Similarly another sociologist, Francis G. Castles, welcomed the work for being 'explicitly comparative, facilitating the assimilation of knowledge

---

8 Stephens 1989, p. 483.
9 Stephens 1989, p. 484; quotation marks in the original.

of the Finnish case into a knowledge-base consisting, only too often, almost exclusively of the experience of the major powers'.[10] He also found essential for understanding Finnish development and its many paradoxes the suggestion of Finland being at the interface between East and West and the ensuing 'subtle interlinkages between endogenous social structures and exogenous factors'.[11] In their reviews, Peter Kivisto and Lauri Karvonen also found the comparative perspective crucial in an investigation focusing (primarily) on one case. Kivisto characterised it 'a comparative history of the middle range', as the author had appreciated historical contingency by adopting 'sufficiently delimited comparative parameters to enhance the distinctiveness of his case study'.[12] Karvonen considered the comparative design the 'most obvious merit of the book', and described its comparative logic by saying that 'the study as a whole lies somewhere in between a case study and a thoroughly comparative investigation'. This logic was evident through the book's presentation of three explanatory factors – the processes of state-making, the external dependence of the country and the Finnish class structure – and two points of historical-geographical comparison: Eastern Europe and Scandinavia.[13]

The comparative framework was also recognised by a number of historians. Anthony F. Upton, the author of the most comprehensive scholarly history of the Finnish Civil War of 1918,[14] wrote, '[t]he merit of Alapuro's book lies not in any new material he presents but in his use of familiar material to produce an explanatory model that can both give a coherent explanation of the pattern of Finland's development and be used to generate generalizations, on a comparative basis, about the politics of small nation states'.[15] Furthermore, David Kirby and Henrik Stenius, two experts on modern Finnish history, found that the comparative perspective produced new insights, a view echoed by Jorunn Björgum.[16]

---

10   Castles 1991, p. 57.
11   Ibid.
12   Kivisto 1989, p. 106.
13   Karvonen 1990, pp. 89–90.
14   Upton 1980.
15   Upton 1990, p. 1237.
16   '[The book] provides a new perspective to Finland's emergence as an independent state; comparisons with other new states are especially valuable' (Kirby 1989, p. 319). See also Stenius 1989, p. 143, and Björgum 1991, p. 892. Of the two established Finnish historians who reviewed the book, Eino Jutikkala, (1989, p. 120) in his rather sceptical review, recognised the fruitfulness of comparisons, whereas his colleague Jaakko Paavolainen (1988) was mostly perplexed by them.

3.2 Problems in the Use of the Comparative Approach

However, the comparative framework failed to receive a positive reception from all quarters. Notably the historian Peter Baldwin voiced criticisms, even though he too considered the idea positive. According to Baldwin, the comparative perspective was the 'main virtue' of the book, and I had 'sought to make Finland a matter of concern even to those of us who are not Finnish specialists, Balticists or even interested in Northern Europe'.[17] Yet for him the problem lay in the application of the comparative approach: the study was limited in originality and 'marred by its disjointedness'.[18] Moreover, he pointed to a lack of consistency in the analysis of the relationship between internal and external factors.

In Baldwin's view, the first half of the book was devoted to 'a summary' that sets the scene for the explanation of the abortive revolution, and it is only in the treatment of the revolution itself that the author 'begins to engage with other scholars' arguments and develop his own'.[19] This may be true in the sense that the book only engages in explicit debate with other interpretations (the prevalence of the 'volcanic' view of collective action, for example) over the events in 1918. This does not mean, however, that the treatment of the developments in the nineteenth and early twentieth century merely summarises earlier research. To take one example, the argument about the nature and position of the upper classes in the nineteenth century and their relationship with popular groups was key to understanding the radical political reforms of 1906 and the nature of the revolution in 1918. Moreover, the nature of the conflict – in addition to Finland's position between Scandinavia and Eastern Europe – arguably helps elucidate Finnish fascism as a general bourgeois reaction at the turn of the 1930s. Thus, the Lapua movement was included in the book as a logical consequence of earlier events rather than being, as Baldwin claimed, 'an afterthought, tacked on for the sake of some sense of completeness'.[20]

---

17 Baldwin 1990, p. 98.
18 Baldwin 1990, p. 99.
19 Baldwin 1990, pp. 98, 99.
20 Baldwin 1990, p. 99. The most appropriate point about disjointedness concerns the chapters on the territorial integration and the regional consolidation of party support (Baldwin 1990, p. 99); Lauri Karvonen (1990, p. 92) shared this opinion. It is true that the narrative could have been told without those two chapters, even though the chapter on regional integration, in particular, adds one dimension to the consolidation of the perspective of Finland being at the interface of East and West. Nevertheless, Peter Kivisto (1989, p. 196) found the discussion of regional differences 'particularly noteworthy' and the descriptions of variations in levels of political mobilisation and allegiance to the Social Democrats or the Agrarian Union 'especially insightful'.

On the key issue of the relationship between external and internal factors, Baldwin stated the following:

> One of the major problems with the book is the ambivalence with which Alapuro reconciles his major tension, that between internal and external factors. It would, of course, have been perfectly reasonable to argue that the story was one of both varieties of influence. The problem is that Alapuro seems to argue both sides of the case with equal conviction, but in different places, coming therefore to no consistent conclusion. His main point, advanced above all in the chapter on the revolution, is that external factors played the crucial role in small and dependent nations … In the conclusion, on the contrary, Alapuro seems to have swung around and now elaborates the significance of internal factors – although this does not prevent him from tergiversating once again and tracing back the determinants of Finnish class structure to external events.[21]

The last comment refers to a passage in which I write, 'It is a reflection of Finland's interface position that even such a crucial internal factor as class structure had its origins in an external influence' (p. 238). The formulation may be misleading, but my point here, as well as in the book more generally, was, contrary to Baldwin's argument, that there simply is no 'consistent conclusion' on the relative role of internal and external factors in the Finnish state-building process. Their respective roles must be analysed in each particular instance separately, as they varied in different contexts and at different levels. In one sense, Finland's position at the interface of East and West is evident in the way the social and economic structures and political institutions established under Swedish rule met Russian autocracy to produce favourable economic development in Finland in the nineteenth century. However, this position is also relevant at a different level, in the way sudden crises in Russia in 1905 and 1917 dramatically affected the workings of the political institutions and popular organisation in Finland.

In my view, variation in the relationship between internal and external factors appears, most graphically, in the role of accident in determining revolutions among the smaller nationalities of Eastern Europe (see p. 246). The precise manner of their unfolding depended, in no small measure, on the internal socio-structural, institutional, and organisational circumstances that *happened to prevail* at the moment of the international crisis, which was largely

---

21   Baldwin 1990, p. 99.

independent of their internal developments; thus, the interplay between internal and external factors varied in those encounters.

3.3   The Unity of the Elites

A number of reviewers commented on my interpretations – based on the comparative perspective – of historical developments or events. Criticism was directed particularly at the treatment of elites. This is important because the perspective I present on elites is crucial for understanding Finnish nationalism, the character of the revolutionary attempt and the Finnish variety of fascism. Upton and Kivisto claimed that I exaggerated their unity by neglecting the importance of the language-related cleavage dividing elite groups during the latter half of the Russian period: 'It might be difficult to find a historian who agrees that the vicious Fennoman-Svecoman polemic and the language disputes that it generated, which still rouse political passions in present-day Finland, could be described as "rather frictionless"';[22] 'In my estimation, he doesn't pay adequate attention to the ethno-linguistic factor ... Alapuro does not deal with the political implications of these divergent positions because he focuses solely on the Fennomen'.[23]

It is certainly true that heated disputes occurred between Fennomans and Liberals, not to speak of the friction between Fennomans and Svecomans, but it is equally true that they never transcended the limits of a basically civilised and regulated political struggle. The intensity of the language conflict should be assessed from a comparative perspective. In earlier historiography, the scale of the conflict tended to be exaggerated, due to historians' involvement, either directly or indirectly, in the dispute itself. Significantly, however, the conflict was a transient phenomenon, thanks to the comparatively easy adoption of the majority language by the educated class. To cite Matti Klinge, one of the foremost experts on the issue, '[i]t is fair to assess that in Finland this process took place rather painlessly'.[24] Klinge continues by asserting that 'internal national consolidation progressed in Finland in the course of the nineteenth century slowly and steadily. Viewed in an international perspective, the development proceeded here without major conflicts'.[25] In his comparative account, Edward C. Thaden stresses the same feature in relation to the Baltic Provinces of Russia: 'The willingness of a significant number of individuals from the Swedish-speaking middle and upper strata of the population to join

---

22   Upton 1990, p. 1237.
23   Kivisto 1989, p. 196.
24   Klinge 1975, p. 42.
25   Klinge 1975, p. 54.

forces with the Finnish national movement tended to alleviate national, class, and economic tensions'.[26]

The claim that the language conflict was relatively minor in scale and thereby limited in its capacity to fuel intra-elite dissent is important for the argumentation of the book in two respects. First, it supports the portrayal of Finnish elites as a group whose structural position was weak – this fragility presumably making them unusually receptive to adopting the language of the majority as their own language. The second point concerns the nature of the failed revolution. Revolutionary upheavals have commonly been preceded by a crisis of elite relationships and the formation of an elite-popular coalition in which discontented elite groups have joined organised popular groups in attacking the authority of the state. Such an intra-elite division was clearly absent from Finland in the approach to 1918.[27]

Lauri Karvonen concurred with Upton and Kivisto on the (dis)unity of nineteenth-century elite, but he presented a more detailed critique by discussing the 1920s and the beginning of the 1930s. Again, I feel that much depends on the framework chosen for judging the degree of unity. From the Eastern European perspective adopted in the book, the most important point is that there remained a rather limited hard core of reactionary forces in Finland – implying greater unity among the Finnish elites than in Hungary or Romania, for example. In my view, Karvonen's observation on the distinctiveness of the right-wing extremism at the turn of the 1930s is reconcilable with my thesis on the decisive role of the civil war experience in its formation. Here, Miika Siironen's recent interpretation of the relationship between bourgeois groups during the two inter-war decades is helpful.[28] In the 1920s, the experience of the civil war maintained the hegemonic position of 'White discourse', which covered all bourgeois groups. It possessed such an aura of sanctity that it seemed impossible to question, and the Civil Guard was its most tangible manifestation. The situation only changed after the emergence of the fascist movement at the turn of the 1930s. The movement attempted to extend White discourse to cover the entire nation, and it turned against the Social Democrats after the Communists had been eliminated from public life. Thereby, it created a demarcation within the bourgeois camp and 'secularised' the White discourse and its central symbols. These were politicised in a new way by becoming attached to one political group, the Patriotic People's Movement. Consequently, the hegemonic force of White discourse dissipated.

---

26   Thaden 1981, p. 6.
27   For more detail, see Alapuro 2011, pp. 140–3.
28   Siironen 2012.

In other words, the rise of right-wing radicalism remained limited, and by 'secularising' White unity, it inadvertently entered a cul-de-sac. This interpretation also stresses the important but transient role of the defeated revolution. It acted as the catalyst for a reactionary wing among the bourgeoisie and undergirded its subsequent position as a part of the White camp. However, at the same time, the crucial role played by the civil war in the promotion of Finnish fascism explains why its influence could not be reproduced. As the war receded into history and the Lapua movement pressed the bourgeois camp to take a stand on its legacy, the quasi-religious aura of White discourse began to wane, and the extreme right wing in the elite was marginalised. To me, the interpretation presented in the book, is entirely consistent with this view.

4 Structures and Actors

This remains the most serious and interesting criticism. It concerns the book's comparative methodology and views on the character of the Finnish revolution. These two related criticisms were not limited to the reviews; they also surface in a number of other comments. At issue was the dynamics of the revolution – the road to it, or its causes and actors. As to the methodological dimension, it is entirely logical for a study that adopts a sociological-historical perspective on revolutions to reflect on causes, preconditions, effects and consequences. Their examination is suggested by the comparative approach implicit in this perspective, even when no systematic comparisons are made.[29] Moreover, when concrete arguments about causality in 1917 and 1918 are presented, these necessarily impinge on the discussion of the conflict as an historical event.

The most extensive comments on my view of the causes of the war were offered by the historian Ilkka Liikanen in the 1990s, and his reflections remain the most perceptive even from the perspectives of today (see below, p. 266). He observed that scholars only began to take the social dimension of the war and its dynamics seriously from the 1960s. Thereafter, notions of the class character of the war gradually found greater acceptance as a part of a more wide-ranging cultural and political liberalisation. Scholars pointed out that the inequalities which had pitted the urban and rural proletariat against other social groups had emerged along class lines, and they emphasised social problems as the factors underlying this clash – both long-term polarisation and hardship, and grievances stemming from 1917. Nevertheless, even though the roots of the

---

29   See, for example, Goldstone 2014.

encounter were now seen to lie in social conditions – in the hardship and distress that had prepared the ground for the upheaval – the genuinely *political* dynamics of the process were not conceptualised or examined. Scholars 'did not study the radicalisation of the worker movement in the light of the organisation process or of the local power relations and political oppositions'.[30] The same held for the Marxist-inspired views of the 1970s: 'Younger scholars hoped to construct as materialist class struggle interpretations as possible and stressed social antagonisms rather than interpreted the revolution as a political process.'[31]

It was against this backdrop that a large-scale research project was launched to study the administration, the army and the local organisation of the short-lived insurgent regime. The findings, published in the 1980s,[32] were significant for highlighting the political dimensions of the conflict by demonstrating that 'mainly the established professional and political organisations of the worker movement' organised the upheaval, even 'with uniquely extensive and unanimous participation'.[33] However, even these findings failed to undermine the 'social background' reasoning used to explain the road to the war. They failed to trigger political-level debate, thereby leaving a 'black hole' in terms of the reasons for the outbreak of the war, which had originally been attributed to such factors as tensions, disorder, or hardship.[34] In other words, the relationship between these factors and the organised worker movement was not seriously analysed.

It is in this context of a black hole that Liikanen placed the reasoning of *State and Revolution in Finland*. He observed that, in considering the war a revolution, the book perceived it, positively enough, as a political process. Nevertheless, he added that the book simultaneously and paradoxically 'draws a picture of a revolution without leaders and masses'.[35] The book's depiction of the revolution appeared to him as a kind of passive takeover, as action without actors.

Liikanen was not alone in levelling this criticism, as similar remarks appeared in several reviews of the book, and it is certainly a highly relevant criticism from the perspective of the dynamics of the conflict. The point was put most bluntly by George Ginsburgs, who wrote, '[a] vital human contest ... is

---

30   Liikanen 1993, p. 573.
31   Ibid.
32   The project was funded by the Finnish government. Its four voluminous accounts are summarised in Lappalainen et al. 1989.
33   Liikanen 1993, pp. 576, 577.
34   Liikanen 1993, p. 576.
35   Liikanen 1993, p. 577.

reduced to the incongruous spectacle of a stage filled with elaborate furnishings and empty of players'.[36] Jorunn Björgum regretted that the book's 'political science framework with its focus on the state [tended] to lose sight of the acting human beings in the rank and file'.[37] Moreover, David Kirby considered the approach to be methodologically problematic:

> A question that is ... waiting for an answer, is ... in which goal the collective action was directed. On this point there is, in my view, a weakness in Alapuro's research method that is above all focused on structures and does not take into the account sufficiently perceptions and attitudes. Did strikes, occupations of public buildings, butter riots, and finally worker guards come up simply due to the absence of coercion and control? ... In other words, I believe that it is also important to call attention to the thoughts which contributed to shape the action ... What we have in the book is an excellent structural analysis of the failed revolution; what is missing is a reference to the character of the revolution, and it seems to me that it is not sufficient to define revolutions solely as a struggle of the state power.[38]

The same issue was central, from different points of view, to three Finnish comments. Raimo Parikka argued that the workers constituted a proactive, in

---

36 Ginsburgs 1990, pp. 158–9.
37 Björgum 1991, p. 894.
38 Kirby 1989, pp. 315–18. The actor-structure controversy was linked to differences in approach between historians and social scientists. Most of those who complained about the absence of acting human beings were historians. Peter Baldwin typified the attitude of many in his discipline when he remarked that sociologists tend to rely on the primary work performed by historians, instead of doing the 'mundane empirical spadework' themselves (1990, p. 100). Moreover, he continued by stating that '[o]n the crucial points where he makes his most important arguments, Alapuro [like many of his colleagues] brings no new evidence to bear. The bulk of his book is based on references to standard printed literature, too much of it is mere summary' (ibid.). One can certainly find examples of superficial exploitation of others' work by social scientists who have made attempts at comprehensive interpretations of historical processes. However, if one accepts synthesis as a legitimate genre, the touchstone is not so much the 'new evidence brought to bear' as the success in constructing a historically coherent story in which familiar elements may have a new or unfamiliar role. Furthermore, those reviewers who were knowledgeable about Finnish history disagreed with Baldwin on this point: 'Comparative studies ... have the quality of pointing at new and interesting aspects of previously known facts and sources, and this is precisely the case with Alapuro's work as well' (Karvonen 1990, p. 89). See also Upton 1990, p. 1237, cited above on p. 255, and, from among the other critics, Björgum 1991, p. 892: 'Alapuro's method is to systematize and interpret in new ways existing research results'.

fact, revolutionary force, and that this was true already in the spring of 1917.[39] He stressed, in turn, their active role in the struggle to dismiss the 'Russified' police, then their participation in the local takeovers during the general strike in November and finally the emergence of a radical nucleus that challenged the party leadership in the autumn of 1917. Parikka's study of a commune on the outskirts of Helsinki provided the stimulus for his objections to my view and for his own interpretation. In this commune he found that the workers' militant spirit was already well developed in 1917 and that it stemmed from a 'culture of contestation', a deeply engrained popular mentality of opposition to those in power.

Jari Ehrnrooth described my position – that the war 'was not based on deep contradictions and no grass-root discontent underlay the Finnish worker revolution' – as a 'reassuring and sympathetic drifting log theory of the worker revolution', in the spirit of reconciliation.[40] He related my work to the social background explanation established in the 1960s and 1970s and the atmosphere of reconciliation which developed at the same time. In Ehrnrooth's view, my approach, which he depicted as downplaying the whole revolutionary fervour and painting in rosy colours the violence and thirst for revenge manifest in the upheaval, took the national consensus project of the epoch one step further. It reinforced the 'interpretation perspective inspired by national integration'.[41] For his part, he wished to stress the centrality of working-class grudges and hatred, released in 1918, in the attempted revolution.

A further criticism, presented by the legal historian Jukka Kekkonen, argued that I presented the upheaval as an 'accidental revolution' (*sattumavallankumous*) resulting from the sum of unfortunate coincidences. In reviewing a local study of mine – whose basic argument was similar to that advanced in *State and Revolution in Finland* – he considered my interpretation 'neo-rightist', in keeping with the political mood of the post-Soviet era, as the study supposedly attributed the war to the collapse in Russia and discounted the role of real hardships and grievances.[42]

---

39 Parikka 1990.
40 Ehrnrooth 1992, pp. 22–3. A part of Ehrnrooth's irony lies in the expression 'drifting log theory', which was originally used in an apologetic attempt to defend Finland's entrance into World War II in 1941 as an ally of Germany. In this view, Finland had no choice, but was driven into the war by greater forces like a log in a torrent (the implication being that the Finnish leaders were not responsible for Finland's decision).
41 Ehrnrooth 1992, p. 23.
42 Kekkonen 1995a; Kekkonen 1995b; also, concerning more specifically *State and Revolution in Finland*, see Kekkonen 2016, pp. 314–15, 435.

What is common to these three comments is that they rely on the 'social background' argument, criticised by Liikanen, whereby the outbreak of the war is primarily ascribed to the grievances and the discontent of the working people and at best secondarily to (unspecified) political processes. Nevertheless, this argument had a different tone in each of the three cases as the working class were variously described as people capable of creation and contestation (Parikka), a social group in which archaic hatred underlies modern class consciousness (Ehrnrooth), and people revolting against difficult living conditions (Kekkonen).

5   The Associational Tradition in the Political Process

What was Liikanen's own view of how to fill the 'black hole' between discontent and the political action it inspired? For him the key factor characterising the political action in 1917 and 1918 were the structural qualities of agency, manifest in the mode of organisation:

> It can ... be noted in a comparative perspective that peculiar to the revolution in Finland was, first, that the established organisations of the worker movement with their unique extent and unanimous support organised the takeover, and, second, that the mobilisation of the population in the revolutionary army and administration was successful in an exceptionally large scale in the basic areas of the revolution.[43]

He even went so far as to maintain that it was the 'exceptionally far-reaching [degree of] organisation' that plunged Finland into war.[44]

In a similar vein, the primacy and nature of the political process appears in a number of publications by another historian, Pertti Haapala. According to him, in late 1917 the country was drifting in a 'strange interregnum', in which the power vacuum was increasingly filled by volunteer guard units, founded on both sides. Two power centres emerged, both based on established organisations, and 'neither the socialists nor the bourgeois parties had exact plans or an idea of the future'.[45] In 1917 the Social Democratic party was the best-organised political force in the country, and in 1918 'the Red Guards and the

---

43   Liikanen 1993, p. 577.
44   Liikanen 1998, p. 28.
45   Haapala 1995, pp. 44, 46.

Red civil organisations ... were based on the organisational structure and activity of the previous years'.⁴⁶

Furthermore, at the local level, the execution of the revolution relied on established organisational models – a crucial point for the argument stressing the continuity in popular action. To cite Liikanen, '[i]n Finland responsible for the organisation of the takeover and the erection of the [local] revolutionary administration were mainly the established professional and political organisations of the worker movement, evolved to the highest degree as a part of the formation of civil society and the nation'.⁴⁷ Indeed, examples of such organisational practices are easy to find.⁴⁸

In my view, the interpretation advanced in *State and Revolution in Finland* is in line with the views of Liikanen and Haapala (despite Liikanen's objections).⁴⁹ Rather than being a deliberate push toward revolution, the conflict indeed emerged and culminated within the associational framework of the Social Democratic worker movement, and it lacked 'exact plans or an idea of the future'. It was the labour movement that primarily channelled the collective action of those suffering hardship and distress in 1917.

This view highlights certain specific features of the Finnish revolution. The collapse of an empire seized the Finnish state and Finnish society, whose cohesion was underpinned by a strong tradition of popular organisation. When the state's ability to act gradually declined, the conflict increasingly crystallised around those actors still able to function in an otherwise disintegrating society. In 1917, both the worker security guards and the bourgeois civil guards evolved from the organisation of civil society, and the same is true for the organisational principles in 1918. The revolution was neither accidental in the sense of being random or arbitrary – even though several 'what if' situations preceded the outbreak of the war⁵⁰ – nor was it predetermined. It was a *contingent* event whose parties emerged within the framework of established organisational activity. Revolutionary determination only developed in the largest urban centres. Agency was not directly based on grievances but on the political process stemming from a crisis in the state's capacity to act. Power was not seized by a revolutionary party with a revolutionary doctrine and a clear polit-

---

46 Haapala 2014, p. 32.
47 Liikanen 1998, p. 27.
48 E.g. Rentola 1992, pp. 625–75; Alapuro 1994, pp. 192–201; Lindholm 2005, 20–89; Hoppu 2009; Heimo 2010, 102–15.
49 It is perhaps no accident that Jukka Kekkonen (2016, p. 435) considers Haapala, besides myself, to be a proponent of the 'accidental revolution' theory.
50 Haapala 1995, p. 154.

ical strategy deriving from it; rather, the working-class movement was drawn into the revolution within a framework established in the preceding decades. From this perspective, it is inappropriate to stress the Social Democratic leaders' capitulation to radical Red guards. On the contrary, the worker movement was able to delay the outbreak of the revolution to the point where it conceived the takeover as a defensive act. The postponement was made possible by the strong tradition of associational organisation.

6   Causes and Scripts

The views of Liikanen and Haapala on the causes and dynamics of the war appeared in the 1990s. Interestingly, they still seem to be the latest serious reflections on the subject; indeed, since the period from the 1960s to the 1990s, no explicit debate on the reasons for the revolution has been conducted. Instead, the subject has assumed a secondary position in the scholarly work of recent decades, or, more typically, to cite one historian, there is simply 'silence on the breakout of the war and its causes'.[51] Thus, the road to war is usually described without explicit analysis of the different (causal) elements or levels in the process.[52] This waning interest in causes seems partly a side effect of the decreasing interest in attributing blame for the war. This is certainly a welcome reorientation: instead of accusing one or another party, even indirectly, scholars have turned to the themes of violence, trauma, and memory; as 'Practically all the major theatres of war have received a detailed analysis of the military, social, and cultural aspects of the conflict'.[53] During recent decades, the war has frequently been approached through individual experiences, with exhibitions, documentaries and novels presenting numerous accounts of local events and stories of victims, executioners and the suffering in the prison camps.

Nevertheless, there are other reasons for the abandonment of reflection on causes, one being a shift in scholarly emphasis. The interest in causes and effects typical of the sociological-historical and comparative perspective of this book has been complemented and in part replaced by perspectives that eschew why-questions in favour of studying actors' experiences and practices and their cultural determinants. 'Theories of revolution are … causal explanations of revolution',[54] but today historically sensitive comparative accounts

---

51 Häikiö 2008, p. 47.
52 Esim. Kekkonen 2016, pp. 43–65, 332–7; Siltala 2009; Siltala 2014.
53 Tepora and Roselius 2014, p. 14.
54 Aya 2015, p. 627.

of revolutions address themselves, for example, to the 'scripts' revolutionaries adopt in their actions, by creatively reinterpreting the unfolding of previous revolutions.[55] This approach feels well-suited to the atmosphere following the 'linguistic turn' and dovetails with current interest in transnational history and conceptual history.

Nevertheless, the two comparative perspectives are not mutually exclusive. For example, in studying the states that were born, reborn or liberated upon the collapse of the Soviet Union, one can reflect both on the circumstances leading to revolution (the stance adopted in this book) and on the notions activists held about those upheavals as revolutions. The former perspective leads to a comparison of post-socialist liberation with the upheavals following the collapse of empires in World War I. The latter perspective focuses on the sources of inspiration – ideological or otherwise – drawn upon by revolutionary actors when defining their situation and on the projected narratives of their actions produced at the end of the 1980s and the beginning of the 1990s.

---

55   See Baker and Edelstein 2015.

Bibliography

Abendroth, Wolfgang 1965, *Sozialgeschichte der europäischen Arbeiterbewegung*, Frankfurt am Main: Suhrkamp.

Ahti, Martti 1982, 'Konspiration – massrörelse – partibildning', in *Kritisk fascismeforskning i Norden*, edited by Håkon Löe and Jan L. Kristensen, Arbejdspapirer fra NSU, no. 11, Aalborg: Nordisk Sommer-universitet, 170–96.

Ahti, Martti 1984a, '"Ohi virallisen Suomen": Konspiratiivinen oikeistoradikalismi 1918–1919', Licentiate thesis, Department of Political History, University of Helsinki.

Ahti, Martti 1984b, 'Skyddskårernas i Finland Förbund – skyddskårsorganisationens dubbelgångare', *Historisk tidskrift för Finland*, 69: 13–37.

Ahvenainen, Jorma 1984, *Suomen sahateollisuuden historia*, Helsinki: WSOY.

Ajnenkiel, Andrzej 1969, 'L' Indépendance polonaise en 1918: Faits et problèmes', *Acta Poloniae Historica*, 20: 31–51.

Åkerman, Sune 1975, 'Swedish Social Development from 1840 to 1970 as Reflected in Emigration', in *Sweden's Development from Poverty to Affluence, 1750–1970*, edited by Steven Koblik, Minneapolis: University of Minnesota Press, 167–79.

Ala-Kapee, Pirjo and Marjaana Valkonen 1982, *Yhdessä elämä turvalliseksi. SAK:laisen ammattiyhdistysliikkeen kehitys vuoteen 1930*, Helsinki: SAK.

Alapuro, Risto 1973a, *Akateeminen Karjala-Seura. Ylioppilasliike ja kansa 1920- ja 1930-luvulla*, Helsinki: WSOY.

Alapuro, Risto 1973b, 'Students and National Politics: A Comparative Study of the Finnish Student Movement in the Interwar Period', *Scandinavian Political Studies*, 8: 113–40.

Alapuro, Risto 1978, 'Statemaking and Political Ecology in Finland', in *The Social Ecology of Change*, edited by Zdravko Mlinar and Henry Teune, Beverly Hills, Calif.: Sage, 109–43.

Alapuro, Risto 1980, 'Yhteiskuntaluokat ja sosiaaliset kerrostumat 1870-luvulta toiseen maailmansotaan', in Tapani Valkonen et al., *Suomalaiset. Yhteiskunnan rakenne teollistumisen aikana*, Helsinki: WSOY, 36–101, 276–80.

Alapuro, Risto 1985, 'Interstate Relationships and Political Mobilization in the Nordic Countries', in *Small States in Comparative Perspective: Essays for Erik Allardt*, edited by Risto Alapuro et al., Oslo: Norwegian University Press, 93–107.

Alapuro, Risto 1988, *State and Revolution in Finland*, Berkeley: University of California Press.

Alapuro, Risto 1994, *Suomen synty paikallisena ilmiönä 1890–1933*, Helsinki: Hanki ja jää.

Alapuro, Risto 2004, 'The Finnish Civil War, Politics, and Microhistory', in *Between Sociology and History: Essays on Microhistory, Collective Action, and Nation-Building*, edited by Anna-Maija Castrén, Markku Lonkila and Matti Peltonen, Helsinki Suomalaisen Kirjallisuuden Seura, 130–47.

Alapuro, Risto 2011, 'The Revolution of 1918 in Finland in a Comparative Perspective: Causes and Processes', in *Revolution in Nordosteuropa*, edited by Detlef Henning, Wiesbaden: Harrassowitz Verlag, 140–6.

Alapuro, Risto and Matti Alestalo 1973, 'Konkreettinen sosiaalitutkimus', in *Suomalaisen sosiologian juuret*, edited by Risto Alapuro, Matti Alestalo and Elina Haavio-Mannila, Helsinki: WSOY, 84–147.

Alestalo, Matti 1977, 'Työväenluokan maailmankuva ja työväenliike', in *Maailmankuvan muutos tutkimuskohteena*, edited by Matti Kuusi, Risto Alapuro and Matti Klinge, Helsinki: Otava, 98–111.

Alestalo, Matti and Stein Kuhnle 1987, 'The Scandinavian Route: Economic, Social, and Political Developments in Denmark, Finland, Norway, and Sweden', in *The Scandinavian Model: Welfare States and Welfare Research*, edited by Robert Erikson et al., Armonk, N.Y.: Sharpe, 3–38.

Alkio, Santeri 1919, *Maalaispolitiikkaa*, Vol. 1, Lahti: Edistysseurojen Kustannusosakeyhtiö.

Allardt, Erik 1962, 'Community Activity, Leisure Use and Social Structure', *Acta Sociologica* 6: 67–82.

Allardt, Erik 1981a, 'Finland mellan öst och väst – De språngvisa omvandlingarnas samhälle', in *Tankar i nutid*, edited by Martin Sandelin, Ekenäs: Svenska Bildningsförbundet, 59–73.

Allardt, Erik 1981b, 'Reflections on Stein Rokkan's Conceptual Map of Europe', *Scandinavian Political Studies*, n.s. 4: 257–71.

Allardt, Erik and Karl Johan Miemois 1982, 'A Minority in Both Centre and Periphery: An Account of the Swedish-Speaking Finns', *European Journal of Political Research*, 10: 265–92.

Anderson, Edgar 1977, 'Die baltische Frage und die internationale Politik der alliierten und assoziierten Mächte, 1918–1921', in *Von den baltischen Provinzen zu den baltischen Staaten. Beiträge zur Entstehungsgeschichte der Republiken Estland und Lettland 1918–1920*, edited by Jürgen von Hehn, Hans von Rimscha and Hellmuth Weiss, Marburg am Lahn: J.G. Herder Institut, 327–77.

Anderson, Perry 1974, *Lineages of the Absolutist State*, London: New Left Books.

Anfimov, A.M. 1969, *Krupnoe pomeshchich'e khoziaistvo Evropeiskoi Rossii (konets XIX–nachalo XX veka)*, Moscow: Nauka.

Annuaire Statistique de Finlande 1922, Helsinki: Bureau Central de Statistique de Finlande.

Apine, I.K. 1970 'Pozitsiia klassov i partii Latvii v natsional'nom voprose nakanune i v khode Fevral'skoi burzhuazno-demokraticheskoi revoliutsii', in *Sverzhenie samoderzhaviia*, Moscow: Nauka, 203–14.

Arens, Olavi 1978, 'The Estonian *Maapäev* During 1917', in *The Baltic States in Peace and War 1917–1945*, edited by V. Stanley Vardys and Romuald J. Misiunas, University Park: Pennsylvania State University Press, 19–30.

Arens, Olavi 1982, 'Soviets in Estonia 1917/1918', in *Die baltischen Provinzen Russlands zwischen den Revolutionen von 1905 und 1917*, edited by Andrew Ezergailis and Gert von Pistohlkors, Cologne and Vienna: Böhlau Verlag, 295–314.

Arter, David 1978, *Bumpkin Against Bigwig: The Emergence of a Green Movement in Finnish Politics*, University of Tampere, Institute of Political Science Research Reports, no. 47. Tampere.

Åström, Sven-Erik 1977a, 'Anlagda städer och centralortssystemet i Finland 1550–1785', in *Urbaniseringsprosessen i Norden*, vol. 2: *De anlagte steder på 1600–1700-tallet*, edited by G.A. Blom, Oslo: Universitetsforlaget, 134–81.

Åström, Sven-Erik 1977b, 'Majmiseriet. Försök till en komparativ och konceptuell analys', *Historisk tidskrift för Finland*, 62: 89–108.

Åström, Sven-Erik 1980a, 'Suurvalta-ajan valtiontalous', in *Suomen taloushistoria*, edited by Eino Jutikkala, Yrjö Kaukiainen and Sven-Erik Åström, Helsinki: Tammi, 1: 294–313.

Åström, Sven-Erik 1980b, 'Suomen asema Ruotsin valtion- ja sotataloudessa', in *Suomen taloushistoria*, edited by Eino Jutikkala, Yrjö Kaukiainen and Sven-Erik Åström, Helsinki: Tammi, 1: 314–21.

Aun, Karl 1982, 'The 1917 Revolutions and the Idea of the State in Estonia', in *Die baltischen Provinzen Russlands zwischen den Revolutionen von 1905 und 1917*, edited by Andrew Ezergailis and Gert von Pistohlkors, Cologne and Vienna: Böhlau Verlag, 287–94.

Aunola, Toini 1967, *Pohjois-Pohjanmaan kauppiaiden ja talonpoikien väliset kauppa- ja luottosuhteet 1765–1809*, Historiallisia tutkimuksia, no. 71, Helsinki: Suomen Historiallinen Seura.

Aya, Rod 1979, 'Theories of Revolution Reconsidered', *Theory and Society* 8: 39–99.

Aya, Rod 2015, 'Theories of Revolution', in *International Encyclopedia of the Social & Behavioral Sciences*, Second Edition, 20, 627–32, Oxford: Elsevier.

Baker, Keith Michael and Dan Edelstein 2015, 'Introduction', in *Scripting Revolution: A Historical Approach to the Comparative Study of Revolutions*, edited by Keith Michael Baker and Dan Edelstein, Stanford, CA: Stanford University Press.

Baldwin, Peter 1990, 'Risto Alapuro, *State and Revolution in Finland*' (book review), *European Sociological Review* 6: 98–100.

Balevits, L.Ia. 1962, 'Sel'skokhoziaistvennye obshchestva v Lifliandskoi i Kurliandskoi guberniiakh v nachale XX veka', *Problemy istorii*, Riga: Izdatel'stvo Akademii Nauk Latviiskoi SSR, no. 6: 165–98.

Barta, I., et al. 1971, *Die Geschichte Ungarns*, Budapest: Corvina.

Bell, John D. 1977, *Peasants in Power: Alexander Stamboliski and the Bulgarian Agrarian National Union, 1899–1923*, Princeton, N.J.: Princeton University Press.

Bendix, Reinhard 1960, *Max Weber: An Intellectual Portrait*, Garden City, N.Y.: Doubleday.
Bendix, Reinhard 1964, *Nation-Building and Citizenship*, New York: Wiley.
Berend, I.T. and G. Ránki 1974, *Economic Development in East-Central Europe in the 19th and 20th Centuries*, New York: Columbia University Press.
Berend, I.T. and G. Ránki 1982, *The European Periphery and Industrialization, 1780–1914*, Cambridge: Cambridge University Press.
Bianco, Lucien 1971, *Origins of the Chinese Revolution, 1915–1949*, Stanford, Calif.: Stanford University Press.
Bjórgum, Jorunn 1991, 'Risto Alapuro, *State and Revolution in Finland*' (book review), *Journal of Social History* 24: 892–4.
Björklund, Joh. 1939, *Suomen papisto 1800-luvulla erityisesti silmälläpitäen pappistarvetta ja sen tyydyttämismahdollisuuksia*, Suomen Kirkkohistoriallisen Seuran toimituksia, no. 42, Helsinki.
Blum, Jerome 1978, *The End of the Old Order in Rural Europe*, Princeton, N.J.: Princeton University Press.
Bonsdorff, Göran von 1954, *Studier rörande den moderna liberalismen i de nordiska länderna*, Ekenäs: Fahlbeckska stiftelsen.
Borg, Olavi 1965, *Suomen puolueet ja puolueohjelmat 1880–1964*, Helsinki: WSOY.
Brass, Paul R. 1980, 'Ethnic Groups and Nationalities: The Formation, Persistence, and Transformation of Ethnic Identities', in *Ethnic Diversity and Conflict in Eastern Europe*, edited by Peter F. Sugar, Santa Barbara, Calif.: ABC Clio Press, 1–68, 447–60.
Brenner, Robert 1975, 'England, Eastern Europe, and France. Socio-Historical Versus "Economic" Interpretation: General Comments', in *Failed Transitions to Modern Industrial Society: Renaissance Italy and Seventeenth Century Holland*, edited by Frederick Krantz and Paul M. Hohenberg, Montreal: Interuniversity Centre for European Studies, 68–71.
Brenner, Robert 1977, 'The Origins of Capitalist Development: A Critique of Neo-Smithian Marxism', *New Left Review*, no. 104: 25–92.
Carlsson, Sten 1968, *Yrken och samhällsgrupper*, Stockholm: Almqvist & Wiksell.
Carlsson, Sten 1980, 'Valtakunnan hajoaminen 1809', in *Suomalais-ruotsalainen historian tutkijain symposio*, Karjaa: Suomalais-Ruotsalainen Kulttuurirahasto, 68–80.
Castles, Francis G. 1973, 'Barrington Moore's Thesis and Swedish Political Development', *Government and Opposition*, 8: 313–31.
Castles, Francis G. 1978, *The Social Democratic Image of Society*, London: Routledge & Kegan Paul.
Castles, Francis G. 1991, 'Risto Alapuro, *State and Revolution in Finland*' (book review), *Acta Sociologica* 34: 57–8.
Chirot, Daniel 1976, *Social Change in a Peripheral Society: The Creation of a Balkan Colony*, New York: Academic Press.

Chirot, Daniel and Charles Ragin 1975, 'The Market, Tradition and Peasant Rebellion: The Case of Romania in 1907', *American Sociological Review*, 40: 428-44.

Chlebowczyk, József 1980, *On Small and Young Nations in Europe*, Warsaw: Ossolineum.

Collins, Randall 1968, 'A Comparative Approach to Political Sociology', in *State and Society*, edited by Reinhard Bendix et al., Berkeley and Los Angeles: University of California Press, 42-67.

Deák, István 1968, 'Budapest and the Hungarian Revolutions of 1918-1919', *Slavonic and East European Review*, 46: 129-40.

Deutsch, Karl W. 1953, *Nationalism and Social Communication*, New York: Wiley.

Djupsund, Göran and Lauri Karvonen 1984, *Fascismen i Finland: Högerextremismens förankring hos väljarkåren 1929-1939*, Publications of the Research Institute of the Åbo Akademi Foundation, no. 94, Turku.

Draudin, T.Ia. 1959, *Bezzemel'noe krest'ianstvo Latvii v bor'be za zemliu i vlast' sovetov v 1917-1919 godakh*, Riga: Latgosizdat.

Droz, Jacques 1971, 'Cisleithanie. Les masses laborieuses et le problème national (1867-1918)', in *Mouvements nationaux d'indépendance et classes populaires aux XIXe et XXe siècles en occident et en orient*, Paris: Armand Colin, 1: 74-92.

Dunn, John 1972, *Modern Revolutions*, Cambridge: Cambridge University Press.

Dunn, John 1977, 'The Success and Failure of Modern Revolutions', in *Radicalism in the Contemporary Age*, edited by Seweryn Bialer and Sophia Sluzar, Boulder, Colo.: Westview Press, 3: 83-114, 305-18.

Eckelt, Frank 1971, 'The Internal Policies of the Hungarian Soviet Republic', in *Hungary in Revolution, 1918-19: Nine Essays*, edited by Ivan Völgyes, Lincoln: University of Nebraska Press, 61-88.

'Editorial Essay: Political Geography – Research Agendas for the Nineteen Eighties' 1982, *Political Geography Quarterly*, 1: 1-17.

Ehrnrooth, Jari 1992, *Sanan vallassa, vihan voimalla. Sosialistiset vallankumousopit ja niiden vaikutus Suomen työväenliikkeessä 1905-1914* [with a summary in English: 'Power of the Word, Force of Hatred: Socialist Revolutionary Doctrines and Their Effect in the Finnish Workers' Movement 1905-1914'], Helsinki: Suomen Historiallinen Seura.

Elder, Neil, Alastair H. Thomas and David Arter 1982, *The Consensual Democracies? The Government and Politics of the Scandinavian States*, Oxford: Martin Robertson.

Élections au parlement de Finlande en 1933, 1934, Official Statistics of Finland XXIX: Elections A: Elections of the Diet and of Presidential Electors, no. 17, Helsinki.

Élections pour la diète en 1907 et 1908, 1909, Official Statistics of Finland XXIX: Elections, no. 1, Helsinki.

Élections pour la diète en 1916, 1917, Official Statistics of Finland XXIX: Elections, no. 7, Helsinki.

Élections pour la diète en 1917, 1919, Official Statistics of Finland XXIX: Elections, no. 8, Helsinki.
Élections pour la diète en 1919, 1920, Official Statistics of Finland XXIX: Elections, no. 9, Helsinki.
Élections pour la diète en 1929, 1930, Official Statistics of Finland XXIX: Elections, no. 14, Helsinki.
Éléments démographiques principaux de la Finlande pour les années 1750–1890, 1899, Vol. 1, Official Statistics of Finland VI: Population, no. 29, Helsinki.
Eley, Geoff 1981, 'Nationalism and Social History', *Social History*, 6: 83–107.
Elovainio, Päivi 1972, 'Tieteiden eriytyminen Suomen korkeakoululaitoksessa', *Sosiologia*, 9: 242–60.
Elvander, Nils 1980, *Skandinavisk arbetarrörelse*, Stockholm: Liber Förlag.
Engman, Max 1978, 'Migration from Finland to Russia During the Nineteenth Century', *Scandinavian Journal of History*, 3: 155–77.
Engman, Max 1983, *St Petersburg och Finland. Migration och influens 1703–1917*, Bidrag till kännedom av Finlands natur och folk, no. 130, Helsinki: Finska Vetenskaps-Societeten.
Engman, Max 1984, 'Finland – ett utflyttningsland. In- och utflyttning under fyra sekler', in *Svenskt i Finland*, edited by Max Engman and Henrik Stenius, Skrifter utgivna av Svenska Litteratursällskapet i Finland, no. 519, Helsinki, 2: 117–64.
Erényi, Tibor 1975, 'The Activities of the Social Democratic Party of Hungary During the First Decade of the Century', in *Studies on the History of the Hungarian Working-Class Movement, 1867–1966*, edited by Henrik Vass, Budapest: Akadémiai Kiadó, 55–88.
Ezergailis, Andrew 1974, *The 1917 Revolution in Latvia*, Boulder, Colo.: East European Quarterly.
Ezergailis, Andrew 1982, 'The Causes of the Bolshevik Revolution in Latvia 1917', in *Die baltischen Provinzen Russlands zwischen den Revolutionen von 1905 und 1917*, edited by Andrew Ezergailis and Gert von Pistohlkors, Cologne and Vienna: Böhlau Verlag, 265–86.
Ferro, Marc 1967–76, *La Révolution de 1917*, 2 vols, Paris: Aubier-Montaigne.
Ferro, Marc 1967, 'Pourquoi Février? Pourquoi Octobre?', in *La Révolution d'Octobre et le Mouvement ouvrier européen*, edited by Victor Fay, 3–25, Paris: EDI.
Fischer-Galati, Stephen 1980, 'Fascism in Eastern Europe: Introduction', in *Who Were the Fascists: Social Roots of European Fascism*, edited by Stein Ugelvik Larsen, Bernt Hagtvet, and Jan Petter Myklebust, Oslo: Universitetsforlaget, 350–3.
Fol, Jean-Jacques 1977, *Accession de la Finlande à l'indépendance 1917–1919*, Lille: Atelier de Reproduction des Thèses, Université de Lille III.
Forsman, Jaakko 1912, *Mistä syystä sosialismi levisi Suomen maalaisväestön keskuuteen?* Helsinki: Otava.

Galaj, Dyzma 1974, 'The Polish Peasant Movement in Politics: 1895–1969', in *Rural Protest: Peasant Movements and Social Change*, edited by Henry A. Landsberger, London: Macmillan, 316–47.
Gallie, Duncan 1982, 'The Agrarian Roots of Working-Class Radicalism: An Assessment of the Mann-Giddens Thesis', *British Journal of Political Science*, 12: 149–72.
Gebhard, Hannes 1913, *Population agricole, ses rapports avec les autres groupes professionels et sa composition sociale dans les communes rurales de Finlande en 1901*, Tilastollinen tutkimus yhteiskunta-taloudellisista oloista Suomen maalaiskunnissa v. 1901, vol. 1, Helsinki: Keisarillisen Senaatin kirjapaino.
Geer, Eric de and Holger Wester 1976, 'Utrikes resor, arbetsvandringar och flyttningar i Finland och Vasa län 1861–1890', in *Österbotten. Årsbok 1975*, Skrifter utgivna av Svensk-Österbottniska samfundet, Vaasa, no. 33: 7–112.
Gellner, Ernest 1964, *Thought and Change*, London: Weidenfeld & Nicolson.
Gellner, Ernest 1983, *Nations and Nationalism*, Oxford: Basil Blackwell.
Germanis, Uldis 1968, 'The Idea of Independent Latvia and Its Development in 1917', in *Res Baltica: A Collection of Essays in Honour of the Memory of Dr. Alfred Bilmanis (1887–1948)*, edited by Adolf Sprudzs and Armins Rusis, Leiden: Sijthoff, 27–87.
Germanis, Uldis 1974, *Oberst Vacietis und die lettischen Schützen im Weltkrieg und in der Oktoberrevolution*, Acta Universitatis Stockholmiensis, Stockholm Studies in History, no. 20, Stockholm.
Ginsburgs, George 1990, 'Risto Alapuro, *State and Revolution in Finland*' (book review), *Journal of Baltic Studies* 21: 157–9.
Goldstone, Jack A. 1982, 'The Comparative and Historical Study of Revolutions', *Annual Review of Sociology*, 8: 187–207.
Goldstone, Jack A. 2003, 'Comparative Historical Analysis and Knowledge Accumulation in the Study of Revolutions', in *Comparative Historical Analysis in the Social Sciences*, edited by James Mahoney and Dietrich Rueschemeyer, Cambridge: University of Cambridge Press, 41–90.
Goldstone, Jack A. 2014, *Revolutions: A Very Short Introduction*, Oxford: Oxford University Press.
Gourevitch, Peter 1978, 'The International System and Regime Formation: A Critical Review of Anderson and Wallerstein', *Comparative Politics*, 10: 419–38.
Gylling, Edvard 1907, *Maanviljelystyöväen taloudellisista oloista Ikaalisten pitäjässä v. 1902*, Taloustieteellisiä tutkimuksia, no. 3, Helsinki: Otava.
Haapala, Pertti 1982, 'Ryhmistä luokaksi – Tampereen työväestön muodostuminen v. 1830–1920', Licentiate thesis, Department of History, University of Tampere.
Haapala, Pertti 1995, *Kun yhteiskunta hajosi: Suomi 1914–1920*, Helsinki: Painatuskeskus.
Haapala, Pertti 2014, 'The Expected and Non-Expected Roots of Chaos: Preconditions

of the Finnish Civil War', in *The Finnish Civil War 1918: History, Memory, Legacy*, edited by Tuomas Tepora and Aapo Roselius, Leiden and Boston: Brill, 21–50.

Haatanen, Pekka 1968, *Suomen maalaisköyhälistö tutkimusten ja kaunokirjallisuuden valossa*, Helsinki: WSOY.

Häikiö, Martti 2008, 'Miksi Suomessa käytiin sisällissota vuonna 1918?', *Työväentutkimus*, Vuosikirja 2008: 47–52.

Hako, Matti 1974, 'Työväenkulttuuri', in *Folklore tänään*, edited by Hannu Launonen and Kirsti Mäkinen, Helsinki: Suomalaisen Kirjallisuuden Seura, 138–50.

Halila, Aimo 1980, 'Oppikoululaitos', in *Suomen kulttuurihistoria*, Helsinki: WSOY, 2: 175–85.

Haltzel, Michael H. 1981, 'The Baltic Germans', in *Russification in the Baltic Provinces and Finland, 1855–1914*, edited by Edward C. Thaden, Princeton, N.J.: Princeton University Press, 109–204.

Hamalainen, Pekka Kalevi 1978, *In Time of Storm: Revolution, Civil War, and the Ethnolinguistic Issue in Finland*, Albany, N.Y.: State University of New York Press.

Harmaja, Leo 1933, *Tullipolitiikan vaikutus Suomen kansantalouden teollistumissuuntaan ennen maailmansotaa*, Helsinki: Otava.

Harve, Paavo 1947, *Puunjalostusteollisuutta ja puutavarakauppaa harjoittavien yhtiöiden maan hankinta Suomessa*, Acta Forestalia Fennica, no. 52: 1, Helsinki: Suomen Metsätieteellinen Seura.

Hautala, Kustaa 1956, *Suomen tervakauppa 1856–1913*, Historiallisia tutkimuksia, no. 45, Helsinki: Suomen Historiallinen Seura.

Hechter, Michael 1975, *Internal Colonialism: The Celtic Fringe in British National Development, 1536–1966*, Berkeley and Los Angeles: University of California Press.

Hechter, Michael 1978, 'Group Formation and the Cultural Division of Labor', *American Journal of Sociology*, 84: 293–318.

Heckscher, Eli F. 1936, *Sveriges ekonomiska historia från Gustav Vasa*, vol. 1: 2, Stockholm: Albert Bonniers Förlag.

Hehn, Jürgen von 1977, 'Die politische Bedeutung des Bauerntums in der unabhängigen Republik Lettland 1918–1940', in *Europäische Bauernparteien im 20. Jahrhundert*, edited by Heinz Gollwitzer, Stuttgart: Gustav Fischer Verlag, 223–41.

Heikkilä, Markku 1979, *Kirkollisen yhdistysaktiivisuuden leviäminen Suomessa*, Suomen Kirkkohistoriallisen Seuran toimituksia, Helsinki, no. 112.

Heikkinen, Sakari 1981, 'Kulutus Suomessa autonomian ajan jälkipuoliskolla', *Historiallinen Arkisto*, Helsinki: Suomen Historiallinen Seura, no. 76: 395–421.

Heikkinen, Sakari and Riitta Hjerppe 1981, 'Den finländska industrins tillväxt och internationella kopplingar 1860–1940', Paper presented at 18th meeting of Nordic Historians, Jyväskylä, Finland, 10–16 August 1981.

Heikkinen, Sakari and Kai Hoffman 1982, 'Teollisuus ja käsityö', in *Suomen taloushistoria*, edited by Jorma Ahvenainen, Erkki Pihkala and Viljo Rasila, Helsinki: Tammi, 2: 52–88.

Heikkinen, Sakari, et al. 1983, *Palkat, toimeentulo ja sosiaalinen rakenne Suomessa 1850–1913*, University of Helsinki, Institute of Economic and Social History Communications, no. 13, Helsinki.

Heimo, Anne 2010, *Kapina Sammatissa. Vuoden 1918 paikalliset tulkinnat osana historian yhteiskunnallisen rakentamisen prosessia* [with a summary in English: 'Rebellion in Sammatti. Local Interpretations of the 1918 Finnish Civil War as Part of the Social Process of History Making'], Helsinki: Suomalaisen Kirjallisuuden Seura.

Heinonen, Reijo E. 1980, 'From People's Movement to Minor Party: The People's Patriotic Movement (IKL) in Finland, 1932–1944', in *Who Were the Fascists: Social Roots of European Fascism*, edited by Stein Ugelvik Larsen, Bernt Hagtvet and Jan Petter Myklebust, Oslo: Universitetsforlaget, 687–701.

Hentilä, Seppo 1979, *Den svenska arbetarklassen och reformismens genombrott inom SAP före 1914*, Historiallisia tutkimuksia, no. 111, Helsinki: Suomen Historiallinen Seura.

Hentilä, Seppo 1982, *Suomen työläisurheilun historia*, vol. 1, Hämeenlinna: Arvi A. Karisto.

Hirvonen, Juhani and Riitta Hjerppe 1983, *Taloudellinen kasvu Suomessa 1880–1940*, Bank of Finland, Research Papers, no. 17, Helsinki.

Hjelt, A. 1893, *Maakaupasta ja krediitti-oloista Itä-Suomessa*, Porvoo: WSOY.

Hjerppe, Riitta 1979, *Suurimmat yritykset Suomen teollisuudessa 1844–1975*, Bidrag till kännedom av Finlands natur och folk, no. 123, Helsinki: Finska Vetenskaps-Societeten.

Hjerppe, Riitta 1981, 'Käsityöläiset uuden yhteiskunnan murroksessa', *Historiallinen Arkisto*, Helsinki: Suomen Historiallinen Seura, no. 76: 213–35.

Hjerppe, Riitta and Sakari Heikkinen 1978, 'Suomen teollisuuden ja käsityön työllisyys 1860–1919', *Historiallinen Aikakauskirja*, 76: 3–25.

Hjerppe, Riitta and John Lefgren 1974, 'Suomen tulonjakautuman kehityksestä 1881–1967', *Kansantaloudellinen Aikakauskirja*, 70: 97–119.

Hjerppe, Riitta, Matti Peltonen and Erkki Pihkala 1984, 'Investment in Finland, 1860–1979', *Scandinavian Economic History Review*, 32: 42–59.

Hjerppe, Riitta, and Erkki Pihkala 1977, 'The Gross Domestic Product of Finland in 1860–1913: A Preliminary Estimate', *Economy and History*, 22: 59–68.

Hobsbawm, E.J. 1972, 'Some Reflections on Nationalism', in *Imagination and Precision in the Social Sciences*, edited by T.J. Nossiter, A.H. Hanson and Stein Rokkan, London: Faber & Faber, 385–406.

Hodgson, John H. 1967, *Communism in Finland*, Princeton, N.J.: Princeton University Press.

Hodgson, John H. 1974a, *Edvard Gylling ja Otto W. Kuusinen asiakirjojen valossa 1918–1920*, Helsinki: Tammi.

Hodgson, John H. 1974b, *Otto Wille Kuusinen. Poliittinen elämäkerta*, Helsinki: Tammi.

Hoffman, Kai 1980, *Suomen sahateollisuuden kasvu, rakenne ja rahoitus 1800-luvun jälkipuoliskolla*, Bidrag till kännedom av Finlands natur och folk, no. 124, Helsinki: Finska Vetenskaps-Societeten.

Hoffman, Kai 1981, 'Työvoimatarpeen kausivaihteluista Suomen sahateollisuudessa ennen I maailmansotaa', *Historiallinen Arkisto*, Helsinki: Suomen Historiallinen Seura, no. 76: 115–34.

Holodkovski, Viktor 1978, *Suomen työväen vallankumous 1918*, Moscow: Edistys.

Hoppu, Tuomas 2009, 'Maalaiskylän sota', in *Sisällissodan pikkujättiläinen*, edited by Pertti Haapala and Tuomas Hoppu, Helsinki: WSOY, 270–9.

Hroch, Miroslav 1968, *Die Vorkämpfer der nationalen Bewegung bei den kleinen Völkern Europas*, Acta Universitatis Carolinae Philosophica et Historica, no. 24, Prague.

Hyvämäki, Lauri 1971, *Sinistä ja mustaa*, Helsinki: Otava.

Hyvämäki, Lauri 1977, 'Fasistiset ilmiöt Baltian maissa ja Suomessa 1920-luvun lopussa ja 1930-luvulla', *Historiallinen Arkisto*, Helsinki: Suomen Historiallinen Seura, no. 72: 113–37.

Ionescu, Ghiţa 1969, 'Eastern Europe', in *Populism*, edited by Ghiţa Ionescu and Ernest Gellner, London: Weidenfeld & Nicolson, 97–121.

Isohookana-Asunmaa, Tytti 1980, *Maalaisliitto Pohjois-Suomessa*, Turun yliopiston julkaisuja C, no. 29, Turku.

Istoriia Estonskoi SSR 1966, vol. 2, Tallinn: Eesti Raamat.

Janos, Andrew C. 1982, *The Politics of Backwardness in Hungary, 1825–1945*, Princeton, N.J.: Princeton University Press.

Jansen, Ea 1985, 'On the Economic and Social Determination of the Estonian National Movement', in *National Movements in the Baltic Countries During the 19th Century*, edited by Aleksander Loit, Acta Universitatis Stockholmiensis, Studia Baltica Stockholmiensia, no. 2, Uppsala, 41–57.

Jelavich, Charles and Barbara Jelavich 1977, *The Establishment of the Balkan National States, 1804–1920*, Seattle: University of Washington Press.

Jokipii, Mauno 1981, 'Finlands väg till självständighet', *Aktuellt om historia*, nos. 1–2: 39–48.

Jörberg, Lennart 1973, 'The Industrial Revolution in the Nordic Countries', in *The Fontana Economic History of Europe*, London: Fontana/Collins, 4: 375–485.

Jörberg, Lennart 1975, 'Structural Change and Economic Growth in Nineteenth-Century Sweden', in *Sweden's Development from Poverty to Affluence, 1750–1970*, edited by Steven Koblik, Minneapolis: University of Minnesota Press, 92–135.

Joustela, Kauko 1963, *Suomen Venäjän-kauppa autonomian ajan alkupuoliskolla vv. 1809–1865*, Historiallisia tutkimuksia, no. 62, Helsinki: Suomen Historiallinen Seura.

Jussila, Osmo 1969, *Suomen perustuslait venäläisten ja suomalaisten tulkintojen mukaan 1808–1863*, Historiallisia tutkimuksia, no. 77, Helsinki: Suomen Historiallinen Seura.

Jussila, Osmo 1979a, 'Kejsaren och lantdagen – maktrelationerna, särskilt ur kejsarens synvinkel', *Historisk tidskrift för Finland*, 64: 105–27.

Jussila, Osmo 1979b, *Nationalismi ja vallankumous venäläis-suomalaisissa suhteissa 1899–1914*, Historiallisia tutkimuksia, no. 110, Helsinki: Suomen Historiallinen Seura.

Jussila, Osmo 1980, 'Förfinskning och förryskning. Språkmanifestet år 1900 och dess bakgrund', *Historisk tidskrift för Finland*, 65: 1–17.

Jussila, Osmo 1981, 'Det finska storfurstendömets skeden 1809–1917', *Aktuellt om historia*, nos. 1–2: 31–8.

Jussila, Osmo 1984, 'Finland's Progress to National Statehood Within the Development of the Russian Empire's Administrative System', in *Nationality and Nationalism in Italy and Finland from the Mid-19th Century to 1918*, Studia Historica, no. 18, Helsinki: Suomen Historiallinen Seura, 91–103.

Jussila, Osmo 1985, 'From Province to State: Finland and the Baltic Provinces (1721–1920). A Comparative Survey', in *Les 'Petits États' face aux changements culturels, politiques et économiques de 1750 à 1914*, edited by D. Kosáry, Sixteenth International Congress of the Historical Sciences, Stuttgart, 25 August–1 September 1985, Lausanne, 55–67.

Jutikkala, Eino 1932, *Läntisen Suomen kartanolaitos Ruotsin vallan viimeisenä aikana*, vol. 1, Historiallisia tutkimuksia, no. 15: 1, Helsinki: Suomen Historiallinen Seura.

Jutikkala, Eino 1939, 'Suurmaanomistuksen historiallinen kehitys Suomessa', in *Suomen kartanot ja suurtilat*, edited by Eino Jutikkala and Gabriel Nikander, Helsinki: Suomalaisen Kirjallisuuden Seura, 1: 13–49.

Jutikkala, Eino 1950, 'The Economic Development of Finland Shown in Maps', in *Proceedings of the Finnish Academy of Science and Letters 1948*, Helsinki, 159–66.

Jutikkala, Eino 1956, 'Ståndssamhällets upplösning i Finland', *Turun Historiallinen Arkisto*, Turku: Turun Historiallinen Yhdistys, no. 12: 113–143 (app.).

Jutikkala, Eino 1963, *Bonden i Finland genom tiderna*, Helsinki: LTs Förlag.

Jutikkala, Eino 1968, 'Suomen rautatieverkon synty', in *Suomen talous- ja sosiaalihistorian kehityslinjoja*, edited by Eino Jutikkala, Helsinki: WSOY, 168–73.

Jutikkala, Eino 1970, 'Laittomat asevelvollisuuskutsunnat ja torpparikysymys', in *Suomalainen Tiedeakatemia. Esitelmät ja pöytäkirjat 1969*, Helsinki: Suomalainen Tiedeakatemia, 173–85.

Jutikkala, Eino 1974, *Säätyvaltiopäivien valitsijakunta, vaalit ja koostumus*, Suomen kansanedustuslaitoksen historia, vol. 4: 3, Helsinki: Valtion painatuskeskus.

Jutikkala, Eino 1977, 'Finland. Städernas tillväxt och näringsstruktur', in *Urbaniseringsprosessen i Norden*, vol. 3: *Industrialiseringens første fase*, edited by G.A. Blom, Oslo: Universitetsforlaget, 95–125.

Jutikkala, Eino 1980, 'Suurten sotien ja uuden asutusekspansion kaudet', in *Suomen taloushistoria*, edited by Eino Jutikkala, Yrjö Kaukiainen and Sven-Erik Åström, Helsinki: Tammi, 1: 147–236.

Jutikkala, Eino 1989, 'Sosiologi kirjoittaa historiaa' (book review), *Kanava* 16, 2: 120–2.
Jutikkala, Eino (ed.) 1959, *Atlas of Finnish History*, Helsinki: WSOY.
Jutikkala, Eino, and Kauko Pirinen 1962, *A History of Finland*, London: Thames & Hudson.
Juva, Mikko 1956, *Rajuilman alla*, Helsinki: WSOY.
Juva, Mikko 1960, *Valtionkirkosta kansankirkoksi*, Helsinki: WSOY.
Juva, Mikko 1962, 'Protestiliikkeet Suomen kirkkohistoriassa', *Teologinen Aikakauskirja*, 67: 185–95.
Jyränki, Antero 1978, *Presidentti*, Suomalaisen lakimiesyhdistyksen julkaisuja A, no. 123, Vammala.
Kahk, Juhan 1982, *Peasant and Lord in the Process of Transition from Feudalism to Capitalism in the Baltics*, Tallinn: Eesti Raamat.
Kahk, J. and A. Vassar 1970, 'Lenini õpetus kapitalismi arenemise kahest teest põllumajanduses ja mõningaid Eesti agraarajaloo probleeme', *Eesti NSV Teaduste Akadeemia toimetised*, no. 19; *Ühiskonnateadused*, Tallinn, no. 2: 150–66.
Kaila, E.E. 1931, *Pohjanmaa ja meri 1600-ja 1700-luvuilla*, Historiallisia tutkimuksia, no. 14, Helsinki: Suomen Historiallinen Seura.
Kalabinski, Stanislaw and Feliks Tych 1962, 'La Révolution des années 1905–1907 dans le Royaume de Pologne', *Annali dell'Istituto Giangiacamo Feltrinelli*, 5: 183–259.
Kalela, Jorma 1976, 'Right-Wing Radicalism in Finland During the Interwar Period', *Scandinavian Journal of History*, 1: 105–24.
Kann, Robert A. 1964, *Das Nationalitätenproblem der Habsburgermonarchie*, vol. 1, Graz and Cologne: Verlag Hermann Böhlaus Nachf.
Karjahärm, T., I. Krastyn', and A. Tila 1981, *Revoliutsiia 1905–1907 godov v Pribaltike*, Tallinn: Akademiia Nauk Estonskoi SSR.
Karjahärm, T. and R. Pullat 1975, *Eesti revolutsioonitules 1905–1907*, Tallinn: Eesti Raamat.
Karma, O. 1963, *Tööstuslikult revolutsioonilt sotsialistlikule revolutsioonile Eestis*, Tallinn: Eesti NSV Teaduste Akadeemia Ajaloo Instituut.
Karma, O. and A. Köörna 1977, 'Suure Sotsialistliku Oktoobrirevolutsiooni sotsiaalmajanduslikke eeldusi', in *Revolutsioon, kodusõda ja välisriikide interventsioon Eestis (1917–1920)*, Tallinn: Eesti Raamat, 1: 48–92.
Karvonen, Lauri 1989, 'Risto Alapuro, *State and Revolution in Finland*' (book review), *Politiikka* 31: 225–7.
Karvonen, Lauri 1990, 'Risto Alapuro, *State and Revolution in Finland*' (book review), *Scandinavian Political* Studies 13: 89–92.
Kaukiainen, Yrjö 1980, 'Suomen asuttaminen', in *Suomen taloushistoria*, edited by Eino Jutikkala, Yrjö Kaukiainen and Sven-Erik Åström, Helsinki: Tammi, 1: 11–145.
Kaukiainen, Yrjö 1981, 'Taloudellinen kasvu ja yhteiskunnan muuttuminen teollistuvassa Suomessa', *Historiallinen Arkisto*, Helsinki: Suomen Historiallinen Seura, no. 76: 39–62.

Kekkonen, Jukka 1995a, 'Suomen synty', *Hiidenkivi* 2, 1: 38–9.
Kekkonen, Jukka 1995b, 'Uustulkintoja sisällissodasta', *Helsingin Sanomat* 27 May.
Kekkonen, Jukka 2016, *Kun aseet puhuvat. Poliittinen väkivalta Espanjan ja Suomen sisällissodissa*, Helsinki: Art House.
Kena, Kirsti 1979, *Kirkon aseman ja asenteiden muotoutuminen itsenäistyneessä Suomessa 1918–1922*, Suomen Kirkkohistoriallisen Seuran toimituksia, no. 110, Helsinki.
Kenez, Peter 1972, 'Coalition Politics in the Hungarian Soviet Republic', in *Revolution in Perspective: Essays on the Hungarian Soviet Republic*, edited by Andrew C. Janos and William B. Slottman, Berkeley and Los Angeles: University of California Press, 61–84.
Kero, Reino 1974, *Migration from Finland to North America in the Years Between the United States Civil War and the First World War*, Annales Universitatis Turkuensis B, no. 130, Turku.
Ketola, Eino 1981, 'Suomen sosialidemokraattisen puolueen itsenäisyyspolitiikan muotoutuminen ja suhde Venäjän vallankumoukseen maaliskuusta kesäkuuhun 1917', Licentiate thesis, Department of Political History, University of Helsinki.
Ketonen, Oiva 1983, *Kansakunta murroksessa*, Helsinki: WSOY.
Kettunen, Pauli 1979, 'Sosialidemokratia ja ammattiyhdistysliike Suomessa 1918–1930', Licentiate thesis, Department of Political History, University of Helsinki.
Kettunen, Pauli 1980a, 'Den finländska socialdemokratins demokratiuppfattning mellan inbördeskriget och lapporörelsens framträdande', *Historisk tidskrift för Finland*, 65: 121–49.
Kettunen, Pauli 1980b, 'Über die sozialen und politischen Bedingungen der Entstehung des Massenanhangs der finnischen Arbeiterbewegung. Der Weg zu den Wahlen des Jahres 1907', Typescript.
Kettunen, Pauli 1984, 'Työväentalo, työläisyhteisö, työväenliike. Kehityspiirteitä ja tutkimusongelmia kansalaissodan ja lapuanliikkeen väliseltä ajalta', in *Työväentaloseminaari HTY:n talolla 16.10.1982*, edited by Simo Laaksovirta and Tero Tuomisto, Työväen perinne ja historia. Tutkimuksia, no. 3. Helsinki: Työväen Sivistysliitto, 35–42.
Kettunen, Pauli 1986, *Poliittinen liike ja sosiaalinen kollektiivisuus. Tutkimus sosialidemokratiasta ja ammattiyhdistysliikkeestä Suomessa 1918–1930*, Historiallisia tutkimuksia, no. 138, Helsinki: Suomen Historiallinen Seura.
Kianto, Ilmari 1957 [1909], *Der rote Strich*, translated from the Finnish by Gustav Schmidt, with revision by Friedrich Ege, Leipzig: Verlag Philipp Reclam Jun.
Kiernan, V.G. 1965, 'State and Nation in Western Europe', *Past and Present*, no. 31: 20–38.
Kiernan, V.G. 1976, 'Nationalist Movements and Social Classes', in *Nationalist Movements*, edited by A.D. Smith, London: Macmillan, 110–33.
Kilpi, O.K. 1913, *Suomen ammatissatoimiva väestö ja sen yhteiskunnalliset luokat vuosina 1815/1875*, vol. 1: *Maaseutu*, Helsinki: Sana.

Király, Bela K. 1977, 'Democratic Peasant Movements in Hungary in the Twentieth Century', in *Europäische Bauernparteien im 20. Jahrhundert*, edited by Heinz Gollwitzer, Stuttgart: Gustav Fischer Verlag, 403–36.

Kirby, D.G. 1970, 'Suomi ja Venäjän vallankumouksellinen liike 1905–1916', *Historiallinen Aikakauskirja*, 68: 106–20.

Kirby, D.G. 1971, 'The Finnish Social Democratic Party 1903–1918', Ph.D. thesis, University of London.

Kirby, D.G. 1978, 'Revolutionary Ferment in Finland and the Origins of the Civil War 1917–1918', *Scandinavian Economic History Review*, 26: 15–35.

Kirby, D.G. 1979, *Finland in the Twentieth Century*, London: Hurst.

Kirby, David 1989, 'Risto Alapuro, *State and Revolution in Finland*' (book review), *Historisk Tidskrift för Finland* 74: 314–19.

Kivialho, K. 1927, *Maatalouskiinteistöjen omistajanvaihdokset ja hinnanmuodostus Halikon tuomiokunnassa 1851–1910*, Taloustieteellisiä tutkimuksia, no. 35, Helsinki: Kansantaloudellinen Yhdistys.

Kivisto, Peter 1989, 'Risto Alapuro, *State and Revolution in Finland*' (book review), *Contemporary Sociology* 18: 195–7.

Klemettilä, Aimo 1976, *Tampereen punakaarti ja sen jäsenistö*, Acta Universitatis Tamperensis A, no. 72, Tampere.

Klinge, Matti 1967–68, *Ylioppilaskunnan historia*, vols. 2–3, Helsinki: WSOY.

Klinge, Matti 1969, 'Suomen kansallisuusliikkeiden sosiaalisista suhteista', *Historiallinen Aikakauskirja*, 67: 185–207.

Klinge, Matti 1970, 'Yliopiston vaiheet', in *Helsingin yliopisto – Historiaa ja nykypäivää*, edited by Niilo Luukanen, Helsinki: WSOY, 9–33.

Klinge, Matti 1972, *Vihan veljistä valtiososialismiin*, Helsinki: WSOY.

Klinge, Matti 1975, *Bernadotten ja Leninin välissä*, Helsinki: WSOY.

Klinge, Matti 1980a, *L'Histoire de Finlande en bref*, Helsinki: Otava.

Klinge, Matti 1980b, 'Poliittisen ja kulttuurisen Suomen muodostaminen', in *Suomen kulttuurihistoria*, Helsinki: WSOY, 2: 11–41.

Klinge, Matti 1981, *Suomen sinivalkoiset värit*, Helsinki: Otava.

Klinge, Matti 1982, *Kaksi Suomea*, Helsinki: Otava.

Knoellinger, Carl Erik 1960, *Labor in Finland*, Cambridge, Mass.: Harvard University Press.

Kollontay, A.M. 1903 *Zhizn' finliandskikh" rabochikh"*, St. Petersburg: T-vo Khudozhestvennoi Pechati.

Koralka, Jiri 1971, 'Social Problems in the Czech and Slovak National Movements', in *Mouvements nationaux d'indépendance et classes populaires aux XIXe et XXe siècles en occident et en orient*, Paris: Armand Colin, 1: 56–73.

Korhonen, Keijo 1963, *Suomen asiain komitea. Suomen korkeimman hallinnon järjestelyt ja toteuttaminen vuosina 1811–1826*, Historiallisia tutkimuksia, no. 65, Helsinki: Suomen Historiallinen Seura.

Koval'chenko, I.D. and L.I. Borodkin 1979, 'Agrarnaia tipologiia gubernii Evropeiskoi Rossii na rubezhe XIX–XX vekov', *Istoriia SSSR*, 23: 59–95.

Kruus, Hans 1935, *Histoire de l'Estonie*, Paris: Payot.

Kühnl, Reinhard 1971, *Formen bürgerlicher Herrschaft. Liberalismus – Faschismus*, Reinbek bei Hamburg, W. Ger.: Rowohlt.

Kuhnle, Stein 1975, *Patterns of Social and Political Mobilization: A Historical Analysis of the Nordic Countries*, Beverly Hills, Calif.: Sage.

Kunnas, Heikki J. 1973, *Metsätaloustuotanto Suomessa 1860–1965*, Suomen Pankin taloustieteellisen tutkimuslaitoksen julkaisuja, Kasvututkimuksia, no. 4, Helsinki.

Kunnas, Maria-Liisa 1976, *Kansalaissodan kirjalliset rintamat*, Helsinki: Suomalaisen Kirjallisuuden Seura.

Kuusinen, O.W. 1919, *The Finnish Revolution: A Self-Criticism*, London: Workers' Socialist Federation.

Kuusterä, Antti 1981, 'Pankkiosakkeiden leviäminen suomalaiseen yhteiskuntaan 1860-luvulla', *Historiallinen Arkisto*, Helsinki: Suomen Historiallinen Seura, no. 76: 367–91.

Kuusterä, Antti 1985, 'The Role of State as Supplier of Capital in Finland During the Latter Half of the 19th Century', in *Economic Development in Hungary and in Finland, 1860–1939*, edited by Tapani Mauranen, University of Helsinki, Institute of Economic and Social History Communications, no. 18, Helsinki, 143–59.

Kuusterä, Paula 1979, 'Maatalouden 1930-luvun lamanaikaisesta protestitoiminnasta Suomessa', Licentiate thesis, Department of Political History, University of Helsinki.

Kyllönen, M. 1975, 'Punaisten ilmastoalueiden synty Pohjois-Suomessa 1900–1910', Licentiate thesis, Department of History, University of Jyväskylä.

Laaksonen, Oiva 1962, *Suomen liike-elämän johtajisto*, Helsinki: WSOY.

Lackman, Matti 1985, *Taistelu talonpojasta. Suomen Kommunistisen Puolueen suhde talonpoikaiskysymykseen ja talonpoikaisliikkeisiin 1918–1939*, Scripta Historica, no. 10, Acta Societatis Historicae Ouluensis, Oulu: Pohjoinen.

Laine, Leena 1983, 'Vapaaehtoisten järjestöjen kehitys ruumiinkulttuurin alueella Suomessa v. 1856–1917', Licentiate thesis, Department of History, University of Helsinki.

Lakio, Matti 1975, *Teollisuuden kehittyminen Itä-Suomessa 1830–1930*, Itä-Suomen Instituutti A, no. 5, Mikkeli.

Lappalainen, Jussi T. 1967, *Itsenäisen Suomen synty*, Jyväskylä: Gummerus.

Lappalainen, Jussi T. 1981, *Punakaartin sota*, 2 vols, Helsinki: Opetusministeriö.

Lappalainen, Jussi T., Juhani Piilonen, Osmo Rinta-Tassi and Marja-Leena Salkola 1989, *Yhden kortin varassa. Suomalainen vallankumous 1918*, Helsinki: Valtion painatuskeskus.

Lemberg, Hans 1977, 'Die agrarischen Parteien in den böhmischen Ländern und in der tschechoslowakischen Republik', in *Europäische Bauernparteien im 20. Jahrhundert*, edited by Heinz Gollwitzer, Stuttgart: Gustav Fischer Verlag, 323–58.

Lenin, V.I. 1954 [1917], *State and Revolution*, New York: International Publishers.
Lento, Reino 1951, *Maassamuutto ja siihen vaikuttaneet tekijät Suomessa vuosina 1878–1939*, Väestöpoliittisen tutkimuslaitoksen julkaisuja A, no. 5, Helsinki.
Liikanen, Ilkka 1993, 'Skuldens långa skugga. Frihetskrigslitteraturens upprorsbild och dess senare skeden', *Historisk Tidskrift för Finland* 78: 562–79.
Liikanen, Ilkka 1998, 'Vuoden 1918 perintö ja perunkirjoittajat', in *Varkaus, Suomi ja vuosi 1918. Kansallinen ja paikallinen vallankumous*, edited by Hannu Itkonen, Varkaus: Varkauden museon julkaisuja 7, 19–30.
Lindholm, Sture 2005, *'Röd galenskap – vit terror'. Det förträngda kriget 1918 i Västnyland*, Helsingfors: Söderströms.
Lindman, Sven 1968, *Eduskunnan aseman muuttuminen 1917–1919*, Suomen kansanedustuslaitoksen historia, vol. 6, Helsinki: Valtion painatuskeskus.
Lindman, Sven 1978, Introduction to *Karl H. Wiiks dagbok från storstrejken till upproret 1917–1918*, edited by Sven Lindman, xiii–xxv, Publications of the Research Institute of the Åbo Akademi Foundation, no. 36, Turku.
Linna, Väinö 1960, *Täällä Pohjantähden alla*, vol. 2, Helsinki: WSOY.
Linz, Juan J. 1976, 'Patterns of Land Tenure, Division of Labor, and Voting Behavior in Europe', *Comparative Politics*, 8: 365–430.
Linz, Juan J. 1978, 'From Great Hopes to Civil War: The Breakdown of Democracy in Spain', in *The Breakdown of Democratic Regimes: Europe*, edited by Juan J. Linz and Alfred Stepan, Baltimore: Johns Hopkins University Press, 142–215.
Lipset, S.M. 1983, 'Radicalism or Reformism: The Sources of Working-Class Politics', *American Political Science Review*, 77: 1–18.
Lipset, S.M. and Stein Rokkan 1967, 'Cleavage Structures, Party Systems and Voter Alignments: An Introduction', in *Party Systems and Voter Alignments: Cross-National Perspectives*, edited by S.M. Lipset and Stein Rokkan, New York: Free Press, 1–64.
Loit, Aleksander 1985, 'Die nationalen Bewegungen im Baltikum während des 19. Jahrhunderts in vergleichender Perspektive', in *National Movements in the Baltic Countries During the 19th Century*, edited by Aleksander Loit, Acta Universitatis Stockholmiensis, Studia Baltica Stockholmiensia, no. 2, Uppsala, 59–81.
Lundin, C. Leonard 1981, 'Finland', in *Russification in the Baltic Provinces and Finland, 1855–1914*, edited by Edward C. Thaden, Princeton, N.J.: Princeton University Press, 357–457.
Lundkvist, Sven 1980, 'The Popular Movements in Swedish Society, 1850–1920', *Scandinavian Journal of History*, 5: 219–38.
Mäkelä, Klaus and Matti Viikari 1977, 'Notes on Alcohol and the State', *Acta Sociologica*, 20: 155–79.
Manner, Kullervo 1924, *Talonpoikaiskysymyksestä Suomessa*, Stockholm: Suomen Kommunistisen Puolueen keskuskomitea.
Mannerheim, C.G. 1953, *The Memoirs of Marshal Mannerheim*, London: Cassell.

Manninen, Ohto 1974, *Kansannoususta armeijaksi*, Historiallisia tutkimuksia, no. 95, Helsinki: Suomen Historiallinen Seura.

Manninen, Ohto 1975, 'Valkoisen Suomen muotoutuminen', *Historiallinen Arkisto*, Helsinki: Suomen Historiallinen Seura, no. 67: 402–71.

Manninen, Ohto 1978, 'Red, White and Blue in Finland, 1918', *Scandinavian Journal of History*, 3: 229–49.

Manninen, Pauli 1976, *Selvitys Suomen elinkeinorakenteesta ja sen tutkimuksesta 1820–1970*, Suomen työväenliikkeen historia -projektin selvityksiä, no. 1, Helsinki.

Manninen, Turo 1982, *Vapaustaistelu, kansalaissota ja kapina*, Studia Historica Jyväskyläensia, no. 24, Jyväskylä: Jyväskylän yliopisto.

Mansner, Markku 1981, *Työnantajaklubista keskusliitoksi*, Jyväskylä: Gummerus.

Markkanen, Erkki 1977, *Maaseutuväestön varallisuusolot ja luottosuhteet Sisä-Suomessa elinkeinoelämän murroskaudella v. 1850–1914*, Studia Historica Jyväskyläensia, no. 14, Jyväskylä: Jyväskylän yliopisto.

Martin, William C. 1970, 'A Sociological and Analytic Study of the Development of the Finnish Revolution of 1917–1918 in Terms of Social Structures', Ph.D. thesis, Vanderbilt University.

Martin, William C. and Karen Hopkins 1980, 'Cleavage Crystallization and Party Linkages in Finland, 1900–1918', in *Political Parties and Linkage*, edited by Kay Lawson, New Haven, Conn.: Yale University Press, 183–203.

Massa, Ilmo 1983, *Ihminen ja Lapin luonto*, Transactions of the Finnish Anthropological Society, no. 12, Helsinki.

Mattila, Aarne 1969, *Työmarkkinasuhteiden murros Suomessa*, Historiallisia tutkimuksia, no. 76, Helsinki: Suomen Historiallinen Seura.

Mauranen, Tapani 1980, 'Kotimaankauppa', in *Suomen taloushistoria*, edited by Eino Jutikkala, Yrjö Kaukiainen and Sven-Erik Åström, Helsinki: Tammi, 1: 436–50.

Mauranen, Tapani 1981, 'Porvarista kauppiaaksi – Kauppiaan yhteiskunnallinen asema 1800-luvun jälkipuoliskolla', *Historiallinen Arkisto*, Helsinki: Suomen Historiallinen Seura, no. 76: 185–212.

Mead, W.R. 1981, *An Historical Geography of Scandinavia*, London: Academic Press.

Meiksins, Gregory 1943, *The Baltic Riddle*, New York: Fischer.

Migdal, Joel S. 1974, *Peasants, Politics, and Revolution: Pressures Toward Political and Social Change in the Third World*, Princeton, N.J.: Princeton University Press.

Molnár, Miklos 1971, 'Mouvements d'indépendance en Europe. Rôle de la question agraire et du niveau de culture', in *Mouvements nationaux d'indépendance et classes populaires aux XIXe et XXe siècles en occident et en orient*, Paris: Armand Colin, 1: 217–27.

Moore, Barrington, Jr. 1966, *Social Origins of Dictatorship and Democracy: Lord and Peasant in the Making of the Modern World*, Boston: Beacon Press.

Moore, Barrington, Jr. 1972, *Reflections on the Causes of Human Misery and upon Certain Proposals to Eliminate Them*, London: Allen Lane.

Moore, Barrington, Jr. 1978, *Injustice: The Social Bases of Obedience and Revolt*, London: Macmillan.

Moritsch, Andreas 1977, 'Die Bauernparteien bei den Kroaten, Serben und Slowenen', in *Europäische Bauernparteien im 20. Jahrhundert*, edited by Heinz Gollwitzer, Stuttgart: Gustav Fischer Verlag, 359–402.

Murtorinne, Eino 1967, *Taistelu uskonnonvapaudesta suurlakon jälkeisinä vuosina*, Helsinki: WSOY.

Musat, Mircea and Gheorghe Zaharia 1980, 'Romania', in *Assertion of Unitary, Independent National States in Central and Southeast Europe (1821–1923)*, edited by Viorica Moisuc and Ion Calafeteanu, Bibliotheca Historica Romaniae, no. 62, Bucharest, 15–55.

Mylly, Juhani 1975, 'Maalaisliiton synty', *Turun Historiallinen Arkisto*, Turku: Turun Historiallinen Yhdistys, no. 30: 82–109.

Mylly, Juhani 1980, 'The Emergence of the Finnish Multi-Party System: A Comparison with Development in Scandinavia, 1870–1920', *Scandinavian Journal of History*, 5: 277–93.

Myllyntaus, Timo 1980, 'Suomen talouspolitiikka ja valtiontalous 1809–1860', in *Suomen taloushistoria*, edited by Eino Jutikkala, Yrjö Kaukiainen and Sven-Erik Åström, Helsinki: Tammi, 1: 333–66.

Myllyntaus, Timo 1981, 'Työvoimapolitiikka autonomian ajan alkupuoliskolla', *Historiallinen Arkisto*, Helsinki: Suomen Historiallinen Seura, no. 76: 155–81.

Nagy, Balazs 1967, 'La Révolution d'Octobre et la République des Conseils en Hongrie', in *La Révolution d'Octobre et le Mouvement ouvrier européen*, ed. Victor Fay, Paris: EDI, 159–72.

Nairn, Tom 1977, *The Break-Up of Britain*, London: New Left Books.

Nieminen, Tommi 1981, 'Ylistaron talonpoikaismarssijat', in *Kansanliikkeitten Pohjanmaa*, edited by Kalervo Ilmanen, Oikeushistoriallisia julkaisuja, no. 2, Helsinki: Helsingin yliopisto, Oikeuden yleistieteiden laitos, 141–76.

Nodel, Emanuel 1963, *Estonia: Nation on the Anvil*, New York: Bookman.

Nolte, Ernst 1968, *Die Krise des liberalen Systems und die faschistischen Bewegungen*, Munich: Piper Verlag.

Noponen, Martti 1964, *Kansanedustajien sosiaalinen tausta Suomessa*, Helsinki: WSOY.

Ojala, Herkko 1962, 'Ensipolven akateemisen sivistyneistön muodostumisesta Suomessa vuosina 1859–1899', in *Historica*, edited by Mauno Jokipii, Studia Historica Jyväskyläensia, no. 1. Jyväskylä: Jyväskylän Kasvatusopillinen Korkeakoulu and Jyväskylän Yliopistoyhdistys, 335–90.

Oksa, Jukka 1978, 'Pohjois-Karjalan kehitysalueongelman yhteiskunnallis-taloudellinen tausta', Licentiate thesis, The Karelian Institute, University of Joensuu.

Orridge, A.W. 1981, 'Varieties of Nationalism', in *The Nation-State*, edited by Leonard Tivey, Oxford: Martin Robertson, 39–58.

Orridge, A.W. 1982, 'Separatist and Autonomist Nationalisms: The Structure of Regional Loyalties in the Modern State', in *National Separatism*, edited by Colin H. Williams, Cardiff: University of Wales Press, 43–74.

Orridge, Andrew W. and Colin H. Williams 1982, 'Autonomist Nationalism: A Theoretical Framework for Spatial Variations in Its Genesis and Development', *Political Geography Quarterly*, 1: 19–39.

Østerud, Øyvind 1978a, *Agrarian Structure and Peasant Politics in Scandinavia: A Comparative Study of Rural Response to Economic Change*, Oslo: Universitetsforlaget.

Østerud, Øyvind 1978b, *Utviklingsteori og historisk endring*, Oslo: Gyldendal.

Osvoboditel'nye dvizheniia narodov Avstriiskoi imperii. Period utverzhdeniia kapitalizma 1981, Moscow: Nauka.

Paasikivi, J.K. 1957, *Paasikiven muistelmia sortovuosilta*, vol. 1, Helsinki: WSOY.

Paasivirta, Juhani 1957, *Suomi vuonna 1918*, Helsinki: WSOY.

Paasivirta, Juhani 1981, *Finland and Europe: International Crises During the Period of Autonomy 1808–1914*, London: Hurst.

Paavolainen, Jaakko 1966–1967, *Poliittiset väkivaltaisuudet Suomessa 1918*, 2 vols, Helsinki: Tammi.

Paavolainen, Jaakko 1971, *Vankileirit Suomessa 1918*, Helsinki: Tammi.

Paavolainen, Jaakko 1988, 'Vuoden 1918 vallankumous sosiologin näkökulmasta. Tulkinta ilman voittajia ja häviäjiä' (book review), *Helsingin Sanomat* 28 August.

Palmgren, Raoul 1948, *Suuri linja*, Helsinki: Kansankulttuuri.

Parikka, Raimo 1990, 'Malmin menetetty maine. Työläisyhteisö ja vallankumous 1917' [with a summary in English: 'The Lost Reputation of Malmi'], in *Arki ja murros. Tutkielmia keisariajan lopun Suomesta*, edited by Matti Peltonen, Helsinki: Suomen Historiallinen Seura, 297–324.

Peltonen, Arvo 1982, *Suomen kaupunkijärjestelmän kasvu 1815–1970*, Bidrag till kännedom av Finlands natur och folk, no. 128, Helsinki: Finska Vetenskaps-Societeten.

Peltonen, Matti 1985, 'Torppari ja markkinat. Maatalouden kaupallistumisen vaikutus 1900-luvun alun tilanosavuokraajan taloudelliseen asemaan', Paper presented at meeting of the Westermarck Society, Jyväskylä, Finland, 8–9 March 1985.

Peltonen, Matti 1986, 'Metsätulot ja maatilatalouden murros autonomian ajan lopulla', *Historiallinen Arkisto*, Helsinki: Suomen Historiallinen Seura, no. 88: 101–14.

Pihkala, Erkki 1969, *Suomen ulkomaankauppa 1860–1917*, Suomen Pankin taloustieteel lisen tutkimuslaitoksen julkaisuja, Kasvututkimuksia, no. 2, Helsinki.

Pihkala, Erkki 1977, *Valtion tulojen ja menojen rakenne 1800-luvun jälkipuoliskolla*, Helsingin kauppakorkeakoulun julkaisuja B, no. 23, Helsinki.

Pihkala, Erkki 1985, 'Relations with Russia, Foreign Trade and the Development of the Finnish Economy 1860–1939', in *Economic Development in Hungary and in Finland, 1860–1939*, edited by Tapani Mauranen, University of Helsinki, Institute of Economic and Social History Communications, no. 18. Helsinki, 25–48.

Piilonen, Juhani 1982, *Vallankumous kunnallishallinnossa*, Helsinki: Opetusministeriö.
Pipes, Richard 1964, *The Formation of the Soviet Union: Communism and Nationalism 1917–1923*, Rev. ed. Cambridge, Mass.: Harvard University Press.
Pipping, Hugo E. 1969, *Kultakannan turvissa. Suomen Pankki 1878–1914*, Helsinki: Suomen Pankki.
Pistohlkors, Gert von 1978, *Ritterschaftliche Reformpolitik zwischen Russifizierung und Revolution*, Göttinger Bausteine zur Geschichtswissenschaft, no. 48, Göttingen: Musterschmidt.
Plakans, Andrejs 1974, 'Peasants, Intellectuals and Nationalism in the Russian Baltic Provinces, 1820–90', *Journal of Modern History*, 46: 445–75.
Plakans, Andrejs 1981, 'The Latvians', in *Russification in the Baltic Provinces and Finland, 1855–1914*, edited by Edward C. Thaden, Princeton, N.J.: Princeton University Press, 205–84.
Pollard, Sidney 1981, *Peaceful Conquest: The Industrialization of Europe 1760–1970*, Oxford: Oxford University Press.
Polvinen, Tuomo 1967, *Venäjän vallankumous ja Suomi 1917–1920*, vol. 1, Helsinki: WSOY.
Polvinen, Tuomo 1980, 'Lokakuun vallankumous ja Suomen itsenäistyminen', *Historiallinen Arkisto*, Helsinki: Suomen Historiallinen Seura, no. 75: 112–22.
Polvinen, Tuomo 1984, *Valtakunta ja rajamaa. N. I. Bobrikov Suomen kenraalikuvernöörinä 1898–1904*, Helsinki: WSOY.
Popkin, Samuel L. 1979, *The Rational Peasant: The Political Economy of Rural Society in Vietnam*, Berkeley and Los Angeles: University of California Press.
Population de la Finlande au 31 décembre 1865 1870, Official Statistics of Finland VI: Population, no. 1, Helsinki.
Population de la Finlande au 31 décembre 1910 1915, vol. 2, Official Statistics of Finland VI: Population, no. 47, Helsinki.
Portal, Roger 1971, 'Balkans. La Participation des classes populaires (masses et cadres) aux mouvements nationaux d'indépendance', in *Mouvements nationaux d'indépendance et classes populaires aux XIXe et XXe siècles en occident et en orient*, Paris: Armand Colin, 1: 93–100.
Pullat, R. 1976, *Gorodskoe naselenie Estonii s kontsa XVIII veka do 1940 goda*, Tallinn: Eesti Raamat.
Radkey, Oliver Henry 1950, *The Election to the Russian Constituent Assembly of 1917*, Cambridge, Mass.: Harvard University Press.
Rajala, Panu 1983, *F. E. Sillanpää vuosina 1888–1923*, Helsinki: Suomalaisen Kirjallisuuden Seura.
Rankoff, Iwan 1977, 'Bauerndemokratie in Bulgarien', in *Europäische Bauernparteien im 20. Jahrhundert*, edited by Heinz Gollwitzer, Stuttgart: Gustav Fischer Verlag, 466–506.
Ranta, Raimo and Sven-Erik Åström 1980, 'Tapulipolitiikka ja Suomi', in *Suomen tal-*

oushistoria, edited by Eino Jutikkala, Yrjö Kaukiainen and Sven-Erik Åström, Helsinki: Tammi, 1: 255-63.

Rantatupa, Heikki 1979, *Elintarvikehuolto ja -säännöstely Suomessa vuosina 1914-1921*, Studia Historica Jyväskyläensia, no. 17, Jyväskylä: Jyväskylän yliopisto.

Rasila, Viljo 1961, *Suomen torpparikysymys vuoteen 1909*, Historiallisia tutkimuksia, no. 59, Helsinki: Suomen Historiallinen Seura.

Rasila, Viljo 1968, *Kansalaissodan sosiaalinen tausta*, Helsinki: Tammi.

Rasila, Viljo 1970, *Torpparikysymyksen ratkaisuvaihe*, Historiallisia tutkimuksia, no. 81, Helsinki: Suomen Historiallinen Seura.

Rasila, Viljo 1982a, 'Kauppa ja rahaliike', in *Suomen taloushistoria*, edited by Jorma Ahvenainen, Erkki Pihkala and Viljo Rasila, Helsinki: Tammi, 2: 89-113.

Rasila, Viljo 1982b, 'Kehitys ja sen tulokset', in *Suomen taloushistoria*, edited by Jorma Ahvenainen, Erkki Pihkala and Viljo Rasila, Helsinki: Tammi, 2: 154-67.

Rasila, Viljo 1982c, 'Liikenne', in *Suomen taloushistoria*, edited by Jorma Ahvenainen, Erkki Pihkala and Viljo Rasila, Helsinki: Tammi, 2: 114-31.

Rasila, Viljo, Eino Jutikkala and Keijo K. Kulha 1976, *Suomen poliittinen historia*, vol. 2, Helsinki: WSOY.

Rauch, Georg von 1967, 'Zur Krise des Parlamentarismus in Estland und Lettland in den 30er Jahren', in *Die Krise des Parlamentarismus in Ostmitteleuropa zwischen den beiden Weltkriegen*, edited by Hans-Erich Volkmann, Marburg am Lahn: J.G. Herder Institut, 135-55.

Rauch, Georg von 1977, 'Die bolschewistischen Staatsgründungen im baltischen Raum und die sovetische Politik', in *Von den baltischen Provinzen zu den baltischen Staaten. Beiträge zur Entstehungsgeschichte der Republiken Estland und Lettland 1918-1920*, edited by Jürgen von Hehn, Hans von Rimscha, and Hellmuth Weiss, Marburg am Lahn: J.G. Herder Institut, 44-69.

Raumolin, Jussi 1981, 'Development Problems in the Scandinavian Periphery', *IFDA Dossier* 22: 2-16.

Raun, Toivo U. 1981, 'The Estonians', in *Russification in the Baltic Provinces and Finland, 1855-1914*, edited by Edward C. Thaden, Princeton, N.J.: Princeton University Press, 285-354.

Raun, Toivo U. 1982, 'Estonian Social and Political Thought, 1905-February 1917', in *Die baltischen Provinzen Russlands zwischen den Revolutionen von 1905 und 1917*, edited by Andrew Ezergailis and Gert von Pistohlkors, Cologne and Vienna: Böhlau Verlag, 59-72.

Raun, Toivo U. 1984a, 'The Estonians and the Russian Empire, 1905-1917', *Journal of Baltic Studies*, 15: 130-40.

Raun, Toivo U. 1984b, 'The Revolution of 1905 in the Baltic Provinces and Finland', *Slavic Review*, 43: 453-67.

Recensement agricole de 1910 1916, vol. 1, Official Statistics of Finland III: Agriculture, no. 9, Helsinki.

Reitala, Aimo 1983, *Suomi-neito. Suomen kuvallisen henkilöitymän vaiheet*, Helsinki: Otava.

Remeikis, Thomas 1977, 'Lithuanian Political Parties and the Agrarian Sector of Society in the Twentieth Century', in *Europäische Bauernparteien im 2.0. Jahrhundert*, edited by Heinz Gollwitzer, Stuttgart: Gustav Fischer Verlag, 242–70.

Rentola, Kimmo 1992, 'Toinen kirja', in Seppo Aalto and Kimmo Rentola, *Karkkilan eli Högforsin ja Pyhäjärven entisen Pahajärven ihmisten historia*, Karkkila: Karkkilan kaupunki, 247–877, 878–912.

Siironen, Miika 2012, *Valkoiset. Vapaussodan perintö*, Tampere: Vastapaino.

Rintala, Marvin 1962, *Three Generations: The Extreme Right Wing in Finnish Politics*, Bloomington: Indiana University Press.

Rintala, Marvin 1963, 'An Image of European Politics: The People's Patriotic Movement', *Journal of Central European Affairs*, 21: 308–16.

Rintala, Marvin 1969, *Four Finns*, Berkeley and Los Angeles: University of California Press.

Rintala, Marvin 1972, 'Finnish Students in Politics: The Academic Karelia Society', *East European Quarterly*, 6: 192–205.

Rinta-Tassi, Osmo 1972, 'Punaisen Suomen keskushallinnon organisaatio', Licentiate thesis, Department of History, University of Jyväskylä.

Roberts, Henry L. 1951, *Rumania: Political Problems of an Agrarian State*, New Haven, Conn.: Yale University Press.

Robinson, Geroid T. 1932, *Rural Russia Under the Old Regime*, New York: Macmillan.

Rokkan, Stein 1969, 'Models and Methods in the Comparative Study of Nation-Building', *Acta Sociologica*, 12: 53–73.

Rokkan, Stein 1970, *Citizens, Elections, Parties*, Oslo: Universitetsforlaget.

Rokkan, Stein 1973, 'Cities, States and Nations: A Dimensional Model for the Study of Contrasts in Development', in *Building States and Nations*, edited by S.N. Eisenstadt and Stein Rokkan, Beverly Hills, Calif.: Sage, 1: 73–97.

Rokkan, Stein 1980, 'Territories, Centres, and Peripheries: Toward a Geoethnic-Geo-economic-Geopolitical Model of Differentiation Within Western Europe', in *Centre and Periphery: Spatial Variation in Politics*, edited by Jean Gottmann, Beverly Hills, Calif.: Sage, 163–204.

Rokkan, Stein 1981, 'The Growth and Structuring of Mass Politics', in *Nordic Democracy*, edited by Erik Allardt et al., Copenhagen: Det Danske Selskab, 53–79.

Rommi, Pirkko 1964, 'Finland', in *Problemer i nordisk historieforskning*, Bergen: Universitetsforlaget, 103–30.

Rosenberg, Tiit 1985, 'Über die Ausdifferenzierung der sozialen Schichtung im estnischen Dorf in der zweiten Hälfte des 19. Jh.', in *National Movements in the Baltic Countries During the 19th Century*, edited by Aleksander Loit, Acta Universitatis Stockholmiensis. Studia Baltica Stockholmiensia, no. 2. Uppsala, 245–58.

Rosenqvist, G.O. 1952, *Suomen kirkon murrosaikoja*, Helsinki: WSOY.
Saat, I. and K. Siilivask 1977, *Velikaia Oktiabr'skaia sotsialisticheskaia revoliutsiia v Estonii*, Tallinn: Eesti Raamat.
Salkola, Marja-Leena 1975, 'Työväenkaartien synty Suomessa 1917 Venäjän helmikuun vallankumouksen ja 13.11. puhjenneen yleislakon välisenä aikana', Licentiate thesis, Department of Political History, University of Helsinki.
Salkola, Marja-Leena 1979, 'Om arbetargardena 1917–1918', *Historisk tidskrift för Finland* 64: 341–61.
Salkola, Marja-Leena 1985, *Työväenkaartien synty ja kehitys punakaartiksi*, 2 vols, Helsinki: Opetusministeriö.
Salokangas, Raimo 1975, 'Maalaisliiton kannatuksen leviäminen Vaasan läänissä 1906–1917', *Turun Historiallinen Arkisto*, Turku: Turun Historiallinen Yhdistys, no. 30: 110–91.
Salomaa, Markku 1983, 'Vuoden 1918 työväenvallan valtioluonne ja esikuvat – oliko niitä?', *Historiallinen Aikakauskirja* 81: 183–97.
Sarajas, Annamari 1962, *Viimeiset romantikot*, Helsinki: WSOY.
Sarmela, Matti 1969, *Reciprocity Systems of the Rural Society in the Finnish-Karelian Culture Area*, FF Communications, no. 207, Helsinki: Academia Scientiarum Fennica.
Schärf, Jacques 1967, 'La Révolution d'Octobre et le Mouvement ouvrier dans les pays balkaniques', in *La Révolution d'Octobre et le Mouvement ouvrier européen*, edited by Victor Fay, Paris: EDI, 195–228.
Schmidt, W.A. 1956a, 'Gammallutherskt kyrkoliv i Egentliga Finland under 1800-talet', *Suomen Kirkkohistoriallisen Seuran Vuosikirja*, Helsinki, 43–44: 83–195.
Schmidt, W.A. 1956b, 'Huvuddragen av Finlands kyrkliga geografi', *Acta Academiae Aboensis, Humaniora*, no. 22: 3, Turku.
Schram, Stuart R. 1957, 'L'Union soviétique et les États baltes', in *Les Frontières européennes de l'U.R.S.S. 1917–1941*, edited by Jean-Baptiste Duroselle, Cahiers de la Fondation nationale des sciences politiques, no. 85, Paris, 23–166.
Schweitzer, Robert 1978, *Autonomie und Autokratie. Die Stellung des Grossfürstentums Finnland im russischen Reich in der zweiten Hälfte des 19. Jahrhunderts (1863–1899)*, Marburger Abhandlungen zur Geschichte und Kultur Osteuropas, no. 19, Giessen: Wilhelm Schmitz Verlag.
Schweitzer, Robert 1984, 'The Baltic Parallel: Reality or Historiographical Myth? The Influence of the Tsarist Government's Experience in the Baltic Provinces on Its Finnish Policy', *Journal of Baltic Studies*, 15: 195–215.
Schybergson, Per 1973, *Hantverk och fabriker*. Vol. 1: *Finlands konsumtionsvaruindustri 1815–1870: Helhetsutveckling*, Bidrag till kännedom av Finlands natur och folk, no. 114, Helsinki: Finska Vetenskaps-Societeten.
Schybergson, Per 1977, 'Entreprenörer inom Finlands fabriksindustri i början av ryska

tiden', in *Från medeltid till 1900-tal*, Skrifter utgivna av Historiska Samfundet i Åbo, no. 9, Turku, 127–49.

Schybergson, Per 1980a, 'Teollisuus ja käsityö', in *Suomen taloushistoria*, edited by Eino Jutikkala, Yrjö Kaukiainen and Sven-Erik Åström, Helsinki: Tammi, 1: 408–35.

Schybergson, Per 1980b, 'Ulkomaankaupan kehitys', in *Suomen taloushistoria*, edited by Eino Jutikkala, Yrjö Kaukiainen and Sven-Erik Åström, Helsinki: Tammi, 1: 451–8.

Scott, James C. 1976, *The Moral Economy of the Peasant: Rebellion and Subsistence in Southeast Asia*, New Haven, Conn.: Yale University Press.

Scott, James C. 1977, 'Peasant Revolution: A Dismal Science', *Comparative Politics*, 9: 231–48.

Screen, J.E.O. 1976, 'The Entry of Finnish Officers into Russian Military Service 1809–1917', Ph.D. thesis, University of London.

Selleck, Roberta Gifford 1961, 'The Language Issue in Finnish Political Discussion: 1809–1863', Ph.D. thesis, Radcliffe College, Cambridge, Mass.

Seppänen, Paavo 1972, 'Finland', in *Western Religion*, edited by Hans Mol, The Hague: Mouton, 143–73.

Seton-Watson, Hugh 1977, *Nations and States*, London: Methuen.

Shorter, Edward and Charles Tilly 1974, *Strikes in France, 1830–1968*, Cambridge: Cambridge University Press.

Sihvo, Hannes 1973, *Karjalan kuva*, Helsinki: Suomalaisen Kirjallisuuden Seura.

Siilivask, Karl 1975, 'Eestin väestön sosiaalisesta rakenteesta 1800-luvulla', *Turun Historiallinen Arkisto*, Turku: Turun Historiallinen Yhdistys, no. 30: 59–72.

Sillanpää, F.E. 1938 [1919], *Meek Heritage*, translated from the Finnish by Alexander Matson, London: Putnam.

Siltala, Juha 1984, 'Lapuan liikkeen joukkokannatus', *Historiallinen Aikakauskirja*, 82: 16–33.

Siltala, Juha 1985, *Lapuan liike ja kyyditykset 1930*, Helsinki: Otava.

Siltala, Juha 2009, *Sisällissodan psykohistoria*, Helsinki: Otava.

Siltala, Juha 2014, 'Being Absorbed into an Unintended War', in *The Finnish Civil War 1918: History, Memory, Legacy*, edited by Tuomas Tepora and Aapo Roselius, Leiden and Boston: Brill, 51–89.

Simon, Walter B. 1978, 'Democracy in the Shadow of Imposed Sovereignty: The First Republic of Austria', in *The Breakdown of Democratic Regimes: Europe*, edited by Juan J. Linz and Alfred Stepan, Baltimore: Johns Hopkins University Press, 80–121.

Simunek, Cestmir 1980, 'Fascisme et sous-développement socio-culturel en Europe centrale et orientale (Slovaquie, Roumanie, Hongrie, Pologne)', *Doctorat de 3° cycle* thesis, École des Hautes Études en Sciences Sociales, Paris.

Skocpol, Theda 1979, *States and Social Revolutions: A Comparative Analysis of France, Russia, and China*, Cambridge: Cambridge University Press.

Skocpol, Theda 1982, 'What Makes Peasants Revolutionary?', *Comparative Politics*, 14: 351–75.
Smith, A.D. 1978, 'The Diffusion of Nationalism: Some Historical and Sociological Perspectives', *British Journal of Sociology*, 29: 234–48.
Smith, C. Jay, Jr. 1958, *Finland and the Russian Revolution 1917–1922*, Athens: University of Georgia Press.
Smith, C. Jay, Jr. 1971, 'Soviet Russia and the Red Revolution of 1918 in Finland', *Studies on the Soviet Union*, n.s. 11, no. 4: 71–93.
Snellman, G.R. 1914, *Tutkimus Suomen sahateollisuudesta sekä sen yhteyteen kuuluvista metsänhakkuusta, lauttauksesta ja lastauksesta*, Työtilastoa, no. 16, Helsinki: Keisarillisen Senaatin kirjapaino.
Soikkanen, Hannu 1961, *Sosialismin tulo Suomeen*, Helsinki: WSOY.
Soikkanen, Hannu 1967, 'Miksi revisionismi ei saanut kannatusta Suomen vanhassa työväenliikkeessä?', in *Oman ajan historia ja politiikan tutkimus*, edited by Lauri Hyvämäki et al., Helsinki: Otava, 183–99.
Soikkanen, Hannu 1975, *Kohti kansanvaltaa*, vol. 1, Vaasa: Suomen Sosialidemokraattinen Puolue.
Soikkanen, Hannu 1978, 'Revisionism, Reformism and the Finnish Labour Movement Before the First World War', *Scandinavian Journal of History*, 3: 347–60.
Soikkanen, Hannu 1981, 'Vanha ja uusi yhteiskunta', *Historiallinen Arkisto*, Helsinki: Suomen Historiallinen Seura, no. 76: 433–53.
Soininen, Arvo M. 1974, *Vanha maataloutemme*, Historiallisia tutkimuksia, no. 96, Helsinki: Suomen Historiallinen Seura.
Soininen, Arvo M. 1981, 'Maataloustyöväen palkat vv. 1878–1913', *Historiallinen Arkisto*, Helsinki: Suomen Historiallinen Seura, no. 76: 91–113.
Soininen, Arvo M. 1982, 'Maa- ja metsätalous', in *Suomen taloushistoria*, edited by Jorma Ahvenainen, Erkki Pihkala and Viljo Rasila, Helsinki: Tammi, 2: 27–51.
Sømme, A., ed. 1968, *A Geography of Norden*, Bergen: Svenska Bokförlaget.
Statistical Yearbook of Finland 1981 1982, Helsinki: Central Statistical Office.
Steiner, Herbert 1967, 'La Révolution d'Octobre et l'austromarxisme', in *La Révolution d'Octobre et le Mouvement ouvrier européen*, edited by Victor Fay, Paris: EDI, 173–94.
Stenius, Henrik 1977, 'Järjestö-Suomen kehityspiirteitä', in *Maailmankuvan muutos tutkimuskohteena*, edited by Matti Kuusi, Risto Alapuro, and Matti Klinge, Helsinki: Otava, 77–97.
Stenius, Henrik 1980, 'The Breakthrough of the Principle of Mass Organization in Finland', *Scandinavian Journal of History*, 5: 197–217.
Stenius, Henrik 1981, 'Finlandssvenska folkrörelser 1860–1917', Typescript.
Stenius, Henrik 1983, 'Massorganisation och nationell sammanhållning', *Sosiologia*, 20: 112–24.

Stenius, Henrik 1989, 'Syntesen av nationens konsolidering' (book review), *Sosiologia* 26: 143–5.
Stephens, John D. 1989, 'Risto Alapuro, *State and Revolution in Finland*' (book review), *American Journal of Sociology* 95: 483–5.
Stormbom, N.-B. 1963, *Väinö Linna*, Helsinki: WSOY.
Strömmer, Aarno 1969, *Väestöllinen muuntuminen Suomessa*, Väestöpoliittisen tutkimuslaitoksen julkaisuja A, no. 13, Helsinki.
Sugar, Peter F. 1969, 'External and Domestic Roots of Eastern European Nationalism', in *Nationalism in Eastern Europe*, edited by Peter F. Sugar and Ivo J. Lederer, Seattle: University of Washington Press, 3–54.
Sugar, Peter F. 1971, 'Conclusion', in *Native Fascism in the Successor States*, edited by Peter F. Sugar, Santa Barbara, Calif.: ABC Clio Press, 147–56.
Sulkunen, Irma. 1977 *Raittiusliikkeen synty Suomessa*, Alkoholipoliittisen tutkimuslaitoksen tutkimusseloste, no. 105, Helsinki.
Sulkunen, Irma. 1980, 'Dryckesstrejkrörelsen', *Historisk tidskrift för Finland*, 65: 18–39.
Sulkunen, Irma. 1981, 'Miksi Suomen työväenliike omaksui kieltolakiohjelman?', in *Sosiaalipolitiikka, historiallinen kehitys ja yhteiskunnan muutos*, edited by Risto Jaakkola, Antti Karisto and J.P. Roos, Helsinki: Weilin & Göös, 98–116.
Sulkunen, Irma. 1983, 'Väckelserörelserna som ett förskede i organiseringens historia', *Historisk tidskrift för Finland*, 68: 1–14.
Sulkunen, Irma. 1986, *Raittius kansalaisuskontona. Raittiusliike ja järjestäytyminen Suomessa 1870-luvulta suurlakon jälkeisiin vuosiin*, Historiallisia tutkimuksia, no. 134, Helsinki: Suomen Historiallinen Seura.
Suni, L.V. 1979, *Ocherk obshchestvenno-politicheskogo razvitiia Finliandii. 50–70e gody XIX v.*, Leningrad: Nauka.
Suolinna, Kirsti 1975, *Uskonnollisten liikkeitten asema sosiaalisessa muutoksessa*, Helsingin yliopiston sosiologian laitoksen tutkimuksia, no. 203, Helsinki.
Suolinna, Kirsti 1977, 'Lestadiolaisuus ja agraarin väestön puolustusmekanismi', in *Maailmankuvan muutos tutkimuskohteena*, edited by Matti Kuusi, Risto Alapuro and Matti Klinge, Helsinki: Otava, 112–20.
Suomen valtionrautatiet 1862–1912 1916, vol. 2, Helsinki: Rautatiehallitus.
Suonoja, Kyösti 1968, *Suomen osuuskauppaliikkeen jakautuminen*, Helsinki: Sosiaalipoliittinen Yhdistys.
Svåsand, Lars. 1980, 'The Early Organization Society in Norway: Some Characteristics', *Scandinavian Journal of History*, 5: 185–96.
Tanner, Väinö 1966, *Kahden maailmansodan välissä*, Tammi: Helsinki.
Tanskanen, Aatos 1978, *Venäläiset Suomen sisällissodassa vuonna 1918*, Acta Universitatis Tamperensis A, no. 91, Tampere.
Tarrow, Sidney 1977, *Between Center and Periphery: Grassroots Politicians in Italy and France*, New Haven, Conn.: Yale University Press.

Tepora, Tuomas and Aapo Roselius (eds.) 2014, *The Finnish Civil War 1918: History, Memory, Legacy*, Leiden and Boston: Brill.

Tervasmäki, Vilho 1964, *Eduskuntaryhmät ja maanpuolustus valtiopäivillä 1917–1939*, Helsinki: WSOY.

Thaden, Edward C. 1981a, 'Introduction', in *Russification in the Baltic Provinces and Finland, 1855–1914*, edited by Edward C. Thaden, Princeton, N.J.: Princeton University Press, 3–12.

Thaden, Edward C. 1981b, 'The Russian Government', in *Russification in the Baltic Provinces and Finland, 1855–1914*, edited by Edward C. Thaden, Princeton, N.J.: Princeton University Press, 13–108.

Thaden, Edward C. 1981c, 'Epilogue', in *Russification in the Baltic Provinces and Finland, 1855–1914*, edited by Edward C. Thaden, Princeton, N.J.: Princeton University Press, 459–63.

Thaden, Edward C. 1984, *Russia's Western Borderlands, 1710–1870*, with the collaboration of Marianna Forster Thaden, Princeton, N.J.: Princeton University Press.

Thaden, Edward C. 1981, 'Introduction', in *Russification in the Baltic Provinces and Finland, 1855–1914*, edited by Edward C. Thaden, Princeton, N.J.: Princeton University Press, 3–12.

Thompson, E.P. 1963, *The Making of the English Working Class*, New York: Pantheon.

Tilly, Charles 1964, *The Vendée*, Cambridge, Mass.: Harvard University Press.

Tilly, Charles 1975a, 'Food Supply and Public Order in Modern Europe', in *The Formation of National States in Western Europe*, edited by Charles Tilly, Princeton, N.J.: Princeton University Press, 380–455.

Tilly, Charles 1975b, 'Reflections on the History of European State-Making', in *The Formation of National States in Western Europe*, edited by Charles Tilly, Princeton, N.J.: Princeton University Press, 3–83.

Tilly, Charles 1975c, 'Western State-Making and Theories of Political Transformation', in *The Formation of National States in Western Europe*, edited by Charles Tilly, Princeton, N.J.: Princeton University Press, 601–38.

Tilly, Charles 1978, *From Mobilization to Revolution*, Reading, Mass.: Addison-Wesley.

Tilly, Charles 1981, *Stein Rokkan's Conceptual Map of Europe*, University of Michigan, Center for Research on Social Organization Working Paper, no. 229, Ann Arbor.

Tilly, Charles, Louise Tilly and Richard Tilly 1975, *The Rebellious Century 1830–1930*, Cambridge, Mass.: Harvard University Press.

Tilton, Timothy A. 1974, 'The Social Origins of Liberal Democracy: The Swedish Case', *American Political Science Review*, 68: 561–71.

Toivonen, Anna-Leena 1963, *Etelä-Pohjanmaan valtamerentakainen siirtolaisuus 1867–1930*, Historiallisia tutkimuksia, no. 66, Helsinki: Suomen Historiallinen Seura.

Tökés, Rudolf L. 1967, *Béla Kun and the Hungarian Soviet Republic*, New York: Praeger.

Toma, Peter A. 1958, 'The Slovak Soviet Republic of 1919', *American Slavic and East European Review*, 17: 203–15.

Tommila, Päiviö 1967, 'Satakunnassa keväällä 1899', *Satakunta*, Helsinki: Otava, no. 18: 130–72.
Tommila, Päiviö 1978, 'Rautatieverkko ja rautatieliikenne', *Suomen sanomalehdistön historia -projektin julkaisuja*, Helsinki, no. 10: 15–31.
Tommila, Päiviö 1984, *Suomen autonomian synty 1808–1819*, Helsinki: Valtion painatuskeskus.
Upton, Anthony F. 1968, 'Finland', in *European Fascism*, edited by S.J. Woolf, London: Weidenfeld & Nicolson, 184–216.
Upton, Anthony F. 1980, *The Finnish Revolution 1917–1918*, Minneapolis: University of Minnesota Press.
Upton, Anthony F. 1990, 'Risto Alapuro, *State and Revolution in Finland*' (book review), *The American Historical Review* 95: 1237–8.
Urbans, Runar 1963, *Suomen säästöpankkilaitos 1822–1922*, Vammala: Suomen Säästöpankkiliitto.
Valkonen, Tapani 1980, 'Alueelliset erot', in Tapani Valkonen et al., *Suomalaiset. Yhteiskunnan rakenne teollistumisen aikana*, Helsinki: WSOY, 181–221, 286–8.
Vattula, Kaarina 1976, *Etelä-Pohjanmaan työväenliikettä viime vuosisadan lopulta nykypäiviin*, Helsinki: Etelä-Pohjalainen Osakunta.
Vermes, Gábor 1971, 'The October Revolution in Hungary: From Károlyi to Kun', in *Hungary in Revolution, 1918–19: Nine Essays*, edited by Ivan Völgyes, Lincoln: University of Nebraska Press, 31–60.
Viikari, Matti 1984, 'Die Tradition der finnischen Geschichtsschreibung und Karl Lamprecht', *Storia della storiografia*, no. 6: 33–43.
Viita, Pentti 1965, *Maataloustuotanto Suomessa 1860–1960*, Suomen Pankin taloustieteellisen tutkimuslaitoksen julkaisuja, Kasvututkimuksia, no. 1, Helsinki.
Vilar, Pierre 1981, 'Réflexions sur les fondements des structures nationales', *La Pensée*, nos. 217–18: 46–64.
Vilks, B.Ia. 1962, 'Zaniatost' naseleniia Latvii v kontse XIX veka (po materialam 'Pervoi vseobshchei perepisi naseleniia Rossiiskoi imperii 1897 goda')', *Problemy istorii*, no. 6: 77–87, Riga: Izdatel'stvo Akademii Nauk Latviiskoi SSR.
Vilkuna, Kustaa 1950, 'Herännäisyys sosiaalisena tekijänä', *Kyrönmaa*, Helsinki: Etelä-Pohjalainen Osakunta, no. 7: 130–77.
Virrankoski, Pentti 1980, 'Teollisuus ja käsityö', in *Suomen taloushistoria*, edited by Eino Jutikkala, Yrjö Kaukiainen and Sven-Erik Åström, Helsinki: Tammi, 1: 240–54.
Wahlbäck, Krister 1967, *Från Mannerheim till Kekkonen*, Stockholm: Aldus.
Wåhlin, Vagn 1980, 'The Growth of Bourgeois and Popular Movements in Denmark ca. 1830–1870', *Scandinavian Journal of History*, 5: 151–83.
Wallerstein, Immanuel 1974–80, *The Modern World-System*, 2 vols, New York: Academic Press.
Waris, Heikki 1932, *Työläisyhteiskunnan syntyminen Helsingin pitkänsillan pohjoispuolelle*, vol. 1, Historiallisia tutkimuksia, no. 16: 1, Helsinki: Suomen Historiallinen Seura.

Waris, Heikki 1940, 'Yliopisto sosiaalisen kohoamisen väylänä. Tilastollinen tutkimus säätykierrosta Suomessa 1810–67', *Historiallinen Arkisto*, Helsinki: Suomen Historiallinen Seura, no. 47: 199–272.

Waris, Heikki 1947, 'Oppikoulu sosiaalisen kohoamisen väylänä industrialismin murtautumiskaudella', *Valtio ja yhteiskunta*, Helsinki: Valtiotieteellinen Yhdistys, 7: 235–46.

Weber, Max 1948, *From Max Weber: Essays in Sociology*, edited by H.H. Gerth and C. Wright Mills, London: Routledge & Kegan Paul.

Weber, Max 1968, *Economy and Society: An Outline of Interpretive Sociology*, vols. 1 and 2, edited by Guenther Roth and Claus Wittich, New York: Bedminster Press.

Weiss, Hellmuth 1977, 'Bauernparteien in Estland', in *Europäische Bauernparteien im 20. Jahrhundert*, edited by Heinz Gollwitzer, Stuttgart: Gustav Fischer Verlag, 207–22.

Wiik, K.H. 1978, *Karl H. Wiiks dagbok från storstrejken till upproret 1917–1918*, edited by Sven Lindman, Publications of the Research Institute of the Åbo Akademi Foundation, no. 36, Turku.

Wilson, William A. 1976, *Folklore and Nationalism in Modern Finland*, Bloomington, Ind.: Indiana University Press.

Winberg, Christer 1975, *Folkökning och proletarisering*, Meddelanden från Historiska institutionen i Göteborg, no. 10, Göteborg: E & B Förlaget.

Wirilander, Kaarlo 1960, *Savo kaskisavujen kautena 1721–1870*, Kuopio: Savon Säätiö.

Wirilander, Kaarlo 1974, *Herrasväkeä. Suomen säätyläistö 1721–1870*, Historiallisia tutkimuksia, no. 93, Helsinki: Suomen Historiallinen Seura.

Wolf, Eric R. 1969, *Peasant Wars of the Twentieth Century*, New York: Harper & Row.

Wuorinen, John H. 1935, *Suomalaisuuden historia*, Porvoo: WSOY.

Ylikangas, Heikki 1979, *Körttiläiset tuomiolla*, Helsinki: Otava.

Ylikangas, Heikki 1981, 'Eteläpohjalaisten kansanliikkeitten selitysmahdollisuuksista', in *Kansanliikkeitten Pohjanmaa*, edited by Kalervo Ilmanen, Oikeushistoriallisia julkaisuja, no. 2, Helsinki: Helsingin yliopisto, Oikeuden yleistieteiden laitos, 225–36.

Zipf, George Kingsley 1941, *National Unity and Disunity*, Bloomington, Ind.: Principia Press.

Index

Academic Karelia Society   187–188, 194
Activists   143–146, 149, 155, 162, 181
   and German intervention   151, 160
Agrarian development. *See* Agriculture
Agrarian Union   108–109, 118–128
   and Lapua movement   192–196
   in White Finland   161, 186–192
Agriculture   26, 29–34
   commercialisation of   30, 40–47, 68, 230
   Hungarian   223
   revolution in   38–41
Albania   6, 202
Alexander I   20–24, 37, 103
Alexander II   30, 242
Allardt, Erik   250
Anderson, Perry   3, 7
Anticapitalism   101, 125, 193
Anti-communism   189–194
Aristocracy   24, 91, 229n
   See also Nobility
Armed forces   107, 134–137, 139–140, 145, 176, 191
   control of   132–134, 191
   creation of   7–8, 37, 146
   lack of   107, 150, 184
   See also Civil Guard; Conscription; Militias; Police; Red Guards; Russian army; White army; Worker security guard
Austria-Hungary   6, 201, 223, 247, 249
   collapse of   135, 201–202, 246–249
Autonomist nationalism   81–84, 91, 201
   Balkan   227
   in Baltic Provinces   202
   Czech   221–222
Autonomy, Finnish   19–22, 24, 27–28, 36, 86, 103, 137, 144–145, 210, 220, 239
Aya, Rod   176–178, 182

Baldwin, Peter   256–257, 262n
Balkan states   8, 11n, 37, 202, 221, 227
   nationalism in   83, 91n
   See also Albania; Bulgaria; Romania; Yugoslavia
Baltic Provinces   4, 8, 9, 21–22, 100, 103, 117, 138, 226, 230–231, 234, 239

Germans in   84, 209–211, 213–214, 231, 233, 238–240, 258
   national movement in   202–210, 245
   revolution in   15, 106, 109, 153, 210–220, 247–249
   See also Estland; Estonia; Kurland; Latvia; Livland
Bendix, Reinhard   95
Berend, Ivan T.   31, 81
Bessarabia   37, 239
Bianco, Lucien   154
Björgum, Jorunn   255, 262
Bohemia   4, 11n, 33n, 91n, 221
Bolsheviks
   in Baltic Provinces   212, 215–220, 230, 231n
   in Finland   152, 156, 181–182
   in Hungary   224, 225–226
   Russian   152–154, 156, 164, 173
   See also Revolution, Russian: of 1917
Borodkin, L.I.   203n
Bourgeoisie   27, 30, 34–36, 141, 143, 150–151, 153, 155–157, 165, 188, 196, 237, 248, 251, 253
   in Baltic Provinces   206, 208–209, 213–215, 220
   and bureaucracy   35
   Czech   221
   and nationalism   82, 91
Bourgeois parties   108, 147, 155, 171, 187, 192, 195, 264
   in Baltic Provinces   215–218
   in government   138–139, 145, 153, 155, 190
   Hungarian   224, 226
   and Lapua movement   189–191
   and Russians   105
Brenner, Robert   237–238
Bulgaria   6, 135, 202, 227, 228–230, 244, 246–247
   worker movement in   228
Burghers   20, 35, 36, 53n, 90, 107, 205
Butter, export of   56, 65, 66, 70

Capitalism   28, 31–34, 39
   agrarian   203, 213
   and class structure   121, 192

INDEX   299

in Finland   40, 101, 125, 192
and nationalism   84
world   28, 81, 81n, 163–164, 168
Castles, Francis G.   99, 254
Chinese revolution   3, 134, 154
Church
    in Baltic Provinces   203n, 205, 206, 208, 211, 216–217
    and Fennomania   87, 92
    in Finland   26–27, 35, 58, 87, 95–96, 100, 122, 127, 186
    national Protestant   4
    and workers   189
    See also Clergy
Civil Guard   162, 185, 187–188, 190–191, 259
Civil guards   107, 150, 156–157, 167, 189–192, 196–197, 265
Class. See Dominant classes; Middle class; Upper classes; Working class
Class conflict   74, 82, 117, 119, 121–122, 124–125, 166, 166n, 174, 180
Class integration   8, 12–13, 15, 94, 131, 179, 201
    and territorial integration   118
    and worker movement   136, 178, 244
Class structure   131, 135, 221, 237, 245
    agrarian   8, 76, 237, 238
    in Baltic Provinces   9, 11, 207, 209, 220
    Finnish   11–15, 32, 49, 74, 79, 84, 119, 203, 210, 238, 240–241, 255, 257
    and market   228, 230
    and revolutions   136, 168–171, 245–246
Clergy   20, 25, 27, 27n, 36, 51
    in Baltic Provinces   206
    and nationalism   35
    and peasantry   35, 88, 95, 121
    and revivalism   87, 124
    in White Finland   186
    See also Church
Coalition party   186–188, 190–196, 196n
Coercion, means of   7, 37, 138, 140, 170–171, 175, 178, 220, 226, 252–254
    See also Armed forces; Police
Collective action   131–132, 242, 250, 256
    against landowners   9, 113, 164, 166
    in latecomer states   1, 3, 9–12, 14, 116, 135, 177, 210, 231, 242, 245–246, 249
    by peasants   46, 113, 123, 125, 135, 167
    and political activity   8–10, 14, 94, 115, 174, 176, 188

and revolution   131, 165, 174, 216, 221, 223, 262, 265
    See also Strikes; Trade unions; Worker movements
Collective farms   218
Colonial states   2, 136, 164, 168–170, 180, 201, 244–245, 249
Communist party
    in Bulgaria   228
    in Finland   119, 161, 180, 185, 190n
    in Hungary   224–226
Communists, Finnish
    and Lapua movement   188–192, 194, 196–197, 234, 259
    in political system   187–188, 190, 196n, 250–251, 253
Congress of Vienna   6, 22
Conscription   22, 37, 104, 107, 138, 160, 166, 166n
    Russian   37, 104
Constitution, Finnish   24, 142, 159, 161–162, 185, 188, 234, 242
Consumer cooperatives   102, 127
Core regions   8, 13–14, 19, 49–50, 54, 58–59, 63, 66, 72–76, 120–123, 125, 128, 157, 237, 247
Core states   248–249
Croats   33n, 229, 229n, 246
Crofters   43n, 44n, 46–48, 51, 110, 118, 121, 121n
    as category of peasants   43–44, 186
    and landowners   26, 41, 43, 45, 54, 74, 109, 207
    political activity of   46–48, 70, 75, 102, 110–113, 116, 120–121, 125, 137, 162–166, 169–170, 172, 184, 213, 227
Culture
    national   15, 85, 87, 89, 166, 171, 180
    Swedish   35, 85, 88
Czech nationalism   221–222, 230–231, 244, 246
Czechoslovakia   6, 91n, 179n, 202, 221–222, 224, 232
Czech territory   221

Dairy farming   40–43, 68, 238
    See also Butter, export of
Democracy   116, 137, 144, 162, 178, 180, 222, 226, 231, 243

Denmark 4, 241–244
Depression, Great 189, 193–194, 196–197, 232–234
Deutsch, Karl W. 80n, 83
Diet. *See* Parliament
Dominant classes 7, 82n, 133, 135, 232
 and fascism 194–197, 231–235
 in Finland 14, 134, 167, 171, 180–181, 194–197
 and nationalism 80, 180
 and revolutions 132–135, 180
 See also Gentry
Dubofsky, Melvyn 248
Dunn, John 2

Eastern (East-Central) Europe 2, 6–13, 170, 236, 252, 255
economic development in 31–32, 38–40, 81, 91, 223, 237
 fascism in 231–235
 national movements in 81–86, 91n
 political activity in 100–101, 111–112, 134–135, 177, 185–186, 201–233, 244–247, 249, 257
 See also Balkan states; Baltic Provinces; *and names of individual countries*
Eastern Finland 51, 51n, 56
 migration from 64–65
 as periphery 63–66, 73–76
 political parties in 124–125, 127–128, 167
Economic dependence 2, 238
 on Western Europe 9, 11, 202, 232–234
Economic development 35, 39, 80, 87, 238–239, 241–242, 257
 See also Capitalism
Education 79–80
 in Balkans 228
 in Baltic Provinces 100, 211, 214
 Czech 221
 in Finland 25–28, 33, 35, 84, 87, 114, 194, 241–242
 in Nordic countries 242
Ehrnrooth, Jari 263, 264
Eight-hour workday 137, 141–143, 145, 153
Elections
 Austrian 221
 in Estonia 209, 215–218
 in Finland 11, 94, 108–109, 123n, 145, 147, 159, 161, 187, 191, 193, 196n
 and Finnish workers' parties 108–109, 116–117, 121, 124, 137, 145, 147, 162, 167, 187, 213, 253
 See also Parliament; Political parties; Social Democratic movement; Suffrage, universal
Emigration 38, 40, 123
 to St. Petersburg 72
 to Sweden 72
 to United States 40, 70–72, 123
Estland 5, 20, 203–204, 206, 214–215
 See also Baltic Provinces
Estonia 5, 6, 202, 202–207, 246
 fascism in 234–235
 national movement in 82, 91n, 203, 208–209, 211, 240, 246
 revolution in; workers' movement in 176, 209–220, 230–231, 236
Ethnicity 239
 and class 9, 239
 and nationalism 6, 9–10, 80–81, 83, 227, 231
Exports 31, 31–33, 42, 50
Ezergailis, Andrew 215

Farming. *See* Agriculture; Dairy farming; Forestry; Peasants
Fascism
 in Eastern Europe 194–195, 202, 231–235
 in Finland 189–197, 253, 256, 259–260
Fennomania 85–93, 185, 207
 and Social Democratic party 102
Fennomans 100, 104, 258
 and nationalism 86–90, 99
 See also Finnish party
Ferro, Marc 133
Feudalism 7, 8, 39, 54, 82, 84, 91, 100, 112, 122, 203, 205, 210, 213, 220
Finland
 autonomy of 19–28, 36, 103, 137, 144–145, 239–241, 252
 constitution of 24, 89, 92, 103–105, 137, 159, 161–162, 185, 185n, 188, 234, 241–242
 as dependent state 2–8, 11, 28, 32–34, 83–90, 145–146
 as grand duchy 22–23, 29n, 55–56, 85, 144, 237, 240, 252

INDEX   301

regions of   49–56, 63–76, 167–168
as successor state   6, 11, 235
See also Parliament; Revolution, Finnish;
    Swedish domination of Finland;
    Worker movements, Finnish; and
    names of specific regions, cities, classes,
    and political parties
Finnish language   86, 90, 93
    and gentry   86–88, 91, 93, 247, 258–259
    and peasantry   87, 88
Finnish party (Old Finns)   90, 104–105, 108–
    109, 118–124, 126–127
    See also Fennomans
Fire brigades   96, 102, 111, 111n
Food shortage   148–151, 173–175, 251
Forestry. See also Sawmill industry; Timber
France   6, 10, 22, 82n, 250
    revolution in   133–134, 180n
    unions in   115
Frank, André Gunder   237

Gellner, Ernest   79, 80, 82
Gentry   25–28, 34n, 35, 92, 99
    and agriculture   35, 55, 91
    language of   35, 86, 88–89, 91
    and peasants   35, 42, 51, 95
    Russian   134
Germans
    in Baltic Provinces   202n, 205–208, 215
    in Czech lands   231
Germany   10, 103, 154, 161, 219, 225, 249,
    263n
    fascism in   195–197, 233
    and Finnish revolution   143–144, 146,
        155–156, 160–161
    Finnish troops in   144, 156, 160
    and Social Democrats   117
Ginsburgs, George   261
Grain
    confiscation of   142–143, 149
    exported   70, 237, 238
    imported   33, 34n, 68, 138, 142, 149
    prices of   193
    rationing of   141–142, 149, 150
    trade of   55, 228
    See also Food shortage
Greece   202, 227, 228
Gulf of Bothnia   19, 50, 54–55, 59, 73n, 74
Gulf of Finland   19, 20, 21, 50, 59

Haapala, Pertti   264, 265, 266
Habsburg Empire   221, 229, 236, 247
    collapse of   202, 227
Hämeenlinna   59, 68
Hechter, Michael   65, 80, 122, 123n, 126
Heckscher, Eli F.   49
Helsinki   23, 43, 46, 50, 58, 86
    guards in   146–155
    population of   55n, 58, 67–68
    railways for   59–60, 68, 72
    and revolution   157–160
    university in   22–23
Hobsbawm, E.J.   24, 80
Hroch, Miroslav   82–83, 85–86, 86n, 91, 208
Hungarian Soviet Republic   225
Hungary   4, 6, 134, 202, 259
    agriculture in   39, 223
    fascism in   231, 233
    independence of   91n, 223, 224
    revolution in   15, 154, 161, 176, 202, 223,
        225–227, 229, 236, 247–248

IKL. See People's Patriotic Movement
Imperial Russia. See Russia; Russian Empire
Industry   26, 29–34, 38–39, 44–46, 54, 59,
    61–68, 72–74, 76, 110, 197, 238
    See also Forestry; Timber; Working class:
        industrial
Inflation   138, 173
Intellectuals   81
    in Baltic Provinces   208–209, 212–213
    and Fennomania   87, 92, 98, 166
    Hungarian   223
    and nationalism   171, 180
    radical   133, 134, 180, 180n, 213
    and Social Democratic movement   112,
        134, 154, 162, 170, 180
    and Whites   166
Iron   29, 45, 63
    exported   33n, 56
Italy   10, 109, 194, 196, 233, 250

Jörberg, Lennart   41
Jutikkala, Eino   118, 255n

Kainuu region   73
Kajaani   73, 74
Karelianism   90
Karvonen, Lauri   255, 256n, 259

Kautsky, Karl 102, 117
Kekkonen, Jukka 263, 264, 265n
Kianto, Ilmari 183, 213
Kirby, David 255, 262
Kivisto, Peter 255, 256n, 258, 259
Klinge, Matti 258
Kollontay, Alexandra 98
Koval'chenko, I.D. 203n
Kühnl, Reinhard 195
Kuhnle, Stein 241, 242
Kurland 203–204, 205n, 215
　See also Baltic Provinces
Kuusinen, O.W. 147, 154n, 159, 170n, 176

Labour
　agricultural 4, 39, 164
　cultural division of 80, 85
　international division of 31, 34
　migration of 30, 38–41, 64–66
　regional division of 49–76
　subordination of 92, 223
　See also Peasants; Trade unions; Worker movements; Working class
Labour movement. See Social Democratic movement; Worker movements
Laestadionism 126, 127
Land, redistribution of 164–166, 211–212, 216–217, 228–229, 232
Landowners and leaseholders 46–48, 74–76, 109, 163–166, 207
Landownership 20, 63–64, 84, 120–121, 128, 202–203, 210
　by peasants 11n, 20, 32–33, 40–45, 66, 74
　See also Peasant landowners
Land reform 40, 186, 229, 232, 232n
Language
　and nationalism 83–93
　and political parties 88–90
　See also Finnish language; Gentry: language of; Swedish language
Lapland 51n, 55, 126
Lapua movement 189–197, 234, 253, 256, 260
Latecomer states 8, 79–80, 134, 177, 236, 242
　collective action in 6, 10, 135
　Eastern European 9, 15, 81, 135, 231, 242, 247, 249

Latvia 6, 246
　fascism in 234
　nationalism in 91n, 202–210
　revolution in 210–220, 230–231, 236, 246
Lenin, V.I. 132, 153, 154n, 212, 217, 230
Liberals 87, 89–90, 92–93, 104, 120, 124, 178, 258
Liikanen, Ilkka 260, 261, 264, 265, 266
Linna, Väinö 184
Lithuania 6, 82, 84, 91n, 202, 234, 246
　revolution in 202n, 236, 247
Livland 5, 20, 203, 204, 206, 214, 215
　See also Baltic Provinces
Lönnrot, Elias 87
Lutheran religion 22, 26, 205
　See also Church; Clergy
Luxemburg, Rosa 222

Mannerheim, C.G.E. 156, 161–162, 180n, 191–192
Manninen, Ohto 166n
Mäntsälä revolt 191, 197
Market. See Capitalism
Martin, William C. 114
Marxism 209
Middle class 41, 88, 90, 96, 108, 221, 232–233
　in Baltic Provinces 206–208, 213–214
　and nationalism 79, 82–85, 92, 245
　and Whites 166, 192–196
Migdal, Joel S. 112
Migration, internal 45, 56n, 63–66, 68–70, 72, 74
　See also Emigration
Military. See Armed forces
Militias 107, 139–140, 142–143, 146–148, 148n, 151, 167–212
　See also Worker militias
Minorities, national 6, 30, 134, 239
Mobilisation, popular 81–82, 132, 134–136, 241–244
　See also Collective action
Modernisation
　and nationalism 79–80
Moore, Barrington 1, 3, 4, 5, 10, 91, 120, 121, 123, 133, 135, 159n, 166n, 171, 172, 195, 204, 206, 250, 251
Moravia 221
Multiple sovereignty 132, 140, 144, 146, 150, 171, 175

Nairn, Tom   81–82, 85n
Napoleonic Wars   6, 242–243, 252
National Coalition party   186
   and Lapua movement   186–196
National integration   8, 13–15, 79, 95, 118, 133–136, 179–180, 185, 196, 201, 207–208, 219, 240
   and class structure   91, 186, 207, 210
   and fascism   189, 194
   and political parties   127, 193
   and worker movement   97, 100, 117, 134, 186, 244, 263
Nationalism   9, 28, 230–231
   in Baltic Provinces   202–210
   as civic religion   14, 80, 82, 84–85, 99, 180, 185, 207, 244
   Finnish   79–93, 99–100, 144, 202–203, 240–241
   Swedish   89–90
   See also Autonomist nationalism
Nationalists. *See* Fennomans; Nationalism
National Progress party   120, 186, 187, 194
Nicholas I   240
Nobility   20, 24–25, 35n, 36, 82, 203, 205, 221, 237
   See also Aristocracy; Dominant classes; Gentry
Northern Finland   51
   as periphery   51, 73–74, 76
   political parties in   120, 125–126
Norway   4, 5, 11, 83, 86n, 241–243
Noske, Gustav   225

Old Finns. *See* Finnish party
Orridge, Andrew W.   83, 84n, 91n
Ostrobothnia   50–58, 70–75, 192–193
   political parties in   120, 122–124
   Whites in   144, 146, 158, 167–168
Ottoman Empire   6, 201–202, 227–229, 236
Oulu   50, 51, 55n, 64, 65, 72, 73–74

Paasikivi, J.K.   114, 240n
Paavolainen, Jaakko   255n
Paper industry   31, 33–34, 45
Parikka, Raimo   262, 263, 264
Parliament (Diet)   24–27, 30, 35, 103–104, 141, 144–146, 155–156, 158–159, 190–191

   composition of   20, 22, 107–109, 137, 187, 189–191
   convening of   26, 30, 35, 43, 57, 95, 137, 152–153
   dissolution of   145–146, 150
   Estonian   215–216, 218
Peasant landowners   13–14, 19–20, 26–27, 32–36, 40–45, 54–56, 68–71, 108, 123–124, 187, 193, 202–203, 237–238, 247
   in Baltic Provinces   205–208, 233–234
   Estonian   214
   and nationalism   14, 85–93, 99, 121–122
   and revivalism   95–96, 99
   and workers   40–48
Peasants   9, 35–36, 163–166
   in Baltic Provinces   212–213, 217–218, 220, 228–231, 239
   in Eastern Europe   111–112, 245
   in Hungary   223, 226
   and Lapua movement   191–194, 197
   and revolution   135, 163–166, 177, 230
   in Romania   228
   in White army   166
   See also Peasant landowners
People's Patriotic Movement   187, 190, 194, 259
Periphery   19, 63–66, 75–76, 125, 248–249
   industrialization of   31, 72
   nationalism in   83, 84
Peter the Great   20, 22, 205
Petrograd. *See* Russia
Poland   4, 6, 33n, 202, 205n, 222, 238, 239, 247
   Congress   23, 37, 239
   fascism in   233
   nationalism in   37
Police   95, 106, 138, 139, 146, 159, 162, 263
   absence of   107, 133, 138–140, 142–143, 184, 190
   Estonian   216
Political dependence   1–2, 24–25, 80–81, 201, 245
   Balkan   227–228
   in Baltic Provinces   230, 208–209
   in Finland   10–13, 83–85, 88–89, 236–237, 241–242, 246–247
   in Hungary   223
   in Poland   222
   See also Autonomist nationalism

Political parties
  Finnish   14, 100–101, 118–128, 241
  Western European   4, 231–232
  See also Agrarian Union; Communist party; Communists, Finnish; Finnish party; National Coalition party; National Progress party; People's Patriotic Movement; Social Democratic movement; Swedish [People's] party; Young Finnish party
Population growth   9, 36, 38, 40, 44, 65, 76, 113, 123, 164, 231
Proletariat. *See* Working class
Provisional Government
  in Baltic Provinces   215, 220
  in Finland   137, 144–146, 151, 171, 253
  See also Russian domination

Railways   30, 48n, 56, 58–60, 64, 68, 72, 74, 112, 123
Ránki, György   31, 81
Rasila, Viljo   173
Red government   158–160
Red Guards   107, 155, 157, 158, 163, 173, 175, 184, 264, 266
Religion   4, 22, 83, 89, 95, 96, 121–122, 125
  and Lapua movement   192, 260
  and revolution   168
  See also Church
Repression   10, 82, 219
  colonial   245
  and revolutions   142, 159, 164, 183, 212, 247
Reval   206, 208, 209, 211, 216
Revivalism   95, 99, 124–127, 167–168, 193
  and church   87, 96, 100, 124
Revolution   131–136
  anti-colonial   2, 227, 244
  in Baltic Provinces   210–220, 230–231
  in Latvia   246
  See also Revolution, Finnish; Revolution, Russian
Revolution, Finnish   10–11, 12, 152–160, 226, 246–249, 252–254
  as civil war   173–174, 179–183
  goals of   158–159
  and working class   162–166
Revolution, Russian
  of 1905   106, 114, 212

  of 1917   133–134, 153, 179–180, 219–220, 216–217
Riga   206, 211, 215, 220
Robinson, G.T.   212
Rokkan, Stein   4, 38
Romania   6, 39, 134, 224, 225, 228, 230, 232n
  fascism in   233
  independence of   202, 227, 244, 246
  peasant unrest in   9, 229
  and World War I   135, 228–229, 247
Russia
  Bolshevik   153
  trade with   31–34, 56–58, 238–239
  See also Revolution, Russian; Russian army; Russian domination; Russian Empire
Russian army   24, 135, 214
  in Finland   138, 145, 146, 151–152, 158
Russian domination
  of Baltic Provinces   206–217
  of Finland   13–14, 19–28, 83–84, 103–107, 116–117, 171–174, 179–180, 236–239
Russian Empire   6, 20–22, 103, 104, 206, 239
  collapse of   14, 131, 168, 171, 201–202, 219, 227, 236, 249

Saimaa Canal   56, 60
St. Petersburg   14, 20, 21, 23, 29, 49, 59, 66, 84, 103, 106, 122, 210
  migration to   55–56, 58–59, 68, 72
Salkola, Marja-Leena   147n
Sawmill industry   31–33, 35n, 36, 45–46, 59, 63, 65–66, 68, 70, 73–74
Scandinavia   4–5, 14, 21, 40, 196, 236, 256
social structure of   11, 13, 32, 35, 197, 241, 244, 247, 255
  worker movement in   14, 94, 99, 116, 137, 178, 241–244, 247
Schools   29, 87–88
  elementary   88, 96, 111
  in Estonia   217
  See also Education
Scott, James C.   183n
Selleck, Roberta   26, 28, 92
Serbia   135, 202, 224, 227–229, 247
Seton-Watson, Hugh   83
Ship-building   54, 70–73
Shorter, Edward   115

Siironen, Miika   259
Sillanpää, F.E.   182, 183, 184n
Skocpol, Theda   3, 112, 135, 168
Slovaks   82, 202n, 225, 230, 246
Slovenes   229, 246
Smith, A.D.   81n
Snellman, J.V.   86–87, 134
Social Democratic movement   241
  in Balkans   228
  in Baltic Provinces   208–213, 218–220
  and crofters   164–166
  Czech   222–223
  and elections   11–12, 108–109, 146–152, 161–162
  in Finland   13–15, 94–117, 220, 222, 246–249
  in Finnish government   131–132, 149–151, 161, 170, 175, 188, 197
  and Finnish independence   144–145, 147, 152
  and Finnish revolution   148, 153–155, 157–160, 170–178
  and Lapua movement   189–192, 197
  membership of   96–97, 140–141
  Polish   222–223
  Russian   209–210, 211
  and strikes   106–107, 114, 141, 153, 188
  support for   11–14, 38, 109–114, 118–120, 227
  in Sweden   242–243
  and wars   249
Socialism. See Social Democratic movement
Social structure. See Class structure
Soikkanen, Hannu   42, 98n
South-western Finland   51–53, 66–70, 74–75, 120–122, 193
Stamboliski, Alexander   228
Stenius, Henrik   255
Stephens, John D.   254
Stockholm   49–50, 56–58, 123
Stock-raising   30, 32, 40, 68
Strike, right to   94–95, 100–101
Strikes   97–101, 114–116, 141, 188–189
  in Baltic Provinces   211–212
  farm   141, 143, 167
  general   106–107, 112, 117, 125, 152–155, 175–176
Successor states   1, 6, 11, 202, 223, 231, 235, 252

Suffrage, universal
  in Austria   221
  in Denmark   243–244
  in Estonia   211, 215
  in Finland   10, 11, 94, 101–107, 244
  in Hungary   223
  in Norway   243
  in Romania   229
  in Sweden   242–243
Svinhufvud, P.E.   161–162, 190–192, 197, 234
Sweden   5–6, 99–100, 241–243
  agriculture in   39–40, 47
  trade with   70
Swedish domination of Finland   13, 19–22, 24, 49–55, 123, 202–203, 238–239
Swedish language   104, 188, 202–203
  and Finnish gentry   14, 19, 24–25, 35, 83–93, 181n, 210, 240, 247
  regions of   51–54, 89, 120, 126
Swedish [People's] party   90, 104, 108, 109, 120, 187, 195, 241

Tampere   45, 46n, 97, 148, 155, 160, 177, 178n
Tar   54–55, 65, 70
Tarrow, Sidney   72
Temperance movement   88, 96–97, 100–102, 111, 127
Tenant farmers   20, 43, 44, 121n, 137, 159, 166
  in Baltic Provinces   203, 205, 211
  See also Crofters
Territorial integration   58–62, 74–76, 118–119
Thaden, Edward C.   19, 239, 258
Third World countries   2, 112, 164, 170
Thompson, E.P.   10
Tilly, Charles   5, 7, 9, 10, 92n, 98, 107, 115, 119, 131–133, 171, 172, 176, 250–251, 253, 254
Timber   41–44, 63–74, 126, 238–239
  See also Forestry; Sawmill industry
Trade   26, 29, 50–51
  with Russia   33–34, 55–56
  with Sweden   29, 54
Trade unions   94–102, 114–116, 140–141, 148, 151, 188, 212
  Hungarian   223–224
  and Lapua movement   189–191, 196–197
  and strikes   141, 155
  in Sweden   243–244
  Western European   94–95, 231

306 INDEX

See also Social Democratic movement;
  Strikes; Worker movements
Treaty of Hamina 22
Treaty of Versailles 6
Treaty of Westphalia 6
Trotsky, Leon 132
Turku 20, 50, 51, 55n, 58, 64–65, 68, 148, 149

Unemployment 138, 140, 143, 150, 173, 251
  in Balkans 228
University 22, 26–27, 36, 58, 87–88, 180
  students 82, 167, 187–188
Untola, Algot 167n
Upper classes 83–93, 104
  agrarian 66–70, 121–122
  culture of 35–36
  in Eastern Europe 201, 230–231, 232–233
  and nationalism 14, 84–93
  and trade unions 98–100
  and Whites 166
  See also Dominant classes; Gentry; Peasant landowners
Upton, Anthony F. 142, 255, 258, 259

Vaasa, county of 51, 64, 65, 72, 124, 158, 161
Venstre 241, 243
Viipuri 23, 36n, 50–70, 75–76, 120, 122, 128

Wages 196–197, 211, 216, 223
Wallerstein, Immanuel 3, 237, 249n
Weber, Max 7, 25, 37, 173
Western Europe 82
  economic dependence on 9, 11, 202, 232–239
  trade unions in 94–95, 100
  working classes in 231
White army 160, 166, 193
Whites 156–160, 179, 181, 190–191, 235, 259–260
  regions under 158, 167
Wiik, K.H. 154n
Williams, Colin H. 83, 84n, 91n
Wolf, Eric 109, 113, 163–164, 177, 211, 251
Wood products 31, 34, 45–46
  See also Forestry; Sawmill industry; Timber
Worker militias 139–143, 147–148, 151, 167
  and strikes 142
  and food shortage 143

See also Red Guards; Worker security guard
Worker movements 9–11, 247–248
  in Eastern Europe 229–231
  and Russian revolution 137
  spread of 112–113, 163
  See also Social Democratic movement; Worker movements, Finnish
Worker movements, Finnish 14–15, 94–102, 143–145, 148, 188–189
  nationalism of 244, 246–247
  and political action 14, 104–107, 114–116
  and revolution 131, 176–179, 227, 249
  See also Social Democratic movement
Worker security guard 148–149, 151–158, 162–163, 167, 173, 175, 177, 220
  See also Red Guards
Workers' halls 113, 116, 189
Working class 38–48, 186, 235
  agricultural 36, 39–46, 48, 70, 74–75, 110–111, 167
  in Balkans 228
  in Baltic Provinces 203–217
  Czech 221–222
  in Eastern Europe 232
  Hungarian 223
  industrial 39–40, 45–46, 61–63, 74–75, 98, 115, 220, 223, 228
  in Latvia 223
  mobilisation of 93, 110
  and revolution 162–167
  and Social Democratic movement 112–113, 118–120
  in Sweden 243
  and unions 114–115
  in Western Europe 231
World War I 2, 6, 11, 14, 170, 172, 201, 233, 246–249
  in Balkans 228
  in Baltic Provinces 214
  in Hungary 229
  and revolutions 131–136, 236
  and worker movement 221
World War II 190, 249, 251, 263n

Young Estonia movement 214
Young Finnish party 93, 104–105, 108–109, 118, 120, 124–125, 186
Yugoslavia 6, 202, 229

www.ingramcontent.com/pod-product-compliance
Lightning Source LLC
Chambersburg PA
CBHW070909030426
42336CB00014BA/2344